D0957236

"Starts quickly and doesn't slow down . . . Phelps consistently ratchets up the dramatic tension, hooking readers. His thorough research and interviews give the book complexity, richness of character, and urgency."
—Stephen Singular

MURDER IN THE HEARTLAND

"Drawing on interviews with law officers and relatives, the author has done significant research. His facile writing pulls the reader along."
—*St. Louis Post-Dispatch*

"Phelps expertly reminds us that when the darkest form of evil invades the quiet and safe outposts of rural America, the tragedy is greatly magnified. Get ready for some sleepless nights."
—Carlton Stowers

"This is the most disturbing and moving look at murder in rural America since Capote's *In Cold Blood*."
—Gregg Olsen

SLEEP IN HEAVENLY PEACE

"An exceptional book by an exceptional true crime writer. Phelps exposes long-hidden secrets and reveals disquieting truths."
—Kathryn Casey

EVERY MOVE YOU MAKE

"An insightful and fast-paced examination of the inner workings of a good cop and his bad informant, culminating in an unforgettable truth-is-stranger-than-fiction climax."
—Michael M. Baden, M.D.

Also By M. William Phelps

Perfect Poison
Lethal Guardian
Every Move You Make
Sleep in Heavenly Peace
Murder in the Heartland
Because You Loved Me
If Looks Could Kill
I'll Be Watching You
Deadly Secrets
Cruel Death
Death Trap
Kill For Me
Love Her to Death
Too Young to Kill
Never See Them Again
Failures of the Presidents (coauthor)
Nathan Hale: The Life and Death of America's First Spy
The Devil's Rooming House: The True Story of America's Deadliest Female Serial Killer
The Devil's Right Hand: The Tragic Story of the Colt Family Curse
The Dead Soul: A Thriller (available as e-book only)
Murder, New England
Jane Doe No More
Kiss of the She-Devil
Bad Girls
Obsessed
I'd Kill For You
She Survived: Melissa (e-book)
She Survived: Jane (e-book)

THE KILLING KIND

M. WILLIAM PHELPS

PINNACLE BOOKS
Kensington Publishing Corp.
http://www.kensingtonbooks.com

PINNACLE BOOKS are published by

Kensington Publishing Corp.
119 West 40th Street
New York, NY 10018

All Kensington Titles, Imprints, and Distributed Lines are available at special quantity discounts for bulk purchases for sales promotions, premiums, fund-raising, and educational or institutional use. Special book excerpts or customized printings can also be created to fit specific needs. For details, write or phone the office of the Kensington special sales manager: Kensington Publishing Corp., 119 West 40th Street, New York, NY 10018, attn: Special Sales Department, Phone: 1-800-221-2647.

Pinnacle and the P logo Reg. U.S. Pat. & TM Off.

ISBN-13: 978-0-7860-3248-8
ISBN-10: 0-7860-3248-0
First Kensington Hardcover: July 2014
First Kensington Mass Market Edition: July 2015

eISBN-13: 978-0-7860-3249-5
eISBN-10: 0-7860-3249-9
First Kensington Electronic Edition: July 2015

10 9 8 7 6 5 4

Printed in the United States of America

This book is dedicated to Diana Ferris, my sister-in-law. Diana was five months pregnant when brutally murdered in 1996 by a perpetrator, I'm convinced, much like the one you will read about in this book. One of the victims in this case, Randi Saldana, reminds me of Diana, whose case remains unsolved.

Author's Note

I think it would be helpful to my readers if I say something about the dialogue and dialect you'll sometimes encounter in this book. Some of the people I've quoted speak in what might seem like confusing, grammatically upside-down sentences. Staying true to the way people spoke to me during interviews and to the dialogue I reviewed from the interrogations and interviews conducted by investigators, I have written much of the book to reflect the language and word choices of these real-life individuals. No disrespect is intended. Furthermore, I did not do this to be dramatic or to add flavor, but to reflect their speech accurately.

PART ONE

THE GIRLS

CHAPTER 1

A striped toe sock. Multicolored, like *Reading Rainbow*. Attached to a foot, a portion of her naked calf sticking up out of the brush on a clear, crisp, chilly day. Her skin was pale, with a reticular, vein-blue tint to it: sheer adolescence juxtaposed against an unthinkable image of horror. A dead teenager's body covered by brush, only her foot visible from the road.

At 1:45 P.M., on the afternoon of October 29, 2009, York County Sheriff's Office (YCSO) detective Alex Wallace, a seasoned, dedicated cop with a dozen years behind the badge, took a call to head out to the 1200 block of Robinson Yelton Road in York County, South Carolina. Wallace referred to this area as "a country . . . gravel and dirt road," same as much of the terrain in this northern part of the state. There were five houses on the road where Wallace sped out to, situated in a fairly secluded section of Clover, the town seat.

When he arrived, Wallace saw other investigators from the sheriff's office standing down in an area off the side of the road. They were huddled around the body attached to that leg poking out from the brush. As a member of the

YCSO's Violent Crimes Unit, Wallace worked death investigations, sex crimes, armed robberies, aggravated assaults, and missing persons cases. The rough stuff. The type of crimes that hardly ever came with happy endings—those cases that keep good cops, like Wallace, up at night, wondering, shaking their heads in disbelief at the terrible things human beings will do to each other.

After parking and getting out of his vehicle, Wallace walked over to where the officers had gathered. There was a "little drainage area" coming from a nearby creek that ran underneath the road. Three ribbed metal pipes, side by side, with several feet of space between one another, directed the water toward the woods, away from and underneath the road.

Looking closely, Wallace saw the girl's toe sock poking up from the weeds. Her body was situated between two of the pipes. There was a surreal quality to the scene: the tranquility of the forest, insects humming, birds fluttering, a farming tractor coughing far away, and this dead teen "in a culvert, amongst some bushes and trees."

"Someone riding an ATV found her," an officer on scene explained to Wallace.

If you stood where Wallace had on this day, staring down into the drain where the three pipes emptied, the young woman's body would have come into view. Although there was a mailbox on the edge of the road, maybe twenty-five yards from the body, there were no houses or businesses close to this section of the road. You're talking thick forest, filled in with dense bushes and tall, dry weeds. There was a house nearby, but not in the eye line of where a potential witness could have seen what happened. It appeared to be a hasty dump site—not the ideal place to hide a body, but also not out in a wide open space, either.

Wallace stepped down into the culvert. The woman's body was bent over. She was naked from the waist down (except for those rainbow-colored toe socks). All she had on was a hoodie.

Within this scene, there was something that struck the detective as he took it all in: "You could see her breasts, butt, and vagina area—there [were] bugs crawling all over her. . . ."

This told investigators the potential existed for her having been down in the small culvert for "a while." She had not been dumped there just recently, it seemed. Possibly not even the night before, and certainly not that day.

Studying her body (she was young, a teenager or early twenty-something, for certain), Wallace saw the girl had "a deep scratch in her side from a claw or something." He noticed this as he got down on one knee. And looking even closer, the detective saw additional marks, maybe three or four "deeper cuts" along her body, "like she scraped across something."

Was she dragged?

There appeared to be some "redness" around her neck, too, just above an area where her sweatshirt had been pulled up to expose her breasts.

Ligature marks? Strangulation?

There was one pressing issue here, however: How to identify her? And a bigger overall question, of course: How to explain to the public that a teenager had shown up dead in a culvert, nearly naked, with scratches all over her and indistinct red marks around her neck?

"Fingerprint her," someone suggested. It was the only way to begin the process of finding out who she was. After all, there had to be someone out in the world looking for this young woman.

CHAPTER 2

As the crime scene off Robinson Yelton Road, located just south of the North Carolina/South Carolina state line, filled in with investigators of all types, and yellow crime-scene investigation (CSI) tape was unspooled and wrapped around trees, the on-scene supervisor called in K-9 sergeant Randy Clinton. The theory was that the rest of the girl's clothing could be somewhere in the woods. But even more shocking: Were there additional bodies out there waiting to be found?

Sergeant Clinton had nearly three decades on the job, the last seventeen dedicated to the YCSO's K-9 Unit. If you were looking for a cadaver, a trail of a criminal at large, the possibility of drugs inside a house or car, the dogs were the go-to team of law enforcement for the job.

"We work on break-ins, armed robberies, anything that a person left on foot, missing persons . . . ," Clinton said later.

The dogs have been trained to pick up a scent and follow it.

"I want you to search along the roads to see if you can find any clothes that might have been tossed out of a vehicle," the captain told Clinton. This seemed like a logical approach. The dead teen was missing some of her clothes. If she had been raped and murdered, as many suspected, her killer might have speedily torn her clothing off and tossed it wherever the attack began. Or taken it with him and tossed it elsewhere. Finding that type of evidence could produce those three magic letters: DNA.

When Clinton met with several other investigators, one suggested walking along the roadside with the dogs. There were three additional officers on scene to assist Clinton. Together, they could cover a lot of ground.

Respectfully, Clinton didn't like that idea. His thought was to have two cars drive along the roadside and conduct a cursory search first, in order to see if they spotted anything out in the open. The incident had likely occurred at night. Out here in these parts of the south, the night sky is a shade under "cave dark." Out in the woods and along the dirt roads, the moon is your only light. There could be evidence left behind in plain sight, which the killer had not seen.

Those in charge agreed with Clinton.

Clinton and a colleague hopped in one vehicle and two other officers in another. Each went their separate ways along Robinson Yelton Road, north toward the state line between North and South Carolina. The small town of Clover is directly south of Gastonia, North Carolina, a mere thirty-minute, twenty-mile ride up Highway 321. These cops see lots of crimes generated by people from nearby Charlotte and other North Carolina towns across the border. Not that there aren't the same types of crooks, dopers, and criminals in South Carolina, but this region of the state is prone to people coming down from the north and bringing their trash and trouble with them.

Clinton and his colleague took off south down Robinson toward Lloyd White Road, the 148. Both cars inched slowly along the side of the road. Officers peered out the windows, looking into the brush and gravel off on the side of the road to see if anything popped out. The thought was: Conduct a passing search by eye first and see what came of it. If they didn't spot anything, they could double back with the dogs on foot and go deeper into the brush and woods along the roadside.

Not long after they started, Clinton and his partner came to a stop sign at Crowders Creek Road, right on the North/South Carolina border.

"Take a right," Clinton suggested. His eyes were focused on the side of the road.

They drove for a mile and a half; Clinton thought he saw something.

"Stop."

They were just beyond a small concrete bridge, now in Gaston County, North Carolina. Something red, with smudges of mud, was half on the edge of the roadway and half in the brush, almost in front of a striped orange-and-black road sign indicating a bridge.

Clinton got out.

"A red shirt!" the cop yelled.

Deputy Mark Whitesides, Clinton's colleague, called it in.

Standing up at the bridge, looking down into the woods, Clinton spotted what appeared to be something sparkling in the sunshine like a disco ball. As they trekked down the hill and searched the immediate area in the woods, a short five-to six-foot embankment from where the shirt was located, Clinton saw a pair of "blue jeans with a diamond-studded belt." The jeans and belt were farther down near the actual creek that the road had been named after.

Upon an even closer examination, the officers discovered that stuffed inside the jeans were a red bra and a pair of black panties with red stripes. The jeans had that diamond-studded black belt inserted around the loops.

When law enforcement looked at the area where the clothing was recovered—the shirt at the top of the ridge near the bridge, the jeans and bra and panties down by the creek—it appeared someone had tossed the items out of a car window while pulled over, or hurriedly flung the clothing out of a moving vehicle.

Or maybe this was where the attack occurred?

Clinton's gut told him the person was fleeing toward North Carolina.

The items matched with the size of the woman found not too far away. They had to be related.

Neither officer touched the clothing. Instead, Clinton had forensics come out and photograph everything before they could look inside the pockets and see if there was identification.

After a meeting and several conversations regarding how they could identify the dead woman, it was decided that the most productive task the YCSO could do was issue a press release and involve the public. If the girl had been missing, and family and friends were out looking for her, they would be watching the news. Additionally, the YCSO had several pieces of clothing, along with some jewelry, that could help with that process.

On Friday, October 30, 2009, as the young woman's body went off to the medical examiner's office for autopsy, the YCSO issued a press release explaining how the body of a young girl found on Robinson Yelton Road was that of an *18 to 28 year old white female approximately 5' 6" tall, weighing 150 to 160 pounds, brown hair . . . and dark eyes.* They published photographs of the clothing on the victim and the clothing located down the road, along with a necklace she was wearing. The YCSO held back the identity of several personal belongings, however, which had been found inside the pockets of the clothing. This might become important to the investigation later on.

"We haven't determined if she was killed where the body was found," a YCSO spokesperson said in a statement released to news outlets. "Part of the reason we need to speak to anyone who has any information is to piece together [answers to] these questions."

An additional motive for going public and hopefully identifying the girl was to try and reach "anyone who can tell us" who she was and where she had been during the final days of her life.

"We want any information about her, period," the YCSO spokesperson said.

Two suspicious vehicles had been spotted on the road during the time her body could have been dumped, the YCSO had learned during early interviews. One was a Ford F-150 red pickup, the sheriff's office reported, almost pleading for someone to come forward. This vehicle had tinted windows and a flatbed liner cover. It had been seen in the area of Robinson Yelton Road between noon and one o'clock on October 27. The second vehicle was a two-tone Chevy S-10 pickup with a blue top and tan bottom, possibly a 1987 to 1990 model. That vehicle had been seen in the area on October 25 and 26, between 9:00 and 10:00 P.M. The YCSO believed, without coming out and stating as much, that the girl's killer was driving one of the vehicles.

CHAPTER 3

She was sitting on top of the knee wall surrounding the carport, her tiny legs dangling, her barefoot heels kicking against the brick, waiting in anticipation for her daddy to come home. She had freckles flanking the bridge of her nose, big, sad brown eyes, and straight, shoulder-length brown hair cut Dutch-boy style. Her rosy smile displayed two missing front teeth, which the Tooth Fairy had scooped up from underneath her pillow one night recently while she slept.

"Man, she sits there every day waiting for you, doesn't she?" his boss asked as they pulled into the driveway.

"Sure does," Nick said. "That's my baby. Daddy's girl."

Nick Catterton had never married his daughter Heather Catterton's mother, Stella (Holland) Funderburk. Stella had a four-year-old boy she brought into the relationship she and Nick had begun in 1983. They lived in South Carolina then, just below the North Carolina border. Stella got pregnant and they had Nicole first, followed by Heather, with her perpetually cheerful outlook on life and lively demeanor.

Nick worked as a plumber on new construction sites. These were long, hard, dusty, and sweaty days. He'd leave the house at six in the morning and not return until six or seven that same night.

"We started off in South Carolina and things [were] going great," Nick later told me. "We were a family."

Whenever work dried up, Nick found it elsewhere. During the early 1980s, Nick packed up his family and moved down to St. Augustine, Florida, where they set up home for about five years, living a mile from the coastline. Sunday was the day Nick and Stella took the kids off to the beach for a fun family day.

"We had to cut back after Heather came along," Nick said in his slow Southern drawl. "But theys was some really good . . . *good* times."

As Heather grew, Nick noticed how different she was from the other kids. Heather exhibited what seemed to be an inherent love for all kinds of people, especially kids her age—seven, eight, nine, ten. At this young age, Heather was already thinking about worldly issues, like poverty and homelessness and starvation. Sure, other kids cared. But with Heather, it came from somewhere deep inside.

"She was a real kindhearted person," Nick said of his daughter. "A real smart girl. She would have graduated high school and went on to bigger and better things."

In a school essay, "What I Would Do to Change the World," which Heather had written when she was eleven, she spoke of a desire to end all war, saying how she *really [didn't] understand why there is a war.* In a profound statement for a child her age, Heather tried to reconcile the idea of how it *really hurts my heart that people are out there trying to save our lives and killing theirs.* She then went on to talk about wanting to meet some of the soldiers fighting for the "freedoms of America," expressing how she loved them very much. Little Heather claimed she *could never be brave enough to go fight for [her] country.*

While in grammar school, after the family moved from Florida to Grover, North Carolina, Heather had such a sophisticated understanding of computers and the skills to back it up that she found herself helping out in class by teaching the other kids how to use the computers.

Nick and Stella had been having problems for a lot of years and they got worse after the family had moved back to North Carolina. When they finally split, Nick took the girls and moved to Gastonia, and Stella and her son went their own way. Over the years, Nick was the first to admit, drinking became an issue for him. Either from genetics or through the course of drinking what Nick described as "a twelve-pack every day, on the weekends a case in a day" for a period of years, Nick's heart grew weak and enlarged.

"I knew the dranking would eventually kill me," Nick said of his drinking.

Both of Nick's parents had died of a heart attack younger than they should have. So Nick knew the physical costs of abusing alcohol, not to mention the emotional toll it had on his family.

Heather grew tired of authority and quite bitter as she entered the junior-high environment—a rather regimented, daily grind that takes dedication and discipline on the student's part to be successful. The peer pressure alone, along with the social ladder, was not something Heather took to. Still, she wanted the knowledge. She wanted to learn. She wanted the benefits an education could give a girl from a small Southern town.

"So she found a family that was homeschooling and she did that," Nick explained. "And I was paying this lady, who had four or five kids, to homeschool her."

As a thirteen-year-old, now uninterested in any type of schooling whatsoever, with her home life in a bit of chaos with Nick's drinking and Stella gone, Heather became part of the social services system.

"She kept running away . . . always looking to come back home," Nick explained.

Contrary to what some would later speculate, Nick said it wasn't Stella, Heather's mother, who turned Heather on to drugs, a path Heather chose as a teenager herself. Heather Catterton was a young, confused human being, enduring the same weaknesses with which many struggle. Albeit misguided, perhaps, she fell into the vicissitudes and ravages of the world around her.

"It was certain friends she hung around," Nick said. "And then when she went to . . . foster homes, you know, you run across kids who do certain things and, well, it is what it is."

It's that innocent image of his daughter, young and full of dreams, sitting, waiting for him to come home from work, that Nick Catterton cherishes more than anything these days. Throughout the years, Nick longed for life to be stuck there, in that moment, frozen. But, of course, that's not how things turned out. People grow and move on. Nick would learn this the hard way.

During the early part of October 2009, Nick became extremely ill. His heart was failing. It would not allow him to do what he wanted anymore. Whenever Nick had problems, he was placed in Carolinas Rehabilitation.

"I couldn't even walk," Nick said, "that's how bad I was when I went in [that October]."

Heather had been in prison, serving a five-month sentence on a probation violation. During the week of October 15, Heather had been released early so she could go see her dad.

They hugged. They talked. But it wasn't a father-daughter conversation like Nick would have later wanted as a lasting memory. He was still very ill. He told Heather to stay out of trouble, but that was something Nick had always told his kids. Funny thing, being a parent, you see your child every day, or once a week, and you never believe that it will be the last time you ever lay eyes on her.

While in rehab, Nick liked to watch the news—it was just something he did as a routine course of his day while he rested and healed.

On October 28, 2009, there was a story the local news had been working on that bothered Nick. Every time an update came on, a new piece of information unearthed, that ache every father has in his stomach reserved for his children throbbed.

Nick's instinct was speaking to him.

The latest report said a girl had been found in a ditch. Dead. Reporters said she was between thirty and forty years old.

Nick breathed a bit easier.

Heather had not been seen by anyone in the family for quite some time. She'd gotten out of prison and had gone to see Nick in the hospital. During that third week of October, she had up and disappeared completely. She'd been gone for quite a while, eleven days at last count by anyone paying attention. This was unlike Heather, to be gone for that long without telling someone. Nick, of course, was in rehab and had not been in the loop back home, so he had no idea that Heather was even missing.

At seventeen, Heather was a minor. Her sister and mother had reported Heather missing during that last week of October. They figured she'd pop up somewhere and explain that she'd been on a bender with friends. It was sad and painful to hear, but Heather had always been truthful. She was caught up in the game, unable to break free from the terrible grip of addiction and running the streets.

On October 29, Nick sat down to watch his daily afternoon news show. He was at home now, just out of rehab. The report started with news of clothing found near the girl in the ditch.

Nick still wasn't alarmed. He'd had it in his mind that she was between thirty and forty. There was no need to be concerned.

Still, something told Nick to pay attention. That parental instinct inside was once again speaking.

Then the report mentioned that the dead girl in the ditch had been possibly wearing toe socks.

Nick stared at the television.

His chest tightened. His face drooped.

Tears.

He asked Nicole, Heather's sister, then Stella: "When was the last time y'all done seen Heather?"

They said almost two weeks ago now.

Nick was devastated. Those toe socks. He knew Heather loved to wear them.

I'm going to wait another day, Nick told himself, *and call the York County Sheriff's Office.*

CHAPTER 4

On that day the girl's body was found in the ditch, Detective Randy Clinton alerted forensics about the clothes and belt he had located on the side of the road by the bridge in North Carolina. Forensics had sent in a photographer and that was how the photos wound up on television. While that unfolded, Clinton turned to YCSO captain Jerry Hoffman, who had secured this new scene, and said, "I'm going back up to start searching the road."

"That's fine."

Clinton walked up the small embankment and started down Crowders Creek Road, on the left-hand side, that same area where the clothing had been found. He headed north.

Fifty yards into his search, Clinton found a white tennis shoe. Investigators knew from this evidence, if it was tied to the DB—the dead body—found in the woods by the drainpipes to the south, two scenarios were possible. Either the girl's killer was heading back into North Carolina, where he had come from, and tossed the items out the window along the way, or he was heading south from the north into the area and tossed the items out before dumping the body. Still, with either scenario, the feeling was that the crime had originated in North Carolina.

Clinton marked the shoe and had forensics photograph it before having it bagged and tagged. After a detailed search of the entire area, nothing else was found.

Once she was brought to the medical examiner's office, it wasn't hard for the YCSO to identify the victim in the ditch as seventeen-year-old Heather Catterton. Heather had been arrested in the past and her fingerprints were on file. When they removed Heather from the crime scene and took her to the Medical University of South Carolina's (MUSC) Department of Pathology and Lab Medicine, the first thing the coroner did was fingerprint Heather and put her prints through the system.

A hit on Heather's name came immediately.

An important piece of the puzzle for the YCSO was how Heather had died. That was where Sabrina Gast and her team at MUSC came into play. Gast had been the York County coroner for three years when Heather's bruised and partially naked body was brought to MUSC. As an interesting aside, Gast had a background in forensic nursing and had worked as a sexual-assault nurse. She knew what to look for in those cases. She had even been certified as a sexual-assault nurse examiner.

Unaware of Heather's identity at the time, Gast had been called out to the Robinson Yelton Road crime scene, where Heather had been found. She'd observed Heather's dead body in situ, which could help now that the actual autopsy had begun.

Near 9:00 A.M., on October 30, the day after Heather's body was recovered, under Dr. Gast's direction and observation, Dr. Cynthia Schandl got to work conducting an autopsy on Heather Marie Catterton. As investigators worked diligently out in the field conducting a victimology, searching

Heather's life for clues to her death by talking to friends and family, Gast and Schandl set out to determine how Heather had died. If they could find out the "how," the YCSO was going to be able to get closer to the "who." It had to be determined first if Heather died accidentally, by the hand of a killer, an overdose, or other means. It was one thing to be a cop out in the field and speculate how you *thought* a victim had breathed her last; it was quite another to allow science to dictate that course.

Dr. Gast, who wrote the report for Schandl, noted that decomposition had set in on Heather's body. *The body is cool to the touch . . . changes of decomposition complicate interpretation,* the coroner wrote.

As Dr. Schandl got to work scanning Heather's body and making notes, she pointed out that Heather's skin had undergone serious *changes in the color . . . that would go along with decomposition.* It's known as "marbling"—*a pattern that forms on the skin from decomposition very early. A fairly prominent area of what we call skin slippage, where the top layer of the skin, the epithelial layer, like if you get a blister, the part that comes off, that part was slipping off* around Heather's neck.

As autopsies go, this one was not going to be easy, mainly because the elements and insects had gotten to Heather.

It appeared from a cursory observation that Heather had been left on the side of the road for some time. The changes Gast noted in Heather's body as decomposition set in told that story: *marbling (left leg and flank),* that spotty skin condition; *green discoloration, (inguinal, abdominal and back); serpiginous skin slippage of the left side and back, multiple additional foci of skin slippage (face, neck, abdomen, extremities), and mild distention of the abdomen.*

What did all of this mean in terms of Heather's condition and determining the cause and manner of death?

Heather's body was deteriorating rapidly. It was a good thing they found her when they had. Another day or two out in the elements and locating any trace or physical evidence (if any had been left behind) would have been impossible. As it were, Gast noted *plenty of insect activity present with fly eggs in the hair, on the abdomen and in the inguinal [groin] region, [along with] maggots in the vaginal and oral cavity.*

The first thing Dr. Schandl did after undressing her was wash Heather's body. There was dirt and debris all over Heather.

Clearly, her body had been discarded more than dumped.

"So having done that, it was apparent that she had a number of bruises and a number of scrapes to the skin," Schandl said later. "She had what looked like bruising to the right side of her face and the inside corner of the right eye, some scrapes to the left side of her face. She also had bruises to the thighs, to the bottom area. She had scrapes on her right side and a couple of scratches in other places."

Heather had gained some prison weight from a recent stay and weighed 161 pounds at the time of her death. She wore it well, but it was above her normal weight. Strangely enough, Heather still wore a metal necklace, loops of silver with tiny silver balls. The photos that forensics snapped of Heather's neck displayed the necklace, along with yellow and white and purple bruises and what looked to be ligature marks directly underneath the necklace. If she had been strangled, that act of violence did not in the least affect the integrity of the necklace.

Schandl moved in for a closer look at Heather's neck and spent a considerable amount of time studying it.

"I had a concern that perhaps there was a violent element to her death," Schandl later explained, "and one possibility that I did not want to overlook was that perhaps she had been strangled or smothered or something to that effect. . . ."

Heather's pupils and cornea were cloudy and "poorly visualized," another indication that she had been dead for some time. This observation is the same as one might hear from a chef looking for fish—if the eyes are cloudy, the fish is not fresh. Based on this observation, it was clear that had it been the middle of summer, there might not have been much left to Heather's body.

The sclerae and conjunctivae (the white part of Heather's eyes) showed "evidence of injury." This type of trauma to the eyes is consistent with strangulation and/or asphyxiation. Forensic pathology 101 says that in manual strangulation, meaning one person using his hands or a ligature, the victim's face, as in Heather's case, is left congested and cyanotic (purplish or bluish) because the main source of blood flow to the brain has ceased.

Schandl was stuck on this. She felt the discoloration around Heather's neck, coupled with the trauma Heather's eyes showed, was significant.

"At this point, when I'm looking just at the outside of the neck," Schandl clarified, "I try not to make any determinations about, you know, how much trauma is involved, but there [was] definitely discoloration, red discoloration around the neck."

Moving on to other parts of Heather's body, Schandl found there were no outward signs of injury to Heather's anus or back area. It was hard for the doctor to tell if Heather had been raped because of decomposition and the presence of maggots in Heather's vagina. It was as equally difficult to tell how many injuries Heather had sustained to her outer body, scratches, bruises, etc., because of the discoloration brought on by decomp. Still, from their experience, both Gast and Schandl were confident that after a thorough examination of Heather's vagina and rectum, there was "no foci" or "laceration" or "hemorrhage."

In her report, however, Gast did make a point to say that "decomposition changes" were apparent in those specific areas.

Nonetheless, Schandl took oral, rectal, and vaginal swabs, along with a saline swab of an obvious and strange pale discoloration on Heather's left breast.

After cutting away the skin on Heather's neck and peeling it back to examine the inner portion of her muscles, neither doctor found evidence of severe asphyxia.

Examination of the soft tissues of the neck in a layer by layer dissection, Gast wrote, *reveals no abnormalities.* She noted that the "hyoid bone" and "larynx" were "intact" and the *underlying firm red-brown musculature is devoid of hemorrhage.*

This information would not be consistent with a violent struggle to cut off Heather's blood flow and oxygen to the brain by strangulation. In many cases, when a person strangles another, he uses more force than is needed. Here, it would almost seem as though Heather had been grabbed around the neck, yet the force was not enough to produce internal injuries.

Dissection of the throat, doctors Dominick and Vincent DiMaio wrote in their informative book *Forensic Pathology, usually reveals hemorrhage, often extensive, into the musculature.* The authors went on to note that depending on the victim's age, the hyoid bone and thyroid cartilage, in particular, generally show signs of fracture if strangulation is the cause of death.

But that wasn't the case here, Gast indicated.

The other possibility—considering the injuries Heather sustained to her throat, neck, and eyes—was asphyxia.

"Suffocation is the exclusion of air from the body," Schandl later explained. "So we all need air and oxygen . . . to live. . . . There are a number of different ways you can achieve this, and some of them will leave traces on the body and some of them won't."

This was one reason why, Schandl added, when forensic pathologists study a body, they "look very closely, because sometimes the evidence can be very scant."

If a person was suffocated to death, her body was deprived of the oxygen it required to survive. This might sound simple, but from a pathologist's point of view in search of a cause and manner of death, it becomes important.

"Every cell in your body needs oxygen," Schandl explained. "If it doesn't get it and you can't exchange the gasses—you're . . . cells will start to die."

For a killer using this method, however, this can take a lot of time.

From the injuries on Heather's upper body, it would appear her killer put something over her head and deprived her body of oxygen while holding the item around her neck just tight enough to cut off her airways, but not tight enough to injure those muscles and vessels underneath the skin.

Schandl filled out a preliminary report, noting that probable cause of death "was pending." At that moment immediately after the autopsy, the doctor wasn't prepared to make an assumption of how the girl was murdered.

Pending means, I haven't been able to determine cause of death definitively . . . the doctor noted.

The doctor wanted "further law enforcement investigation" before making the determination. Medical examiners do this routinely. Schandl also sent blood and tissue samples to the lab. She wanted those toxicology reports back before she made a determination. There was nothing worse than (and no need for) a rush to judgment.

Regarding manner of death, Schandl also wrote "pending" in her report. She believed the death to be a homicide—just as law enforcement investigating the case did—but until further investigation could yield results, the doctor wasn't comfortable making a final call. Complicating matters further, early lab tests proved Heather had high amounts of cocaine and amphetamines in her system at the time of her death.

CHAPTER 5

It was the call no father wanted to get. His daughter, his baby, was dead. Nobody knew how. Nobody would tell Nick anything. Nick looked out his window and stared at the media trucks parked across the street. He wondered how his life had become a breaking news story he had only seen on CNN or FOX News.

Is this real? Is this my life now?

"My heart was broke," Nick said through tears as he recalled those harrowing, gut-wrenching days after his daughter had been found in a ditch.

Heather had no reason to be in South Carolina, Nick knew. Moreover, Nick felt that if she had overdosed—which he knew to be a possibility because of the lifestyle she was leading—the police would have already told him.

Which left only a few different possibilities.

The one on Nick's mind as he considered the days, weeks, and months ahead—and surely on the minds of the reporters camped across the street—was that a vicious murderer was stalking the streets of Gaston County, North Carolina, and quite possibly searching for his next victim.

CHAPTER 6

Confirming what they knew already, Heather's aunt called into the YCSO and said the family had recognized the clothing the YCSO had published in the newspapers and had shown on television.

"She's been missing for twelve days," the aunt told police. "She was last seen wearing a Hollister sweatshirt matching the one in the pictures."

In fact, it was Heather's sister Nicole's boyfriend—a forty-seven-year-old local man, Danny Hembree—who had actually encouraged the family to report Heather missing. Family members had feared the worst. When they saw the clothing, all those nightmarish images they'd had became a reality. Heather had never been gone without communicating for that long a period of time.

Heather's aunt was at Nick's. He took the phone from her. As the YCSO had suspected since finding the body in its jurisdiction and Heather's clothing in North Carolina, just over the border, Heather lived in Gastonia, an eleven-mile, twenty-minute ride from Clover, South Carolina, where Heather had been found.

Nick was obviously broken up about his daughter's death.

His phlegm-riddled, scratchy voice told that story. When he collected himself, Nick asked, "How did she die?"

"The cause of death is unknown at this time, Mr. Catterton."

Later that afternoon, two YCSO investigators caught up to Nicole's boyfriend, Danny Hembree, at Jacob's Food Mart out on York Highway. Danny was the type of guy who knew the streets, knew people, and might have some information that could help. He was a career criminal. He was as good as any other resident in town to start with. In addition, Danny knew Heather and the Catterton family quite well. He had offered to be a pallbearer at Heather's funeral. He said he wanted to help out the family any way he could. He told Nick repeatedly how sorry he was for the loss of his youngest daughter.

Nick appreciated that.

Danny had been dating Nicole for a few months and hung around Nick's house and even stayed over some nights.

At Heather's funeral, Danny signed the guest book. When it came time to carry Heather's casket, however, the idea that initially seemed like a good one scared Danny enough so that he left and blew off the service completely.

"I don't know why he did that," Nick remembered. He assumed that Danny, same as everyone else, was broken up over Heather's death.

Nick wasn't paying too much attention during those early days to what was going on around him. He was in that fog of grief, struggling with heart issues. By most accounts, his daughter had been murdered and died a lonely, brutal death in a ditch in the middle of nowhere. Nobody was giving him answers.

Danny talked with investigators at the Food Mart and mentioned the last time he saw Heather, saying, "The eighteenth, near two in the morning." He said something about partying with Heather, a girl named Sommer Heffner, and Sommer's boyfriend. He didn't want Nicole to find out. He admitted to having sex with Heather that same night.

"How'd the night begin?" an investigator asked.

"Nicole and me, we got into a fight. She wanted [something]. She wanted me to get it for her. I told her I wouldn't."

Investigators asked about the Catterton family in general.

"Look," Danny said, "I've had sex with Heather, Nicole, and their mother, Stella."

An entire family? Interesting. The guy certainly gets around.

"Had you seen Heather?" The cop meant between the time she disappeared and wound up dead.

"Lots of people been asking me about Heather. . . . I been asking around, you know." Danny stubbed out a cigarette on the tar. He spoke with a terribly hard-to-understand Southern brogue, slow, drawling out his words. "I could not find anyone who done seen her."

"Any ideas?"

Danny thought. "There was this one guy. He been looking for Heather. They call him the Marlboro Man. He drives a red Dodge. I done seen him, oh, near the seventeenth. He was looking for Heather."

That was good information, considering the YCSO had reports of a truck with that description in the neighborhood where Heather had been found.

One of the investigators asked Danny where he had been that week.

He answered he was working; and that when he got off work, he would go to his mother's house and eat dinner, then drive over to Nicole's. According to him, he did this just about every day—facts that had been confirmed by Nicole and Danny's employer, a report from the conversation with Danny stated.

CHAPTER 7

Sommer Heffner, Heather's best friend, walked out her screen door and sat on the porch of her home. It was the morning of November 1, a Sunday. Sommer picked up the newspaper and opened it. She took a sip of her coffee.

To her shock and sorrow, there it was: confirmation. Not Heather's name, but a story about a young girl found in a ditch. Sommer read what the girl was wearing, along with the clothes cops had recovered not far from her body.

Sommer, who had seen Heather get dressed in those same clothes on the night she disappeared, lost control of her emotions. She started bawling.

Her boyfriend came out.

"What's going on?"

"That's Heather," Sommer said, jabbing her finger into the text of the article. She handed him the story of the girl in the ditch. "That. Is. Heather."

CHAPTER 8

It's not every day, week, month, or even year that a body is discovered in your jurisdiction. Law enforcement personnel come under a tremendous amount of pressure to solve a case as the media and downtown brass begin to ask questions about the investigation and what stage it's at—no matter how early or far into it you are.

"The YCSO was working around the clock on this case," one law enforcement official told me. "By the end of the first week, with no real leads, they were tired and beat down."

They didn't have a clue as to what happened to Heather Catterton.

No one knew it then, but as the second week of the investigation came to a close—and there were still no viable suspects on the radar—the unbelievable happened. It was a scenario that would ratchet up the investigation ten notches and turn it into a multijurisdiction, multiagency search for a potential serial killer. All while a ticking clock worked against law enforcement in what seemed to be a bogeyman on the loose, preying on women in Gaston County.

CHAPTER 9

On the night Heather Catterton's identity was released publicly for the first time, her photograph was displayed on the nightly news. Randi Saldana, a twenty-nine-year-old (soon to be thirty) local Gastonia woman, sat in the living room of her sister, Shellie Nations, watching television. The two of them, close as sisters could be, talked as if it was just another normal night together, enjoying each other's company. But as the news came on, Randi was quickly distracted by that image of Heather.

"I know her," Randi said. It was the face. She had seen Heather somewhere.

"Where?" Shellie asked.

Shellie, called "Shell" by her sister, did not recognize the photo. Heather was, essentially, just a child, and her pudgy, bubbly face indicated as much. Randi and Shellie were much older. Randi hung around different circles. But they had lived in Gastonia, nonetheless, which was where Heather had spent most of her life.

"I got it," Randi said, snapping her fingers. "Jail." Randi had done some time just recently for several misdemeanors, drug possession, and fighting.

"You mean it? You talked to her, too?"

"Yeah." Randi had also seen Heather around town, from time to time, she explained to Shellie. "And you know," Randi added, "she would not have gone down like that without a fight. She was a *tough* chick."

Shellie listened as the newscaster explained what law enforcement chose to release publicly. By now, it was being reported that Heather's death was considered a "homicide investigation." She had been dumped on the side of the road in South Carolina; some of her clothing was found just to the north, in North Carolina. They also cleared up a notion that Heather had been officially reported missing, saying there was never a missing persons report filed.

Shellie knew Randi was running around town with some shady characters lately. With the news of Heather's body dumped on the side of the road Shellie grew worried.

"Listen to me, Randi," Shellie said, stopping and looking Randi in the eyes, "whatever you're doing, you need to stop. You have to understand *that*"—Shellie motioned to the television—"is what we're scared could happen to *you*."

Randi turned pale. She felt the seriousness of Shellie's concern. Randi was aware of walking that fine line between dabbling in things she could control and others that could turn ugly at any given moment. It seemed to hit her right then that she was living a high-risk lifestyle, same as Heather, and her behavior could ultimately have consequences.

The sisters didn't say much after that. What else was left? Shellie was the big sister; she was the one who looked out for Randi.

The worrywart.

Randi got up, hugged Shellie, and then turned to leave. She didn't have to say it, but she did, anyway: "I love you, Shell."

"Randi, I'm serious. I love you, too."

"Will you take me to my friend's house, Shell?" Randi

asked. She had been living with a guy since breaking up with the father of her youngest child.

"Yes, Randi."

As they walked out the door together, they made plans to meet up for Randi's birthday in a few days.

Shellie pulled up to the house. Randi stared out the car window, almost as if questioning whether to get out of the car.

Before opening the door, she turned to Shellie. "I love you, Shell."

"I love you, too, Randi."

Randi was somber. As though Shellie's words back at the house had impacted her way of thinking.

Randi got out. Walked into the house.

Shellie drove away.

CHAPTER 10

They had met back on October 29 to celebrate Shellie's birthday. But now it was November 2, just a few days after Heather's body had been found, and that conversation Randi and Shellie had about Randi's lifestyle rang in their ears. Randi had always stopped by to see Shellie on her birthday and bring her a little something.

"Let's go out and eat! My treat," Randi had said on that October 29 night when she stopped by to wish her big sister a happy birthday. Their birthdays were so close, it was always a celebration.

"No, Randi, you don't have that kind of money. Let's just hang out and talk."

"Nothing big," Randi said. "Just some tacos. I really want one."

"I'll tell you what," Shellie said, "I'll bring you some tacos on *your* birthday."

Shellie promised she'd drive to where Randi had been living with a guy named Tim, her current boyfriend. Shellie told Randi that in just two days, November 2, she'd arrive with a box full of Randi's favorite tacos, ready and prepared to celebrate Randi turning thirty. A milestone.

"I like that idea," Randi had said.

Randi had a glamorous, *Vogue*-like, supermodel smile that nearly everyone she came into contact with noticed immediately. It juxtaposed seamlessly against her deep, penetrating light blue eyes and porcelain skin. She was one of those women who always took the time to wear the perfect amount of eyeliner and makeup, accentuating her faultless facial features. Randi was not merely beautiful; she was gorgeous, turning heads wherever she went.

As kids, Randi and Shellie, one year and a few days apart, were like twins. Whatever one did, the other was right behind. It had been that way all their lives. They looked out for each other. They knew that men would come and go, even their girlfriends, but they would always be there for each other. No one could take that bond of being sisters away.

"Randi and I both grew up in Gastonia, North Carolina," Shellie told me. "We had good lives. We were raised for the majority of our lives by our grandmother. We lived a very religious life."

They attended the local Pentecostal Church of God every Wednesday and Sunday with their grandparents. There were never any drugs or alcohol around the home, Shellie recalled. It was as straight a life as one could lead: prayer, family dinners, more prayer, cookouts, TV, lemonade, Bible talk, and laughs.

"There was never anything that we could complain about, growing up," Shellie added. "We had good schooling. Good home."

It was the kind of life one imagines in the small-town south. Gastonia, the largest small town in Gaston County, has been branded the "All-American City" three times and received the U.S. Conference of Mayors Livability Award. Its slogan spells out the feeling you get, many claim, from walking around town: "Great Place. Great People. Great Promise." The city's website says that because of Gastonia's "strategic location," just minutes west of Charlotte and midway between Atlanta and North Carolina's Research Triangle, Gastonia has become a bastion for attracting "both industry" and "new residents."

For Randi and Shellie, Gastonia had always been, and always would be, home.

On November 2, at some point late into the afternoon of Randi's birthday, Shellie's phone rang. Looking down at the caller ID, she smiled.

"Hey, Randi . . ."

"Shellie, I need you to come and pick me up."

"I told you I would bring you some tacos—I'm on my way."

Shellie pulled up and parked her car in front of where Randi was living. She was excited to see her sister on her birthday.

Because of that strict but formidable lifestyle they had lived as kids growing up with God-fearing grandparents, Shellie and Randi never got into much trouble throughout their youth and into junior high.

"We were very obedient. My grandmother would not have tolerated anything else," Shellie said.

As Randi grew older, however, she fell into a group of kids at school that dabbled in those temptations just about every kid, at some point, faces. Shellie never went the way of drugs or alcohol; Randi, on the other hand, couldn't resist.

Still, Randi was one of those girls in junior high and high school who became a magnet, attracting others who wanted to be around her. She had that glow about her that drew people toward her. You wanted to know Randi. You wanted to be seen with her. You wanted to be her friend. She made you feel alive and loved and important. She made people laugh and allowed them to be comfortable with who they were.

"Her dream," Shellie recalled, "was to do hair and makeup, to go off to cosmetology school and learn the trade."

That vocation fit Randi so well.

Randi and Shellie's grandmother had a large spread of land with a lake, and Shellie recalled how her fondest memories of her sister included going down to the lake, just sitting, staring out at the water, and talking like young girls do.

"We'd always go there swimming with our cousins and cook out right by the lake. We had a lot of family time. It was never many outsiders. It was always family."

Randi had an inherent goodness in her. Whenever she met people for the first time, she would not judge, as though anyone and everyone were not only equal, but loved by her in a special way.

There was one woman Shellie met years later who shared a story about Randi. The woman was crying. The story had conveyed the type of person Randi was.

"What's wrong?" Shellie asked.

"Aren't you Randi's sister?"

"Yes, I am."

"If it hadn't been for Randi, I don't know where I'd be today."

The woman explained that when she arrived in Gastonia for the first time, she didn't know anyone. She met Randi.

"Randi gave me ten dollars and a place to stay," the woman said.

The woman now had a job, a new home, and was doing better than she could ever recall. All because Randi reached out and showed her love.

"If it had not been for Randi," the woman concluded, "I do not know where I'd be today."

"She accepted people for who they were," Shellie said. "If they were down and had nothing, Randi wanted to help."

Shellie and Randi spent November 2, Randi's birthday, together. It was one of those days Shellie remembered later with a gleam: two sisters enjoying each other's company.

They ate tacos. Talked. Drove around. Laughed.

They didn't get a chance to see their mother much; but on this day, Shellie drove over to her and Randi's mother's house and they all sat and chatted.

At one point, Randi started crying.

"What's wrong?" Shellie asked.

"I need you to do me a favor, Shell. Will you?"

"Of course, Randi. Yes. What is it?"

Shellie knew Randi was in a tight spot and didn't like to talk about her life and where it had been lately, not where Randi saw herself headed. Since he had been two years old, Shellie had custody of Randi's middle child. Randi had signed over that custody. It was the right thing to do for Randi. She realized she couldn't handle the child at the time and knew that by leaving the child with Shellie, Randi could see him whenever she wanted. For Shellie, family looked out for one another.

When she entered high school, Randi was passionate about hip-hop dancing, along with hanging out with the popular crowd, since she was one of them. As far as boys and dating, Randi was not one of those girls dreaming of one day marrying Prince Charming and riding off into the sunset. Sure, she wanted that white-picket fence, same as most people, but there was something inside Randi that told her not to allow herself to be tied down—at least not at a young age. She was determined that before settling down, the love between her and her partner needed to be genuine. It should not be just the "next thing to do" in life, nor just because she'd had children at such a young age.

For years, Randi considered how people dated. They'd graduate college together. Then they would move into the working world, believing the next "thing" to check off the list was marriage and kids and SUVs and Little League and PTA meetings. It was almost as if their lives had been scripted.

And then the bubble burst at some point and they found themselves staring at each other one day across the dinner table, realizing they were following a path set before them by others and not listening to their hearts.

Randi didn't want that. She yearned for love at its core. If she didn't feel it, she wasn't sticking around and wasn't going to kid herself into believing that just because a man fathered her child, he was "the one."

"What is it, Randi?" Shellie pressed.

Randi was still crying.

Shellie and her mother looked on, wondering what was going on. It was Randi's birthday. She was supposed to be celebrating. She should be happy.

But there was a certain darkness hovering over Randi. Shellie could feel it.

"Randi, talk to me. . . ."

CHAPTER 11

Sisters Randi and Shellie hung out with the same group of friends while in high school. Being so close in age, they did just about everything together. High school, however, changes kids—more choices to make, more temptations. Teenagers begin to think as though they're adults. It's nature. It's all part of growing up.

"Randi was never one to get out there and start trouble with people," Shellie said. "It just wasn't in her. But, look, if someone brought trouble her way, she was not going to back down. She would stand her ground. Still, Randi was brought up in a godly way. She had more sympathy for people than anger or animosity. She never really wanted to be ugly to anyone."

While in high school, Randi got pregnant.

"And after she had Brendon (pseudonym), these people, that crowd, started coming around and causing problems for her and her boyfriend, and it wasn't gonna work out."

Sometime after giving birth to Brendon, Randi stopped by to see Shellie.

"I want to go to Michigan," Randi explained. She was

looking for approval from Shellie—the okay. They had family up north.

Randi wanted to get away from Gastonia and take some time in another place, a location away from all the drama and bedlam of her life. The last few years of high school had been rough. It started out slowly, but after falling in with a certain group, getting pregnant, and then beginning to dabble in the drug culture, Randi needed a break.

"Do you think it'd be okay if I took Brendon with me?" Randi asked Shellie.

"Of course, honey. He's your son."

Randi left.

When she got out there, Randi found out that the father of her child and his family weren't happy about it. To them, it seemed Randi had run off with the kid. To add to Randi's problems, she had been in some trouble with the law for fighting. She'd had a court date she skipped out on.

All of that worked against her.

Randi was picked up and the child went to the father's family. In jail, Randi couldn't do much about it.

According to Shellie, this was a turning point: "They took him and wouldn't allow Randi to see her own child."

As Randi emerged from jail, she'd hit a dark, bottomless pit without any boundaries or safety nets. Randi hadn't been on any type of hard drugs then. It was only after the father of the child took Randi's firstborn away that things went south. She fell into a depression that drugs deceivingly lifted her out from under.

"She felt like she had lost *everything*," Shellie told me.

The drugs Randi took numbed the pain of losing her child. She could forget about life for a while.

Shellie tried as best she could to rescue Randi, but what can a sibling do for a sister who has basically given up?

In Shellie's case, only pray.

The family allowed Shellie to pick up the child. When

she did, Shellie brought the child to see his mother. Randi, Shellie said, was never high when Shellie brought the boy around. Randi knew better and would never allow her problems to infiltrate the life of her son.

"Losing that child like that, it broke her," Shellie recalled. "To Randi, she had already lost her life."

Randi worked as a power washer for the big rigs, eighteen-wheelers. That's hard work. It wasn't easy. And it wasn't as if Randi had fallen into a deep drug addiction and lived on the street. She was deadening the pain and escaping her problems, holding down a job as best she could.

"You have to understand," Shellie clarified, "as a family, we never knew that Randi was doing these drugs. She had so much respect for us that she never came over here or came to see any of us when she was on drugs. She never asked us for money."

They would wonder, of course, but Randi was an adult. She did what she wanted to do, suffered, and dealt with the consequences. Family would help, but Randi had to make the first move.

With Randi hiding her drug use, it made it easy for her family not to see the full grip the drugs had on Randi until later.

Then she had two more kids. One of the fathers, according to Shellie, liked to drink, and Randi found that alcohol served the same purpose for numbing the pain as drugs. Randi fell into drinking.

Life with the new man took an even faster downward spiral for Randi. She knew the relationship wasn't going to work.

"I don't love him," Randi told Shellie one day. She didn't feel anything for the man. They had drinking and arguing in common, but not much else. "I don't want to be with him."

"You don't have to stay with him, Randi," Shellie said, comforting her.

"I'm afraid he'll take the children away from me."

There was that pain from the past coming back to hold Randi down. Randi felt trapped. If she left, she'd be in a battle for her kids.

Shellie pressed Randi about what was wrong. Why was she so upset? Crying on her birthday?

Randi relented. It was the child Shellie had taken care of since he was two years old. Randi was feeling as though she'd abandoned him and he would never know she was the birth mother.

"Do me a favor," Randi said through tears.

"Sure, honey, what is it?"

"Make sure he knows I'm his mother one day. Please do that for me?"

Where had this come from? Why was Randi feeling as though she was not going to be around to tell him herself? Confused, Shellie asked Randi why she felt this way. They had always agreed that at the appropriate time, Randi would sit the boy down and explain it herself.

"It was so odd," Shellie later said. "I just found this statement to be very odd. Because Randi knew that when the time was right, she was going to tell the child herself."

Staring at her sister, Shellie thought something terrible was going on and she didn't know about it. Something Randi wasn't sharing. The way Randi cried and carried on about telling the child who his mother was made Shellie wonder what Randi had gotten herself mixed up in.

"What is it, Randi?" Shellie asked.

"Please, please do me this favor and just make sure he knows I'm his mother."

"Of course, of course, Randi, when the time is right. But why not tell him yourself?"

"I just want to make sure that he is going to know."

"Yes, Randi, he is going to know."

As the night wore on, Randi made a point to tell her mother how much she loved her. The way she sounded, it was as if Randi was saying good-bye.

For good.

They stayed a while longer and Shellie drove Randi home.

"I love you, Shell," Randi said before getting out of the car. Randi was still feeling that talk back at her mother's house. She seemed so sad.

"I love you, too, Randi. More than you'll *ever* know."

They said their good-byes and made plans to stay in touch by phone and hook up for dinner soon.

CHAPTER 12

Katherine "Kat" Sturgell spent the morning of November 15 with her sister-in-law, Linda Franks. It had been a fairly mild start to the day, about 62 degrees Fahrenheit, no wind, some bright sun (for that time of year) poking through the opaque clouds. Kat and Linda were riding down Apple Road, inside the limits of Kings Mountain State Park in Blacksburg, just south of the Gaston County, North Carolina, border. This is a massive state park encompassing some twenty-plus miles of hiking trails, along with 115 campsites.

Kat and Linda were trotting down Apple Road on horseback, lost in the beauty of what is fifteen miles of park equestrian trails. Earlier, Kat and Linda had ridden the trails with Kat's husband and niece, both of whom had gone back home by late morning, early afternoon. Now it was Kat and Linda out on the trails alone.

As they were trekking up Apple Road, Kat saw something that didn't seem so strange at first glance, especially inside a state park.

"Look," Kat said as she passed the area before Linda, pulled back, slowed her horse, turned around, and went to check it out more closely.

On the ground between the woods and the road, there was a large burn spot between some leaves and a downed tree. It was easy to see from Kat's vantage point of being high on her horse: a black patch of what looked to be terribly charred leaves or pine needles by a tree, with something strange-looking inside the ring of ashes.

Kat got down off her horse and approached the area. Something didn't feel right all of a sudden. One of the worst things for a state park is to have an abandoned fire pit, smoldering. One gust of wind and it could swallow up the whole park within a few days.

Linda was just coming up behind Kat. She stayed on her horse as Linda approached the scene.

"What's up?" Linda asked.

"I don't know. It's a burn spot in the ground. Looks like somebody tried setting the woods on fire," Kat said, walking closer.

Kat tied off her horse and approached the burn. She stood by what she described as "the foot" of the patch of scorched ground, just a bit larger than the size of a human being. There was something inside the ring of char, faceup, although the face was blackened and perhaps melted completely off. There was also what looked to be a human arm sticking up in the air, stiffened with some type of black soot melted onto it. The entire "thing" was draped over a rotted log. There was some type of blanket or tarp melted onto the thing itself.

Kat thought she was staring at a mannequin. Clearly, she could now make out that the *thing* was in the shape of a human being, with several sections of what appeared to be unburned skin exposed. The vaginal area was visible and unburned. One breast was exposed. A leg was burned at the foot and thigh. The entire neck and shoulders and head were charred and red, some melted completely. It wasn't clear if the mannequin's clothing made the blackened, melted mess all over it, or it was from the mannequin's plastic flesh, but it had definitely been wrapped in a blanket at some point.

Kat never mentioned seeing this, but the feet of the "mannequin" were bound with some type of copper wire or cord, the plastic outer coat burned away.

"Someone set a mannequin on fire," Kat yelled up to Linda. "That's what it looks like."

To be sure, Kat walked up to the torso section of the mannequin—which was red and burned, but still very much intact. Then she touched it.

"I wanted to make sure. . . ."

She poked at it like rising dough.

And that was when Kat knew right away that it wasn't a mannequin, after all.

"Call 911!" Kat yelled.

"What?" Linda said.

"It's a body."

When she touched it, Kat was certain it was a real woman because, she later said, "it felt like human flesh."

CHAPTER 13

Captain of the YCSO Detective Division (DD), Jerry Hoffman, along with several officers, raced toward a SWAT call when dispatch radioed to tell Hoffman that the emergency situation had been resolved.

This was a good thing. Anytime cops disengaged from what could be a volatile and potentially violent scene, there is a fleeting moment of celebration.

A moment later, however, dispatch called back, indicating the celebration on this day would be short-lived.

"Go ahead . . . ," Hoffman said.

"There's a body been found out on Apple Road."

Hoffman hit his lights and headed toward the park, arriving at 12:25 P.M., just over ten minutes after the 911 call from Linda and Kat had been made.

There were two patrol officers on scene when Hoffman pulled up. The first thing that struck the investigator as he drove up to the scene was how secluded the area was where the body had been found.

"This is a very rural area," Hoffman said. "There is only one residence on it that I know of. It runs through the state park, and the area . . . It's a pretty isolated area. . . ."

In other words, a good place to burn and dispose of a body.

As Hoffman got out of his vehicle and walked up to the body, one of his officers said, "I think it might be a mannequin, Captain."

"Like somebody pulling a prank or something?"

"Yeah."

The scene had a surreal vibe to it. The body, if one didn't know any better, seemed as though it could be a mannequin. Kat had thought so.

Hoffman approached the body, getting himself close enough, he said, "to see, like, a ridge detail on the bottom of the foot."

Staring at it, Hoffman knew then that "it was, indeed, a person."

Mannequins don't have that type of feature.

The captain told his officers to get some crime scene tape up around the area and watch it closely. He didn't want anyone unassociated with the investigation to enter the scene and possibly contaminate it. Just because a body had been burned, it did not mean there wasn't trace evidence and possibly DNA left behind.

Hoffman noted that whoever placed the woman here had bound her legs together with some type of wire or cord. To Hoffman, this meant they were looking at the potential cover-up of a violent murder.

When members of the DD realized they had a second body found in a wooded area within a few weeks' time, alarm bells went off that they might be looking at a serial killer working in the area. Here were two dead females; each was found under similar circumstances, about ten miles apart (depending on which way you drove); both areas were just below the North Carolina border; both victims obviously were murdered in one location and dumped in a second.

Not to mention, with a second female having been burned the way she had, did this indicate that perhaps her killer, after realizing his first body had been found so easily in that culvert, had now figured out that he might want to try and get rid of his victims from this point on?

CHAPTER 14

On Monday, November 16, Shellie Nations was at home, keeping herself busy doing what housewives and mothers do. She had been thinking about the last time she saw Randi on Randi's birthday and how sad Randi had seemed. Some weeks had gone by. They'd spoken on the phone a few times and made plans to see each other, but life had gotten in the way and priorities kept them apart. What Shellie didn't know—and how could she?—was that Randi's life had been on a fast-moving, downward trajectory over the course of the past few months.

Randi had been living with a boyfriend, Tim Gause, in a house they had emptied out because it was being foreclosed on. She had been running with some of the same people Heather Catterton had. The sting of drug addiction for Randi had become infected. She had been doing things that, had it not been for the drugs, she would not have ever thought of attempting. Randi essentially had become the type of person she had once helped out. Tragically, she managed to keep it all hidden from those in her life who could have helped her.

What was she thinking? Shellie thought as an item on the

nightly news caught her attention. Shellie had just sat down, happy to be off her feet for the first time that day, when the newscaster reported another body had been found in York County, South Carolina, just below the North Carolina border.

When Shellie heard of possible ties to Gastonia, she paid attention.

The YCSO had released a photograph of a tattoo found on the woman's body—one of only a few sections that had not been burned or charred beyond the recognizable beauty and ceramic-like texture of the woman's skin. What greatly worried investigators was how the woman's killer had wrapped her in a blanket and bound her legs with what they now knew to be a piece of cut electrical cord. This was not some sort of overdose or accidental death being covered up by a group of dopers, a gallon of gas and a stupid idea. That deduction was clear from the evidence thus far.

"York County was greatly concerned," said one North Carolina law enforcement official, "that they had a serial killer on their hands and he would soon strike again. And when they discovered that both victims lived in Gastonia, that was when they called on the Gaston County Police [Department] for help."

Shellie was listening to every word spoken by the newscaster, who was reporting from as close to the Kings Mountain State Park crime scene as cops would allow. In the background, as the reporter told a familiar tale, you could see the yellow crime-scene tape flapping in the wind, marking off the area. A black char mark on the ground was visible in the distance.

Then the news showed a photograph of the tattoo. Investigators were hoping the victim's family would recognize it and call in.

That tattoo looks very familiar, Shellie thought, staring at the television. The YCSO had released a partial photo, actually: just the green leaf section of what had been a red flower.

Shellie called out for her husband.

"Yeah?" he responded, walking into the living room.

"I really want you to watch the news. This tattoo they're showing really looks familiar to me."

It was 5:30 P.M. As each moment passed, Shellie was beginning to worry more.

"We need to go find Randi *right* now," she told her husband. Shellie wanted Randi in front of her, so she could see her and hug her and know—without a doubt—that this was all just a terrible coincidence. She wanted to convince herself that the way she felt was how several other people watching might be feeling, staring at the same tattoo.

"Sure, Shell. Let's go."

Shellie and her husband searched all the places she knew Randi either hung out or had spent time at. Randi had been so mobile over the past few months that it was hard to track her down to any one spot.

"We could not find her," Shellie recalled.

Shellie and her husband returned home near midnight. As the time passed, Shellie went through a roller coaster of emotions.

"My mind was telling me she was all right," Shellie said. "But my heart was telling me something different."

Shellie's and Randi's mother had severe heart problems. She'd been struggling with those issues for many years. Shellie didn't want to concern her mother, but she did want to tell her what was going on.

It was the tattoo. Shellie kept seeing it in her mind.

That . . . *coincidence.*

"Listen, Mom," Shellie told her mother that night, "they found a girl over at the [park], and I cannot find Randi." Shellie's voice told her mother how concerned she was that her sister was not around and she hadn't heard from her.

"Oh, Shellie, she's all right," her mother said. "You worry too much."

Shellie stood with the phone in her hand. She felt a "pit," as she described it later, in the middle of her stomach. "And I knew," Shellie said later, "that it was *not* all right."

CHAPTER 15

The following morning, Shellie woke after a night of tossing and turning, staring at the ceiling. She immediately called Crime Stoppers. She wanted more information about the tattoo and the girl found in the woods. Shellie knew Randi had a second tattoo of a sun with a smiley face on the right side of her upper back. If she could confirm that the girl found in the woods did *not* have that same tattoo, she could go back to her life and stop worrying.

"I cannot share any of that information with you, nor do I know," the Crime Stoppers operator said. "But I can have an investigator call you back."

Shellie figured it would take forever. Something also told her that when Randi found out all the trouble Shellie was going through in searching for her, "she was going to be really pissed off at me." There was a little angel of optimism whispering in Shellie's ear that Randi had run off somewhere and would find out about all of this and become angry with Shellie for inviting the cops into her life. Yet, it was a risk that Shellie was willing to take to curb the anxiety of thinking that Randi was in the morgue.

"At the same time, however," Shellie admitted, "my heart was telling me something was wrong. I just knew."

Within five minutes, an investigator called Shellie back. This was exceptional, Shellie knew.

Five minutes?

"Can we speak to you in person?" the investigator asked. He wanted Shellie to meet him and another investigator.

"Sure, sure . . . ," Shellie answered. "I'm on my way."

And with that, Shellie recalled, she breathed a sigh of relief. She honestly now believed they had found Randi. They had located her in a jail somewhere and Shellie needed to go and bail her out. It was actually a weight off Shellie's shoulders to hear the investigator say he wanted her to meet him downtown.

CHAPTER 16

Dr. Sabrina Gast was overseeing the autopsy of the latest girl found in the woods. Here it was a few weeks later and now two women had been found. The attending pathologist on this new case was Dr. Nicholas I. Batalis. He would conduct the autopsy at the Department of Pathology, on the University of South Carolina campus.

As Batalis got to work, unlike in Heather Catterton's case, it became clear within no time at all that they were dealing with a homicide. The cause of death, undisputed among doctors, was strangulation.

From a careful observation of the body and how it had been burned, the doctor determined that the woman's killer had wrapped her in a comforter. The burns were postmortem, most likely, which gave everyone some relief that she had not been burned alive.

Portions of a burned comforter, Batalis noted, *accompany the body and are on the left side of the face, under the body, and on the left leg.* The doctor also identified several pieces of "burned fabric" and an "identifiable brassiere," along with *a copper colored metal wire [wrapped] around the lower extremities, just below the knees.*

In his notes, Batalis described a tattoo of a "red flower with green leaves," a portion of which had been publicized on the news. He also found a tattoo of a "sun with a smiley face" on the woman's "upper right side" of the back. There was a third tattoo of "a band design" (barbed wire) on her upper right arm, "nearly circumferential."

The next section of Batalis's report was under the title EVIDENCE OF INJURY—and there it was: "strangulation." Batalis was certain, adding: *The inferior right eyelid has scattered purple petechiae.*

Petechiae are small red or dark-colored spots indicating hemorrhage. There are only a few reasons why someone would have these types of spots (broken capillary blood vessels) in their eyes. Trauma was on the top of the list.

The discovery that caused Batalis to consider that she had been strangled to death was a *faint 2 ½ inch area of blue contusions . . . on the lateral left side of the mandible and neck—approximately ten red contusions, up to 1 inch, are on the anterolateral left side of the neck.*

When Batalis cut and then filleted her neck back and examined the muscles, tendons, and tissue, he found additional hemorrhaging, along with several fractures. Unlike Heather Catterton, who might have been choked and then killed by asphyxiation (a bag or a pillow over her face), this woman's killer kept up pressure on her neck, choking her until she died.

Moving forward with the theory they were looking at the work of one killer, the question became: Had he learned from his earlier experience with Heather? Serial killers, any armchair profiler can reckon, evolve from one murder to the next, even if they choose the same MO.

There were other injuries Batalis noted: contusions on her tongue, back, arms, one ear, legs, left eye, nose, and additional places.

With this, and no further explanation, it appeared her killer had savagely beaten her, too.

* * *

YCSO Forensic Investigator Brian Bagwell attended the autopsy. Bagwell was there to collect any evidence that he could take back to the lab for further testing. Part of Bagwell's job was to identify victims of murder. Bagwell was on the team that had taken Heather's fingerprints and identified her after putting them into the Automated Fingerprint Identification System (AFIS).

"AFIS is a computerized system that basically searches all of the criminal arrest records and police records in South Carolina," Bagwell explained. "We have access to the federal, as well, throughout AFIS. But what it does is allow us to enter fingerprints in and plot points of minutiae on it. And the computer, through its little magic and rhythms that it uses, it looks at those points that we have plotted and tries to find matches for us."

Sort of—but not exactly—like the procedures chronicled on dramatic television series, such as *CSI* and *NCIS,* which exaggerate the tool a bit, but under the guise of factual significance.

Bagwell did the same with Randi as he had done with Heather: He submitted her fingerprints into AFIS. He also collected her clothing (what was left of it) and any fabric debris left over from the fire, the copper wire ligature unbound from her legs, some "pulled scalp hair," oral, vaginal, and rectal swabs, along with a tube of blood.

Regarding the victim's anus and vagina, Batalis indicated that he did not find any evidence of violent sexual behavior. Similar to Heather's case, Randi's killer did not appear to be sexually motivated. His MO was not to rape or sexually torture these women. He was not a sexual deviant in the sense that these women were there for his sexual pleasure. When that type of killer was done with the sexual aspect, he would murder and discard them—an uncontrollable urge many serial killers exhibit.

No intact spermatozoa are identified on vaginal, oral and rectal smears, Batalis noted.

From all outward signs, this killer was much more dangerous than your sexually motivated serial, because here, it appeared, he was driven entirely by the kill itself—at least the way things looked at this stage. And any time investigators stared down the barrel of that type of serial killer, they knew a race was on: Because if this guy was getting off on the act of strangulation alone, or watching as these ladies suffered horrible deaths, he was more of a danger than most. What made his clock keep time, in other words, was a sheer determination to kill. Nothing else. He liked to put his hands around women's throats and play God. Stare at them in the eyes as he took their lives. A guy like that cannot stop. Killing, in turn, becomes as addictive as a drug.

CHAPTER 17

Shellie was not in a melancholic mood or worried about Randi as she drove toward her meeting with two YCSO investigators on the morning of November 17, 2009. She was hopeful. That call she took from an investigator somewhat convinced her there was soon to be a reunion with her sister.

All right, Shellie told herself. *Randi's in jail and I'll have to get her out.*

There were worse things. Randi would be upset. They'd talk it out, but everything would be okay.

Shellie pulled into the parking lot and saw two investigators standing by an unmarked police vehicle.

"They had no expression on their faces," Shellie remembered.

She parked, got out of her vehicle, walked over to the men.

They introduced themselves.

The tallest one asked, "By any chance, did your sister have a sun tattoo—a picture of a sun, on her back?"

This stunned Shellie, stopping her in her tracks. A brick wall.

By instinct alone, Shellie walked backward. Her hands flew over her mouth; her mind shouted, *No . . . no. . . . Please, no. Not Randi. . . . No. Please . . . God. No. No.*

A barrage of tears then came on. Shellie ran, but did not get too far. Her legs gave out and she collapsed on the pavement. She was weak from emotion, not enough strength even to get up off the ground. An overwhelming amount of grief took control of her body. It crushed her.

The detectives rushed over and picked Shellie up off the ground.

They didn't say much. They didn't need to.

It didn't seem real—like one of those numbing moments in life when time stands still. In this situation, your mind wants to tell you that it must be some mistake. There is some other woman out in the world with the same tattoo, the same color hair, the same eyes, the same lovable demeanor.

The same name.

But Shellie knew better. Denial would not serve her right.

"Come on, Mrs. Nations. We cannot let you leave here like this."

It took some time, but Shellie got herself together the best she could. She was going to get through this like she'd gotten through every other traumatic moment of her life. Shellie had the will of a lion, the heart of a lamb. She was strong. The big sister. She had to be there now for Randi in other ways. It was going to hurt like hell once this settled, but she needed to pull herself together, at least for the moment.

The children.

"You cannot tell my mother about this right now," Shellie told detectives. "Her heart is weak. She'll have a heart attack."

More tears.

My God . . . Randi. No.

That ripple effect of one murder: Shellie was living it. She was feeling it.

Shellie explained that she wanted to be the one to break the news to her mom.

They agreed.

Shellie drove out of the parking lot and decided she'd better go over and talk to her mother now, before the woman saw it on the news.

Her mother lived in a house with three steps leading up to the front door. Shellie got out of her car, feeling emotional pain pulling her down weightily. She said, "I could not even make it up three steps. I had to crawl into my mother's house."

The pain was unbearable. Randi was gone. As it hit her, Shellie crumbled. No more tacos on their birthdays. Laughs. Serious talks. No more watching TV together and chatting about their lives. All those thoughts and memories any one of us would think of in this situation ran through Shellie's mind. Her only sister—they were so close in age—was never coming home. And now Shellie had the grave task of revealing this information to their mother.

Shellie's mother had never seen her daughter in this state of total emotional devastation. The loss was written all over Shellie's face.

"Shell, what is wrong with you?" her mother asked.

She told her.

Shellie's mother walked from one end of the house to the other, not knowing what to do with herself, where to go.

"I felt so helpless," Shellie said later. "It was horrific."

Then Shellie had to tell Randi's oldest boy, just fourteen then. He was visiting at the time.

Shellie sat him down at the dining-room table. "It's your mom, honey. She's been . . . she's been killed."

The boy turned pale. He took a moment. His lower lip quivered. He was trying to hold it together.

"I really thought you were going to tell me that Mom was in jail," he finally said.

Telling a fourteen-year-old that his mother had been murdered, Shellie said later, "was the hardest thing I have ever had to do in my life."

CHAPTER 18

Nick Catterton was looking for his daughter Nicole as news spread of another body found under similar conditions and circumstances to Heather's. Most everyone believed Heather and Randi's killer was the same man and that he might have known both women.

When Nick saw Randi's picture on the news, he thought, *Shit. I know her. She's been over to my house.*

Nick was also beginning to think he knew Heather and Randi's killer. *Florida,* it occurred to Nick. Nicole had taken off to Florida with her boyfriend, Danny Hembree. She said something about going down there to pick up some of Danny's belongings.

Nicole had called one day. She and Danny were actually in Florida.

Nick was beside himself. He called his daughter. He said, "That girl Randi y'all know, her body done just turned up, Nicole."

Nicole had no idea. She had not heard.

"Nicole, listen to me. Something's funny about this thing. Look, all this stuff is coming up. . . ."

Nick was talking about learning recently of Danny Hembree's past arrest record and his overall creep factor. Not to mention all of the coincidences between Danny and the two girls, which Nick was going over inside his head: Danny knew both girls. He had been with both girls shortly before they wound up dead.

"What are you talking about, Daddy?" Nicole asked.

"I bet Danny had something to do with this, Nicole," Nick said.

Nick couldn't get that final image of Randi out of his mind. He had gone over it before calling Nicole. Danny, along with Randi, had been at his house one day not long ago. Nick had caught them smoking dope inside Nicole's room. Nick had to kick them out of the house. Nick watched as Randi left his house with Danny. Then someone had said the last person to see Heather was Danny.

Nick's mind went wild with possibilities. He knew there was no harm in being wrong about something like this.

"You need to get away from him right now," Nick explained to his daughter. There was pure panic in Nick's voice. He was scared for his only living daughter. Was Danny on some killing spree? Was Nicole next?

Nicole didn't seem too worried. "Daddy—"

"No, listen, Nicole. You done need to get to the darn police station. Let them know what's going on and then have them contact me, and I'll send you a bus ticket."

"No, Daddy."

"Come on now, Nicole. You need to get away from him. Now!"

"They's found Randi's body?" Nicole asked, sounding almost as if she thought her father had been lying about it.

Nicole wasn't alarmed, and she didn't seem to be too hung up on any connections between her boyfriend and her dead sister and Randi Saldana. She had been with Danny Hembree just about every day, for weeks and months. He was no killer. He was a lot of things, Nicole believed, but a serial killer?

No way.

They hung up.

Nick spent the night worrying. Since the day he had found out his daughter was dead, Nick gave up drinking and hadn't touched a drop. Now he was worried sick that his only living daughter was going to wind up in a ditch somewhere between Florida and North Carolina.

What Nick didn't know then was that law enforcement had the same concern.

"We worried Nicole was going to be next," one detective told me. "The clock was ticking."

CHAPTER 19

A cold chill fell over those towns within the York County boundary where Randi and Heather had been found. Not from the weather. This was an ominous, gloomy, unspoken sentiment: It appeared that a sadistic serial killer was roaming the streets in search of his next victim. Residents looked at one another squint-eyed and accusatory: *Is it you?* After all, until this guy was behind bars, it didn't seem young females were safe to walk the streets. Over at the Bear's Den, a local bar outside one of the gates into the park where Randi had been found, patrons did a lot of head shaking, wondering to themselves what was going on within their otherwise calm, pleasant Southern community. One guy, taking a moment from his drink to talk to a local reporter, couldn't believe what he'd heard. Right there, just beyond the doors of the tavern, someone had tried covering up a murder by burning a human body—a woman, no less.

"I'm worried for all the small girls," that man told a local-television news outlet. "That's who they seem to be hitting on, and like [everyone] said, it might be a serial killer."

Law enforcement didn't want to take chances. Police departments sent out warnings. More than they had in the past, men probably said "I love you" to their daughters and wives whenever they parted ways. Several women went on record to the local newspapers saying how scared they were, but they did not want to use their names, fearing, of course, that a serial killer was watching, listening, targeting.

The YCSO caught up with Tim Gause, the guy Randi had been living with at the time of her disappearance. In speaking with Tim, the YCSO was able to pinpoint that on the previous Thursday, November 12, at some point that evening, Randi left the Shannon Bradley Road home in Gastonia she was staying at, a solid fifteen-mile ride north of Apple Road in Kings Mountain State Park, where her corpse had later been located.

Tim was an obvious first person of interest. When the YCSO caught up to him, he explained that Randi had left the house on Thursday night to "go see a friend." He didn't say who it was, or where she was headed.

"I would never hurt her for nothing in the world," Tim told reporters. "I would never put my hands on her."

There was a corner gas station just down the block from the house that Tim Gause and Randi Saldana lived in. Investigators picked up surveillance-camera footage from the store from a camera pointed toward their residence. Disappointingly, however, there was a tree in the way of seeing if Randi had left the house when Tim said she had.

The next few days were busy for the YCSO. There was a lot of work to do, on top of getting the word out that a potential serial killer was stalking women of the region. They were challenged to accomplish this without spreading total fear and panic throughout the community. There was a fine line in that regard. People needed to know—especially young females living high-risk lives, but investigators didn't want to send the community into a frenzy. That would scare away potential witnesses and deter them from coming forward.

"Before another girl comes up missing," Heather's grief-stricken father, Nick Catterton, came out and told a local-television news station, "somebody needs to find out who this guy is."

Nick thought he knew the perp personally, but he wasn't saying it publicly. He'd tagged Danny Hembree as the guy—that creep who'd been hanging around Nick's house and taking off with his daughter, Nicole. She had since returned from Florida with Danny, telling her father he was crazy for thinking her boyfriend was a serial killer.

As Nick began to consider the chilling reality that Heather's and Randi's killer was sticking close to him and his family, he thought back to how Danny had offered to help carry Heather's casket during her funeral, but then he bailed out on the service at the last minute.

For a serial killer, there can be no other high than hanging around the family of one of his victims. In law enforcement's view, as one detective standing on the periphery of this case for the time being, later told me, there were good reasons for this behavior: "He wants to know what the family knows. Keep track of the investigation from the inside out. Be one step ahead at all times."

CHAPTER 20

Early in the morning, November 17, YCSO investigator Alex Wallace called Danny Hembree. There was a feeling among investigators that they had to scratch him off their list, or put him at the top. There were too many coincidences surrounding Danny Hembree to simply write him off: his connection to Heather and his overall life of crime. He had alibis for both cases and was open to talking to police. But how much of what Danny was saying turned out to be truthful? And who could verify his alibis besides him and his girlfriend, Nicole?

"Listen, Danny . . . how are you?" Wallace said, opening up the conversation. Danny was familiar with Wallace and the YCSO.

"Good, good," he responded. "What can I do for you?"

"I'd like to know if you'd come on into the sheriff's office and take a polygraph for me and clear some things up. We just want to confirm some information we have."

The main thrust of the YCSO asking Danny Hembree to take a polygraph was based on the information they had regarding him being the last person to see Heather on the night of October 18. The YCSO had heard this from a credible source.

"I've been forthcoming with information," Danny explained. He was clearly a bit agitated. "I'm getting pissed now, though. Y'all got me fired from my job."

The YCSO had put some pressure on Danny Hembree since Heather's disappearance. They followed him and asked around town about him. They'd questioned some of his friends and party buddies.

"How so, Danny?"

"Y'all went up there to my work site and talked to my boss."

Wallace tried to say something.

Danny interrupted, speaking over him: "My mom is thinking of kicking me out of the house, too."

"Come on, Danny—" Wallace started to say, but he couldn't get a word in. Danny was on a roll.

"Y'all went to my momma's house and you done told her I was smoking crack!"

"We never went to your job site, Danny—and we did *not* tell your momma anything that she didn't already know."

Danny took a moment. Then he got loud; pure rage spewed out of him: "Fuck you! Don't call me again!"

He hung up.

CHAPTER 21

Tim Gause claimed to have nothing to hide. On Wednesday, November 18, the YCSO approached Tim and asked him if he was willing to take a polygraph. There was something about the guy that investigators just didn't like. He seemed sketchy, acting odd during those immediate days after finding out the woman he claimed to have loved had been found murdered, her body torched. The key here for investigators was that Randi's body had been burned, meaning that her killer was desperately trying to hide evidence. This indicated that perhaps Randi knew her killer. Or was worried his DNA could be traced easily back to him.

"I have nothing to hide," Tim announced.

What's more, Tim and Nick both claimed that Randi and Heather knew each other casually from the street—that they weren't simply acquaintances from jail, as some had suggested, but had actually hung out together.

"She stopped by our house," Nick said, talking about Randi. "She came by to see Heather."

Nick had no idea how the girls might have met, but he was certain they had been together in those days before Heather was last seen. He explained this to the YCSO.

"I think Randi and Heather knew 'of each other,' had some mutual friends, but did not *know* each other, hang out, et cetera," a law enforcement official told me. "There was a big age difference between them. . . . If you are involved in the world of drugs and have been to jail, you tend to know the other people involved in the same activities."

Tim voluntarily went into the YCSO on Friday, November 20. Of course, they asked him several questions, but the main reason for the visit was put to him across the table quickly: "Did you have any role in the deaths of Heather Catterton and/or Randi Saldana?"

"I did not hurt either girl," Tim replied.

He was asked the same question again.

"No," Tim said a second time.

Once more.

"No!" Tim stressed.

Tim Gause had been talkative with the local media. He came out that same night of his polygraph and discussed it with a local television news station. Beyond saying how he had responded "no" to hurting either of the girls, Tim sent a warning out to the public, "If I was a female friend of Randi's . . . I would be *very* afraid right now."

The sense was that Randi and Heather's killer was targeting a certain group of local girls. He was choosing each girl. It was almost as if he was at home, sitting, tacking up on a wall the photos of each victim. A spread of additional photos—future victims—on the table in front of him. He instilled fear—not only with the female population in town, but with law enforcement, too, many who now felt they were working against a clock.

"I don't know if it was the lifestyle, or if it was where they were going," Tim told local television news station WCNC. "I wish I knew more."

An aunt of Randi's came out and told the media that Randi had fallen "into a rough crowd" lately, and her lifestyle had made it such that she was around some of the seedier characters in town. Investigators knew that lifestyle choices can result in death.

In this part of the state, the failed economy had taken a drastic toll on locals. Hard-core drugs were more prevalent than they had been in the past. In this regard, as Gaston County law enforcement sniffed around and became more interested in the people associated with the cases, they were now sending messages into the community when the opportunity arose.

Whenever a sheriff found a girl walking by herself, he or she stopped. "Hey, be cautious. And always let someone know where you are and where you're going."

Sage advice. That clock *was* ticking. Everyone felt it. And if this maniac wasn't stopped soon, another body was certain to show up.

CHAPTER 22

Twenty-eight-year-old Gaston County Police Department (GCPD) detective Matt Hensley was at SWAT school during the second week of November when news of a potential serial killer roaming the streets of his jurisdiction broke. Hensley had heard about Heather's murder and the ensuing YCSO investigation. However, when a second body turned up, and it was learned that she was also from Gastonia, the case took on an entire new level of intensity for all law enforcement within Gaston County.

Once a year, cops head out and undertake firearms and tactical exercises in several different areas—i.e., SWAT school training. There are various competitive sessions during the week. In this day and age of terrorism (both homegrown and international), law enforcement has to be ready and trained for anything. Not to mention those types of routine calls that law enforcement agencies receive: such as a suspect holed up in a house or hotel with an arsenal of weapons, looking to go out in a blaze of bloodshed.

Hensley was a North Carolina transplant, yet no stranger to the South, having grown up in Chattanooga, Tennessee.

His family moved to Gaston County when Hensley was in his teens. It wasn't some sort of childhood dream to become a cop. Hensley went to college and majored in business. His first job out of school was with Lowe's Corporation in its corporate offices near Mooresville, North Carolina. Yet, after a short stint at Lowe's, working within that corporate environment, Hensley found the work to be rather unfulfilling.

"I wanted to become a detective," Hensley realized. He craved excitement and the pressure of performance. Toiling inside a cubicle farm all day, counting beans—with all due respect to his former coworkers for their chosen profession—wasn't what Hensley realized he wanted to do. He wanted to be out in the world, solving puzzles, dealing with the public, helping people. Not to mention, within his family, Hensley had a pedigree to fall back on. Effectively, it was that law enforcement bloodline Hensley could not escape.

While away at SWAT school, Hensley had heard how several of his GCPD colleagues were at the Heather Catterton crime scene in North Carolina. Gaston County law enforcement had been called in on that original case to support the YCSO. Hensley read about the case in the papers while away at training school and heard various insider bits of info from colleagues.

When he returned to work, Hensley was brought into the case because of the connection both victims had to Gastonia. Hensley was deeply engrained in the Gastonia drug culture; he had informants on the street. He knew people. With Heather and Randi being Gastonia residents, the case was setting itself up to become a collaboration of agencies. The YCSO had been bringing witnesses and even a few early suspects (who were quickly ruled out) into the GCPD station house in downtown Gastonia to question. The GCPD had the facilities for videotaping and recording interviews, along with being close to Heather and Randi's stomping grounds.

It was a natural fit to use the GCPD facility and its resources.

With a second body now found, along with early reports of the two girls running in somewhat similar circles, the YCSO was leaning toward forming a task force. Two weeks, two bodies. They did not want to see—but anxiously feared—a third body showing up soon.

"Both Heather and the second girl, Randi, had the same sort of people they interacted with," Hensley explained. "So the idea for York County was to form this task force, which consisted of them, us, the Gastonia Police, and even law enforcement from Charlotte. We all needed to figure out the next course of action."

The YCSO did have a prime suspect they liked for the crimes. However, Hensley pointed out, "There was so much information coming up on the girls and other people as possibly having motives or being seen with the girls, we needed to hunt down those leads as well."

As an investigation such as this begins, sometimes it can be hard for law enforcement to keep track of all the information coming in. You have two victims, two crimes scenes (and in this case, both crime scenes were secondary scenes, or dump sites, not murder scenes), two different states, all sorts of seedy drug-culture characters involved, on top of witnesses coming forward.

None of that, of course, mattered to the families of the victims, who wanted answers. It didn't make any difference that these women might have done things for drugs they weren't proud of, or that they knew scuzzy people. They were human beings with loved ones, people who missed them, and their murders were being felt by everyone in the community. Law enforcement, moreover, looked at these victims as women and members of the community and did not define them by their behavior.

*   *   *

On November 23, Matt Hensley acquainted himself further with the case. He sat in on an interview that the YCSO conducted with Stella Funderburk, Heather's mother, which took place inside the GCPD station house.

Hensley was in the sergeant's office watching the interview on a closed-circuit video monitor. He was with YCSO detective Alex Wallace, who briefed Hensley on all they knew by then about each case, bringing him up to speed on every detail of the investigation.

Wallace mentioned a few names to Hensley, saying, "We served a search warrant on Tim Gause's house. He's been our focus really." Wallace also talked about Nick's prime suspect, Danny Hembree, who was a repeat violent offender. The YCSO had learned that Danny Hembree had been in and out of jail and prison for most of his adult life. Law enforcement knew his name well.

"Hembree's the boyfriend of Nicole Catterton, Heather's sister," Wallace explained. "According to several people we interviewed, he was the last person to be with Heather, along with a few other people."

"Where's Hembree living?"

"He's been staying with the Catterton family."

Hensley was immediately interested in Danny Hembree, as was the YCSO. Anyone involved in the amount of crime that Danny had been connected to needed to be looked at closely. There was also a report, Wallace added, that Danny Hembree had been seen with Randi before she disappeared. But they were looking to track down the source of the information and button it up. If true, the evidence was overwhelming on that alone: Same guy last seen with two dead girls. What were the chances he didn't have anything to do with their deaths?

"He drives a red four-door Ford Escort," Wallace explained, looking at his notes from the case as they talked. "Nicole and Hembree, they lived at the house with Heather and Nicole's father, Nick."

Nick was probably as good a source as anyone else to interview.

Hensley and Wallace turned their attention to the interview the YCSO was conducting with Stella Funderburk, who had explained how she'd been hanging around the house one day earlier that week and something happened she thought might be important. Stella was still feeling the effect and sting of her daughter's death. Heather's murder had been devastating to her family, an already broken bunch. They had no idea how to deal with it. Not being the mother she had dreamt of being to Heather, Stella was dazed by the blow.

Nicole had walked into the room where her mother sat, Stella explained to detectives, as Hensley and Wallace looked on from the other room. Nicole was wearing what Stella described as "new jewelry." This was something in the Catterton house everyone noticed: It wasn't every day that Heather or Nicole wore flashy jewelry. So it stuck out, Stella said, when one of them had something new.

Nicole never had any money, so Stella asked about the necklace.

"Where'd you get it?"

Nicole said, "It's Randi's."

Nicole had been wearing a piece of Randi Saldana's jewelry.

This was a major lead, if it was true.

"We spoke to Randi's family," Wallace told Hensley as they watched. "They claimed that Randi was very protective of her jewelry, especially, and would never give it to anyone."

Law enforcement brass was in the midst of creating a task force, figuring that to catch a serial killer before he killed again, two hands were surely better than one, but a dozen was even better than that.

"There's a meeting tomorrow morning," Wallace told Hensley.

Hensley said he'd be there.

"You know," Hensley commented later, "South Carolina had two bodies, and with this task force, they were hoping to stop another body from showing up before it happened. Of course, we found out that both the girls were drug users . . . and ran in similar circles. We needed to look at their lives. . . . When both were last seen, we confirmed, each had been with Danny Hembree."

Danny Hembree seemed like the perfect candidate to place inside the box (interrogation room) and interview. If nothing else, they needed to conduct a complete study of his life of crime and interview people who knew him. Find out what he's been up to the past few months—a guy like Danny Hembree, he could be ruled in or out quickly.

Law enforcement decided that a search warrant of Nick's house was in order. It was based mostly on that devastating (and quite promising) information from Stella that her daughter was in possession of Randi's jewelry. This was potentially explosive evidence. Why in the world was the sister of one dead girl wearing the necklace from a second dead girl?

But then you added the common denominator to that question—Danny Hembree—and it all seemed to come into focus.

Hensley and Wallace agreed to sit on the Catterton house as they waited on the warrant. They would park down the block and keep an eye on the ebb and flow of the residence.

CHAPTER 23

Sommer Heffner was a stunningly attractive, petite seventeen-year-old girl with shiny brown hair, bright and alluring aqua-colored eyes, along with the perfect little nose and high chiseled cheekbones some actresses might spend tens of thousands of dollars trying to obtain. Sommer had grown up with Heather. They had known each other, Sommer later explained in her cute, comforting Southern accent, "since we was kids."

Sommer called Heather "my sister," describing Heather as "outgoing" and "fun" to be around. "She wouldn't never hurt nobody," Sommer told me. Another common phrase associated with Heather from Sommer's perspective was "heart of gold."

The rainbow-colored toe socks Heather wore on the day she was murdered summed up the life Heather had dreamt of for herself.

"Heather wanted to work with kids, actually," Sommer said. "Special-needs kids."

Like those toe socks, Heather's dreams were vibrant and varied. There wasn't one particular color that best depicted Heather's usual upbeat, jovial demeanor, her far-reaching cheerful attitude, and her optimistic outlook on a life that had pretty much been stuck since as long as anyone who knew her could recall. The color missing from that rainbow, the darkest shade of black, represented the thunderstorm of trouble Heather had been mixed up in during those days before her death.

"You could have the worst day in the world," Sommer said, "and there was Heather to put a smile on your face."

Mud pies and water sprinklers and chasing boys were the things Heather and Sommer did as kids. They built Legos. They weren't the type of girly-girls to play with Barbies or baby dolls. One of Sommer's fondest memories was the two of them as very young kids planting sunflowers together, something they did every spring, a sign of a new beginning, a rebirth.

Heather's desire to work with children was born from having to take care of her sister Nicole's two kids, when Nicole wasn't around.

"She was only, like, twelve or thirteen," Sommer explained, "and she was taking care of her sister's two babies."

Nicole was sixteen when she had her first child; she was seventeen when she had her second.

According to Sommer, who witnessed most of it firsthand while hanging out at Heather's house as a child, it was the "environment she grew up in" that introduced Heather to the bottomless, merciless world of hard-core drugs. It was all around her, Sommer said. Everyone in Heather's life was doing it.

The girl didn't have a chance.

"And she never really got away from it until she went into foster care," Sommer said.

Heather stayed with one foster family for a few years.

"But she did miss her own family," Sommer remembered.

And it was that blood bond that ultimately pulled Heather out of a calm, unchaotic, healthy atmosphere of a family unit enjoying a quiet, normal life. As warm and caring as her foster family was, Heather missed her mother, father, sister, and especially "her [step]brother" and her sister's babies, Sommer said. That pull, for some, is too much. They often jump back into the dysfunction, even knowing how bad it is for them.

"She missed her [step]brother the most. She was very close to him," Sommer said. "And she just got tired of that environment [at the foster family's home] because it just wasn't what she was used to."

Sommer was describing how codependency works. Dysfunctional families breed codependency. If left untreated, experts say, codependency gets worse. General symptoms include low self-esteem, not knowing (and exhibiting poor) boundaries, caretaking, control, obsession, denial, not being able to experience intimacy, not being able to take rejection, abandonment, people-pleasing. This was a script for Heather's life—only she didn't know it.

Sommer slept over at the foster family's house one night. She and Heather sat on the bed in Heather's room and talked about boys and crushes. Sommer wanted to know about the boys Heather liked.

Heather had something else on her mind, however. "I'm running away from here," she said. "I need to see my [step]-brother." Heather was tired of the structured, disciplined atmosphere of a foster home and missed her family terribly.

So Sommer and Heather busted out a window and took off with the clothes on their backs. They were fifteen.

Heather never went back. She fell deeply into her addictions and started to sleep at friends' houses and other family members' homes. She was classified as a runaway child, now part of an institutional system she would begin to spend time locked up in.

"She just went from house to house to house," Sommer said. "And that was when she started smoking crack."

The life destroyer.

Crack.

Poison.

Heather was a fragile girl who had experienced a lifetime's worth of grown-up activity (and emotional pain) by the time she hit puberty. Now she was messing with one of the most addictive drugs (cheaper than alcohol) the street had to offer.

CHAPTER 24

Back on October 17, the day before Heather went missing, Sommer took a call from her best friend. "I just got out [of jail] and I'm at my dad's house," Heather explained. She sounded defeated and tired, but was happy to hear Sommer's voice. It was clear Heather wanted to see her BFF. "I need you to come here now."

"I'll be right over."

Heather and Sommer often met at Nick's house in Gastonia, using the house as a staging area to decide where they were going to party for the night. It was early afternoon on this day. Sommer was with her boyfriend, George Baston (pseudonym). They had no way of getting over to see Heather, so they started walking from George's house.

As they trekked down the road toward Nick's, Danny Hembree came rolling up. Danny was the type of guy that preyed on the young girls around town and lured many of them to have sex with him by providing drugs. He had a fixation with this: paying girls to pleasure him.

"He's a sex addict," said one girl who knew him.

Violent sexual deviant was more like it.

Danny Hembree was driving down the road and spotted

Sommer and her boyfriend walking. He pulled up beside them.

"Hey, I'm Danny," he said, with his arm hanging out the window. There was that pronounced Southern drawl, obvious in every word he spoke. "Where y'all going?"

Sommer explained.

"Heather sent me to pick y'all up," he said. "I want to take you to see her. Get in."

Sommer looked at her boyfriend, who deferred to her judgment.

"Okay," Sommer said. "That's fine. Save us the walk, anyway."

Weirdo was what Sommer thought upon seeing Danny Hembree that first time. He just had that look in his eye, she later said. Like in his mind, he was always up to something, contemplating, scheming.

Of course, Danny knew the Cattertons. He was a regular fixture over at Nick's these days. He had dated Stella Funderburk, Heather and Nicole's mother, and had known Stella "since [we] was kids growing up." Sommer didn't know it, but Danny was dating Heather's sister, Nicole. Sommer had heard of Danny Hembree, but this was the first time she had met him.

The backcountry, simple way Danny once explained how he had gone from dating a mother to her daughter sounded as though he was doing them both a favor by gracing each with his presence: "I had promised Stella some things that I was now giving to Nicole."

As they drove, he took a different route from what Sommer knew would take them to Nick's. She looked over at her boyfriend, wondering what was going on, and then asked Danny, where was he headed?

"Momma's house. To see my daughter," he said. Danny had that hard, weathered prison look about him: a somewhat-crater face, at times a ragged gray-and-brown mustache (which he dyed tar black on occasion), dark (almost black) beady eyes, greasy dark grayish brown and black hair (with streaks of gray and white), and a strange, cocky smile off to the side of his face, indicating how his mind was always cooking up something that was probably illegal. His criminal record was longer than a college transcript. The guy had spent more time in prison than he had out of prison. He fashioned himself a badass, someone to be feared. He believed—and there can be no doubt about this fact—that he was better than anyone within his circle of friends and family.

The Hembrees lived in an area of Gastonia known as Chapel Grove, named after the main road in town. It is a section of town where bursts of well-populated Southern-style neighborhoods blossom around acreage of thickly settled woods. At the corner of Camp Rotary and Chapel Grove Roads is the Chapel Grove Baptist Church. Beyond that is the church's day care center. It's quiet here. People keep to themselves and generally take care of one another. The word "serial killer," or even "killer," is not something locals think about. Those types of evil things, as they say, happen somewhere else. God is a driving force in this community. People fear Him. They worship regularly.

As they pulled up to Danny Hembree's mother's house, Sommer and her boyfriend saw a rather pleasant home, all considering. The house was small, one of those redbrick, ranch-style box homes with black shutters. The yard and outside of the home (in the front) were kept up rather well. The backyard showed some suburban decay: fence that needed painting and repair, porch stairs that needed replacing, an empty in-ground pool, its liner ripped and cut, various brush and leaves scattered about. Danny lived here, too. He had a bedroom and den area to himself down the hall from where his mother slept.

Danny told Sommer and her boyfriend to wait in the car. He said he wouldn't be long. "Just running in to get some money and see my daughter."

They waited about thirty minutes. While alone with her boyfriend, Sommer said, "He's weird, huh?"

"Sure is," George replied, staring at the house.

("You know how you can just *tell* when people are strange?" Sommer later commented. "*That* was Danny Hembree.")

Sommer wasn't the only one who later described a suspicious, peculiar vibe emanating from Danny Hembree. Women, mainly, felt an odd sense of unkindness and nastiness when they were around the guy. Many said it was hard to explain, but think about someone you've met for the first time and there was a wisp of immorality in the air hovering over them—a gut response that there's something wrong with them.

Danny returned to the car, said nothing, and proceeded to Nick's house.

"With their upbringing, the Catterton sisters were doomed, essentially," said one law enforcement official. Heather had tried time and again, but the pipe had gotten hold of her at that young age and would not let go. According to Sommer, Heather did what she needed to do in order to fund her habits, same as a lot of girls in Heather's position. But quite contrary to what the media and others would later say, Heather had never been arrested or charged with solicitation or prostitution.

It was a sad story, and yet one that played out across America in towns where the economy had ravaged families, education budgets were slashed, and help for the poor and starving was just not there anymore. In many cases, kids only do what they are taught by those in charge of rearing them. Often drugs become a way to deal with the pain of growing up in a home where love is not enough to overpower the pull of addiction and abuse.

At the Catterton house, Danny, George, and Sommer got out of the vehicle and walked in. Danny went about his business of hanging out with Nicole, while Sommer's boyfriend sat in the living room. Sommer found Heather in the wash-room, taking a warm bath. As Sommer later put it, she was "getting ready for the night."

This was the first time Sommer had seen Heather since Heather had been released from jail. Heather had done a stint of several months after being convicted in February (2009) of possession of drug paraphernalia and felony pos-session of a controlled substance. She'd put on some prison weight, but she was still strikingly attractive, and yet as much a child at seventeen as any kid her age.

Heather and Sommer hung out in the washroom and talked while Heather finished bathing. Sommer had been clean for a time and had not used drugs. She was drinking that day, however, and they talked about what they were going to do to celebrate Heather's homecoming. As they conversed, Danny and Nicole walked in on the conversation.

Nicole asked, "What are you guys up to tonight? You have plans?"

Heather and Sommer didn't seem too interested in hang-ing out with Nicole and her weird boyfriend. Neither of them could reconcile why Nicole, so young herself and at-tractive, was dating the guy, anyway. He was twice her age. There was no doubt Danny had some sort of sexually trans-mitted disease—his skin was as yellow as a summer squash at times. Perhaps the jaundice was connected to hepatitis. He had no job, and got up in the morning with a beer in one hand and went to bed with a crack pipe in the other. What in the hell did he have to offer anyone?

Nicole picked up on the cold shoulder and walked away.

Danny waited until Nicole was out of earshot before he spoke. "Y'all want to come off and get high? Come on. I'll buy some dope." He paused a moment. Let it sit. Then, when Heather didn't respond: "I promise a good time if you come." He had that devilish, cocky look about him. This was Danny's pickup line: "I'll buy the dope if you come and party with me." He knew and understood the girls' weaknesses and exploited each one of them any chance he got. Crack was Danny Hembree's carrot; he knew the girls in town who could not resist.

Sommer believed Danny was making the offer to Heather. He knew Sommer was with George. So his plan was to party with Heather, who thought Nicole was also included. But according to everyone in that circle, Nicole did not smoke crack.

Danny liked what he saw in Heather. She had just gotten out of jail. Heather didn't have a lot of street miles on her. She had been sober for months. In his way of speaking, she was "clean." He wanted her.

"I ain't going anywhere without Sommer," Heather said. "Get your ass outta here."

Danny took a look at Sommer, eyeing her. "I don't mind her going."

"I don't know you," Sommer piped in. "I'd never go with you, without my boyfriend."

"Get outta here," Heather told Danny again. She was in the tub. No free shows for her sister's boyfriend.

"Oh, well," he said, shrugging, walking away.

Heather got herself out of the tub and went into her bedroom.

Sommer followed.

Looking through her drawers, Heather pulled out a Hollister hoodie, a strapless red bra and panties to match, blue jeans, and a diamond-studded belt. Then she put on white tennis shoes.

As Heather got dressed, Danny walked into the room. He shut the door behind him. "Come on. Come with us," he said to the two girls. He made it sound as though Nicole was going along, too. Clearly, he had something on his mind other than getting high.

They told him no. Sommer, for one, certainly wasn't going anywhere with Danny unless her boyfriend and Heather went along.

"I'm not going anywhere without George," Sommer said again.

"All right," Danny gave in, "your boyfriend can come."

Heather and Sommer looked at each other.

They agreed to go.

According to Sommer's recollection, Nicole stayed behind and knew nothing about what her boyfriend had offered the two of them.

Earlier, the girls had heard Danny and Nicole arguing. It was one of his central behaviors in this situation: Whenever he wanted to part ways with Nicole, he'd generate a fight.

"Nicole wanted me to buy her [something]," Danny Hembree would say later, recalling this night. "I told her no. She got pissed."

Sommer later said Nicole talked about heading out by herself that night.

So Heather, Sommer, Danny, along with Sommer's boyfriend, George, took off to a local store in the area known as the place in town to score some prime dope.

Danny pulled up. Some dude came out from underneath his rock and walked up to the driver's-side window. He and Danny exchanged a few words—both men very familiar with the other—and Danny gave him cash for a small tinfoil of crack.

Party time.

From the store, Danny drove to a friend's house out on Chapel Grove, a trailer park on Only Street. His pal was home. But as soon as Sommer, Heather, Danny, and Sommer's boyfriend arrived, Danny's pal took Danny's car and left—almost as if planned beforehand.

Danny wanted to be with Heather. He had a thing for her, many later claimed. When they arrived at the trailer, he knew what Heather wanted; and he also knew how to get what he wanted by dangling the drugs in front of her.

"So they went off into a bedroom," Sommer said.

Heather and Danny were gone for thirty minutes. At one

point, Sommer walked into the bedroom to see what was going on. Make sure things were okay. Sommer did not trust Danny.

"They was just butt naked," Sommer said. "On the bed. Heather seemed fine."

George walked toward the room, but Sommer stopped him before he could go any farther than the doorway. "They'all's naked, George. Let 'em be now."

"That's fine," Heather said. "He can come in."

"And afterward," Sommer said, "when they was done, we all got high."

After smoking that first round, Heather and Sommer wanted more. A crack high lasts about five to ten minutes and then, if you don't continue, that big crash comes on like a stomach bug. The world ends. You want to strangle yourself. The depression is so all-consuming, those who smoke say, you'll do whatever you can to continue. For an addict, the goal is to keep that high going as long as possible. And yet, as most addicts will agree, it is an itch that one cannot scratch hard enough, no matter how hard one tries. In many ways, you're constantly chasing that first high. Problem is, you never catch it.

Danny told everyone he wanted to go hang out inside another trailer. It was nearby—a particular trailer that had been abandoned. It was a filthy mess. Beer bottles and empty crack foils and vials were everywhere. There were blankets, dirty and bug-infested and musty, broken glass, boarded-up windows. No electricity. Mold. Mildew. And the smell—rotten, like a flooded basement in the middle of summer.

When they got inside, Danny indicated he wanted Heather and Sommer to have sex together so he could watch. And if they wanted to smoke more dope, they'd get on with the show right away.

"So Heather and me," Sommer admitted, "we put on a show."

After another round of smoking, the dope was gone.

When they finished partying in the abandoned trailer, Danny had a suggestion.

"Me and Heather, by ourselves, we's going back to my mother's house so I can get some more cash to continue the party. Any y'all got a problem with that?"

Sommer and George said they didn't; they'd wait inside the trailer.

CHAPTER 25

On November 23, Hensley and Wallace sat inside an unmarked police vehicle in the parking lot of a bowling alley down the street from Nick Catterton's home. The YCSO and GCPD had good information that Nicole had a piece of jewelry that had belonged to Randi. There wasn't a judge in the county who wouldn't sign a search warrant for the Catterton home and Nicole's body after being told of the events leading law enforcement to this place on that day.

"That looks like Hembree's Ford Escort right there," Hensley pointed out to Wallace.

The car was parked in the Catterton driveway.

"Hembree must be in the house," Wallace said.

Hensley called GCPD CSI detective Chris McAuley, who was in the process of getting the search warrant for Nick's house signed, and told him to add the red Ford Escort to the warrant. Thus, when McAuley arrived with the warrant near eight o'clock that night, not only was the body of Nicole, whose actual name on the warrant was "Wendy," and Nick's residence part of the search, but it now included the red Ford Escort and any other vehicles "located on the curtilage."

What a bonus.

Beyond Wallace, Hensley, and McAuley, Sergeant Myron Shelor joined an additional investigator to help with the search.

Nick answered the door. Because the Catterton house was located in Gastonia, a part of Gaston County, the GCPD—not the YCSO—had to serve the warrant. McAuley, who knew Nick from his days of neighborhood policing and local drug investigations, said at one point, "I'm just here tagging along."

"I haven't vacuumed the house . . . ," Nick said. The comment kind of broke up the moment, relieving any tension that might have been present. Searches can go two ways: resistance or surrender.

"Can we go on in and search your residence, Mr. Catterton?" Hensley asked.

"Yeah, go on in. I'll help you out any way I can," Nick said, eager to assist.

Hensley said Nick was "very cooperative and wanted to help us out in the search. He was encouraging us to find out who killed his daughter."

Nick's house is located just a few steps from the heavily traveled Highway 321. The house is sandwiched between the 321 and a mostly inactive train track out back. Inside the house was close quarters. You walk in through the front door and there's a small foyer area where a washer and dryer sit crouched together. The one bathroom is on the right. A few steps beyond that is a small kitchen. Take a right from there and head into a bedroom where, just outside that, another bedroom, a wee bit bigger than a closet, is situated. It's a square little house—homey, cute, but rather nondescript. A lot of the houses in this section of town share the same characteristics.

As they headed inside, someone asked Nick who lived in the house with him.

"Me and Nicole—and Danny. He been staying here," Nick said. "But mainly just me and Nicole and, well . . . Heather."

Heather—the reason why they were all there.

Nicole was twenty-three years old at the time police searched her father's house, just about to turn twenty-four. Nicole had flowing brown hair, charming green eyes, and a clear complexion. She was a quite attractive young woman, and the resemblance between her and Heather was impossible to ignore. Later, Nicole would deny being Danny Hembree's girlfriend, telling law enforcement and reporters, "We was just friends." But it was a proven fact that she and Danny had been together since Nicole walked out on her other boyfriend earlier that year.

Nicole had her share of physical difficulties. Just under her neckline, she sported a rather large flower tattoo. Above that was a hole in the center of her throat, a tracheotomy Nicole had to have in order to breathe properly. Nicole had been hit by a car while crossing the street in front of her house. (This happened on three separate occasions!) She had been badly injured, had undergone several surgeries, and was scheduled for several more. She had to use a tracheotomy because "her throat had been paralyzed," a friend later told police.

The street outside the front door of Nick's home, Highway 321, was a main thoroughfare between North and South Carolina that people traveled all day long. Some of these motorists drove very fast. Although uncommon to be struck two times—better yet three—it's one of those streets that if you stood for a time and watched cars go by, you could picture someone losing her balance or not paying attention to where she was walking and being struck.

"Some of these cars that go by here," Nick explained to one investigator as the search inside his house began, "they fly."

Nicole was every bit the big sister to Heather, looking

out for her at times while dealing with personal issues herself. Nicole had known Danny Hembree for years and never knew of him being anything other than a good soul, she later claimed.

"He was always nice . . . ," Nicole remarked, adding that she'd never seen him get violent with anyone and certainly never felt threatened by him in any way. She didn't understand what all the interest in the guy was lately.

As the team of investigators walked about the home, Danny came out from a bedroom and sat down on the couch in the living area. He seemed agitated. He focused on the television set and hardly ever looked at investigators as they searched the house around him.

Hensley asked Nick to sign a consent-to-search form.

"No problem," Nick said.

Danny Hembree and Hensley stared at each other. Danny had a brash arrogance about his gaze, as if taunting Hensley for some reason.

"He seemed to be disgusted that we were there," Hensley said later.

"Just out of curiosity," Danny said at one point, "what in the world are y'all looking for?"

"We want to be able to say that in all the locations where Heather was, we looked—we're just covering our bases," said an investigator.

"Yup," Hensley reiterated.

This seemed to satisfy Danny Hembree.

In an audio recording of the search, the television set came across loud. Nick walked from room to room with investigators, helping out where he could, pointing out areas where they might find what they were looking for.

Wallace and a colleague took Nicole into her bedroom and asked about the necklace Stella had reported was Randi's. Could Nicole produce it, or were they going to have to turn the house upside down?

Hensley stayed behind, searching in the living room, keeping a close eye on Danny Hembree.

"He ignored us most of the time and watched TV," Hensley recalled.

As he watched Nicole enter her bedroom with investigators, Danny yelled out, "What are y'all doing, going in there?" Then he directed a comment at Nicole: "You don't have to let them to go in your bedroom."

Nicole didn't respond.

Hensley laughed.

"Unless they give you a paper, they cain't do the search, Nicole," Hembree uttered with a sneer in his signature drawl.

They had that *paper,* as Hembree referred to it. Nicole knew this. She had no trouble adhering to the law. ("Nicole never revoked consent and was very cooperative," Hensley said.) Nicole and Nick wanted authorities to find Heather's killer. Why was Danny Hembree being so belligerent and unhelpful? Was it just his nature to butt heads with cops?

Nicole and Nick wrote off Danny's attitude as a characteristic "bad guy" versus "good guy" showdown. Their houseguest hated cops because they disrupted his lifestyle: burgling, robbing, smoking dope, and drinking.

Inside her bedroom, despite Danny Hembree's verbal resistance, Nicole broke out all of her jewelry.

"We can search your room—you don't have a problem with that, Miss Catterton, right?" one of the investigators asked.

"No, no . . . ," Nicole said. "Of course not."

At first, this comment made investigators wonder about Stella and the information she had given them. With Nicole being so willing, if she knew she had a dead girl's necklace in her possession, would she be so eager to roll out the red carpet for a look at her personal belongings?

Hensley soon found his way into Nicole's room and got busy, asking Nicole, "Can I go into the closet?"

"Yeah, sure," Nicole said. "Some of that stuff is Danny's, though. It's not all mine."

Detective Hensley went to work.

Nicole helped him.

"Can you explain for me, if you can, what's yours and what's Danny's?" Hensley asked.

Hensley looked on as Nicole felt around inside the closet. On the opposite side of the room, investigators were busy bagging and tagging other items, including several cigarette butts from an ashtray.

"DNA, right?" said one investigator to the other, out of Nicole's earshot.

"Yeah . . . Hembree's in CODIS."

CODIS (or the Combined DNA Index System) is a national FBI database set up for ongoing investigations (and cold cases), giving investigators a direct link to repeat offenders. It's a computer software program operating under local, state, and national databases, indexing the DNA profiles of convicted offenders, unsolved crime scene evidence, and missing persons information. If a cop develops evidence from a crime—DNA, hair, trace, blood, etc.—out in the field, the first thing he or she would do is pop it into CODIS to see if a connection to an offender or an open, cold-case crime within the database pops up.

As Nicole went through the items in her closet, Hensley spotted something of interest. He bent down.

"That's not mine!" Nicole said. She stood by Hensley, who was staring at a piece of cut electrical cord. That was something you don't find every day in a person's closet.

"Whose cord is this?" Hensley asked.

"That's Danny's," Nicole said.

CHAPTER 26

Sommer Heffner and her boyfriend waited at Danny Hembree's friend's trailer well into the night of October 17, 2009. Danny and Heather had gone off to his mother's house in search of more cash so he could buy more rock. Danny said something about $200 or $300 in cash his mother had stashed inside the house.

Near eight o'clock at night, Danny and Heather returned.

"It seemed like forever," Sommer remembered.

Danny produced a large jug of pennies, explaining it was all he had left to his name. They hadn't located any cash back at his momma's house.

Someone suggested they find one of those turn-change-into-cash machines at a local supermarket and pour all of the pennies into it so they could come away with some party money. There was no drug dealer on the planet who wanted twenty pounds of pennies.

By eleven at night, they had exchanged the change for cash at a supermarket and Danny purchased more crack cocaine. It was time to party once again.

That abandoned trailer wasn't going to do at this late hour, however. So Danny took everyone over to his mother's house. If they were quiet, they could party downstairs in the basement. It was warm. It didn't smell as bad as the abandoned trailer, and there was also the potential they could help him find that $200 to $300 he knew was in the house somewhere. But damn it all, he warned everyone, you had better be on your best behavior in Momma's house.

As they partied in the basement of his mother's house, on October 17, the idea was for Danny and Sommer's boyfriend to swap Sommer and Heather. However, it didn't work out so well. "Because, you know, crack cocaine makes it to where men can't perform right," Sommer explained.

So, instead, they smoked more rock.

When the crack was gone, Danny revisited that earlier idea. He was fixated on the money he believed his mother had hidden. He could not let it go. With the fever of crack he started smoking earlier that day running through his blood, Danny wanted more. He needed more.

"Look, there's like two hundred or three hundred dollars stashed somewhere in the house," he explained. "We just need to find it." He sounded like he was sending everyone on a treasure hunt.

It was enough money, Danny knew, to buy a lot of dope—enough to last well into the next day. Plus, dangling that much rock in front of them—after giving the girls a taste—he could get whatever he wanted, whenever he wanted it. Though he wasn't telling anyone, Danny also had a plan to get rid of George so he could be all alone with Sommer and Heather.

They all went about "ransacking" the house in search of the money.

When they failed to find any cash, there came a point when Danny "began to get real violent" with George, Sommer said. A switch had flipped in Danny. He had gone from hunting down money, willing to buy cocaine for everyone, to a pulsating maniac, blaming everyone around him for not being able to purchase more rock.

Danny soon went after George, charging at him, saying quite angrily, "I'll shoot you, man. I'll whip your ass, stab . . . cut . . . kill you!"

He was in a violent rage. He was a different person. He had suddenly turned into that guy everyone had heard about: the violent sociopath who just didn't give two shakes about anyone else when a volcanic fury, pent up inside, erupted. He had turned, just like that, into a monster that didn't care about anybody but himself and his needs.

Danny locked George out of the house after accusing him of finding and stealing that money.

"Please, Danny," Sommer pleaded. "What are you doing?"

"I'm getting the fuck out of here," Heather announced. Heather and Sommer were scared. Danny was seething. Something had come over him from deep within. Heather had not seen this side of him. Not ever.

George, who had found a stash of booze earlier, was blasted drunk, coming down from a crack high. Now he was locked outside.

Total chaos had exploded within the blink of an eye.

"It's freezing cold out there, Danny," Sommer said. "Please." She put on her shoes. "I'm just gonna walk home if you ain't gonna let George back in."

Danny approached the door and stood before it; then he opened the door and motioned with his hand for George to come back in.

"You sit on that couch," he said in a clenched-jaw, gruff voice. It was clear he meant what he said. Here was a guy who had been in and out of prison all his life and learned the hard way how to take care of himself. He didn't muck around when it pertained to getting his way: Danny Hembree always struck first.

"You do not move and you do not leave this living room," he said as George sat down. "You fucking understand me?"

Danny Hembree was impatient and furious, more so because he couldn't find that money and needed to get high.

Paranoid, he also mentioned again and again that perhaps George or one of the girls had found the money and kept it.

Sommer ran over and sat down next to her boyfriend, now concerned that George was going to say something to Danny that he didn't mean.

Heather and Danny, after he suggested it, continued to search the house for the money.

"Look, it has to be here somewhere," he said.

By now, it was after midnight.

"Let's go," Danny ordered after the latest search proved fruitless.

"Where we going?" Heather asked.

He explained, and then added, "Alone, just you and me."

Heather looked at him. She thought about it.

"I'll be back," she told Sommer. "I'm going with Danny."

CHAPTER 27

Hensley and his colleagues kept a close eye on Danny Hembree as he sat on the couch inside Nick's house on the evening of November 23. The YCSO, along with members of the GCPD Detective Unit (DU) and CSI, continued a search now focused specifically on a closet inside Nicole's bedroom.

With the cause and manner of Heather's death classified as undetermined throughout the time period before Randi's body had been found, the YCSO didn't know if Heather had been murdered. It had always been a pressing question: Had Heather been walking down the road, for example, had a seizure and suffocated to death? Had she tripped and fallen and couldn't breathe?

"They certainly felt like she had been pushed down into that culvert or dumped there," one law enforcement official explained. "But there was just no clear sign of murder."

After Randi's body was recovered, however, it was the beginning of what looked to be a pattern, and the course of the investigation into Heather's death changed. Heather's injuries and death were looked at now under different circumstances. Her death had context.

Hensley assisted another detective in writing up a property list invoice for Nick, noting all the items they had confiscated from his house, along with the jewelry taken from Nicole's possession and inside her bedroom. The one item on Hensley's mind as they concluded the search inside the house (there was still Danny Hembree's vehicle in the driveway to go through) was that electrical cord. Or, rather, *cut* electrical cord.

Hensley couldn't shake a feeling he had of why a person would hold on to an electrical cord that has been cut from a lamp or some other appliance. It didn't make sense to save it. The item had no practical use. In his short career as a detective, Hensley prided himself on his instincts. He listened to his gut.

Hensley's dad was transferred to Gaston County from Tennessee when Hensley was in high school. The family has lived there ever since.

"Look, I bleed orange," Hensley said of his Tennessee roots.

It was 2004 when, Hensley said, "I decided to try the police thing out." Hensley wanted to be one of the good guys, chasing all those bad guys he had heard so much about as a kid. He had law enforcement and public service coursing through his veins. Hensley's uncle was the chief of police in a small Southern town and also fire chief, and his cousin made assistant chief of the Chattanooga Police Department. So serving the public had been in him all his life, Hensley felt while growing up.

The thing that had actually turned Hensley off from a career in law enforcement early on, and as he entered college, was his mother telling him, "You're not going to be a police officer."

"She had grown up around it, and was always right there

with the family as they went through it. She tried to engrain it within me that I was going to do something else."

The GCPD had jurisdiction over the county—responsibilities beyond the Gastonia Police Department (GPD)—serving the communities outside the bounds of the city. The GCPD DU focuses on major crimes: murder, organized crime, missing persons, sexual and serious assaults.

Hensley felt comfortable within the DU, having joined the team on July 16, 2008, after four years of patrol. And wouldn't you know it, on that same day he was sworn in as a detective, he found himself working on the Lucy Johnson case.

"It's really not anything like the glamour that you see on TV," Hensley said with a respectful laugh. Asked if the DU was what he had expected, Hensley said, "I guess the answer's 'yes' and 'no.' It's what I expected, to a certain extent. I wanted to be involved in cases like [the Lucy Johnson case] and there I was. I had input. My opinions mattered. That's where I wanted to be. That's what I wanted to do and there I was doing it."

Johnson, thirty-one at the time of her death, was pregnant. She had been shot in the head twice—that is, before the home in which she lived was set on fire. Her fiancé was later charged in the case but found not guilty.

This was Hensley's inauguration into the DU. So, as he said, it didn't take long for "the newness" to wear off. "I wasn't the primary detective on [Lucy Johnson], but that's what I walked into on my first day."

All that experience, all that thought he had put into police work, it came back to Hensley on days such as the one he spent at Nick's house, bagging and tagging a piece of cut electrical cord he had found extremely attention-grabbing.

"Would you come down to the Gastonia PD and have a chat with us?" Hensley asked Nicole. Hensley wanted Nicole to speak with the YCSO without Danny Hembree hovering over her. They wanted to lock Nicole down to a statement. The case was going somewhere. Hensley had been with the DU only a little over a year, but he knew when a case—he could feel it—was about to take a turn.

The cut cord.

Danny stood up from the couch after hearing what Hensley asked Nicole and walked over. He said: "You don't have to go!" He wasn't being loud or obnoxious, but was merely voicing his concerns.

Nicole seemed torn. Hensley could tell she wanted to go, but she also wanted to be loyal to her boyfriend.

Danny sat back down. Hensley chatted with Nicole a bit more.

"Look, go ahead," Danny finally said with a smile from the couch, apparently giving Nicole "permission" to go down to the station house and give a statement.

"He seemed to change his mind and approve," Hensley later commented.

One of the detectives standing in front of Danny asked him if he would give them consent to search his vehicle. A search warrant was one thing, but getting people to consent verbally on top of the warrant is ironclad.

He shifted in his seat. Took a pull from a cigarette. Exhaled the smoke overdramatically. The guy was haughty and smug, obviously reveling in this one particular moment.

Control: Danny Hembree thrived on it.

"Sure, go ahead," he said after a beat. "Y'all can look inside my car."

CHAPTER 28

Danny Hembree was your quintessential loner type, wandering through life concerned with only himself and his needs. He later claimed that during the period of his life when Heather was murdered and Randi's body was found, he had "four or five" different residences where he'd spend his nights. In fact, he drifted from place to place. He had not worked a steady job (nine to five, clocking in and out) in many years. For money, he said, he would "go out and look for a house that had some damage done to a roof or porch or something, go talk to the people, offer my services, give them a reasonable price, and do the job for them."

By August 2009, he had found somewhat steady work in Charlotte at an apartment complex. They'd hand him what he called a "punch list" of things to fix—leaky ceiling, electrical wiring, a cracked window, caved-in piece of Sheetrock—and he'd go on, checking off each job from the list as he did it.

One of the reasons why Danny had trouble keeping a full-time job, he claimed, was because of substance abuse issues that had plagued him his entire teen and adult life.

"Just about anything you could get high on or drunk," he

once said. "Alcohol was my drug of choice, but crack cocaine, Ecstasy . . . I mean, *anything. . . .*"

Danny claimed that throughout his life he had been prescribed "hundreds" of prescriptions and had, at one time or another, taken every psychiatric and narcotic drug made. During those months leading up to the fall of 2009, however, he was supposed to be taking Neurontin and Ultram. When prescribed with other drugs, Neurontin is used to treat seizures associated with epilepsy in adults. Ultram is a narcotic-like pain reliever.

Danny said he was prescribed the drugs—both of them—"for neuropathy" in his feet and joint pain.

According to Danny, his first brush with any mental-health medication came when he was "thirteen or fourteen years old." As far as his drinking, he said he'd buy a twelve-pack of beer and a fifth of liquor every day and drink "until it was time to go to work."

During this time when he was drinking enough booze to pickle a leather shoe, he took a call one night. It was August 2009, though he did not recall the exact date. It was a friend of his.

"Nicole had a run-in with her boyfriend's mother and she's standing outside her trailer," the guy said. "Can you go over and get her?"

Danny had heard of Nicole Catterton. He knew the family. He'd dated Nicole's mother, Stella.

"Yup," he said. "But I don't have a car."

Danny arranged for a friend to come and get him. When they arrived where Nicole was waiting, he saw she had a "trash bag" with all of her belongings inside. She was leaving her boyfriend.

They dropped Nicole off at Nick's.

A week or so later, Danny was driving north on the 321, not far from the Catterton home. He had his cousin and his cousin's son with him. Driving down that busy road, he spied Nicole walking.

"Hey, hey," he told his cousin. "I'm pulling over here."

Parking in front of where Nicole walked, he blew the horn.

Nicole waved at him.

Later, in court, Danny claimed that his "cousin's son wanted to be with her."

So they brought Nicole to that abandoned trailer and left Nicole and the boy there for "a date."

Nicole began staying at Danny's friend's house after that. A woman friend of Danny's, whom he had known for thirty-five years, then took Nicole in. Danny went over one night and partied with her and the others.

As he was ready to leave, he claimed, Nicole grabbed him by the shirt. "No, I want you to stay."

"I ain't got me no way home," he responded.

"Come on, spend the night."

He thought it over. "That's cool."

Later, Danny Hembree said: "I spent the night with her, and we stayed in her bed. And from that point . . . I was pretty much with Nicole."

CHAPTER 29

As investigators piled out of Nick's house, Danny Hembree stepped outside. He walked over to where Detectives Chris McAuley and Myron Shelor stood. McAuley wore a wire and recorded parts of the search. Hensley and the others were over by Danny's vehicle, preparing to go in and have a look. It was explained to Danny that it wasn't going to take long.

He said, "Go ahead, take your time."

Mr. Calm, Cool, and Collected.

Standing with McAuley and Shelor, Danny seemed to be relaxed and rather willing to chitchat. They began their conversation talking about cars.

"I'm thinking about rebuilding the suspension on one of mine," McAuley said.

Danny mentioned a bit of work he needed to do to his car, but then he changed the subject, bringing it back to him, of course, and his latest dilemma.

"I was working, but y'all made a call over there, and because of that, I got fired."

"Oh, geez. Why'd they tell you they fired you?" McAuley asked.

Danny spoke of a phone call that cops had made to his boss. "And he told me he didn't need that shit over there."

"Where'd y'all work?"

Danny said he was a contractor, a handyman. He fixed things. He added, "Fourteen dollars an hour," with a tone that indicated this was a lot of money to a guy like him.

"You did plumbing, carpentry, things like that?" McAuley asked.

Cars whizzed by Nick's house—the common noise of life—as they continued talking. The sound of their voices was drowned out from time to time by the fast-moving traffic and roar of engines. Neither man spoke louder than he needed.

As several dogs barked in the background, Danny said: "Oh yeah. You know, [my boss] had a granddaughter seventeen years old and, you know, well, I used to be with Heather . . . and I think he had a problem with all that. It ain't none of his business, though. Hell, I'm forty-eight years old." (Hembree rounded up; he wouldn't turn forty-eight for another month, on December 19.)

Radio static and sporadic dispatch calls from a police car in the background gave the scene a feeling of gravity. Several cops and a suspect in two murders might have been standing around and shooting the shit like old bar buddies, but these cops were paying close attention to everything Danny had to say, analyzing him and everything about his demeanor. They were on top of their game here, despite sounding as if it was a routine search.

Danny Hembree gave the impression that he was angry with law enforcement riding him over the past week or so.

"I can understand," said one detective, "you've had the *poe-lease* crawling up your ass lately."

"Oh yeah," Danny said, taking the bait, "they's been harassing me."

"These guys," said McAuley, referring to the YCSO,

"they've been up, what, every day for four or five weeks now working on these cases."

"Well, you know," Danny said, "I understand."

"We appreciate y'all helping us out, you know. It makes things so much easier." McAuley was speaking of Danny Hembree not putting up a stink about searching his vehicle.

"I know, I know," Danny said. "Nick, he needs some closure on this thing." He paused. Then, hoping they'd bite, he said: "That damn Stella."

"Why do you say 'damn Stella,' Danny?"

" 'Cause she's the one who done gotten Heather into all that."

They talked about Nick next. How he was doing. Danny seemed to care for Nick and his well-being, however superficial it came across. Then, for a time, they talked about local Gastonians they both knew, the bars in the area, and what was happening currently within the drug culture. What types of drugs were kicking around and who was selling them. Danny mentioned how he'd picked up some girl at a local dive one night recently and she tried to push "some Oxy" on him. So he pulled his car over and "kicked her ass out" of his vehicle. He laughed while telling this story.

There was an obvious cockiness about Danny Hembree as he talked about other people—especially females. You could tell the guy looked down on women in general. And if they did things—sexual favors—for dope or a ride or some pocket money, he thought even less of them. It was as if he was better than all of the people he ran with—even Heather, Nicole, Stella, and Nick. He sounded as though he was doing all of them a favor by being their friend.

Danny brought up Nicole and explained how she had been doing well in certain areas of her life.

"That's so great to hear," McAuley said. "She's a real good girl."

"I know, I know," Danny said. He paused. Then: "Boy,

these five minutes is sure taking a long time." He was talking about the search of his car—which was only just now about to get started.

"Yeah, well," McAuley said.

Nick came outside.

"We're gonna be done soon," the detective told Nick.

"Okay."

Two investigators, Hensley one of them, stood by Danny Hembree's vehicle. Hensley asked the YCSO investigator helping with the search, "Do we know what we're looking for in here?"

"Rings, necklaces, jewelry," the cop said. "Stuff like that."

"Got it. Might as well get in there and start digging," Hensley announced.

CHAPTER 30

Detectives searched inside Danny Hembree's Ford Escort for any items that might help connect him to either of the two girls. YCSO investigators had no better suspect on radar at the current time than Danny. In fact, the closer they looked at him and placed him (and his previous crime record) within the framework of both deaths, the more it seemed plausible that he was the only man with motive and opportunity.

Nothing of significance was found inside the car, but when they popped the trunk open and poked around, Hensley hit pay dirt.

"Another cut piece of electrical wire," Hensley said.

"Look at this," McAuley announced to an on-scene YCSO investigator. The same cop had been involved in Randi's case. He had seen the electrical wire used to bind Randi's legs.

"That's quite similar to the piece of wire used on Randi Saldana's legs," he related to McAuley.

When Hensley heard this, he felt that Danny Hembree—a guy who had seemed to enjoy the cat and mouse of cops searching Nick's home and his car—had murdered Heather and Randi. Hensley needed no additional evidence than these two seemingly insignificant items and the fact that Danny was the last person to be with both women.

"My suspicions are like everyone else's at that time," Hensley remarked. "Hembree killed Randi, took her jewelry, and gave it to Nicole." But it was the cut cord that became the most important piece of the puzzle at this stage. "I've searched a lot of houses and vehicles and we typically don't find a lot of lamp cords that are cut," Hensley explained. "I don't know of many people that cut electrical cords off lamps or other appliances."

Especially when you place the electrical cord into the context of a homicide victim bound by what appeared to be the same material.

And then the necklace that Nicole supposedly had.

There are no coincidences in murder—only evidence.

Why else would Nicole have Randi's necklace? Hensley kept asking himself.

Still, none of this was enough to haul Danny Hembree in. Yet, it was certainly plenty to begin an arrest warrant narrative. With Nicole heading down to the GCPD for an interview, things were shaping up.

Hensley could hear Nicole now . . . *"Danny gave that necklace to me."*

If true, they had enough to bring Danny Hembree in and interview him on suspicion of murder. At least in Randi's case.

As they finished the search of the vehicle, Hensley noted how Danny Hembree was standing off to the side, talking to McAuley and Shelor. That was a good sign. The guy, it seemed, wanted to play.

"I recall them speaking to Hembree the night of the search warrant at the Catterton home," Hensley commented, "as we searched his vehicle. But he was not formally interviewed, by no means—more like friendly conversation while we searched his car. He was our primary suspect, but our purpose for being there that night was Nicole and the jewelry. Hembree just happened to be there when this all went down."

Sometimes, all a cop needs is a little luck.

CHAPTER 31

Y CSO detectives asked Nicole to sit down inside an interview room at the GCPD. Nicole had pieces of this puzzle—no doubt about it. The most pressing—and important—question centered on the jewelry. And yet, one had to be careful with a witness like Nicole. She was close to Danny Hembree. Her sister had been murdered, or so the YCSO now believed. Nicole had a record herself. There was a fine line between getting Nicole to open up, getting her to believe that law enforcement was on her side, and alienating her.

Danny Hembree had already tried to influence Nicole. As they began the interview, investigators considered that if Danny was brazen enough to try and control Nicole in their presence, what would he do when he got her alone?

Hensley sat and watched from a separate room. York County continued leading the investigation.

Nicole was asked about the jewelry.

"I traded that with Randi," she said.

This was not what everyone expected to hear.

Nicole explained that she had been with Randi at a friend's

house in Gastonia one night shortly before Randi went missing. They were partying.

"We were together part of the night and this was when we traded jewelry."

Hensley was confused by this statement, but not in a way that threw him off. He went through scenarios in his head, comparing those theories with the information Nicole was sharing, along with the information they had developed.

"If you believe that Danny Hembree killed Randi," Hensley explained, referring to what he was thinking as he watched Nicole's interview, "and gave Nicole Randi's jewelry, then you would *have* to believe that Nicole was either involved in the murder or knew exactly what Danny had done to Randi."

Taking it one step further, you would also have to consider that Nicole was part of her own sister's demise—certainly something no one was keen to believe.

Or maybe she was being intimidated by Danny Hembree? Threatened?

"You'll be next, bitch."

"When we looked at the case at this time," Hensley said, "and began to focus on Hembree, we were actually surprised that Nicole was still alive."

That ticking clock: the need to arrest Danny Hembree before he killed again.

Over the course of a few hours, Nicole talked her way through her life with Danny and the events of the past month.

"When did you last see your sister?" an investigator asked.

"It was a Saturday, I think," Nicole said. "We were at the house. She was in the bathtub. I left the house to go across the street to the Mighty Dollar to meet someone and buy some[thing]."

"How long were you gone?"

"About thirty minutes."

"Did you return home?"

"I did. When I walked in, I asked my mom where Heather was. She said Heather left with Danny, Sommer Heffner, and Sommer's boyfriend."

"Boyfriend's name?"

"I don't know, sorry."

"Who is Sommer Heffner?"

"She and Heather have been friends for a long time."

Investigators wondered: Why hadn't Nicole run off to party with her boyfriend and the others?

"I didn't know they was leaving," Nicole said. "I figured that they had left to go cop some crack to smoke."

Investigators wanted to know who had the money that night. Who financed the party?

"I think Danny had money, because he got paid from his job."

Nicole talked about where she thought Danny worked. But then she said she believed he financed the crack party with "money" he got from "his mother."

The subject of Nicole's boyfriend leaving with Heather, and no one seeing her sister again, came up. Nicole was asked what she knew about it.

"I spoke to Danny later that night on the phone," Nicole said. "I called him. I asked him where Heather was."

"Did he tell you?"

"Yeah, yeah. It was about eight or nine (when they first spoke) and then later on, about eleven or twelve, and he said he dropped Heather off at the Mighty Dollar," located just across the street from the Catterton house. "I didn't speak to Danny until the next day."

YCSO detective Mike Baker asked Nicole, "Did it make you mad that Danny left you there at the house and took off with Heather and Sommer and her boyfriend?"

"I was mad, yeah," Nicole said. "But Danny knows I don't smoke crack. And it wasn't uncommon for Heather to ask Danny to buy crack for her. . . ."

"But it *did* make you mad, right?"

"I was jealous they left together, sure. Mad too."

The theory of Danny Hembree having a thing for Heather came up next.

Nicole said, "I know he's had sex with Heather before. My mother told me Heather and Danny had sex on Valentine's Day this year."

Heather would have been a minor then, just sixteen. What in the world was going on within this family? YCSO investigators wondered.

"I didn't have a problem with Danny and Heather having sex then," Nicole responded. "I wasn't dating Danny back then." She went on to say Heather was sleeping with him for drugs. That was the only reason. She added, "Look, my own mother even had sex with Danny—but it was all about drugs."

"Tell us about Mr. Hembree."

Nicole explained that she'd started "dating" him a few months ago. "I trust Danny to be alone with other women. I don't think he'd have sex with Heather now, because we're dating."

"How does he treat you?"

"Danny? Oh, he's good to me. He treats me like a woman. Even when he smokes [crack], he doesn't get aggressive or anything." The way she described the guy, it seemed he had never gotten violent with her, and he was a stand-up guy who would never raise a hand.

"You and your sister get along?"

"Yes, of course. I had a good relationship with Heather. She was a good person." This brought on a bit of sadness for Nicole to talk about Heather in the past tense. "She was streetsmart, you know. Always careful." Nicole said Heather was tough. She was a "fighter."

Hensley looked on and had a few theories developing. Danny Hembree was two different people: one around these girls, another when not with them. He was also the Svengali type while with the girls, the provider of a good time. And it appeared that the girls turned to him when they wanted drugs, a ride somewhere, or even money.

"You recall what your sister was wearing that night she left with Hembree?"

"I don't, sorry. But those clothes she had on and the clothes found near her body—they was hers, I know that. I bought Heather that Hollister sweatshirt myself. The pants and belt, I know was hers, too. The New Balance sneakers, she got those, I remember, when she got out of jail."

Important information: Here was another source putting those clothes found down the road from Heather's body on her. That fact alone of Heather not having all of her clothes on where she was found was a red flag, despite what the autopsy could not prove at this point.

Detective Baker asked Nicole what she thought might have happened to Heather.

"She was murdered," Nicole said without hesitating.

"How do you think she might have been murdered, Nicole?"

"I think somebody choked her or put a bag over her head."

Either scenario worked with what the autopsy proved.

All of the detectives in the room were struck by this—how could Nicole have known? The autopsy results (and theories being explored by law enforcement) had not been released. And there was no specific cause of death mentioned in the final autopsy report.

Nicole then added something else: "She could have been shot. I believe she was raped, too."

"Why do you feel she was raped?"

"Because her clothes were off and her shirt was up around her head."

Talking more about this, Nicole explained that one of the investigators told her certain facts about Heather's body and the autopsy, which explained why Nicole was so well informed.

"Did you know Randi Saldana, Miss Catterton?" Baker asked.

"Um, not that well. But I'll tell you this, whoever killed my sister also killed Randi."

"Did they know each other?"

"Yeah, they did. I know that Randi and Heather hung out at Shorty's house," Nicole said. "And I think maybe someone was watching [his] house. . . ." She broke down. Then: "Whoever done this, they deserve to die, like Randi and Heather done died. They deserve the electric chair."

"Shorty" (pseudonym) was the nickname for a local guy named Bobby Mercer (pseudonym). Shorty's house in town was a known hangout and a place to purchase cocaine. Heather, "as a friend," Shorty later explained, lived at his house "every now and again." Heather would come by and sometimes "she didn't have nowhere to go, so I let her stay there," Shorty added. He was one of Heather's dealers, but he was also someone who liked Heather. He claimed to care about her. There was a "rumor on the street" that Heather would trade sex for cocaine, Shorty said. If she did that, "I didn't treat her that way."

Between January and October 2009, Heather had been dodging various violations of probation charges and often hid at Shorty's when she felt cops were after her. The YCSO had actually found Heather at Shorty's that August and hauled her off to jail.

"I mean," Shorty said, "she just stayed there [with me]—she was good people, man. Everybody had put her down."

Detective Baker asked Nicole who she thought killed Heather. Could Danny Hembree, the same guy Nicole had been sleeping with and allowing inside her home, be capable of killing her sister?

"I have suspected Danny," Nicole said. "I have. Since this happened, I thought about Danny being with both Randi and Heather before they went missing. . . ."

If that was the case, why would Nicole ever go near

Danny Hembree again? Why in the hell was she still with the guy?

Every investigator in the room, along with Hensley, was greatly concerned for Nicole's safety. Many believed Danny was going to kill her next. Thus, detectives encouraged Nicole not to go back to him that night. He could be dangerous—even more so, now that the pressure was on. There was no question he was going to interrogate Nicole when she returned. He would demand to know what she told police. Did Nicole truly want to subject herself to that kind of torment?

"Let us take you somewhere safe for the night," Baker said to Nicole. There was a shelter for women in town.

"No!"

"You should consider this."

"No, take me home. I'm not scared of Danny."

Going back was Nicole's prerogative. Investigators had gone from interrogating Nicole, as though she might have had a hand in Randi's murder, to being concerned she was going to be Danny Hembree's next victim.

"I want Danny to take a lie detector test tomorrow," Nicole said.

"We're not sure that—" one of the investigators began to say.

"If not, I'll get a restraining order against him."

They talked a bit more and one of the detectives drove Nicole home.

Hensley was worried, along with the rest of the team, that Danny Hembree—if he was indeed their guy—would kill Nicole that night or certainly within the next week. So it became a race to gather enough evidence to arrest Danny Hembree.

CHAPTER 32

On the morning of November 24, a meeting took place at the Moss Justice Center out on York Highway. The YCSO had been serving South Carolina in York County since 1786. Within the infrastructure of the YCSO existed a series of squads: Violent Crimes Unit, Crimes Against Property Unit, Drug Enforcement Unit, Forensic Services Unit, Polygraph Unit. The YCSO was equipped to investigate just about any crime committed within its boundary lines. The deaths of Randi and Heather, however, called for a broader level of investigation involving other jurisdictions. Thus, the YCSO wanted to form a task force in search of what most believed was an evolving (and quite possibly highly experienced) serial killer.

Earlier that morning, while conducting a thorough background check on Danny Hembree, it was learned that he had been questioned back in 2007 as the primary suspect in the 1992 murder of another local Gastonia girl. As each layer of his record peeled back, darker and more sinister secrets rose to the surface.

Hensley sat and listened as detectives from several local agencies shared what they knew about the cases. Sitting in on the meeting was a behavioral analyst—some might call him a "profiler"—from the South Carolina Law Enforcement Division (SLED). He took in everything being said regarding how the bodies were found, where, when, by whom, on top of the condition of each victim and state of decomposition, along with the latest information the YCSO had compiled on their suspect.

Additional info was shared about Heather as the meeting focused on her victimology. There was no painting Heather in the light of a princess here—the team concentrated strictly on the facts. Anything less would have not served the victim well. The better an investigator is informed about a victim's life, the better his chances of zeroing in on her killer. This might sound awfully simple, but there's no other way to solve cases of this caliber.

According to Hensley's final report of the case, York County investigators advised the group that Heather "had been a prostitute since the age of twelve." When that information was presented, a certain pall came over the room. Of course, cops had heard far worse. But twelve years old and selling her body? It was a nightmare life that ended, apparently, with the bogeyman chasing Heather in those dark dreams. Heather had been placed in group and foster homes most of her childhood. She had run away from just about every one of them.

The term "prostitute" was probably not the best way to describe Heather's behavior. Heather had never been formally charged with the offense as an adult. It wasn't as though Heather put on high heels, a miniskirt, too much makeup, and went out walking the streets. She might have traded—and several reported this—her body for drugs at times, but it was not some sort of pimp/prostitute life of working the streets at specific locations and times, or even advertising as an escort on Craigslist or Backpage, same as many girls do.

"Heather was a drug user," said an investigator running the meeting, "crack . . . being her drug of choice. She is . . . a person who is pleasant to be around and easy to get along with." Heather would date drug dealers, it was reported, and "align herself with drug suppliers. . . . [She] was known to date white and black males and had been in lesbian relationships."

"She was," said the same investigator, reading through Heather's victimology report, "known to rip off customers. Before her death, Heather had recently been staying with [Shorty]."

An investigator laid out the case as it stood. From all the information the YCSO had collected thus far, it was clear Danny Hembree was the last person to see Heather alive on October 18. He had admitted (during that impromptu interview in the driveway of Nick's house) that he dropped Heather off at the Mighty Dollar across the street from her home. Heather's friends and family had last seen her on the night of October 17. Her body was found twelve days later, on October 29.

What happened between October 18 and October 29 was an obvious question that needed an answer. Where had Heather gone? Better yet, where was Danny Hembree during that time?

"Basically, the behavioral analyst," Hensley later said, "confirmed what York County already knew—that Danny Hembree was looking like our main guy."

Many in the room believed their main suspect was a serial killer, especially since there had been a third body connected to him back in 1992. Over the past twenty-four hours, the YCSO and the GCPD had dug up all they could on Danny Hembree. It was extreme. Murders aside, he was a very bad man, indeed. Far beyond what anyone close to him had ever known.

CHAPTER 33

Stella Funderburk had known Danny Hembree for as long as she could recall. "Maybe thirty years," Stella testified later.

They had gone to school together in Gastonia.

During her lifetime, Stella had little trouble admitting in court, she'd struggled with substance abuse issues. However, she stipulated, "I wouldn't say I had an addiction."

Still, she admitted to using "crack cocaine and alcohol." And her big sister, Cynthia Patterson, backed that up by stating later that Heather had even used crack in front of Stella.

Anyone analyzing Stella's (and Cynthia's) comments can reckon that crack cocaine is not a drug one uses socially. With crack, you're all in, once you pick up that pipe. To make her point, Cynthia testified that although Heather was no walk-the-block working girl, she did often "trade sex for crack cocaine and/or sex for money."

Stella was not romantically linked to Nick any longer, but she still went over to the house and visited the girls, hung around, and, because of his bad heart, helped Nick out when he needed.

There was some indication Stella had dated Danny Hembree at one point in her life, but not while he was with Nicole, Stella made a point to say when asked by law enforcement. Regardless, Danny was Stella's, Nick's, Heather's, and Nicole's source of transportation a lot of times. He often gave them rides wherever they needed to go, albeit always for a price, one way or another.

Danny generally never had an issue doing favors (especially rides) for any of them—until, Stella claimed, the week Heather went missing.

On November 11, 2009, a day and night that would turn out to be a focal point for cops in their investigation, Stella and Nicole went over to Shorty's house to get something, Stella later said. "It was when I met Randi."

Randi was at Shorty's that night, according to Stella and several others hanging around the house. Randi and Shorty knew each other. It wasn't a strange circumstance for Randi to be at Shorty's.

Danny brought Stella and Nicole to Shorty's. While Stella was at Shorty's with Nicole, Nick called.

"I need to go to the hospital." He sounded out of breath and scared.

"We'll be right there," Stella told him.

According to Stella's recollection, Danny drove her, Randi, and Nicole to Nick's. She never said why Randi went along for the ride, but others claimed Randi was in the mood to party that night and Danny always had the money to buy the dope and dangle it in front of the girls.

Nick was in trouble. He needed to get to a hospital.

Upon their arrival, Randi had even "given her condolences" about Heather to Nick. She told him how sorry she was for his loss, which was obviously taking an unfavorable toll on the guy's health. Nick had taken Heather's death particularly hard.

"Danny, can you take me?" Nick asked him.

"No," he answered, refusing to drive Nick to the hospital. The request for the ride was in that control zone that Danny loved to work in. He knew the ride was another bargaining chip he could use that night to get what he wanted out of the girls.

"Come on, Danny," Stella pleaded.

He shook his head. He coldly said again, "No."

Stella watched as Danny, Nicole, and Randi walked into Nicole's bedroom. Stella knew what they were going to do.

"Stella, what are they doing in there?" Nick asked.

"I don't know, but maybe some drugs."

One thing Nick hated was when the kids did drugs in his house. He frowned upon it. If they were going to destroy their lives, he was not going to sit by and be a party to it.

Nick got up. He walked over to the bedroom and opened the door.

"I saw Danny sitting there with a crack pipe in his mouth."

Nick was pissed. "Oh no!" he said. "Get out of my house. I don't want that shit in here. Y'all gotta go. Right now."

So Danny took off, with Randi and Nicole, and went back to Shorty's.

"We'll come back later and give y'all a ride to the hospital," Danny said as they were leaving. Stella knew they were heading back to Shorty's to party.

Stella couldn't wait. She wouldn't wait. Danny Hembree was being the power-hungry prick that he could be. Nick was huffing and puffing. Catching them smoking dope didn't help. So Stella called an ambulance.

After the ordeal inside the ER, doctors gave Nick the okay to go home and told him to take it easy. Nick and Stella did not have a ride back to Nick's house. Stella waited with Nick inside the reception area. She wanted to make sure Nick was going to be all right. It was near midnight. Nick was falling asleep. Stella called Danny Hembree.

"No," he said to a ride home from the hospital.

Danny, Randi, and Nicole were with Shorty inside his house, partying. All four were on a bed in a back room, sitting, talking, laughing, joking, and smoking (except Nicole, everyone later said). There was even a moment, Shorty later claimed, when he saw Randi and Danny mocking Nicole behind her back, making adolescent gestures to each other and laughing at Nicole.

Nicole figured it out and got pissed at them. "Assholes," she said. "Stop it."

"I'm leaving, anyway," Randi said.

Randi got up and made a call; then she told Shorty she was taking off. She had someone coming to get her. She was meeting her ride up the street. She didn't say who, though.

Shorty followed Randi out the door.

"Stay here, Randi," Shorty pleaded. (Shorty liked Randi.)

"No, I can't. Thanks, though. I'll see you later."

Randi took off, walking up the road.

Sometime after that, Shorty walked up the same block toward another friend's house, four houses away.

After hanging out a bit at that house, Shorty walked back toward his party house. As he was coming down the street, a figure came up the same street toward him: Nicole.

"She were mad, talking junk," Shorty recalled.

Nicole was upset about Randi and Danny teaming up on her. She thought that maybe Randi and Danny had a thing going on behind her back. The way Shorty saw it, Nicole and Danny had an obvious blowup. Shorty guessed it was over Randi and all that goofing around earlier, along with the possibility that Randi and Danny were sleeping together.

As they talked in the street, both saw Danny drive up the road in his red car. Strangely enough, though, when he spotted them in the road (he did not expect to see Nicole and Shorty), he abruptly made a U-turn and drove away.

"Back down the same way Randi had gone," Shorty said later.

Nicole got a ride to the hospital. She walked in, upset.

"What's wrong?" Stella asked.

"Danny and me, we's been fighting," Nicole explained.

Stella called Danny on his cell to find out what the hell had happened. It was near one in the morning. Everyone was tired. It had been a long day and a longer night. Stella still needed to get Nick home.

"Yeah?" Danny said, answering.

"Where are you?"

"At Momma's." He sounded winded, out of breath, Stella recalled. He didn't want to talk. He was preoccupied. He was in a rush to get off the phone.

"Can you give us a ride home, Danny?"

"No," Hembree said. It was clear he did not want to be bothered. He hung up.

CHAPTER 34

As that task force meeting continued on the morning of November 24, it became clear to everyone that the common denominator in the deaths of Randi and Heather was Danny Robbie Hembree. There was Nicole, too, but law enforcement didn't think Nicole had a hand in murdering her sister and Randi.

The investigator running the meeting explained how Danny Hembree admitted he had last seen Heather when he dropped her off at the Mighty Dollar on October 18, late that night, after another round of partying.

"Mr. Hembree is known to use crack cocaine, drink . . . and pick up prostitutes," he explained, adding how the suspect had a penchant for girls who sold their bodies for drugs. It was maybe even a fixation—a morbid, twisted fascination he couldn't control. It was an obsession for Danny Hembree, some said, to have two or three girls at once, but they had to be girls whom he paid for and bought with drugs or cash.

Profiler of serial killers, psychotherapist, social worker, certified addiction specialist, and fellow at the American

College of Forensic Examiners, John Kelly (who studied this case for me and is my profiling guru for *Dark Minds* on Investigation Discovery) said guys like Danny Hembree give themselves away in their behavior. They cannot hide from who they are; it always comes out.

"Mr. Hembree is a power and control–focused killer," Kelly commented. "The killer that likes to use drugs as payment is extending his pleasure, by extending his time and length of power and control. This is very different than the killer that shows a victim a twenty-dollar bill and gets her in a car, drives to a location, and kills her. That's too fast for these guys. More time equals more power and control—which, in turn, equals more pleasure."

John Kelly was, in fact, one of the first clinicians to label serial killing an addiction in his 1993 published paper, "The Alcohol/Drug Serial Killer Connection."

Danny Hembree fit into this mold: He enjoyed every bit of dangling drugs in front of the girls and making them beg for it, once he hooked them with a free hit.

"By having control over two women who are drug users," Kelly added, "and who would do anything for the drug, he doubles his pleasure." Consider Sommer and Heather. "He enjoys watching them grovel and beg. He would get double, maybe triple, the sexual gratification and excitement by having two people, under his power, doing his bidding. For these types of serials, the more people you control in a degrading manner, the more gratification you get out of the experience."

Kelly said Danny Hembree's fantasy "was fetish-driven," by controlling the girls' sexual performance on each other.

"In many cases, these guys ejaculate watching the fetish phase take place and can't get an erection afterward. One serial killer whose fetish was bondage, the girls later said, if you did what he wanted and allowed him to tie you up and control you, that was enough for him, and he had an orgasm. Problems took place and he got violent only when they didn't obey him. Some killers are impotent as well, which enrages them, and just can't get an erection."

In those cases, "they blame the girl," Kelly said.

If you place Danny Hembree into a clinical structure, he becomes the poster child for what experts determined a serial killer was during the 1990s (criteria that has changed somewhat since those days, but has, likewise, stayed the same in many ways): white, middle-age, lives with parents, drinks alcoholically, frequents areas where prostitutes hang out, addicted to hard drugs, criminal history, violent (sudden) rage that, to those around him, seems to come up out of nowhere, loner type who chooses carefully the people he hangs around.

"There's an indication that Mr. Hembree visited some relatives in Florida after Miss Saldana's body was uncovered," said the task force investigator to his group.

Matt Hensley took extensive notes during the meeting. It was almost a certainty that he was going to become one of the lead investigators in the case as it now seemed to be focused on Gastonia, where both women had likely been murdered.

One of the big reveals from this meeting was how Danny Hembree had been questioned in that 1992 murder. With three bodies connected to the same guy in various degrees, how could they not focus on him?

That 1992 case involved another man, who had been brought into the investigation by Danny Hembree. It was a guy named James Swanson. He and Danny knew each other, but they were not friends—still, Danny tossed James Swanson's name out when questioned. Thirty-year-old Deborah Ratchford was found in a Gastonia cemetery (a wooded area) in 1992 with nasty slashes all over her body and neck. Not the same MO as Randi and Heather, but the dumping of the bodies was similar. On top of that, serials evolve: Danny Hembree could have started out using a knife and realized it was dirtier and messier and turned to strangulation and/or asphyxiation. Many serials begin killing one way, realize it is going to get them caught, and so they choose a different manner that is more conducive and necessary to the way in which they stalk and pick up their girls.

In addition, there were several cases dating back to the early 1980s that he would later admit to being involved in with another man, where the victims were terrorized and beaten savagely and left for dead. These cases fall in line with the way in which Deborah Ratchford was murdered.

"When Hembree went out there [to the Ratchford crime scene] with . . . officers, he was *very* particular about where the murder took place, about this, about that," one of the prosecutors in the Deb Ratchford case later told me. "It wasn't like he was saying, 'Over there and here. . . .' He was very particular about the area. And he was right on about it. Another thing was his details. If you are going to make something up and lie, you don't give as much detail as he did. He gave us details about, 'Yeah, we picked her up. I was irritated because I had to get out of the car to let her in the backseat. . . .' We were like, why would he say this stuff if he wasn't reliving it back in his head as he told us?"

James Swanson was arrested and charged in early 2007, but those charges were dropped two weeks later when investigators could not find a shred of evidence linking him to the murder (other than his co-perpetrator saying he was involved).

Danny Hembree had a reputation for planting notions in investigators' minds to throw them off. That was another textbook trait for a serial killer. He liked to toss out red herrings and send cops on wild chases. He thrived on the back-and-forth aspect with cops that went along with being involved.

On paper, Danny Hembree was not stupid. He had dropped out of high school as a teen, but he later obtained a GED while in prison. He had not failed any of his grades in school. He had an IQ, said one source, of 90. An IQ of 80 to 90 is considered "dullness," while 90 to 110 is "normal or average intelligence." It's not until one reaches the 110 to 120 and above that superintelligence comes into play. So an IQ of 90, if he scored in that range, did not mean he was unintelligent.

In the relationship department, Danny had been married for fifteen years, from 1980 to 1995. He had three kids (two sons and a daughter). He had a brother, David, who died in a car accident in 1999. (It was David who had been good friends with James Swanson.) Danny's father died a year after his brother.

"He has an extensive criminal record," said the task force investigator running the meeting. "Been in and out of prison most of his life."

Burglary and robbery were his crimes of choice. Violence was there, within the infrastructure of his criminal past, but it was thieving—and maybe killing—that he lived for.

When they finished discussing Danny Hembree, the meeting then moved on to Randi Saldana. At the time of her death, Randi was thirty, five feet seven inches tall, 125 pounds. The task force described Randi as a "crack cocaine user . . . that was known to use heroin on occasions." Randi had an arrest record dating back to 1997: robbery, forgery, larceny—all common crimes that chronic drug users often commit.

"Randi Saldana was not a prostitute," said one law enforcement official. "Mr. Hembree claimed that she was, but really there was little proof to that. . . . She was convicted of misdemeanor larceny in 1998, 2007, and 2009, Intoxicated and Disruptive in 1998, Misdemeanor Simple Possession of Marijuana in 2001, Driving While Impaired in 2002, Resisting an Officer in 2002."

"Randi was known to run in the same circles as Heather Catterton," the task force manager told the group. "People who knew Randi said she was not afraid to fight. . . ."

This was an important point, Hensley noted. Randi was someone who could take care of herself. She was not a naïve girl, running in a crowd where she couldn't handle the issues that came her way. It was one more reason to believe Randi's killer knew her—because Randi walked into a trap. There was no doubt in Hensley's mind. She was lured to her death, same as Heather.

The task force manager said, "Randi . . . was last seen on November eleventh at . . . Shorty's, with Shorty, Danny Hembree, and Nicole Catterton."

This fact was indisputable.

It was the night Stella, Nicole, and Randi had all partied at the same house with Danny and Shorty, and he and Nicole had that blowup. It was the same night Nick ended up in the hospital.

"According to witnesses, Randi was last seen walking down the street leaving [that house]. It has been confirmed through phone records that Randi made three calls to [the father of her first child] from Mr. Hembree's cell phone. [He, the father,] told us she asked that he come and pick her up. But when he got there, she was gone."

It felt as though all they had to do was connect the dots and Danny Hembree would be wearing metal bracelets by the end of the week.

Hensley got up as the meeting adjourned and felt good, as did just about every investigator involved from that first moment when Heather's body appeared out of the brush.

And yet no sooner did everyone have their mind set on Danny Hembree, when a tip came into Crime Stoppers that would throw the investigation into somewhat of a tailspin and send Hensley and two detectives heading in another direction entirely.

Anythink Commerce City

7185 Monaco Street
Commerce City, CO 80022
303-287-0063
Tues and Thurs., 11AM-7PM
Wed, Fri, Sat, 9:30AM-5:30PM
Sun and Mon, Closed

Date: 7/23/2019 Time: 1:47:19 PM

Items checked out this session: 1

Title: The killing kind /
Barcode: 33021031987891
Due Date: 08/13/19

Page 1 of 1

... where anything is possible.

CHAPTER 35

Some point after Randi's body was recovered and word hit the street that Heather and Randi knew each other, if only casually, Bobby "Shorty" Mercer called Danny Hembree.

"Meet me on Butler Street. I need to talk to you."

"I'll be there," Danny responded.

Shorty was pacing, walking back and forth as Danny arrived. There was something on Shorty's mind. He wasn't happy.

Danny asked Shorty what he wanted.

"You killed them—*didn't* you?" Shorty snapped. Inside each of his jacket pockets, Shorty had two knives. He gripped both knives with each hand as Danny approached him.

Shorty noticed that Danny Hembree "would not look" him in the eyes as Shorty accused him of killing the girls. Instead, he was staring at the ground, then at the cars going by, nearby buildings, lighting a cigarette. Anything else but the accuser in front of him.

There was some silence, followed by Danny shrugging it off.

"You killed them, didn't you?" Shorty asked again. (Shorty wanted him to man up, so he could maybe stick him.)

Danny Hembree got back into his vehicle and took off.

Shorty watched him drive away. He had sent a message to Danny that he was watching him. Danny thought he was playing a game, laughing at everyone else; but there were others, Shorty had made it clear, friends of the girls, who would not be intimidated by Danny Hembree.

CHAPTER 36

Detective Matt Hensley headed out with two YCSO investigators to speak with a young guy who had called into the Crime Stoppers tip line with what felt like a promising lead. His name was Mark Bailey (pseudonym) and he told the Crime Stoppers operator that he had gotten into an altercation recently with someone he knew and the kid blurted out how he knew something about the "two girls that got killed." The impression was that as they fought, the kid had killed twice already and was not afraid to do it again.

The YCSO called the number they had been given.

Mark answered.

"I never called that tip line," he claimed.

They visited Mark at his home.

"I suspect someone called in, using my name," Mark suggested.

Hensley checked out Mark's caller ID and his phone history. Mark Bailey had made no calls to Crime Stoppers, either on his cell or landlines.

They asked Mark what he thought was going on.

"I bet it's a neighbor of mine," Mark said. "He's trouble. I don't like him."

Mark gave Brad Kelp's (pseudonym) address to the officers.

Hensley and his two colleagues went over to speak with Brad. His mother answered the door and said her son wasn't home. "Come on in."

They told the woman why they were there.

"Brad's recently undergone a psychological evaluation," she said. "I've had to have him admitted, since he's threatened (and even attempted) suicide."

The call to Crime Stoppers did not surprise Brad's mother, she said.

"He needs to call us, ma'am," Hensley indicated, handing her a business card.

Later that day, Brad went into the GCPD voluntarily. "I didn't call a tip into Crime Stoppers," Brad said. Then, after being asked if he knew anything about the recent girls being found dead, Brad explained how he and another friend had seen a young female one night wearing a hoodie and jeans near the time Heather went missing. The girl had been walking along a road in town. He thought it might be Heather.

"What'd she look like?"

"We never seen her face."

Brad gave them his friend's name and number.

After speaking with the friend, who knew Heather from high school, investigators realized it wasn't Heather they had seen.

"Brad lies a lot," that friend further explained. Brad was one of those guys who wanted to be involved. He couldn't help himself.

"It was all nothing . . . and had nothing to do with anything," Hensley said later, commenting on how they had spent a day tracking down dead leads.

Ninety percent or more of what cops uncover during those early days of a murder investigation leads nowhere. It's part of the process of solving cases. You can't get to your location without walking through the muck. This particular

Crime Stoppers tip showed how fluid investigations of this nature become, even though you have a viable suspect looking good on paper.

The following morning, Hensley and two colleagues ran down another erroneous lead after sitting and watching the Catterton home from down the block. As they spied on the movements surrounding Nick's house, they witnessed "several subjects in the backyard stripping wire." As they looked on, it seemed as though it might lead somewhere.

So they followed the group to a scrap yard, where they turned in the wire for some chump change to go out and, most likely, buy drugs.

"Again, it had nothing to do with our murder investigation," Hensley said.

CHAPTER 37

That first real break did come, however, on November 25. YCSO detectives Russ Yeager and Alex Wallace had Sommer Heffner come in for an interview. Matt Hensley was there, too, again monitoring from another room. The YCSO was still not handing over the investigation to the GCPD. For now, it was a dual effort, with the YCSO leading the way.

Sommer sat down and told her tale of the last night she spent with Heather—the last time, in fact, she had seen Heather alive. It was that night Danny Hembree picked Sommer and her boyfriend up while they were walking and drove them over to Heather's. Heather was taking a bath, getting ready for the night.

This narrative gave investigators more ammo for their warrant, placing "Danny Boy," as Sommer said Danny liked people to call him, and also referred to himself, as the last person to have been with Heather. Now they had a witness making the claim in a formal interview. This was a statement Sommer would sign.

Sommer went into detail about the night. As he listened, Hensley was particularly interested about one event that

Sommer described. After convincing her boyfriend that she was going to have sex with Danny, and her boyfriend was going to have sex with Heather (the swapping part of the night), Sommer recounted how "angry" Danny Boy became when he couldn't get an erection. A switch had flipped inside him when he couldn't get it up, almost as if he blamed the girls for what the crack cocaine had done to him.

After Sommer admitted watching Danny and Heather have sex, investigators asked about the sex itself and if there was anything significant she could offer. Was he a normal guy in that regard?

"As a matter of fact," Sommer explained, "he liked *rough* sex. . . . I noticed him pulling Heather's hair."

"Pulling on her hair?"

"Yeah, but I ain't never done seen him strangling her or anything like that."

Sommer explained what happened as the night turned into the next morning. She recollected everything that occurred before and after they left Danny Boy's mother's house, including that fiasco with Danny locking her boyfriend out, as well as all of them ransacking the house in search of the money that he was certain his mother had stashed.

"We all went to the store to get more beer," she said. That was when things got creepy.

After pulling up to the store, Danny told Heather's boyfriend, George, to go in and get some beer, saying, "We'll wait here for y'all."

As George walked into the store, Danny took off.

Leaving George at the store alone, Danny drove to one of his dealers' houses and "bought an eight ball of cocaine" (an eighth of an ounce), Sommer said.

When he got back into the car, he told Sommer, "You can come with us, or I will take you to [your boyfriend's] house."

By then, Sommer had spoken to George. He was home, and really pissed off.

"Take me to George's!" Sommer demanded. She was upset that Danny had left George at the store by himself.

"Come with us and party," Danny said. It was something he had wanted all night: to be alone with Heather and Sommer. When the night had started back at Nick's, Danny had made it clear he didn't want George around. But Sommer insisted she wouldn't go unless George went, too. Danny gave in, but now he had the opportunity to get the girls alone.

Sommer told him to take her to George's house right away.

"Stay with us," Heather pleaded with Sommer as Sommer got out of the car at George's.

Sommer hugged Heather. "I love you." It had been a long night. She kissed her friend on the cheek. Heather looked scared.

Heather hugged her friend back, whispering in her ear, "Please come with us. . . . Please don't leave me with him. Something doesn't feel right."

"Please, please, please, Heather, just come with me," Sommer pleaded in turn. "Do not go with him. You can sleep here. We'll get up in the morning and get something to eat. We'll do something."

George was seething, pacing in the driveway, still upset at Danny for leaving him behind. George had gone from being wasted (earlier at Danny's mother's) to sobering up some.

Danny Boy was enjoying himself, laughing at George.

"No," Sommer said. "Heather, don't go with him. Stay with us."

Sommer knew Danny Hembree was mean-spirited and could not have cared less for Heather—all he wanted was for Heather to give him sex in exchange for the dope. Sommer knew this. She wanted nothing to do with the guy.

The pull of the drug was too much for Heather, however. He had a night's worth of rock. If they paced themselves, the eight ball would take them well into the next day. He and Heather could stay high for a very long time.

("She had smoked dope and had sex and been alone with Danny prior to this night," Sommer told the YCSO. "She was in it strictly for the drugs.")

"Stay with me and George," Sommer pleaded once more.

Heather said she couldn't.

"That was last time I done seen her," Sommer explained.

Staying there at George's, not giving in to the desire to smoke more rock, was a decision that probably saved Sommer Heffner's life.

It was two days later when Sommer went over to the Catterton home in search of her friend. She knew something was up, because she had not heard from Heather.

"I just had that feeling that she was dead," Sommer said through a barrage of tears.

She was surprised she had not seen Heather since that night with Danny and George. It was unlike Heather. She had just been released from jail. She and Sommer had not spent a lot of time together over the past several months. ("It was so unlike her not to go home and at least take a shower or get some sleep.")

Sommer saw Nick. "Where is she?"

"She was never dropped off the other night," Nick said. "She ain't done come home."

"Last time I seen her she was with Danny . . . and, uh, Nick, the last thing she said to me was that she was scared of going with him. It don't sound right, Nick."

A few days after this visit, Sommer went back to Nick's. Stella was there.

"You see Heather?" Sommer asked.

"No, I was going to ask you the same thing," Stella said.

"Last time I saw her, she was with Danny," Sommer said.

Just then, Danny Hembree came walking out of the Catterton home.

"What did you do with Heather?" Sommer shouted at
him as he came toward her.

Sommer knew. She could tell he was rustling his feath-
ers, rubbing their noses in it without coming out and saying
anything. It was in that smirk of his, the cocky walk.

"What the hell you talking about?" he snapped. "I
dropped her off at the Mighty Dollar that night. I ain't done
seen her since."

During the interview on November 24, with Hensley
looking on, YCSO investigators asked Sommer, what did
she think about Danny Hembree?

"When I done seen it in the papers where a body had
been found, and they's released what she was wearing, I
knew it was Heather. And I immediately suspected Danny
had something to do with it."

"You seen Danny around lately, Sommer?"

"I spoke to him yesterday," she said, meaning the day before the interview.

"He say anything?"

"Oh yeah. He done said that since he was the last one
with Heather, and the last one to be seen with Randi, he's the
main suspect. And you cops think he's a serial killer."

"He say anything else?"

"He's been telling people to keep quiet about what they
know—especially Nicole."

CHAPTER 38

Hensley and the YCSO had an idea. Sommer claimed to have been inside the Bi-Lo in Gastonia, a grocery store, on the night Heather was last seen. If they had cashed in those pennies, as Sommer said, Hensley knew video surveillance from the store would corroborate Sommer's account. Not only would it tell them how truthful she was being, but they might be able to get a bead on Heather's movements before her death. And with any luck, they could put Heather with Danny Hembree on tape on the night she disappeared.

More narrative ammo for an arrest warrant.

After watching the Sommer Heffner interview for a second time, Matt Hensley thought Sommer could be a turning point in the investigation.

"For me, that's where I found an opportunity to kind of take charge on something," Hensley said later, "and that's when I kind of really involved myself in this."

Hensley focused on the coins and how Sommer had talked about going to that supermarket and exchanging the pennies for cash in one of those Coinstar machines.

The other part of Sommer's interview that interested Hensley was how she talked about the trailers she had visited with Danny Hembree, her boyfriend, and Heather. That one particular abandoned trailer especially piqued his interest.

Crime scene, Hensley considered.

"Hembree's cutting off pieces of rock for them to smoke inside that trailer," Hensley said. "He's having sex with them. . . ."

That trailer seemed like a good place to murder someone. Had Danny taken Heather back there after he left Sommer at her boyfriend's? After smoking that eight ball, trying to have sex, but not being able to get an erection, had he blamed Heather for his sexual dysfunction? Had she made fun of him? Hensley could picture Heather saying something to Danny, and then him blowing his top, lashing out in a fit of rage.

It was just a theory.

Hensley and another investigator got hold of the Bi-Lo's manager and asked about the video.

"We do," the manager said.

Hensley and his colleague went to Bi-Lo's to have a look and, lo and behold, there was George standing at the Coinstar machine, feeding a bucket of pennies into the mouth of it. George looked wired, on edge, in a hurry.

Sommer's credibility factor shot up the moment they saw this.

As they watched the video, something else caught their eye. At one point, two girls walked into the supermarket past George, toward the restroom. Both came out of the restroom not long after and stopped to talk to George.

Heather and Sommer.

Bingo!

The last images of Heather before she disappeared and wound up dead in a South Carolina culvert.

"We need to seize the video," Hensley told the manager.

"We have footage of the parking lot area, too," the manager said.

Even better.

"I viewed that footage," Hensley said, "which was poor quality. I didn't see Hembree or his vehicle."

When Hensley got the videos downtown and had a better look, he noted the times: At 8:22 P.M., George entered the store and walked to the Coinstar machine. By 8:34, Heather and Sommer went to use the restroom. Two minutes later, they exited the restroom and walked up to George. Then, at 8:37, Heather and Sommer exited the store as George continued to feed the coins into the machine. Nine minutes after that, at 8:46 P.M., George presented the cashier with his receipt for the cash and exited the store.

But here was the most crushing part of this video: As Heather walked out, it was clear she was wearing a gray Hollister sweatshirt, blue jeans, and those white tennis shoes. These were the same clothes she died in.

This video, Hensley knew, was probably taken hours before Heather was murdered.

Hensley asked himself, *What happened in those hours after they left this store and partied, and Hembree dropped Sommer off at George's, and the moment someone tossed Heather in that ditch?*

CHAPTER 39

Any good cop listens to his gut. To a certain extent, he might even rely on it. Yet, within that investigatory DNA we could argue great cops are born with, he never allows his instinct to overshadow where the evidence leads him. Being in his late twenties, with just over a year behind the gold shield, Detective Matt Hensley had a lot to prove, perhaps. Still, within just a short time, Hensley had developed a sixth sense for major crimes. There are some guys who take to the job so naturally they find themselves getting up every morning and going to work with a feeling that catching bad guys is the reason they were put on this earth. For Hensley, it was more than just his calling; it was something he *had* to do.

"Detective Hensley is one of a kind," said Gaston County assistant district attorney (ADA) Stephanie Hamlin, who has worked side by side with Hensley on many cases (and would soon step into the current investigation involving the murders of Randi and Heather). "He is able to get people to open up and talk to him."

Some in the district attorney's (DA) office call Matt Hensley the "perv whisperer," a strange nickname that might sound a bit unusual to the outside world. However, when you have a guy like Hensley with a reputation and "such great success in getting sex offenders to confess to him," Hamlin added, you reward him with a moniker.

"Hensley is a very hard worker and perfectionist," Hamlin offered, "but never talks down to others and always approaches his work with an open mind. He is always willing to lend a hand to anyone who needs help."

Some might claim Hamlin has a biased opinion, but you ask people in Hensley's circle about him and you'll hear different versions of Hamlin's statement.

That abandoned trailer gnawed at Hensley after he viewed the Coinstar video a few times and took in all of what Sommer had to say. The way Sommer explained it was that she and Heather, while inside the trailer with Danny and George, "put on a show," and the trailer seemed to be a fairly significant place to their older friend. He was familiar with it. He felt comfortable there.

Knowing that Danny Hembree had a prolonged, perhaps fetish-like relationship with prostitutes, picking them up and plying them with dope, Hensley thought: *This trailer might be a common place for Hembree to take his girls.*

More than that: *a possible crime scene.*

Hensley tracked down the owner of the trailer.

"I own all those trailers . . . ," the guy said. "That one in particular there, it's been vacant for quite a while."

Hensley only gave the guy the details he needed to know without any particulars involving the YCSO's growing suspicions and case against Danny Hembree. All detectives involved worked under the assumption that their suspect knew all the players and had consistent contact with them. He was the intimidating type, for sure. He'd threaten. Once Hembree realized it was focused exclusively on him, he'd meddle in the investigation.

"Sure, go on ahead and search the trailer—you have my permission. I got no problem with you looking in that one or any other trailer on the lot."

"Can you meet us out there?" Hensley asked.

"Not now, I'm having a Christmas party."

Two YCSO detectives drove to the trailer park landlord's house and had him sign a consent-to-search form. Hensley headed to the trailer park and waited for YCSO detectives to arrive with the signed warrant. As Hensley waited, he couldn't help but think about the case and where they were.

"When Sommer started talking about these trailers," Hensley recalled, "you know, criminals generally behave the same. If something is working, they are going to continue to do it. It's what they're comfortable with. If Hembree was comfortable taking druggies and prostitutes . . . over to those trailers, I'm thinking, *This could definitely be where the murders took place.*"

Matt Hensley was familiar with the area. He knew if Danny Hembree was murdering girls inside one of the trailers, nobody was likely to hear a struggle for life and death. And serials, especially, once they get cozy within a kill zone and it's "working for them," as Hensley pointed out, they rarely deviate from it—until, that is, it stops working.

One of the early assumptions Hensley had when he stepped into the case turned out to be a miscommunication between agencies, a common problem before so many different agencies huddle up together to form a task force and share information.

"Look," Hensley noted, "I thought Hembree's house had already been searched. Part of everything that had been going on, I just worked under the *assumption* that Hembree's house had been searched."

There was so much interest, in other words, in Danny Hembree as a suspect, Hensley took it for granted that the YCSO had served a warrant on his house, searched it, and came out of it with nothing. That made Hensley consider with even more certainty that the trailers were a good bet for a crime scene.

As he learned, however, the YCSO had searched Danny Boy's mother's house, but "it was kind of a hasty search with the consent of his mom. A walk-through of the upstairs."

This was not taking a jab at the YCSO, Hensley was quick to make clear.

"I had asked them if they searched the house, [and] they said they did. I didn't say, well, how *good* did you search it, or how thorough did you go through it?"

Regardless, when the YCSO went knocking on the Hembree home, it was early in the investigation. They did not have enough information leading them to do a complete rip-through of the Hembree residence, turning over cushions, emptying drawers, looking in closets, and so on.

Hensley was thinking now about how Sommer and Stella had put Danny back at his mother's house on the night Randi went missing *and* on the night Heather went missing. So things had changed a bit. What's more, they had spoken to Sommer's boyfriend, George Baston, and independently confirmed everything Sommer had given them.

That Hembree house needs to be searched thoroughly, Hensley told himself.

Next door to the abandoned trailer, where Hensley waited for the YCSO to arrive, was where Danny, Heather, George, and Sommer had started out the night. Gavin Compton (pseudonym), Danny's friend, was home when Hensley pulled up.

Gavin came out when he saw Hensley sitting there.

"How's it going?" Hensley asked, getting out of his car. He could tell Gavin had been drinking. The guy was stumbling.

"What are y'all doing?" Gavin asked. His speech was slurred.

Hensley explained, somewhat.

Although amped up on booze, Gavin guarded what he knew. Hensley could tell that he was being mindful of what he said.

"Danny Boy's crazy," Gavin said.

"Yeah, how so?"

"I been battling with DSS (the state child and youth services) over my kid because of Danny. I got in a fight with Danny."

Hensley wanted details: When? What happened?

But Gavin didn't want to explain.

"I don't want no trouble, man."

"No, course not," Hensley said.

Gavin Compton went back inside his trailer.

Armed with a consent-to-search form, investigators pulled up just then. They had someone in the car with them.

Sommer.

She got out and walked over to the trailer in question, pointing out the exact one they had partied in. "That's it. Right there."

As they made their way to the trailer, Hensley looked around. The street was short, the tar broken up and in pieces. The trailers were old and in need of maintenance, to put it kindly. All around the back of the park, which consisted of about nine trailers on foundations, was a dense wooded area.

Walking around, Hensley saw smoke. He found the trailer park's maintenance man, who was burning some items behind one of the trailers.

"What'a y'all doing over here?" Hensley asked.

The guy claimed he was cleaning out a few trailers, burning some trash, and putting some in a Dumpster on site. "The landlord asked me to clean them out."

"Can you show me that Dumpster?"

The man explained that it had already been emptied for the day, earlier that morning.

"Can you tell me if you cleaned anything out of 107?" Hensley asked. That was the trailer in question—the one Danny Boy had taken Heather, Sommer, and George to.

"I removed a blanket . . . but don't recall much about what it all looked like or anything."

"What about 103?" Hensley queried, asking about another trailer Sommer had pointed out.

"There was furniture in it left by the previous tenant, but I tossed that out in the Dumpster."

"You know a guy by the name of Danny Hembree?" Hensley asked. Worth a shot. People around here seemed to know him, since he was one of those hard-to-forget guys.

"I know Danny and his cousin Manny Alverez (pseudonym). They hang out at Gavin's quite a bit."

There was smoke billowing all around them. It smelled toxic, like melting plastics and metallic.

Hensley asked about Danny and what he did when he came around.

"Danny and his cousin, they liked to take girls in the trailers and use drugs and have sex with them." The guy walked out from around the trailer, where they stood. He pointed to another trailer over by the two they were focused on. "I just done seen Danny parked between those two trailers there [101 and 103] and he was with a girl. It was early in the morning."

"Can you tell me what she looked like?"

"I don't remember."

Hensley believed him. It wasn't as though the guy was trying to cover for anyone. The conversation didn't have that feel to it.

"I can tell you that I am sure he had a girl with him," the man continued, "and he was parked like he was trying to hide his car. I saw him walk into 103, the vacant one. I noticed it was Danny. Then I saw him leave."

"Thanks."

Hensley walked over to unit 103. Sommer was standing

outside the door. She was talking about a blanket she remembered seeing inside the trailer.

This was important. Maybe blood? Maybe semen? Maybe a mixture of the two? If they could put Danny Hembree here with one of the victims, they had him.

Inside the trailer they uncovered all sorts of items. Fibers from the carpet indicated evidence of drug use. That blanket Sommer described wasn't there, however.

"We also found this," said a YCSO investigator.

Hensley walked over to have a look.

It was a small blood spot found in the rear bedroom, near the center of the floor.

The only bit of blood found in the entire trailer.

PART TWO

THE PLAYER

CHAPTER 40

Danny Hembree was a man who viewed life through a prism of events that he could manipulate to his advantage. Born six days before Christmas, 1961, Danny grew up in a home with an alcoholic father, he later told Dr. Claudia Coleman, a psychologist he began to see in 2009. It wasn't long after, Coleman later noted after speaking lengthily with him, when Danny hit his teens and was "viewed as possibly having bipolar disorder." There wasn't an actual diagnosis, but Coleman believed after reading through his psychiatric history that his early behavior showed clear signs of the disorder.

Lithium was a drug that Danny became acquainted with before he was out of his teens. Lithium is serious medication; according to most reputable medical websites, *[it affects] the flow of sodium through nerve and muscle cells in the body.* It's the sodium in the bloodstream that creates "excitation" or "mania." Essentially, when a child or adult is exhibiting severe and even routine episodes of manic depression, and nothing else works, lithium is prescribed. The list of behaviors and characteristics associated with mania include hyperactivity, rushed speech, poor judgment, and reduced need for sleep, aggression, and explosive anger.

According to Dr. Coleman, Danny Hembree displayed all of these symptoms. And as he grew, he developed antisocial disorder, personality disorder, borderline personality disorder, and, of course, substance abuse.

Dr. Coleman, who earned a Ph.D. and her undergraduate degrees in clinical psychology from the University of Mississippi, had thirty years' worth of experience by the time she met Danny. What interested Coleman after evaluating him was the range within his intelligence tests.

"His overall score was in the average range at ninety," Coleman indicated. "But the . . . part that was most salient to me was the fact that his verbal skills were higher than that at one hundred five, and his performance or mechanical skills were at seventy-five. That kind of thirty-point difference is extremely rare, except for individuals who have brain dysfunction. . . ."

As a child, Danny worked in "the family machine business." However, he had trouble holding down jobs because of his explosive fits of rage. Kathy Ledbetter, Danny's younger sister by four years, a psychiatric nurse by trade, said in court, "In a lot of ways, we thought we were like everybody else." She was referring to the Hembree family growing up together. "We had two parents, my mom and my dad." She described her mother, Jacqueline, as "very stoic. She doesn't show a lot of emotion—she never has. I think we always felt she loved us, but she was not affectionate."

Their father "was affectionate," Kathy recalled, although the man "was a very severe disciplinarian." Although he "was an alcoholic," Kathy added, she didn't "think the alcoholism had anything to do with the discipline. He was a severe disciplinarian regardless of alcohol."

On the one hand, Kathy said: "I can't sit here and say he went out, got drunk, and beat his family, because that's not how it was. How it was, he would punish Danny and David [their brother] for things that he thought they did wrong. . . . He thought he was disciplining them, [that] he was justified in doing what he did."

What type of "discipline" did Mr. Hembree inflict on his boys?

"He would whip them with a belt," according to Kathy. "He would beat them. He thought he was doing what was right. It was wrong. He did later regret that."

This wasn't, Kathy went on to say, the sort of old-school whipping whereby a man places his boys over his knee and unleashes a few pats on the ass with an open hand. No. For Mr. Hembree, Kathy claimed, he committed the abuse often and hit the kids with a belt "from shoulders to feet. They would have to lean over the bed. . . ."

Kathy said she was never allowed to watch. But worse, "Mostly, I heard it. I was sent to my room, and I would hear it more than I would see it."

It was the slaps of the belt hitting the boys' skin that tore through the house and pierced her ears, Kathy explained.

"I would hear the screams."

She was five years old when her father started beating the boys. She recalled the day she first learned of it. After school one day, she came home to the house.

What in the world is going on? she asked herself while walking up the house path. She could hear screaming coming from beyond the front door.

So she ran inside.

It had been report card day. The boys' grades weren't up to snuff, apparently, because Mr. Hembree was whipping both of them savagely with his belt as they screamed in terror.

Like most of the times he whipped them, the beatings went on for "fifteen to twenty minutes," Kathy remembered.

There was only one time, she explained, when she was

subjected to a beating herself. She'd lied to her parents. Some kids from school had stolen her candy. Embarrassed, she told her parents she lost it.

Her dad found out and got the belt out.

When little Danny heard his sister being whipped, he ran into the room and began crying and screaming for Pops not to do it.

"And my dad stopped," Kathy said.

And never hit her again.

"Once or twice a week," Kathy concluded, "I would say between [the ages of] nine and sixteen," the boys were beaten.

A day that crushed Danny Hembree and his sister, despite being beaten by the same man while growing up, took place on December 29, 2000. It was Danny, his mother, and his sister in the hospital room. By then, Danny's brother, David, had been killed in an accident. They stood over the Hembree patriarch and, together, removed the ventilator keeping the old man alive. He'd developed pneumonia and sepsis, shock from an infection. Suffice it to say, it was a hard thing to do; Mr. Hembree had a strong heart and would not go into cardiac arrest.

"In fact," Kathy recalled, "his heart was so strong they had to OD him on the morphine so that the death process would not be horrific, because they said he would gasp for air."

With Danny's brother and father now gone, it was Danny whom the women in his family looked up to for guidance, protection from the outside world, and masculine love. Danny was the be all and end all in the minds of these smart women—a fact that would become utterly apparent as their lives together carried on.

While interviewing Hembree, Dr. Coleman noticed an inherent narcissistic characteristic he could not hide from. Danny Hembree had been known by then to have admitted to crimes he had not committed, and Coleman wondered why he would do such a thing.

"I might be given more consideration by authorities," he explained.

Manipulation. Danny was an expert at it.

When he lied to authorities and, in his mind, built himself up into something he wasn't, Danny told Coleman, it resulted in "providing him with more amenities or different custody placements when he was incarcerated."

Danny Hembree got something out of lying and controlling the situation. The more he did it, the better he became at doing it—and the rewards became better. Through this, Danny learned he could control the system by telling them what they wanted to hear. If authorities believed he was confessing to crimes, he thought they'd ply him with what he desired. Lots of criminals develop this tactic.

"I also want to die," he told Coleman during a session one afternoon. They were talking about how he felt about himself, how he viewed himself in the world.

"Die?"

"I have created stories and lies about myself all my life," he said, "in order to bolster myself because I have always felt so insignificant."

Later, Coleman would say his "narcissism is kind of the over-the-shell overlay of the insecurity."

His father, it was a good bet, made Danny feel as though he was an object—a "thing" with which the old man could do what he wanted. Danny would go on to treat women he viewed as below him and "his kind" on the social scale in this same way.

As far back as 1986, his mother is on record saying her son would lie to hospital staff whenever he was committed and often "exaggerated about his behavior." This so-called false confession history he had throughout his career as a criminal was something Coleman later explained in court:

"Well, oftentimes [they do this] to build up [the] ego. They like the excitement of it. They want attention. They have a high desire for attention from others. They typically make those claims repeatedly over time. It's usually not just one instance, and it is usually for some sort of short-term incentive or gain without any consideration of long-term consequences."

After speaking with her patient on four separate occasions, Dr. Coleman established how difficult it was for her to determine if he suffered from bipolar disorder because of a severe substance abuse problem, which often masked itself in symptoms similar to bipolar disorder. So Coleman was not confident in making that diagnosis. What Coleman was certain of, however, was that Danny Robbie Hembree had "long-standing difficulties with impulsivity," a "low tolerance for frustration," an "unstable mood," plenty of "self-defeating behaviors," a terrible "disregard for the rights of others," in addition to acting out "in antisocial ways."

Coleman concluded in her assessment that Danny Hembree frequently found a way to manipulate "the legal and prison systems for personal gain," and he had been somewhat successful at it throughout his life.

The more pressing issues Coleman had firm opinions about pertained to his being perhaps "insane," or out of his mind. Did the guy suffer from mental illness that seemed to control his thoughts and actions, literally disallowing him to be responsible for what he did? Was Danny Hembree crazy?

No opinion can be made, Coleman wrote in her report.

The idea was that Danny Hembree had lied so often, so many times, twisting the truth in ways that served his purposes and desires, that his behavior indicated an "underline" narcissistic personality disorder.

But Danny Hembree knew what he was doing. He understood right from wrong.

When one looked at this report, the only conclusion can

be that he was a ticking time bomb. The trigger for him, generally, was women he viewed as below him on the social ladder, and what they said and did. If he didn't approve of what a female in his life did, that fuse—so short—was lit. And if you were near him when the fuse reached its end, guess what?

You wound up dead.

CHAPTER 41

O n Friday morning, November 27, Detective Matt Hensley took a call from a York County investigator. "We're picking Hembree up . . . and want to question him at your department."

Game on.

YCSO detectives Mike Baker and Russ Yeager hauled Danny Hembree into the GCPD and sat him down in the box. Staring at the suspect on a video monitor from an adjacent room, Hensley had no doubt he was looking at Heather and Randi's killer. The cop felt it. Hembree had a way about him: a hubristic swagger to his walk and demeanor as he made his way into the nondescript interrogation room and sat down. He had a look in his eye as though he wanted to play. This sort of thing was fun to a guy like Hembree. He enjoyed the process.

As he waited for investigators to come in and question him, Danny picked at his cuticles and sat calmly, an elbow on the arm of his chair at times, or cradling his chin, as though the entire moment was under his total control. He smoothed his mustache with two fingers and was no doubt going over in his mind what he was going to say, how he was going to stage it, believing unreservedly he was going to be able to outsmart these cops and feed them a line of bullshit they would eat up.

The interview suite had whitewashed walls with nothing on them but paint, bare as a sheet of paper. There were four cushioned chairs set up around a small table, one of which Hembree sat in. He wore a dark gray—almost charcoal black—shirt and pants. He sported dyed black hair, same as his black mustache and eyebrows. There was a pasty quality to his skin—especially his face—as though he'd been on a binge and was perpetually hungover. As intense as this moment was (after all, he was there to be questioned about two murders, there could be no mistaking that reality, no matter how law enforcement had packaged the interview to him), he didn't flinch. It seemed to him to be just another day.

This space was familiar to Hembree. He had been questioned by police about crimes ranging from rape to robbery, and seemingly everything in between, more times than he could recall. The cops interviewing him on this day no doubt knew of his wide-ranging history of violence and lawbreaking. Hembree was a serious offender, quite capable of the crimes he was being asked about.

"Mr. Hembree was charged with assault in the 1980s against a man," said one law enforcement source. "And then a rape/assault against a female and even admitted to it later—but was never charged with that crime." Hembree had a codefendant in those cases, and his "codefendant . . . was interviewed [later] and admitted to the horrible acts they committed. . . . His [rape] victim remembers the case vividly and it still haunts her to this day (twenty years after). She is lucky to be alive. The male victim was a black man, and Hembree and his codefendant brutally assaulted him."

* * *

Detective Mike Baker explained to Hembree that he was not under arrest and could leave at any time. The YCSO appreciated him coming in to talk.

"Can you tell me what you got?" Baker asked Hembree.

"You ask the questions and I'll answer them best I can," Hembree responded firmly. He wasn't about to start offering up anything.

"Well, you said you thought you had some information."

"Just what I've already told you," Hembree said, using a hand to gesture a "let's get this thing going here" type of rolling motion, before beckoning a familiar name Hembree liked to bring up whenever he was being backed into a corner regarding Heather: "Stella . . ."

Danny told a story about how, when he first got out of prison after his last bid in January 2009, he "boarded" with Stella. And while he was living there, he did a roofing job for a local guy, which put some money in his pocket. When Stella found out, she asked him if he would take her out.

"And when I got up there and went to pick her up, Heather came running out," he explained. "And I didn't know Heather was her daughter. Because a week prior to that, I had seen Heather inside a hotel room and I wouldn't let her go with me because she didn't have no ID on her. She looked like she was twelve years old. So I left her up there." He continually used his hands to make his points, gesturing with them at times, using a chopping motion, *1-2-3,* on the table at others. "Anyway . . . we got down there, about eight or nine of us, and I bought Stella [some things]. . . . So me and Heather and Stella, we go to a back room and, well, I feel like I'm getting played now." The resentment and anger in his voice was obvious and intense. You could tell he was restraining himself because he was sitting in front of cops. But there's no doubt he wanted to unleash and relive those moments when Heather and Stella pissed him off. He was pinning all of the drug use and whatever else went wrong on Stella and the others. None of it, he insinuated over and over, was his fault. He was simply being a nice guy and buying dope for everyone, same as he generally did.

As Danny Hembree continued to tell this story, he stared into space and at the wall in front of him. Within every lie, any cop knows, there's a grain of truth. And here was Hembree, making sure the right lie was told at the right time.

"As Stella got into the bathtub," he continued, "Heather, she took off her top."

"What's up?" he asked Heather as she stood there before him with her breasts exposed. (Mind you, this was a girl he claimed to believe was only twelve.) "What's up?" was street-speak for, Hembree explained, "What is it you want me to do?"

"Well," he claimed Heather said to him, "aren't you and my momma kind of dating?"

"Yup, but we ain't married. So what's up?"

Hembree walked over and sat on the bed in the room. He said Heather came over to him and "started to give me a hand job"—and he used his hands again to explain what he was saying—"and I said, 'No, no, no . . . *hell* no.' "

Just then, a second investigator walked into the room and handed Baker a Diet Coke, breaking up Danny Hembree's story.

Baker asked the detective: "Hey, maybe y'all want to sit in, since you two knew each other back in the day?"

"No, no," the detective said. "I got some other stuff I gotta do." He walked out of the room.

Continuing, Hembree said he walked over to Stella, who was still bathing in the tub, and said, "You got a problem with me fucking Heather?"

Hembree claimed that Stella said, " 'Give me a hit.' "

So Hembree gave Stella the crack pipe.

After that, "she got upset about it." He meant Stella. "And she left."

Which gave him, Hembree said, the opportunity to take Heather and get another eight ball.

After copping the crack cocaine, Heather and Hembree went back to the room and "we rolled, and I ain't done seen her since she got out of prison."

"That was back *when*?" Baker asked.

"That was Valentine's Day—because it was Stella's birthday."

"So what you're saying is that Stella basically *offered* her to you?" Baker wanted this clarified. After all, the way Danny Hembree worded it, he was accusing Stella of selling her daughter for a hit of crack.

Before answering, Danny Boy shifted in his seat and sat up straight, a clear indication that this question—or the behavior itself—rattled him. In his mind, the idea of Stella selling her daughter's vagina for a hit of crack cocaine was revolting. Every nuance of his body language as he spoke of this event communicated that feeling.

"She's been tricking them girls out for a long time," Hembree answered.

CHAPTER 42

Detective Mike Baker found a groove Danny Hembree seemed to feel comfortable in. So Baker next asked Hembree if he could talk them through that time when Heather got out of jail until the last time he saw her.

Hembree broke into a familiar story to investigators by now: picking Sommer and her boyfriend up that day on the road and driving over to the Cattertons' house; seeing Heather in the tub getting ready for the night; then ditching Nicole and taking Heather, Sommer, and George out to that trailer to party.

Listening to Hembree, monitoring his temperament and bodily semantics, a fact emerged: The guy had a fixation with Heather Catterton. It was clear in the way he responded, his movements, his speech patterns, and the words he chose. Danny had a thing for Heather.

As he told the story, Hembree mixed up Sommer and Nicole at times, interspersing the names. Baker corrected him when he did, and Hembree responded as if their names or who they were didn't matter. The story was a shorter version of the events Sommer had described. Hembree stuck mostly to that script, taking it one step further into the night, adding, "When we got back to my mom's, we was there about forty-five minutes, and I told Heather just to go to bed, because that's what she said she was gonna do, but she done said she wanted to make some more money. . . . She was going to call the Marlboro Man."

Hensley looked on from that second room and thought how Hembree often implicated this "Marlboro Man" in things to bring in another potential suspect. "The Marlboro Man is a person Danny just threw out there at us to try to throw us off track," Hensley explained. "We found out the Marlboro Man was a guy that would give cigarettes to the girls in exchange for sexual favors. That's how he got his nickname."

When Heather said she was thinking of going to see the Marlboro Man, Hembree responded, "Well, I'm not gonna take you back up to your house because Nicole already done called and left me messages threatening to knock the windows out [of my car]."

The mention of Heather going to see the Marlboro Man angered Hembree. It was as if he had a thing going on with Heather that night, that she was his girl. There she was at his mom's house, getting ready to nestle up to him in bed and spend the night. The Marlboro Man, clearly, was not part of the fantasy Hembree had envisioned.

Nicole, on the other hand, was mad because her boyfriend had taken off earlier that night without her.

Hembree skipped right to dropping Heather off at the Mighty Dollar, across the street from her house, sticking to a familiar story surrounding that night he had already planted for investigators on several other occasions.

"I pulled in and let her out," Hembree said. "And that was the last time I done seen her."

"What was she wearing that day?"

"Ah, she had on a gray hoodie," Hembree said, staring off into space again, "and a . . . a . . . a pair of jeans." He then looked over at Baker to gauge his reaction to the statement.

After all, Hembree had just described what Heather was wearing on the day she died.

Smartly, Baker kept his poker face.

There was an awkward moment of silence.

"The reason I know that," Hembree offered without being prompted, "was because Nicole said theys was her jeans."

"Where were y'all at when you were at your mom's doing all that?"

"In the den and another room. . . . Well, me and Sommer, and me and Heather and Sommer, when we was together, we was in a room beside the den."

"Your bedroom? Or what?"

"That is my bedroom, but I sleep in the den mostly."

Baker and Hembree talked about the information Danny had left out of his narrative, which the YCSO had obtained from other sources. Hembree cleared up the confusion. Moments before this explanation, another investigator, Detective Russ Yeager, walked into the room and sat down, not saying a word. Instead, Yeager got comfortable and opened the lid to a sixteen-ounce cup of Dunkin' Donuts coffee and, taking a sip, stared at Hembree.

In all of Hembree's explanations, whenever he talked about Nicole, Stella, Sommer, and Heather, there was a steely crassness to his voice, as if to suggest he was better than those women.

"Was there anything else about that night you can recall and tell us about?" Baker asked.

"Just that Sommer's boyfriend was an asshole . . . and he couldn't do nothing"—get an erection—"and so I wound up with Heather and Sommer."

The braggart: Hembree routinely touted himself as "Mr. Love Machine." Here was that arrogance and grandiosity of Hembree's. The reality was far different. Sommer had told police it was also Hembree who could not get an erection that night.

After dropping Heather off at the Mighty Dollar, Hembree explained, "I went back home to my momma's and stayed till about . . . ten o'clock [the next morning], when my son came over. And then Stella's boyfriend . . . called and that's when he came up there."

Returning home from dropping Heather off, Hembree explained, he "watched some porn" and fell asleep. It was strange that he mentioned this detail: Why not just say television? Why porn specifically?

According to expert John Kelly, "It seems Mr. Hembree always had an interest in porn. In fact, you could say he was addicted to it. His porn viewing, I suspect, escalated to where it became boring to watch it on television. Being bored by the television version of porn, he upped his excitement and fantasy levels, as we see in him watching it up close and personal." (Kelly was referencing when Hembree would ask Sommer and Heather and other women to perform sexual acts in front of him.) "Having the drug-addicted females perform live for him while he controlled them with drugs shows his progression to sexual control, the sexual degradation of the women. . . . Most power and control serial killers are hypersexual. It's a murderous progression. They can't get enough. As the sexual fantasy escalates, so does their controlling and murderous sexual behavior. Ted Bundy is a good example of this. There are many more."

During the interview, Hembree said he was upset that Heather left him that night; but it was something she had done before. He wanted her to stay. Without realizing it, delving back into that fantasy he had built around him and Heather, Hembree said he wanted to cook Heather breakfast when she got up the next morning. But the fairy tale of them sleeping together, spooning all night, waking up, and then having breakfast like a real couple was quashed when, he said, Heather bailed out (after the drugs were gone). He insisted that she asked to be dropped off at the Mighty Dollar. This request told Hembree that Heather was with him *only* because he was providing her with drugs.

The next morning, Hembree saw his son and then drove to Nicole's house.

Stella had called. "Nick's not mad at you anymore, Danny," she said. "Come on over."

He arrived at noon.

"That Nicole sounds pretty rough," Baker said as Yeager stared, taking a pull from his coffee. "Now, you don't seem like the type of guy that somebody would mess with, but everybody round here been talking 'bout how Nicole slaps you and, well, she rules the roost."

"Yup, well, you know, I love her. I pretty much get my way. And she don't hurt me none, or anything like that. She wrecked my phone and kicked my windshield and kicked my radio. No big deal."

"Is she just that jealous or what?"

Hembree took a deep breath. He looked to his side, then down at the carpet.

"She's obsessive. . . ."

CHAPTER 43

"We're continuing to build this circumstantial case against Danny Hembree," Matt Hensley explained, "and we were going to continue to do that until the leads ran out."

The momentum of the investigation tipped toward Hembree. He was involving himself in the investigation, taunting cops with his macho, catch-me-if-you-can manner.

Danny immersed himself into the growing suspicion surrounding his potential involvement as the interview with York County went on for two-plus hours. He actually enjoyed himself, sitting, believing he was controlling every aspect of the interview. There was a hard edge to him that gave him an air of sovereignty as he spoke. He talked fast and skipped over pivotal portions of a preplanned narrative he was laying out for cops.

In his mind, Danny wanted to keep them guessing. He spoke with an increasing amount of delight in taking part in the progression of the case. His narcissism was evident and obvious, as if what he had to say was the most important information to date. These cops were going to sit and listen, no matter what he had to say, because he was driving this bus. And yet within all of his hubris, the one clear, undisputed indication was that Danny Hembree knew exactly what he was saying and why he was there. If the guy ever planned to stage a mental-illness argument, this one interview, in all of its candidness and simplicity, spoke of a man not insane or mentally ill, but rather someone carefully and excitingly flexing his self-absorbed, ego-driven muscle.

Danny Hembree, after all, could have gotten up and walked out of there or asked for an attorney at any moment.

He never did.

After Heather went missing, Danny Hembree took Nicole on a road trip to Florida. Investigators had gotten wind of this trip and wanted to know from Hembree why he decided to head south. The insinuation was: *Were you running?*

"When I first got out [of prison], I lived down there about three months," Danny explained. "I took all my winter clothes and stuff down there and I been meaning to try to get back down there and we decided to just go . . . load up my stuff and just come back."

Baker brought up Shorty and "that night," as he called it, that Danny spent with Nicole and Randi and Shorty. Baker, however, never mentioned Randi Saldana by name.

"Y'all talking 'bout with that Randi girl?"

This was Danny Hembree: "That Randi girl?" He was speaking as if he barely knew her.

"Uh-huh," Baker said, shaking his head.

Hembree took a deep breath; then he looked off to his left side and told his version of the night. He explained that he and Nicole were driving around with Stella, and Stella, Hembree said, "wanted to get [something]. . . ."

When they got to a particular drug house, which Hembree claimed he had "never been" to before that night, "that girl Randi was there." Hembree said he'd seen Randi before, "way back in January." She was with "Stella and Nicole."

Randi was "breaking bread with everybody" on that night, Hembree said. Sharing the dope she had, in other words. Randi had a bottle of liquor "because she knew Nicole. She don't do crack."

He skipped over the entire party. Then: "We went over Nick's house. When we got to Nick's house, that girl Randi gave Stella a piece. . . ."

Hembree recollected how Stella "got pissed" over something and ran off and told Nick they were smoking rock in his house.

Nick made everybody leave, Hembree confirmed.

Leaving Nick's, they went to find Shorty and headed over to that dope dealer's house, where they'd started the night.

Inside the house, Hembree said, he and Nicole, along with Randi, retreated to a back bedroom and partied. He also clarified that it wasn't Shorty's house they had all gone to (which was the one differing fact from what the others reported).

"Shorty kept coming back in there because he was the one scoring the dope."

At this stage of the interview, Hembree said something quite interesting, which came out of him almost as an afterthought. It was as if he wanted to make sure Baker and his YCSO boys had this information: "And we was back there talking and I think they's swapped a necklace or ring or something like that. [I wasn't paying no attention.]"

Randi then talked about an Alcoholics Anonymous coordinator she had to call. So Hembree let her use his cell phone, he said, picking his cell up off the table and referring to it.

"I gotta go. . . . I gotta go. . . . I gotta go," Randi kept telling Danny and Nicole.

Forty-five minutes went by. They had not seen Shorty in that time, so Hembree figured he'd left.

Then Randi said it again, "I gotta go." She walked out of the room.

"I seen the way she was looking at you," Nicole said to Danny.

"What? Come on?"

Nicole then slapped him, Hembree claimed.

So he left and went to look for Randi. Finding her, Danny brought Randi back into the room to tell Nicole, "That shit ain't right."

The owner of the house told Hembree to get out.

"So I just got in my car and took off. I done that a lot."

Baker asked Hembree about Randi. "You give her ride" when you left?

"I didn't see Randi no more after that," Hembree said, shaking his head slowly, right to left. His hands were folded; his fingers were crisscrossed and set on his lap. He was comfortable.

"What was she wearing?"

Hembree shook his head and looked off to the side. "Dark clothes . . . I . . . That's all I can tell ya."

"She was a sharp-looking girl, right?" Baker asked.

"Oh yeah, Randi was pretty sharp. I don't think she looked as good as Heather when Heather was fixed up. . . ."

"What else can you tell me about Randi?" Baker pressed.

"That's basically it. I know she talked about wanting something better for herself and she said that a . . . a . . . The next day was her two-year-old son's birthday. Other than that, I didn't pay no attention."

While reaching to take a sip from a Mountain Dew he had in front of him, Hembree mumbled something along the lines of "You hear shit so much." It was obvious Hembree was casting a line.

Baker took the bait. "Well, what have you heard?"

"What do you mean, *what* have I heard?" Hembree snapped.

"Well, you say you hear shit. What does that mean?"

Hembree paused. He took a pull from his soda, staring at Baker the entire time. Then he placed his drink down slowly, saying, "I've been hearing so much shit. . . . I heard that . . . the girls coming out of [Shorty's and the other guy's house] are being targeted . . . but that's bullshit. . . . Shorty told me hisself that when he found out who did Heather, he was going to do him. . . ."

As long as Baker allowed Hembree to think he was in control, the guy was going to keep talking.

Watching from another room, Hensley shook his head. He knew what Hembree was doing. "To him," Hensley commented, "he had all the power and control during those interviews. He loved talking to investigators and would, as long as he felt he was in control."

Baker asked Hembree where he went when he left the dope house.

"I went home," Hembree said. Then he told the story of Stella calling from the hospital and asking him to pick her and Nick up. "And I told her if he's out by one-thirty to call me back . . . and I'll come and get ya."

Again, in Hembree's narrative, he never put himself in a position of being the bad guy. He was always the innocent bystander doing dope because of the peer pressure (the girls pushing him) within a circle of dopers that he hung around. He wanted to come across as a man who never raised his voice or became aggressive.

For the rest of that night when Randi went missing, Hembree said, he was at home and "passed out" by two or three in the morning. The following day, he got up and drove to Nick's.

"So you went home, home—Momma's home?" Baker asked.

"Yeah."

"Was Momma home?"

"Oh yeah, Momma let me in."

"Where'd you stay at then—in your room, in the den?"

"I stayed in the den."

For whatever reason, perhaps his sheer willingness to up the cat-and-mouse angle, Hembree said out of nowhere: "There was another girl up there. . . ." He was referring to the night he got in that tiff with Nicole and Randi and left them at the dope house. "And for a twenty-dollar bill, I took her down the road for a little while. . . ."

"And she gave you a blow job?" Baker asked.

"Yup," Hembree said, nodding his head.

Then the question came up why he would go off with someone else (and pay) when he had Nicole and "other girls," each of whom he could have easily gotten oral sex from (according to him).

"I don't know . . . she's a pretty good old girl," Hembree remarked, referring to the girl he paid $20. It came across as though he was doing her a favor.

"So, what do you think happened to Randi?"

Hembree did his characteristic look off to his left side, a clear indication that this question made him uncomfortable and he had to think about what he said before he said it.

A pause.

Then he picked at his fingernails.

Finally: "I have no idea. . . . Somebody said that she"— and here Danny looked at Baker squarely, as though taunting him—"got set on fire."

Baker shook his head.

Game on.

Danny Hembree stared Mike Baker down. In a near whisper, Danny repeated himself: "I. Don't. Know." He paused.

"In my honest opinion, I don't think Shorty had anything to do with it." And his reason for thinking that, Hembree said, was nothing in particular. "Just a gut feeling."

"Is there anybody that you do suspect of it?"

Hembree mentioned how the circle he ran in was "so deep. . . . It's just what they do."

If you ran with the Devil, Hembree seemed to say, you sometimes got burned.

CHAPTER 44

The interview with Danny Hembree could have carried on all night, perhaps. Hembree was used to the structure of the box. If Baker and Yeager thought they were going to get him to give it up by tiring him out, they thought wrong.

At least, it appeared to be the case on this day.

Hembree knew how to spoon-feed detectives just enough information to keep them guessing, but also come across as though he was answering their questions. And yet, while Hembree played a game of his own, Yeager, Baker, and Hensley were doing the same thing. While around Hembree, the detectives displayed a set demeanor, Hensley later explained: The idea that they were hot on Hembree, sure; but they were also still digging and confused about the cases. Outside the box, however, all three detectives worked under the assumption that Hembree was their guy and it was only a matter of time before his shoulders dropped, he took a deep breath, wiped his brow, and gave it all up.

Certain cops can smell an admission before it arrives.

Baker and Yeager had questioned lots of suspects. They knew what to do with a guy like Hembree, how far to push, and where to take things.

Baker mentioned how odd it seemed that with so many people in that circle Danny ran with, someone had not known what happened to Heather. Maybe Randi wasn't such an engrained part of the group he hung around every day, but Heather was. Baker pointed out that with a tight group of dopers hardly ever leaving their comfort zone of a few houses around town, why was Heather's body found in South Carolina? That part of the scenario didn't make sense, Baker explained. The dump site was only ten miles away; but in the confined world of a doper, it might as well have been in Los Angeles.

"Well, Heather's gone down to York . . . a couple of times, from what I understand," Hembree offered, again looking off to his left side before taking a pull of his Mountain Dew.

"What do you know about that?"

"All I know is that her brother . . . told Nicole that she was at a hotel in York." From there, Hembree tossed Nicole's brother into the flames by telling Baker and Yeager where they could find him and how he had a "bunch of copper" he was scrapping for cash. Hembree said he wanted no part of stealing copper. "I don't want to go back to jail."

It got to a point where Baker needed to get things moving. After explaining how the YCSO and GCPD had gone around and around with these cases, studying them backward and forward, no matter which way they disassembled the homicides, it always circled back to one guy.

"I already know I'm the number one suspect," Hembree acknowledged.

Baker nodded his head in agreement.

"I ain't had nothing to do with it!" Hembree announced emphatically. "I ain't got nothing to hide. Y'all do whatever y'all gotta do."

Baker asked about a fresh DNA sample from Hembree.

Hembree balked a little at first, but then he said, what the heck, the Department of Corrections (DOC) has his DNA on file, anyway. "So I ain't got no problem with that."

This request made Hembree particularly uncomfortable. It rattled him. He shifted in his seat several times and rubbed his chin nervously. The walls were closing in. He felt the pressure. His mind raced. And it was obvious he was thinking about his next move.

After sitting, staring off into an empty space, Hembree shifted to the other side of his chair and again spoke while staring at the wall, away from Baker's line of sight.

Hembree decided he had to tell them. He had no choice.

"The only thing that you're gonna find is that both of those girls . . . was in my car right before they disappeared. And you know, I'm not a rocket scientist, but I'm not stupid, neither. And I'm not a killer, neither. As far as women goes, I'm not . . . I take . . . I'm one of those, whatcha call it . . . gigolo types of deals. There's places I can go lay down and that's because I done treat people right."

In one breath, the guy had gone from placing the girls in his car to comparing himself to Richard Gere's character in *American Gigolo*. What in the name of Southern barbeque was Danny Hembree talking about now? Did he even realize what he had said? Did he know what the word "gigolo" meant?

It came out of him as if he couldn't help it: Hembree wasn't the lonely troll people were making him out to be, some Green River type, driving around, picking up girls, killing them for sport. He qualified that argument by telling Baker to check each one of his robberies. There they'd find that Hembree, as he claimed, had "never used a real gun" in any of them.

The mention of taking a DNA sample put Hembree on the defensive. Agitated now, he wanted to know why the YCSO was running around telling people he was their main suspect. He had an accusatory tone in his voice.

"Well—" Baker started to say.

"Did you talk to Nicole and tell her you wanted to get her into a shelter?"

"Yup, yup, we did." Baker explained why, saying if they believed Hembree was a suspect in two homicides, why would they want to put Nicole's life in danger, too? They wouldn't be responsible cops if they didn't think ahead.

Using a finger to articulate a circle on the table, Hembree said: "Well, I want y'all to get everything you need today . . . because I'm all done. . . ."

That was it, Hembree said. This would be the last time he sat with detectives and talked about these cases under these circumstances.

Wearing a button-down blue shirt, tie, and dark slacks, Matt Hensley walked into the room with a buccal swab DNA kit and read the consent form to Danny Hembree, who then signed it. It was perfect timing. Hensley entering the room broke up Hembree's negative burst of energy.

Baker said something to Hensley about taking Hembree's car in for a more thorough forensic search. Hembree said he didn't mind: "As long as y'all fill it up with gas." It was on *E* and he was busted, no cash.

The way Hembree begged for gas sounded pathetic. Here was a grown man, forty-seven years old, no money, no job, providing dope to down-and-out females (some of whom were clearly underage) in exchange for sex, smoking crack every chance he got, drinking alcohol every day, living in his mother's house.

Nothingman.

As Hensley prepared the DNA kit, Hembree mumbled how they were likely going to find his DNA on Heather because he'd had sex with her three times that night. On each occasion, he felt the need to announce, he had ejaculated in her mouth and vagina without using a condom.

Sommer's interview, they all knew, contradicted this statement.

"What about Randi?" Baker asked.

"I've *never* had sex with Randi."

Hembree went quiet; he was thinking. Then, rather randomly, he said how Randi had rubbed his arm that night, suggesting that they might find his DNA on her because of this subtle touch.

Hensley didn't say anything. He finished swabbing Hembree's cheeks—which made Hembree tense up—and left the room.

"So there shouldn't be any of your DNA, sperm, saliva, nothing like that, on Randi at all?" Baker asked, clearly letting Hembree know that a rub of the arm was not enough of an exchange to leave DNA.

"No, no. . . ."

"Nothing?"

"Well, there might be a little from a kiss on her neck or something." It seemed that Hembree then realized what he had said: *neck.* Then he quickly added: "Or on her *cheek.* But there shouldn't be—"

"So you never had sex with Randi?"

"Not that I know of. I only met her twice. You guys gotta understand. I've been with a *lot* of women—three or four a day for a while."

While Mike Baker continued interviewing Danny Hembree, Hensley and Yeager found out that Hembree's vehicle was parked at Nick's. They had consent from Hembree that as long as they filled his car up with gas upon returning it (Hembree actually wrote this as an addendum on the consent form), they could tow it to the GCPD and give it a thorough forensic sweep.

CHAPTER 45

Back inside the box, Baker took out his calendar book to make sure he was working with the right dates. Hembree had been unclear about certain dates. Baker, alone with Hembree now, wanted clarification.

Baker asked if anyone had heard from Heather during that time period Hembree said he had dropped her off at the Mighty Dollar and eleven days later, when she was found dead in that ditch.

Using his fingers to count them off, Danny rolled out several times that Nick, Nicole, and Stella had told him they'd seen Heather (or someone they knew had seen Heather) "at some dude's house" and several other places, including Shorty's.

"She was always doing dates," Hembree added, meaning trading sex for dope.

They talked about where Heather stayed. Hembree said Shorty's, mostly. Then he told Baker they (Shorty and Heather) were making "pornographic movies" with "a lot of them girls who's underage."

They talked about this for a while. Russ Yeager came

back into the box, sat down, and stared at Hembree without speaking.

Baker asked Hembree if he liked Heather.

Hembree took his time. "Yeah, uh . . . as somebody to hang out and party with. She's sweet. She's innocent in her own little way. Yeah, I liked Heather."

"You like her as much as you like Nicole?"

"Oh, hell no. Nicole's got a chance. She's getting her GED and all that stuff."

The tone Hembree used to describe his girlfriend, it wasn't clear if he was dissing or complimenting her. "She's got a low standard, but there's something about her. There's potential. There's something different there."

After talking about his future with Nicole, Hembree digressed (as he often did) and explained how he once thought about putting Heather and Sommer up in a trailer. Hembree said he had been discussing it with Heather, especially.

It was a strange comment, considering that he had only met Sommer one time and had, just before talking about it, told Baker how much he adored Nicole.

Baker picked up on this thread and asked about Sommer.

"Sommer's been calling me," Hembree claimed. "She told me if she found a place to go, she'd dump that old boy she's with . . . and I told them (Sommer and Heather) what I wanted."

"What is it you wanted?" Baker asked. After all, Hembree was not going to be paying the girls' rent without getting something for himself, Baker knew.

"I told them both it was like this," Hembree explained. "I want eggs, when I get up. I want the house clean, when I get there. I want sex, when I want sex. And what y'all do when I'm gone, do it discreetly. And everything's fine."

As the interview continued, Hembree said he met a girl at Heather's funeral and ended up partying with her.

Baker asked who she was in relation to the Catterton family.

"Heather's lover—"

"Her *lover*?"

Hembree said yes. He did not elaborate.

They talked about what Hembree might have been doing during those days while Heather was missing, but he conveniently couldn't recall exact dates, where he had gone, and what he had done. It was very telling to Baker how Danny Hembree could talk candidly about what he and Heather and Sommer and Stella and Nick and Nicole had done in those days when Heather first got out of jail (in detail); but as soon as Heather went missing, Hembree had developed a case of amnesia.

"Heather would jump in the damn car with the ice-cream man," Hembree said, referring to when she wanted dope. He said he warned Heather and Nicole about "getting into the car with anybody." He told them they shouldn't do it, "especially in South Gastonia. She (Heather) was just young and she didn't think it could happen to her."

"It." Subtle word choice there.

Baker asked Hembree if he had any idea who "did this" to Heather.

"I figured she . . . [Someone] told me she OD'd and the way it looked someone woke up and panicked. . . . Y'all hadn't even told us how she died, so I don't know—how did she die?"

"Well, that's what we're trying to figure out."

"What do you think?" Hembree asked.

"Well, what I'd like to do is get what *you* think. "

Hembree said he could "not see her OD'ing" because of how used she was to smoking rock.

"How do you think she died?" Baker asked after explaining he couldn't tell Hembree everything they knew about Heather's death.

Hembree played with the cap from his Mountain Dew in one hand and shook his head. "I don't know. I can't see anybody murdering her without her pants on. [I know someone who] said she wasn't raped, so . . . I mean . . . I don't know. . . ."

Why in Clover, South Carolina, and that general area? Baker wondered.

"Well, whoever it was didn't have no place to take her so they put her out there."

"Why do you say that?"

"I mean, it's obvious. It's secluded. If they had a place to take her, they would have put her *there*. If they had a place to bury her, they wouldn't have just shoved her off in that field there."

Baker went back to something Hembree had said earlier about Heather not having pants on. He was confused. He wanted Hembree to elaborate on his "theory" of what he thought happened.

Hembree looked straight ahead, past Russ Yeager, who sat more relaxed, elbows on his knees, hands folded, staring at Hembree. Danny said, "I mean, if *I* was gonna kill somebody . . . I wouldn't kill them with their pants *off*."

"What if I got all mad at her and pissed off or something?" Baker suggested.

"Then she would have marks or something. She didn't have marks, according to [what I heard]."

If it was an accident, Baker tossed out, why wouldn't the person she was with call 911?

"That's what I would have done," Hembree said twice.

Someone had gone out and purchased a coffee for Hembree. Yeager and Baker then walked out of the room as Hembree prepared his coffee with milk and sugar. Hembree put his jacket on; and when Baker returned, he indicated he wanted to go outside and smoke a cigarette.

*   *   *

After his smoke, Hembree was back in the box.

Baker wanted to clarify. "There's nothing that I missed." He looked at his notes.

An interesting fact about Hembree's life came up and Baker wanted to know how Hembree picked up his girls. There had been so many, according to Danny. But that one girl walking down the street—what about her?

Hembree said he didn't know her name, where she was from, or much else about her, adding, "She was just walking down the road and I asked her if she was working, and she said 'yeah,' and I said, 'Well, I got a hit. . . .' "

So there was Hembree's pickup line: "I got a hit."

He took her to his favorite spot—that abandoned trailer.

The anecdote Hembree gave Baker showed how little Hembree valued the lives of the women he had sex and partied with. He viewed these women—Sommer, Heather, Nicole, and Randi included—as lowlifes: females he could do what he wanted with because they were out there in the world smoking dope. In Hembree's skewed view of life, they were below everyone else. They didn't matter because of the choices they made.

Hembree was asked again what he had done during the weekend of October 24 and 25.

He kept saying he couldn't recall. "I'll have to talk to Nicole and figure it out."

Two hours and four minutes into the interview, Hembree stretched. "Look, man, if we're gonna do something, let's *do* it," he said. "Because I'm about tired of hanging out in here."

The interview ended as Hembree stood and popped a cigarette in his mouth. They left the box without a confession. Yet, in the days to come, Danny Hembree's vanity would be his worst enemy. His unchecked narcissism would come back to bite him.

CHAPTER 46

Working out of the Gaston County Police Department headquarters, YCSO investigators picked Shorty up and brought him in. Shorty's name had come up so often within the scope of the investigation that law enforcement knew he was going to become a good source for intel inside that tight-knit group of Gastonia dealers and dopers. Still, had investigators focused on Hembree too closely and missed something with Shorty? Had Shorty, a guy with a soft spot for Heather, someone who had wanted to "rescue" her from the street life, become jealous and enraged by the lifestyle Heather was involved in?

Average height, at about five feet nine inches, quite scruffy around the edges, fifty-year-old Shorty, an African American, was one of those old-school Southerners who had a thick, hard-to-understand accent that sounded as if he spoke a language of his own. Shorty had his own problems with the law. He'd been arrested and charged with drug possession. He later admitted that while Heather, Randi, Danny, and Nicole were hanging around his house, he was providing them with controlled substances. Despite his reputation as a dealer, Shorty said he had never gone to Heather and traded drugs for sex. There was a certain type of scourge that did that sort of thing, and Shorty made it clear he wasn't it.

The main theme Shorty got across became that Heather was someone many, many people took advantage of, especially the older women Heather hung around with. They used her. They abused her adolescence and lack of street smarts.

"People would come to my house looking for her and I would turn them away," Shorty said.

After being asked, Shorty gave investigators the first glimpse they had into what Heather did on the morning before she was last seen alive. This was important. It was another piece of the victimology puzzle, another piece of Heather's life before she went missing that law enforcement could now fill in.

Heather had been over at Shorty's that morning. She'd been hanging around, as usual. Stella, Danny, and Nicole came by soon after Heather woke up and picked her up. Shorty had no idea where they ran off to, but he guessed they took Heather back home (to Nick's).

Nicole called Shorty later that day; through that conversation, Shorty learned Heather had taken off with Sommer and Sommer's boyfriend, George. Nicole never mentioned Danny as part of the crowd, or the one who actually came up with the idea to take off without Nicole.

Shorty went about his day. As the night progressed, Sommer called several times. Each time she called (Shorty never said why), he asked to speak with Heather to make sure she was okay.

"But Sommer wouldn't let me talk to her."

Then Sommer called back and asked Shorty, "Can we come over there?"

"Sure," Shorty said.

"But they never showed up," Shorty told investigators.

What made Shorty think something was wrong took

place the following morning. Heather never called. By then, he was used to Heather checking in with him at least once a day, if not several times. Not calling "was unlike her."

After Heather was considered missing, Shorty said, he worried something had happened. No one had heard from her. This was important to Shorty, who knew Heather could not go a day without talking to someone from that group.

Shorty talked about a friend of his—a real piece of garbage—who had sold his truck after Heather disappeared. It seemed suspicious, he explained, because he knew the guy and his girlfriend had been with Heather at some point during those days before she went missing.

"Why? What would be their motive?"

"Competition," Shorty explained. The guy's girlfriend, according to Shorty, was jealous of Heather because guys generally chose Heather over her. The indication was that the two of them—the guy who sold his truck and his girlfriend—hated Heather.

After a simple check, Hensley and the YCSO learned that the property where Heather's body had, in fact, been found was owned by a relative of the girl's.

Coincidence?

Shorty thought it just might be.

Why?

Because he believed in his heart that Danny Hembree had murdered both Heather and Randi.

"Danny was raised in those areas where both bodies was found," Shorty said.

Red flag.

Shorty talked about the night he last saw Randi (giving investigators details about that fight Nicole and Hembree got into after Nicole found out Randi and Hembree were making fun of her behind her back). Listening, detectives realized Shorty was confirming lots of details from the night that others had reported. Three people now said Hembree had taken off in his vehicle toward the direction where Randi had left the house and started walking.

"I saw Danny turn around and drive toward where Randi was walking," Shorty said. He was certain of this. "I believe Danny picked her up."

"Why?"

"I done put two and two together," Shorty said.

"Two and two?"

"I think Randi and Danny planned it together in the room without Nicole knowing."

So that fight Nicole and Danny had after Nicole caught them making fun of her was staged—a plan by Danny and Randi to take off and go party together. This was the first time law enforcement had heard this theory.

It sounded plausible.

"Randi looked clean that night—she looked good!" Shorty said.

Hembree liked this about her: the same as when Heather had gotten out of jail and bathed and cleaned herself up.

Hembree didn't like being turned down, Shorty explained. He hated when girls told him no. He believed he was entitled, as long as he had something to give them.

Motive.

There was another girl Hembree had wanted to take out and trade drugs for sex. Hembree had just met her. She knew Randi and Heather. Shorty said when the girl refused Hembree, he became enraged and "bucked at her," threatening to pummel her. They were at Nicole's house. Nick was gone. Nicole was out. Danny and the girl were alone in the house. He placed a "couple of hits of crack" on the kitchen table.

"What's your price?" he asked the girl.

"I ain't no call girl, asshole!"

"Everyone's got her price. If I done had me a thousand dollars, you'd take it."

"I would not. I'm no call girl."

Hembree exploded. He grabbed a kitchen table chair and slammed it on the floor.

("He was enraged," the girl later told Matt Hensley after he tracked her down. "Danny is *crazy*.")

Scared of Hembree, she ran out of the house.

CHAPTER 47

Inside Danny Hembree's vehicle, forensics found several carpet fibers that did not match anything else in the vehicle.

"We knew they were from somewhere," Hensley later said. "We just didn't know where."

This particular trace evidence was no good to them—unless they could come up with trace evidence to match it to, but it was a start.

As the first week of December brought some cold weather to the region, that noose the GCPD, while working with the YCSO, had put around Hembree's neck was about as tight as it could get without Hembree being totally depleted of oxygen. It was time, they all knew, to ask a judge to sign off on an arrest warrant and get Hembree in the box answering questions once again, but this time while under arrest. With a little prodding, Hensley, Baker, and Yeager were certain, Hembree would crack.

Yet, as it would turn out, shocking everyone involved, Danny Hembree would do the heavy lifting himself. No arrest warrant would be needed.

CHAPTER 48

Detective Matt Hensley attended a narcotics meeting on December 2 with several local Charlotte narcotics officers involved in a local heroin ring investigation. This drug brought communities to their knees. Where there was heroin, there was organized crime (be it gangs or the old-school Mafioso). Death seemed to follow this drug's path more than any other: overdose, unpaid drug debts, taking out street pusher competition, or some form of all three.

One particular group of junkies had been stealing over-the-counter medications as a side business to fund their habits. They had been taking the stolen medications to a local drug dealer and trading. One of the subjects interviewed as part of this operation, Hensley found out during the meeting, knew Heather and Randi.

After the meeting, Hensley tracked her down, which turned out to be easy enough. She had been popped on a shoplifting charge and was sitting in Gastonia County Jail.

"Nothing," she said.

She didn't want to get involved. She didn't know anything. She only knew the girls from hanging around certain people. That was how the street life worked.

Everybody knew everybody. Nobody knew anything.

"I have no information about how they died or who killed them," she said.

Hensley scratched his head. Conducting this interview had given him an idea, however. Look over Randi's visitor list the last time she was in jail.

Names.

People always help move an investigation along. It might take talking to ten people, maybe twenty; but by crossing names off a list, you get to know the victim better.

Hensley had never met Heather or Randi. He had never seen them around town, or run into them when they got into trouble. But as the investigation into their murders continued, Hensley felt a bond on top of that voice of the victim calling out. Cops describe it candidly. They begin to think about the voice. Work under it. Feel it. The victim—or, in this case, victims—speak from the grave. There is no one else there to represent them. Cops have to take it on. And every time Hensley spoke to a friend or street buddy of one of the girls, he felt closer, not only to catching their killer, but to the real person behind the madness that their lives had become.

On December 3, Hensley conversed with Russ Yeager, who had recently gotten hold of several photographs found inside a camera Randi owned. Randi appeared to be inside a motel room in some of the photos, lying on a bed "with an unknown black male subject," a report indicated. They couldn't tell when the photos were taken.

What interested Yeager and Hensley most was the bedding. With Randi being found wrapped in a blanket and burned, the bedding in these photos was a potential lead. Were these photos the last pictures of Randi Saldana?

"We have to see if we can match the design of the print on the blanket or comforter Randi was found in," Hensley said.

Hensley and Yeager found out the photos were taken inside a seedy "Motel Hell" on Highway 321, near Highway

74. It was one of those motels to take a date for a few hours. You could rent weekly, and would probably want to wear a full-body condom upon entering the rooms.

The manager was helpful. He handed over records of visitors and tenants during those weeks before both murders.

Hensley, along with two other investigators, sat down and went through the paperwork.

Nothing. Not one player in the drama they were investigating popped out from the documents. That didn't mean Randi, Shorty, Danny, Nicole, Heather, or anyone else within the group hadn't changed his or her name. These are the types of motels that don't much care about having a credit card or proper identification. You have cash; you get a room.

"Can we take a look inside a room?" Hensley asked.

"Sure. Go ahead."

They took the photos and visited several rooms, trying to match up the bedding, bed, and headboard, all of which were visible in the photos.

No match.

As they drove away from the motel, the investigation seemed to be leading nowhere. The only real leads they had led back to Hembree. They were still waiting on a signed arrest warrant.

What now?

They didn't know it, but patience was all they'd need.

PART THREE

THE MOTHER

CHAPTER 49

There is something extraordinarily insidious and unique present within the eyes of a man who's taken a human life. Perhaps it's the cold, deep murkiness running through the sclera (white), which is set against atlas road map–red bloodshot streaks. Or the temperamental depth of blackness in the iris. But it is always there. Unmistakable. A steely, emotionless gaze only a certain part of society maintains. Some say it's the Devil's way of projecting evil into the world, laser-like. Whatever it is, there's no mistaking this presence if you've ever had the opportunity to witness it firsthand.

On December 3, 2009, there was that same hollow stare looking back at investigators as they studied several photographs taken from surveillance cameras set up inside two IHOP restaurants in Charlotte, North Carolina. Within all of the suspicion surrounding him and his potential role in the deaths of Randi and Heather, Danny Hembree decided to commit several armed robberies.

The behavior seemed so, well, stupid, especially in the scope of where Hembree's life was then. Here was Danny fingered on those surveillance cameras and caught, essentially, red-handed. The images of a yet-to-be-identified Hembree were e-mailed around to scores of local law enforcement agencies to see if anyone recognized the man.

It was YCSO detective Eddie Strait who saw the images roll across his computer screen and immediately knew who it was: a familiar face to the YCSO.

They had Hembree right where they wanted him.

Backing up the notion that the image was no doubt Hembree, witness reports matched Hembree's vehicle leaving the scene of both robberies.

An officer from the Charlotte-Mecklenburg Police Department (CMPD) created a photo lineup, in which Danny Hembree's recent mug shot was included. They tracked down one of the witnesses from IHOP. At 7:15 P.M., on December 4, two Charlotte-Mecklenburg police officers met with the witness and placed the lineup in front of him.

"That's him," the man said. "He's the one."

He was positive. The witness pointed to suspect number two in the lineup.

"He's the one that robbed me. He had a silver pistol, like a silver revolver. I recognize his facial characteristics."

They asked him if there was anything else.

"The eyes," the witness said.

Indeed, there was no mistaking the eyes of the Devil.

The eyes belonged to Danny Hembree.

CHAPTER 50

The Gastonia Police Department picked Hembree up at his momma's house and transported him to the Charlotte-Mecklenburg Police Department. Hembree was sleeping when he arrived at the CMPD garage and was greeted by fifteen-year-veteran armed-robbery CMPD detective Ryan Whetzel. It was 12:20 A.M.

After being woken and escorted out of the vehicle, Hembree said, "Where are we? Is this the jail or the detectives' building?"

"The jail's about a block away," Whetzel explained. Hembree was handcuffed behind his back. He wore blue jeans. A checkered flannel shirt was flanked over his shoulders like a cape. "But we're going in here because I need to talk to you about a few things."

"I want you to know that I am invoking my constitutional rights and you need to walk me over to the jail."

"I need to take you in here first before I can transport you over to the jail," Whetzel said.

Hembree didn't balk.

Whetzel and Hembree, along with a uniformed officer, exited the prisoner elevator on the second floor. Whetzel wanted to get Hembree into an interview suite, sit him down, and give him a few moments by himself to think about things. Whetzel had seen this scenario likely hundreds of times before: Some doper is busted for a robbery. After a few moments inside the box, he's ready to give it up. Hembree could make this easy on himself and admit to the robberies. They had him nailed. With Hembree's history of burglaries and robberies, he was facing serious time. Playing stupid and saying he didn't do it would only make matters worse.

As they walked down the hallway toward the box, Hembree spoke without being asked. "I think I might just done changed my mind, depends on what you want to talk about. You know, and how nice y'all are."

Clearly, Hembree had a plan. He was setting the hook.

"I'm real nice, Danny," Whetzel said.

They were in the box. Hembree was a bit out of it, more sleepy than spent. He wasn't as alert as he had been with Baker and Yeager the previous week. With his arms cuffed behind his back, that plaid shirt draped over him, he sat in one of four chairs around a small table. The room was about the size of a large closet.

"Well, if you're nicer than the others," Hembree blurted out before breaking into a rant, slurred as it was, about "those other boys. . . . You give them a shirt and badge and they get that God thing going. . . ."

What this comment was in reference to had never been established or discussed. Maybe it was the way Hembree had been picked up and handled that night. In any situation he found himself, Hembree was all about maintaining power and control. He had proven this during the Baker/Yeager interview. And here he was again taking control of the situation with Whetzel, merely seconds after sitting down. All of it recorded on video cameras set up around the room.

Whetzel tried shackling Hembree's legs around the chair, but it wouldn't work.

Hembree let out a big yawn.

Whetzel uncuffed his suspect, who let out a sigh as the cuffs came off. Hembree then dropped his head and hugged himself, as if he was cold.

"I'll be back in a minute, all right?" Whetzel said.

Hembree didn't respond.

Whetzel said it again, louder.

Hembree looked up. "Yeah, man. . . ." Then he dropped his head.

Whatever Hembree was going to talk about, Whetzel wanted it recorded under the support of a formal interview. If Hembree was going to admit the robberies, they needed it on record.

Hembree, of course, had other things on his mind. But for right now, as he waited for Whetzel, he put his head down on the desk in front of him and slept.

CHAPTER 51

Danny Hembree was sound asleep when Ryan Whetzel returned to the box at 12:32 A.M. It was now December 5.

"All right, Danny . . . ," Whetzel said. He had a pad and several sheets of paper.

Hembree didn't move. He had his head resting on his folded arms on top of the desk, like a kid sleeping during detention.

"Danny!" Whetzel said louder, knocking on the table.

Nothing.

"Danny!"

Pause.

"Danny!"

Pause again.

"Danny!" Whetzel screamed.

Finally, after Whetzel yelled for a fourth time while grabbing Hembree by the arm, Danny snapped out of it. He rubbed the sleep off his face with one hand. Then he acclimated himself to his surroundings, as if realizing all over again where he was.

"Can you wake up for me, buddy?"

"Yeah, maybe," Hembree said.

"You want to talk . . . and get all your eggs in one basket? Let's get it over with . . . ," Whetzel said. It was clear Whetzel wanted to do this the easy way. He didn't want to play games with Hembree by sitting there for six hours in a stand-off.

Whetzel had Hembree sign a Miranda warning form, indicating that Hembree had been read and clearly understood his rights. Then the cop said he wasn't going to waste time. He wanted to know if Hembree was willing to put his cards on the table now.

"You know what we want to talk about?" Whetzel said.

"Yup," Hembree answered. "Them robberies . . ."

"Okay . . . which one would you like to talk about first?"

Hembree leaned back in his chair and took in a deep breath. "Y'all get them from York County up here, and y'all get me something to eat, and let's talk about those murders. . . . I'll tell y'all about them two girls."

CHAPTER 52

Detective Ryan Whetzel sat stunned. After taking in what Hembree had just announced, Whetzel said the only thing he could think of at the time: "Okay. . . ."

Hembree stared at Whetzel. The felon's shirt was pulled up over his head like a hijab. His arms were folded in front of himself. He leaned back in the chair.

Control.

"Hang tight," Whetzel told him.

Hembree stared at the cop.

Because he had not gotten any response from Hembree, Whetzel said: "You gonna wake back up now?"

"Sure," Hembree responded immediately. "Look, I'm just tired, *not* under the influence."

Whetzel thought Hembree had passed back out. After establishing that Hembree was wide-awake and alert (and staring blankly at him), Whetzel said it would take time to get that meal.

Full of surprises on this night, Hembree blurted out: "Actually, York County . . . theys wasn't killed there—theys was just *dumped* there. Theys was killed in Gastonia."

Whetzel again seemed shocked. "O . . . kay," he said slowly.

Whetzel left Hembree in the box for a few hours while he got hold of two York County detectives. All three went in and sat down with Hembree, who seemed more with it now that he'd had a few hours of uninterrupted sleep.

"You requested York County," one of the investigators said, "well, we're here."

"Them girls wasn't killed in no York County," Hembree said. At times, when he spoke, Hembree hammered the tip of a finger angrily into the tabletop.

"No?"

"Nope! I's just *dumped* them there."

The way he used the word "dumped"—there was no doubt that these girls were mere garbage to Danny Hembree.

"Where did it happen at?"

"I killed them at Momma's. . . . I killed Heather downstairs in the laundry room, and I killed Randi in my den. You'll find their blood all over the couch."

"At your momma's?"

"Yup."

"Does your mom know?"

"Nope."

"Anybody else know?"

"Nope."

Hembree talked about killing two women as though he was describing a trip to the supermarket. Casual. Detached. No emotion. It was as if he was excited to get the opportunity to talk about it finally. To relive it. Their lives, clearly, had no value to him. There was no remorse. No tears or even a faint, phlegmy scratch to his voice. It was all business for Hembree. Here was a killer talking about his work.

Hembree talked about killing Randi in particular and how the YCSO could go downstairs in his mother's house and find "where she bled and I tried to clean it up. . . ."

"Was that blood from her nose?" one of them asked.

Hembree coughed into his fist and folded his arms. "Yeah, uh . . . I punched her in the nose after she was dead. I didn't figure she'd bleed or nothing."

He remembered the exact time he killed Heather. "It was four-thirty on the eighteenth. And I dumped her body . . . that Sunday. . . ."

After a bit of discussion over where he killed Heather, one of the investigators asked, "What brought that on?"

"I killed Heather 'cause, um, I don't know—I just did. I just wanted to. And I killed Randi for the same reason. I just wanted to."

He said he used a bag on Heather. "And it took a long time."

Next he told the group how he, Sommer, and Heather, on that night, "had sex six or seven times." Moments after that, he said: "She (Heather) was a whore and she wouldn't quit. And she was having to sell her body to the niggers every now and then . . . and I just, uh, I *released* her from that. I wasn't mad at her or nothing. She's just better off."

Then came what every investigator working the case had suspected as the weeks passed and Hembree was still walking the streets. Who was his next victim?

Hembree took a breath. He scratched his nose with the back of his hand. In a voice full of grandiosity and arrogance, he said, "I was gonna get her momma this week!"

Stella Funderburk didn't know it, but she was lucky to be alive.

CHAPTER 53

It was 3:30 A.M. Matt Hensley was sound asleep when a ringing cell phone woke him.

Hensley opened his eyes and stared at the caller ID.

York County?

"You talk about waking up quick," Hensley said later.

Indeed. There would be only one reason why the YCSO was waking him up in the middle of the night.

A break in the case.

YCSO detective Eddie Strait was on the other end. He had some news about a suspect Hensley would be interested in. "Eddie Strait here. We have Danny Hembree in custody at the Charlotte-Mecklenburg PD for armed robbery. And he's confessed to both murders."

"What?" Hensley responded.

This was certainly not a fist-pumping moment. It was much too early in the morning for that. But what Strait told Hensley next made Hensley sit up and take immediate notice.

"Hembree said he wanted someone to come speak to him about the murders before he said anything about the armed robberies."

Hembree was so schooled in the law, having been arrested and jailed for so long, he knew a Gastonia investigator would ultimately need to hear his confession before the legal ball rolled.

"Russ Yeager and myself have just finished speaking with Mr. Hembree and he's confessed to killing Heather Catterton and Randi Saldana."

Hensley couldn't believe it. The guy wouldn't talk about an armed robbery, but he had confessed to killing two women?

"Said he killed both at his mother's house and dumped their bodies in York County."

"He say how?"

"He claimed to have suffocated Heather, strangled Randi."

Strait gave Hensley a few additional details and said they were on their way to a restaurant in York County where Hembree said he tossed some evidence in a Dumpster.

The case was unofficially in the hands of the GCPD. Hensley needed to secure murder warrants for Hembree on both girls so he could make the trek over to Charlotte and get Hembree picked up. The last thing they needed now was for Hembree to go before the magistrate in another county. If that happened, it'd be a legal battle, which could take days or weeks, before they'd be able to get him back to Gaston County to answer for the murders. By then, Hembree would be lawyered up and likely not want to talk anymore.

"I need a few hours," Hensley told Strait.

Strait spoke to his superior. When he came back on the line, he said they'd wait.

CHAPTER 54

The Charlotte-Mecklenburg PD is a whitewashed, stone-and-marble building, with perfectly groomed maple trees, red bark mulch at the trunk base, greeting visitors as they take the four steps up in through the front doors. The state flag stands proud and nearly as high as the building to the right of an old-school noir-style streetlamp. A block away, heading northwest on East Trade Street, is the Time Warner Cable Arena, the glitz and fine hospitality of the Ritz-Carlton hotel just beyond that.

With his partner, Michel Sumner, Matt Hensley parked his Crown Vic and headed into the building to meet Yeager and Strait. It was shortly after five in the morning. Hensley had obtained the two murder warrants he needed. As Hensley did that, a colleague, GCPD CSI detective Chris McAuley, secured a search warrant for Hembree's mother's house.

After Hensley and Sumner sat down with Yeager and Strait, they explained what Hembree had admitted to. It became obvious there was certain to be more evidence at Hembree's mother's house than just a shoe and some blood.

"He said he kept Heather in the closet for a week," Strait explained.

"Damn, a week."

"Randi he kept for 'a few days.' "

Hembree said he dumped Heather's clothing off Crowders Creek Road by the bridge, her shoes down the road. He placed Randi's clothes in that Dumpster.

"He say why he killed them?" This bothered Hensley. What was Hembree's motive?

"He said he killed Heather because he wanted to 'free her from her lifestyle.' "

"Randi?"

"Said he didn't like her."

It was more than that. During the initial interview Hembree gave on December 5, when he first admitted killing both girls, he said (without being asked), "Randi was just a whore who fucked niggers, and I just didn't like her."

As Hembree had said during that initial interview, he helped Randi sneak into Momma's house through a window. They hung out in his bedroom. "I went in there. . . . She was in there about ten minutes. She thought I was going to give her some crack, but I didn't. I just killed her."

Hembree said that while he was at someone's apartment the night before his recent arrest, December 4, "Shorty was supposed to come over there . . . and I was gonna kill him, too. . . . Heather hated Randi. They fought over the same nigger, Shorty. . . . He fucks all them young white girls, and he's fiftysomething. He gave them crack."

Taking his deep-seated racist commitment a step further, part of his hatred for Randi, he clarified, was centered on "when she was around a nigger, she tried to talk like a nigger. . . ."

Hembree despised this about Randi. It disgusted him.

After he murdered Heather, Hembree put her in the closet. His comment was chilling: "I then went upstairs, watched me some TV, and made me something to eat."

* * *

Detective Michel Sumner and Matt Hensley worked cases together. Sumner, nearly a decade older than Hensley, had joined the DU a few months after Hensley. Sumner's background was in sales; he had aspirations once of becoming a pharmaceutical-sales rep. But after interviewing with several major companies, he realized he lacked the core component of the job: sales experience. Born in Winston-Salem, North Carolina, Sumner moved around the state as a child and landed in the Gastonia region as a teen, attending high school and subsequently Belmont Abbey College in Charlotte. Within his path of choosing a career, Sumner later said, "Not once, ever, did I consider law enforcement." But 9/11 happened. Sumner wanted to make a difference. He was determined to become a federal agent. "And in order to become a federal agent," he said, "I thought local law enforcement would be the right direction or the right step to go into that field."

What Sumner didn't realize until Hembree became part of his life was how much he would rely on that background in sales in order to get suspects to talk, and keep talking.

The plan was to pick Hembree up and get him down to the GCPD and allow him to say whatever he needed to say. As a cop, if you have a suspect talking, you let him ramble for as long as he'll continue. There's no telling what tomorrow will bring—especially when dealing with such an unpredictable, volatile guy like Danny Hembree.

One of the last things Hembree told the YCSO before they handed him over to Hensley and Sumner was "Y'all would have never figured it out." Hembree took pride in the fact that he had gotten away with the murders; it was important to him that he admitted to killing the girls—and that cops didn't figure out he was the killing kind.

Even as he went down in flames, Danny Hembree maintained that balance of power.

He liked playing the role of the serial killer, a family member of Hembree's later wrote to me in an e-mail. *I be-*

lieve Danny wants [the publicity]. It scratches [an] itch. No, you should not believe him. If anything was true . . . [it's] that he is a liar.

"We deal with bad guys on a daily basis," Hensley commented. "Mr. Hembree proved to be a different breed altogether."

Law enforcement was spot-on with its assessment of Danny Hembree. Because what no investigator knew then was that Hembree wasn't finished giving up bodies.

There would be more.

CHAPTER 55

Danny Hembree was sleeping when Hensley and Sumner woke him at 6:39 A.M. on December 5.

Ryan Whetzel met them outside the door. "He's been sleeping for several hours. I recorded the interview. I'll get you a copy as soon as I can. The tech guy, who does that, only comes in one day a week."

"Thanks. You can't get me that right now?"

"No."

Thus, Hensley and Sumner were not going to be able to have a look at Hembree's confession before they interviewed him. And they had no time to wait for the DVD.

This made Hensley a bit uncomfortable.

"I would have liked to have known what he had told them exactly," Hensley said. "So I could design my questioning around what he'd already said. But sometimes you don't have all the luxuries you want and you have to make do with what you have."

"He's fine with y'all coming to get him—he knows," Whetzel said.

Quite contrary to what some close to Hembree later said about him lapping up the media attention that becoming known as a serial killer would yield, one of the first things Hembree said to Hensley upon greeting him was "I'll tell y'all everything, but no media. Y'all keep the media away."

"He was firm about this," Hensley remembered. "He did not want a camera in his face."

After Hembree used the restroom, he asked Hensley to loosen his handcuffs. "They's hurting me."

Hensley didn't see a problem. Hembree realized he controlled the what, where, when, why, and how. As long as he talked, everything was going to be done on his terms.

"He started making demands," Hensley said. "We had to give him what he wanted. We had no reason not to make him comfortable, because we're anticipating that he's going to tell us he killed these girls, but, more importantly, maybe give us corroborating information."

Hensley had heard Hembree only wanted to discuss the murders with Gaston County. Hensley wanted to know if this was true. Had Hembree actually felt that way?

"Yup," he confirmed. They walked out of the building. "It was never theirs in the first place."

Hembree rode by himself behind a cage in a patrol car, while Hensley and Sumner followed. The game plan they discussed along the way was simple: Allow Hembree the comforts he desired, as long as he talked.

They arrived at 7:39 A.M., according to Hensley's report. The next few days would be well documented by videotape, audio recordings, and written reports detailing every move Danny Hembree made, along with everything he said.

"Can I have some coffee?" Hembree asked. He sat down in what was now a familiar chair inside the box at the GCPD.

"You want us to get you something to eat?" Hensley asked.

Hembree wanted to wait on the food.

By 7:50 A.M., Hembree was Mirandized.

Hensley sat back, relaxed. "Well, man, what do you want to tell us? Is there something in particular?"

Hembree broke into the same story of seeing and talking to Heather that night while she was in the bathtub. He explained what happened on October 17 in detail, same as he had to the YCSO, backing up, pretty much, what Sommer Heffner and her boyfriend had told police. But it was that time period after Hembree dropped Sommer off at her boyfriend's house and he took off with Heather alone that Hensley and Sumner were interested in. What took place between the time Hembree was alone with Heather and ten days later, when Heather's body was found in that South Carolina ditch? That was the question.

Hensley and Sumner waited.

Hembree took a breath and explained in detail how he killed Heather Marie Catterton.

CHAPTER 56

Hembree pulled up to his mother's house around 4:30 A.M. on October 18. He had already decided Heather was going to die. He wasn't "mad at her," he claimed. Nor was he angry. He wasn't in some sort of violent rage, pissed off that Heather would not do what he said. He wasn't obsessed with Heather. Nor did he have some secret fantasy focused on her—at least, none that he admitted. Hembree said he loved Nicole. Heather's death had nothing to do with any sexual gratification or sexual fantasy. Instead, Hembree decided, he was going to save Heather from a life of hell that he knew was ahead. It was a life on the streets, Hembree claimed, that had started back when Heather was twelve years old.

Hembree's extreme racist slant on life in general was evident as he talked about how, because Heather was "never going to stop fucking niggers," he needed to swoop in and rescue her. He could not allow her to continue with the lifestyle she had chosen for herself. It wasn't right. It wasn't what she wanted deep down inside.

Hembree believed he was doing Heather and her family a favor.

Inside the house, they hung out in Hembree's den, a part of the house near his bedroom that Hembree and his mother had designated for him alone. Hembree had sex with Heather, he claimed. When they finished, he thought: *She's too heavy to carry down the stairs—how am I going to get her into the basement?* He didn't want to kill Heather in his bedroom or in the den. He decided the best place was downstairs in the basement. He had planned on storing Heather downstairs after he killed her, anyway, but never said why.

"Hey, Heather," Hembree said after sex, "we've got us some lighters downstairs in a cabinet inside the washroom. Can you go and fetch me one?"

Heather got up and walked down into the basement. All she had on, Hembree said, was that Hollister hoodie and toe socks. The rest of her clothes were on the floor in his bedroom.

Hembree's mother was not home. She had gone away for a few days.

With Heather downstairs, Hembree got up. Without saying anything, he approached Heather from behind. She had a flashlight in her hand and was searching a dusty shelf in the basement, looking for a lighter.

With "some kind of cord" (he could not recall what it was exactly), Hembree walked up behind Heather without speaking and, placing the cord around her neck, pulled it tight, choking her.

Heather reacted by thrashing her arms and swinging the flashlight and smashing Hembree in the head. ("It wasn't hard enough to hurt, though," Hembree felt the need to add as he told this story.)

Heather tried pulling at the cord with her hands as she struggled for air.

Hembree wrestled her down to the concrete floor.

Within a few moments, Heather stopped fighting.

But she was not dead.

Hembree let go of the cord and placed both his hands on

her nose and mouth and pushed down tightly. He was simultaneously trying to cut off her air and hold her down.

As one final reaction, Heather's legs kicked and her body convulsed. She was fighting for her life, instinctively. The way Hembree talked about this moment, he described it as calm and not at all violent. As he talked about it, with his hands handcuffed, Hembree acted out the "process"—the perfect word choice—of murdering Heather, saying coldly that it wasn't "easy."

"She just wouldn't die. . . ."

Cutting off Heather's air supply—effectively suffocating her to death—took "ten to fifteen minutes," Hembree explained. He even placed his bare foot on her neck at one point to hold her down. "And she still wouldn't die. . . . I mean, I didn't want to hurt her or nothing—I just wanted her to go to sleep."

If Hembree's description of the murder is true, Heather suffered horribly—all while staring into the eyes of the man taking her life.

Because it was so difficult to suffocate Heather with his bare hands, Hembree grabbed a plastic shopping bag nearby and placed it over her head, pulling it tightly around her neck as he held her down.

This method seemed to work better; but, still, Heather wouldn't die.

So as he struggled to suffocate Heather with that plastic bag, her legs and arms still flailing wildly, Hembree hauled off and slammed the middle of Heather's chest with a hammer fist, hoping to stop her heart.

According to Hembree's recollection, this worked.

Heather, just a child, was now dead.

Confident his victim had breathed her last, Hembree walked upstairs. He sat down in front of the television and watched TV.

Feeling famished, he then made himself a sandwich.

A foot was visible in the brush just off a dirt road in York County, South Carolina, where the half-naked body of an unknown female was discovered on October 29, 2009.
(Courtesy of State of North Carolina, 27A Prosecutorial District)

Down the road from the body, clothing was found and the York County Sheriff's Office investigators believed they were now searching for a killer.
(Courtesy of State of North Carolina, 27A Prosecutorial District)

A red shirt was discovered beside a bridge on the
North Carolina/South Carolina border, leading investigators to
believe it belonged to a young female found in another jurisdiction.
(Courtesy of State of North Carolina, 27A Prosecutorial District)

The unknown female's clothing was displayed
for the media to help identify the victim.
(Courtesy of State of North Carolina, 27A Prosecutorial District)

Growing up, Heather Marie Catterton was known as the girl with "the smile of an angel." Heather often helped other students with homework and dreamed of one day working with special-needs children.
(Courtesy of Nick Catterton)

Heather Catterton always
found a reason to smile.
(Courtesy of Nick Catterton)

Heather was 17 years old when
her body was found; she had been
strangled and asphyxiated.
(Courtesy of Nick Catterton)

Nearly two weeks after Heather Catterton's body was discovered,
the badly charred and burned remains of another woman were found
in a state park in the same county.
(Courtesy of State of North Carolina, 27A Prosecutorial District)

Stunning and beautiful, with a million dollar smile, Randi Saldana was a mother, sister, and daughter. Randi's remains led North and South Carolina law enforcement to believe a serial killer was prowling their streets.
(Courtesy of Shellie Nations)

Randi's sister, Shellie Nations (with long blond hair), would prove to be Randi's voice when her killer was later brought to trial.
(Courtesy of Shellie Nations)

Gaston County Police Detective Matthew Hensley was determined to see Randi and Heather's killer brought to justice.

Assistant District Attorney Stephanie A. Hamlin, a pivotal player in the prosecution of Danny Hembree, would become embroiled in the serial killer's wicked, made-up tales as his case went before a jury.
(Courtesy of Debbie Gulledge)

Detective Matthew Hensley (left) and his partner,
Michel Sumner (right), question main suspect
Danny Robbie Hembree (top) about his role in
the murders of Randi Saldana and Heather Catterton.
(Courtesy of State of North Carolina, 27A Prosecutorial District)

Forty-seven-year-old
career criminal Danny
Robbie Hembree was arrested
on December 6, 2009, for
the murders of Randi Saldana
and Heather Catterton after he
admitted killing both of them
and three additional women.
*(Courtesy of State of North Carolina,
27A Prosecutorial District)*

Inside a closet in the basement of his mother's house, among stuffed animals and children's toys, Danny Hembree kept the bloody bodies of his victims hidden.
(Courtesy of State of North Carolina, 27A Prosecutorial District)

The blood-soaked couch in the den of his mother's house where Hembree said he often watched porn—but also strangled Randi Saldana and beat her in the face.
(Courtesy of State of North Carolina, 27A Prosecutorial District)

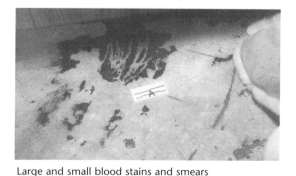

Large and small blood stains and smears were found on the carpet in the basement of Danny Hembree's mother's house.
(Courtesy of State of North Carolina, 27A Prosecutorial District)

The basement of his mother's house was where Hembree stored his victims' corpses for several days. *(Courtesy of State of North Carolina, 27A Prosecutorial District)*

This laundry area in the basement of his mother's house was where Hembree suffocated and strangled Heather Catterton as she searched for a cigarette lighter on a nearby shelf. *(Courtesy of State of North Carolina, 27A Prosecutorial District)*

The severed lamp cord Hembree used to bind Randi Saldana's legs together before dragging her out of the basement and into his vehicle. *(Courtesy of State of North Carolina, 27A Prosecutorial District)*

Danny Hembree's blood-stained boots — evidence he was proud
to show off for law enforcement.
(Courtesy of State of North Carolina, 27A Prosecutorial District)

Danny Hembree, inside his mother's house with detectives
Matthew Hensley and Michel Sumner, explained where they could
find his bloody boots.
(Courtesy of State of North Carolina, 27A Prosecutorial District)

On December 6, 2009,
after spending hours admitting
the murders of Randi Saldana
and Heather Catterton
(along with three other women),
Danny Hembree took detectives
on a guided tour of his
mother's house, explaining
where and how he murdered
Randi and Heather.
*(Courtesy of State of North Carolina,
27A Prosecutorial District)*

Standing outside his mother's house talking to Michel Sumner, Danny Hembree admitted to a vicious rape and attempted murder —and then told Detective Matt Hensley where to find several "trophies" he kept from Randi Saldana's murder.
(Courtesy of State of North Carolina, 27A Prosecutorial District)

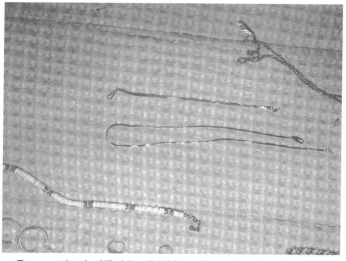

To prove that he killed Randi Saldana, Danny Hembree hid these "trophies" (necklaces and bracelets belonging to Randi) inside the glove compartment of his vehicle.
(Courtesy of State of North Carolina, 27A Prosecutorial District)

The changing faces of Danny Hembree: with a mustache in 2007; without in 2010. *(Courtesy of State of North Carolina, 27A Prosecutorial District)*

Seventeen-year-old Heather Catterton was murdered because her killer believed he "was doing her a favor." Heather's father says there's not a day that goes by when he does not shed a tear for his little girl.
(Courtesy of Nick Catterton)

CHAPTER 58

Hembree drove up on Randi as she walked down the street away from Shorty's. According to him, he didn't need to ask her to get in. Back at Shorty's, they'd planned to go hang out and smoke some drugs.

As they drove, Hembree said he knew immediately he was going to kill Randi. But instead of taking Randi to his mother's house (Momma was home), Hembree drove Randi out to that abandoned trailer. He gave no purpose for taking Randi there as opposed to his mother's house, other than Momma being home.

By nature, serial killers rely on comfort zones they feel safe in, either as a dump site or a kill space. This trailer was a place where Hembree felt he was able to control his girls and whatever situation came up. If Sommer's boyfriend, George, was not with Heather, Sommer, and Danny as they partied inside the trailer, the possibility existed that Hembree would have murdered Sommer and Heather that night there.

"Serials always want to be in their comfort zones—which means places they feel safe and have less chance of being caught," John Kelly later commented. "Inside an abandoned trailer, Mr. Hembree could pretty much do what he wanted."

Indeed, Hembree was master of that domain.

With Randi walking into the trailer beside him, Hembree reveled in that feeling of power he craved so much. Now all he needed was a trigger—something to convince himself it was the right time to take Randi's life.

At one point, Randi "had made some statement about Heather's death" that riled Hembree. There was that impetus, putting him in the mood. He didn't recall exactly what Randi had said, but the implication was that Randi had either asked him if he killed Heather, or accused him of the crime. There were other triggers within this moment that Hembree later talked about, but this one had stirred Hembree's thirst for blood the most.

Once inside the trailer, he did not waste time. As soon as Randi turned her back, he grabbed her by the neck with two hands and "choked her out." Randi was so scared, Hembree claimed, "she done pissed herself."

"What are you doing?" Randi managed to say as Hembree lunged at her.

Choking her unconscious, Hembree knew Randi wasn't dead.

So he sat and stared at her.

When Randi "came to," she said, "Why'd you do that?" She was coughing and gagging, trying to catch her breath. She was spitting mucus on the floor.

"What you said about Heather. You disrespected me."

"I didn't mean it that way. Get me out of here," Randi demanded. "I don't want to be trapped inside here with no killer."

"Look, everybody got me down as a suspect who done killed Heather," Hembree said.

"I'm sorry," Randi replied. "I didn't mean it that way."

Randi must have known by then that Hembree was capa-

ble of murder, after he choked her unconscious solely because she had mentioned Heather.

"Look, you want me to just take you back up the road,"
Hembree suggested. "Or do you want to go over to Momma's
house?"

"It's cold in here . . . ," Randi said, hugging herself. She
had dirt all over her from being on the floor. Her short-
cropped hair was matted in the back. She had marks on her
face. Her neck was sore. Her pants were soaked in her own
urine.

After a brief moment, Randi said, "Take me to your
momma's."

"Okay."

"Can I take a shower when we get back there?"

"Yeah. But we gotta wait until Momma goes to sleep so I
can sneak you in."

When they got to Hembree's mother's house, Danny
parked his car and told Randi to be quiet. He needed to
sneak her in through a window on the side of the house. He
gave police no reason why.

They tiptoed through the yard like burglars, brittle leaves
crunching underfoot. Then they made it over to Hembree's
bedroom window.

"Shhh," Hembree said, a finger to his lips. Tree branches
cracked and popped like burning firewood as they moved
around. In the deep darkness of the night, far away, a dog
yelped. Beyond that, it was quiet. Suburban serenity. All of
Hembree's neighbors were sound asleep.

Hembree pushed open his window, helped Randi get up
onto the edge of the windowpane, and pushed her on the ass,
heaving her into his room.

He then climbed in behind her, so he claimed. And as he
mentioned this fact during the interview, something hap-

pened. Hembree stopped himself. He stared at the table. He collected his thoughts for a brief moment as he took that carefully constructed pause (perhaps realizing that this part of the story didn't gel), and then blurted out, almost as a correction, "I climbed back *out* [the window] and went in [through the back door] and told Momma I was home."

He then walked from his mother's room down the hallway into the den just outside his room. Randi was sitting on the couch.

Hembree turned on the TV in the den. Momma was reading in bed, maybe thirty feet away.

"Momma never comes down there, because she know I like to watch porn and shit," he told Hensley and Sumner.

After watching television for "ten minutes," while sitting on the couch next to Randi, Hembree presumed Momma was sleeping. Without saying a word, he reached over and, without warning or fanfare, strangled Randi down to the floor.

He gave no explanation regarding what he was thinking at the time. All Hembree could recall from this chilling moment was "She went pretty fast. A *lot* faster than Heather did."

Hembree didn't know, however, if Randi was alive or dead moments later when he cocked his fist back and punched her as hard as he could, right above her nose, between her eyes.

This injury caused a tremendous amount of blood, which now spilled all over the couch. The floor. All over Randi.

Shit . . . , Hembree thought.

He looked for a comforter or blanket, found one, and placed it over Randi.

Then he went into his bedroom and rested for "two or three hours," or until he was certain Momma was sleeping deeply. During the ordeal, Hembree later claimed, Momma never left her room.

When he went back for Randi, he stripped off her clothes,

rolled her up in the blanket, hoisted her over his shoulder like a sack of potatoes, and walked her through the house. As he got to the kitchen, he realized she was still bleeding and had left a trail of blood throughout the house from the den to the kitchen.

Son of a bitch.

After Hembree had murdered Heather and gotten himself something to eat, he went back and checked on Heather to make sure she was dead. Downstairs in the basement of his mother's house was a closet. Hembree had placed Heather in the closet and left her there. It was days before he removed Heather from the closet and dumped her in that South Carolina ditch. Considering that it had worked for him once already—serial killers always fall back on the comfort of routine—he dragged Randi down the same basement stairs after, he said, cleaning up the "damn mess she made" (blaming the victim, of course!).

Then he stuffed Randi in the same closet.

She stayed there for several days.

"Danny, what's all that blood on the couch in your den?" Hembree's mother asked him a day after he murdered Randi. Hembree had tried best he could to clean it up, but there were stains on the couch itself, two of the cushions, a pillow, and the rug. None of the stains would come out.

"Uh, Momma, just a bloody nose I done got. Nothing to be worried about."

Hembree spent the night of November 14 at his friend's trailer (the trailer next door to the abandoned one) with Nicole. He had decided to dispose of Randi's body in a way that law enforcement would not find her. His objective with leaving Heather outside in that ditch was to allow law enforcement to find her. He didn't want Heather's family to wonder. The way he made it sound was as if he was doing a good deed by not burying Heather somewhere where she would never be recovered.

Wide-awake on the morning of November 15 by "seven

or eight," Hembree rustled Nicole up and told her he was going out. Nicole mumbled something and went back to sleep.

Hembree's friend was already up. "I'm gonna go get some cigarettes," Hembree told him as he walked out the door. "I'll be back."

By himself, he drove to his mother's house with a plan: He would take Randi out into the woods and set her on fire.

Arriving at Momma's house, Hembree walked out to the mailbox and retrieved the mail. He saw a neighbor as he walked back toward the house.

"Hey, how's it going?" Hembree gestured as if it was any other day.

The neighbor said hello.

Hembree put the mail on the kitchen counter and went downstairs. There were several old lamps hanging around. He cut the cords off several and used them to tie the blanket around Randi's body. In the closet, where he'd hidden Randi, there were copious amounts of coagulated blood in the corner by the wall—thick, tacky, and saturated into the carpet.

After securing the blanket, Hembree hoisted Randi up over his shoulder—"Her body was still dripping," he claimed—and placed Randi in the backseat of his car, which he had driven around and backed up to the basement door. On the night he killed Randi, after stripping her clothes off, Hembree had taken all of her jewelry and put it in a bag. He kept one bracelet and hid it inside the glove compartment of his car.

A serial killer's trophy, no doubt.

Hembree said he purchased a gallon of gasoline from the Creekside Store on Chapel Grove School Road, not far from that trailer park, at some point that morning.

It was a lie.

"And I already knew where I was gonna take her," he said.

When he arrived with Randi's corpse in the backseat of

his vehicle on Apple Road inside Kings Mountain State Park, however, Hembree ran into a problem. It was mid-morning. There were several horse trainers and riders out and about. People were coming and going. It was too busy. How was he going to ignite a corpse with all of these people around? Burning human flesh had a distinctive smell—not to mention the smoke and fire itself.

CHAPTER 59

Hensley and Sumner listened as the man in front of them described murdering two young women and then disposing of their bodies as if he was talking about a football game he had seen the night before on television. To Hembree, the act of murder and getting rid of the bodies was so mundane, so easy to talk about, that at one point during the interview Hembree sounded as though he was bored with it all.

As he first assessed Hembree, Michel Sumner couldn't help but think, "Here was a guy who wanted to make sure we knew he was in charge. This was his idea [to talk], and he wanted to let us know that we would not have caught him if it were not for him! . . . I remember taking a look at the characteristics of a sociopath—and Danny Hembree was dead on."

"Oh yeah," Hembree said as an afterthought about an hour into the interview, just as he took a sip from a large coffee in front of him, "her blood (Randi's) is also going to be found on my boots in the closet, where I put her." He greedily slurped a sip of coffee. "But all the DNA you'll need is on the couch in the den and down in that closet."

The arrogance and pure narcissism Hembree exuded as he admitted to killing the girls was not something Hensley necessarily noticed or took note of while the moment was happening in front of him. He and Sumner were there to get all they could out of Hembree and allow him the comfort and space to talk through it.

Be his buddy. Tell him what he wanted to hear: "Sure, Danny, no problem. More coffee, Danny? Wanna smoke? Need a light?"

Part of this strategy, Sumner explained, was to allow Hembree to think they were country bumpkin cops who didn't know what they were doing.

"I noticed he was giving us tidbits, just bits and pieces," Sumner said. "And when I would ask him for more information, he would only give us so much. We were afraid of losing him. And he knew this. So we kind of had to play the part and act like the dumb detectives he thought we were."

The information Sumner mentioned that Hembree was holding back was in reference to the Deb Ratchford case and a few Florida murders he had supposedly committed. Hembree had been giving them a point-by-point narrative of the murders of Randi and Heather, where they could locate evidence, and why he had done certain things. But with Florida and with Ratchford, he held back.

Bargaining chips.

"He wanted something in exchange," Sumner observed. "He wasn't going to tell us about the others until we were able to get him what he wanted."

When Hensley looked at tapes of the interview later, the obvious enjoyment Hembree displayed while talking about such horrifying moments was overwhelmingly clear. Yet, something else became evident to Hensley: "Even when Mr. Hembree is going down, he thinks he has control of his destiny."

This comment would never be more evident than in the coming weeks, months, and years as Hembree slithered his way through the legal system—all the while thinking he could manipulate, control, and make a mockery of justice.

CHAPTER 60

A s Hembree waited in the woods on November 15, with
Randi's corpse in the backseat of his vehicle, he smoked
a cigarette. His eyes darted from one area to another as
horseback riders strode around him.

Impatient and scared of being caught in the act, Danny
drove a "mile or two" away from there and found a secluded
area.

Many who have tried think that lighting a human body on
fire is as easy as pouring gasoline over the flesh and flicking
a match, vis-à-vis a scene from a Hollywood movie. Yet, if
they hang around the scene long enough, most realize quickly
that the human body, as complex and durable as it is, does
not burn easily. To ignite a human body (which is basically
85 percent water) takes long periods of sustained tempera-
tures in the range of 1,400 degrees Fahrenheit, hence the
need crematoriums have for a furnace.

Hembree parked and grabbed Randi's body. He placed
her on the ground about fifty yards away from his vehicle.
He did a complete three-sixty with his eyes to make certain
he was alone.

He then poured gasoline all over Randi.

Confident no one would see the fire, he lit "a piece of paper or tissue" and watched as a ball of flames engulfed Randi's body and made a black puff up into the forest sky.

Hembree, however, did not wait around to watch her body burn: "I went to [my friend's trailer] and got back into bed with Nicole."

CHAPTER 61

Hensley and Sumner were curious about the conspiracy Hembree had mentioned. "Basically," Hensley asked Hembree, "Randi was set up?"

"I killed her for money, or dope, whatever you want to call it," he claimed.

As Hembree talked about the alleged conspiracy involving Shorty, Stella, and Stella's sister, it became clear that he was trying to bring down those he hated. He offered no evidence other than his word and a motive that Stella and her sister believed Randi had had something to do with Heather's murder.

Hensley and Sumner listened, but they had a tough time with this story.

"I didn't believe him," Hensley said. (And later, as Hensley investigated this allegation Hembree had made, the detective spoke to all three and proved it was nothing more than Hembree having a little fun. Furthermore, as law enforcement asked Hembree to give up details regarding the time, place, and when the first conversation about a conspiracy occurred, Danny could not do it.)

Hembree got back on track, talking about the facts of

Randi's murder and where they could find evidence. Randi's blood, he said, would be all over the inside basement closet, where he had placed her body. He had "covered [the blood] with plastic and . . . stuffed a teddy bear in the corner to keep Momma from finding [it]. And Randi's boots are downstairs. . . ."

To Sumner and Hensley, it was obvious Danny Hembree didn't want to disappoint his mother in any way. He'd mentioned this several times. It was strange, seeing that he'd killed two women and stored their corpses inside Momma's house. Yet as Hembree talked through his crimes, Sumner believed there was something deeper there between Danny and his mother.

"At some level," Sumner said later, "he and his mom definitely had a relationship that was not like a normal mother/son relationship. But it also seemed like he had some type of respect for her, because he would say things like, 'I didn't want to wake up Momma.' Yet here he was killing these girls—at least one of them—while she read in [her] bedroom down the hall."

Sumner asked Hembree if he could explain where the scratches Heather had on her side came from. They believed she had been dragged through the wooded area, where she was found.

Hembree got excited, actually, wasting little time: "Yeah, that's from the tacks in front of where the closet's at there. There's . . . some of those old rug tacks. . . ."

Hembree had dragged Heather over the tacks as he stuffed her into the closet. She sustained the injuries, Hembree thought, after she was dead. He added as an insult, "You see, I had to drag Heather because she was so heavy."

"We had heard," Sumner stated, "that you had wanted to kill Stella. Is that true?"

"Yup," Hembree said, nodding his head in agreement. "I was gonna kill Stella."

"Why is that? Is it because of who she is?"

"Well, that, yes, and she's been running her mouth."

"How so?"

"Just getting into mine and Nicole's business and shit."

"What about [Shorty]?" Hensley asked. "Did you have plans on killing him a certain way?"

"I was gonna kill him today."

Getting more into the specifics surrounding Heather's murder and why he did it, Hembree said, "Look, I didn't plan on killing Heather." Then, quite coldly, he offered: "It just seemed like the thing to do at the time."

Imagine, taking a seventeen-year-old girl's life—so young, she had decades to rebuild and start over, to love and be loved, to have children, to find a husband, to get a job and live a healthy life—was boiled down for Danny Hembree into eleven words:

"It just seemed like the thing to do at the time."

He explained how hard it was to kill Heather. He said she went unconscious while he suffocated her with that plastic bag, but her body "wouldn't stop breathing." Then he added how he had to place his bare foot over her neck.

As Hembree talked through it, he had trouble explaining how he'd accomplished certain tasks. So he made a suggestion: "I can take you there and walk you through the whole thing. . . ."

Hensley nodded.

"But I don't want my mother there. I'll show you where the blood's at. I'll show you where *everything's* at."

This was not a hard call to make. Break out that video camera and make sure the battery was fully charged. And yet one had to wonder: What was Hembree planning? What was his motivation for bringing these two cops into his mother's house to show them where he had committed two murders? Glorification? The sheer comfort of knowing he was in control of this interview?

Before they could promise a car ride and walk-through, Sumner brought up something Hembree had told the YCSO.

"You mentioned to York County that there were some murders in Florida?"

Hembree paused. His demeanor changed. "I don't want to talk about that."

"Okay."

"That took place earlier this year . . . ," Hembree added without being asked. "And then there's also that [African-American girl, Deb Ratchford], who was found murdered in that-there cemetery in Gastonia in 1992."

If true, that brought his total to five . . .

. . . that they knew of.

CHAPTER 62

Shellie Nations was suffering greatly from the loss of her sister. As she went about her days after Randi's murder, waiting and wondering when an arrest would be made, hearing rumors that someone named Danny Hembree was a person of interest, all Shellie could do to lessen the impact of her sister's death was think back about Randi and the good times. Stay focused on those memories that made Shellie smile—the days when they were two innocent kids having fun.

There was one of those times, Shellie recalled, when Randi had a sleepover. At some point during the night, Randi made up her mind that she was going to do one of the girls' hair. You know, fix it up. Comb it out. Break out the hair spray and tease it up. Sleepover stuff.

As nothing more than a practical joke, Randi decided to switch the bottle of shampoo for a bottle of Nair hair remover. She thought it would be hilarious. She was so naïve then that Randi had no idea what a bottle of Nair would do to a head of hair. She thought maybe the girl would lose a few hairs and they'd all have a laugh.

The girl never lost any of her hair, but Randi and her

friends had that laugh at how strangely dark and sinister Randi's sense of humor was.

"She didn't mean no harm," Shellie said. "It was all in good fun, and nothing happened to the girl."

Thinking back on that moment made Shellie smile; she felt warm inside. There was so much information going around town, Shellie was beside herself with unanswered questions and thoughts about what had happened. When she heard it later, Shellie was sick to her stomach that Danny Hembree had murdered Heather, and not only slept in Heather's bed at Nick's house afterward, but offered to be a pallbearer at Heather's funeral, too.

At Randi's funeral, Shellie watched as people passed by her sister's closed casket, pondering those she had never seen before and did not know.

Is it you? Are you the person who took my sister's life?

Law enforcement, a presence at Randi's wake and funeral, explained to Shellie that the type of person who murdered Randi was perhaps the same type to show up at his victim's funeral and take pleasure in watching the suffering of Randi's friends and family.

"That scared us," Shellie said.

Along with the idea that Randi's killer was still at large—an additional fear Shellie suffered from, and one that tears victims' families down as they go through the grieving process—were those memories that came on without warning. You could be walking down the street and a recollection of a bridal shower or a party came over you unexpectedly, like a hot flash. In Shellie's case, it might be just a snapshot of an image: Randi and her unforgettable smile. Randi sleeping. Randi walking out the door saying, "Bye, I love you, Shell." Or maybe a song on the radio and Shellie was back to a day when she and Randi sang along together in the car, giggling, enjoying life. Those were the toughest moments—the simple ones, the times most everyone else takes for granted.

At home, Shellie was trying to cope with the sting of losing her sister, waiting for that call to tell her Randi's killer was behind bars. On edge, Shellie had no idea that Danny Hembree, at that very moment, three weeks before Christmas, was describing how he had planned, plotted, and carried out Randi's murder methodically, maliciously, and evilly because he believed Randi, in his language, was a "whore," who needed redemption and—oh yeah—he just didn't like her.

CHAPTER 63

"We're ready to go, Danny," Hensley said.

"Where?"

"Momma's house."

While Hensley and Sumner interviewed Hembree inside the box, several investigators served a search warrant at Hembree's mother's house and were already digging around, looking for those items that Hembree had discussed during his confession. They were having some difficulty locating some of the items Hembree had mentioned. It was important for the GCPD to corroborate as much as it could with regard to what Hembree had admitted. Investigators didn't want Hembree jerking them around, telling them one thing, wasting time, while the facts lined up differently. There had been enough evidence never released publicly to check against Hembree's story. Every law enforcement agency held back details of crimes for this very reason. Most of it seemed to line up with Hembree's revelations. But inside Danny Hembree's mother's house, according to Hembree, that was where they'd find the evidence that could end Hembree's life by lethal injection—and maybe Hembree didn't realize that as he sat and discussed how he murdered two women in cold blood. The information Hembree was sharing, especially in a state like North Carolina, was enough to place him on death row if convicted.

"I want some things from y'all, too," Hembree said after Hensley brought him a fresh coffee. After brushing his hands off, as if they were dusty, he said, "I want *all* my property released to my mom—my cell phone, a little bit amount of cash." He slapped his hands together as if to say, "Hey, pay attention now." It was just Hembree and Sumner. Hensley had gone off to check on the status of them taking a trip out to Hembree's mother's house. "I want you to impound that car. . . . I used it during the murder." He talked about the outrageous financing he was being charged after having to put a new motor in the car recently. "And I want you guys to auction it off and let them all fight for it." The way Hembree spoke so straightforwardly and confidently about his personal issues, it seemed he had thought about all of this beforehand and had a plan going into the confession.

No sooner was he making demands than Hembree began rambling on about not having any sleep for the past five days, having been "smoking dope constantly."

Hensley came back into the room. He had his jacket on. "Let's go."

CHAPTER 64

As they pulled up to Momma's house and looked at the yard, it had the feel of autumn, with the sunburst-colored leaves from the maples strewn about all over. The stray tree branches, dead and fallen, lay about the grass like the limbs of rusted and fallen old-school TV antennas. Although winter, indeed, there was a fall essence to the look of the Hembree home.

It was 9:41 A.M. when Hembree, Sumner, and Hensley arrived at the redbrick ranch house that Hembree lived in with his mother. A third investigator had gone along beforehand and documented a walk-through on videotape before Hembree and the others arrived. The video is eerie, displaying how the simplest, most basic, everyday items, under such a dark context, can magnify into creepiness when you know what happened. For example, a green plastic watering can sitting on the entrance porch into the Hembree home, a half-opened umbrella hanging off the railing, a shaky hand behind the video camera capturing the images as the cameraman walks into the house, all now had an ominous, almost surreal, black-and-white *Blair Witch Project* effect.

There was no narration or explanation of what was being

filmed, just a video of the inside of the home. The GCPD wanted a clean copy of the house, as it was when they arrived.

The house could have used a makeover. Carpets were old; curtains were faded and dirty; closets overflowed with clothing and other common household items; graffiti had been written on the inside of one closet; linens, a touch out of date, were dirty; the kitchen overflowed with clutter. Yet, there was still a someone-lived-here sense to it all. This was a home. It wasn't until the den that blood showed up on camera. The one piece of furniture in the den—a blue couch, with white polka dots—had a few obvious dried bloodstains. There was a pillow that seemed to have plenty of blood spatter and drippings. Likewise, the carpet had several areas where dried blood could have been present. Luminol would tell that story later, and when the lights were turned off and the chemical reacted to the bodily fluids, it would probably illuminate the room like the Milky Way galaxy.

Down in the basement, stuff was strewn everywhere: black garbage bags filled with clothes and odds and ends, old appliances that no one used anymore, books, hubcaps, old lights, laundry baskets, chests, and other items most people would have tossed into the garbage long ago. Of interest to the man behind the camera were dried spots of blood spread about a large area on the concrete flooring. There were also white garbage bags with blood droplets on them, and then a pillow without a case. Blood turns almost black when dried and coagulated, days or weeks old. On this pillow was what seemed to be an enormous amount of dried blood.

Back upstairs in the den, the cameraman found a pair of Hembree's work boots with specks and spots of dried blood around the toes.

And then the video tour was done.

Cut and print.

* * *

Hembree got out of Hensley's Crown Vic and popped a cigarette in his mouth, lighting it as he walked up to the front door. Obvious was an incredible swagger. Danny Boy Hembree was in his element here: the cat bringing his master his catch of the day. He was gloating (buzzing) as he walked, no doubt thinking that all of this—cops, their cameras, their questions, their eagerness while awaiting his responses—was all by his design.

I did this.

It's my work.

This time, right now, is mine.

No one can take it away from me.

Indeed, this was "The Danny Hembree Show." He led the way.

It was one thing walking through a crime scene with a video camera and taking images of empty spaces and what might have happened here or there. It was quite another when you had a killer walking you through that same scene, pointing things out, talking about what he did.

Hembree wasted no time in getting right down to it, stepping into the house with a lit cigarette, nearly running down the hallway toward the den, stating, "Right here . . . this is where I strangled Randi."

The first words out of his mouth.

"This is where I strangled Randi." It said a lot about the mind-set of the guy as he walked into his home for what was likely going to be the last time.

Officers lifted the cushions off the couch. With his hands cuffed, Hembree spouted off: "Blood there . . . *there* . . . right *there* . . . that, right there, that's her blood, too. That's blood," he said loudly, pointing to the corner of the couch. Then he stood up straight, looked down on the carpet below him, pointed, and proclaimed: "And that-there [spot] is where she shit."

It seemed the amount of blood Hembree described coming out of Randi had to be generated by more than a bloody nose or cut above her brow from a fist blow to the head. But no one was going to challenge Hembree here. Not now. This was his game.

They were curious about the stain on the carpet in front of the couch, where Hembree said Randi had moved her bowels.

"Was she naked when you strangled her?" Hensley asked. This was not what Hembree had said back in the box.

"No."

"Well, at any point, did you, um, take her clothes off—"

Before Hensley could finish, Hembree said, "I stripped her down, took all of her jewelry and everything off." Hembree stared at the floor as he described the moment, reliving it. "Carried her down and put her in the closet."

Sumner watched and listened. He took note of how "detailed Mr. Hembree was as he explained things to us. But what I noticed, too, was how emotionless, flat, and so very nonchalant. On the inside, we were kind of freaked out by that."

It was chilling to hear Hembree talk about such horrifying moments with such a stark, cold demeanor. He didn't care. He had no feelings for these girls and the way he treated them. They were things.

Objects.

Hensley indicated he wanted to head into the basement. As the detective led the way down the stairs, he asked Hembree, who was following closely behind, "Any weapons down here?"

CHAPTER 65

First things Hembree pointed out while walking Hensley and Sumner around the basement were Randi's boots. "Some of her shit might have spilled out in there." He pointed to a box next to the boots. "Because that's where I had her stashed, getting ready to move her."

As Hensley took in the basement, he understood why Hembree chose to put the girls here. The driveway went behind the house and there was a space to pull a car under the back deck and up to a door that led into the basement. Thus, there was hidden access to the basement. The closet he put the girls in was down the hall from the exit, but it was easy for him to drag the girls down the hallway, out the door, and place them into his car without being seen.

The question Hensley and Sumner asked themselves, although they never posed the theory to Hembree: "Why hadn't anyone smelled the girls?" Both were in the Hembree house long enough for their bodies to decompose. Why hadn't Hembree's mother smelled the odor of rotting flesh? Why hadn't anyone visiting the house noticed an odd smell?

Hembree had no trouble finding those areas where he hid the bodies and some of the women's clothing and pointing out the blood left behind. By the washer and dryer, he acted out killing Heather, step by step, hand motions and all, as if auditioning for a play. There was one area where he showed Hensley a large spot of blood in the shape of Florida on the concrete floor. As he talked about murdering Heather, what made Hembree's explanation so unsettling—and maybe ironic—was the presence of a children's bible on a desk right above the blood spot.

As he talked, Hembree chain-smoked, sometimes lighting one with the next.

"So far, everything I've told you today has been the truth," Hembree said just after discussing how he had killed Heather.

He inhaled a drag, blew it out slowly, as if taking a very deep breath.

"Thank you for that," Hensley and Sumner said. "That's what we're looking for."

Sumner asked Hembree about a mark they had found on Randi's back.

"Tramp stamp," Hembree said.

"Huh?"

Hembree was referring to a tattoo.

"No, a red mark," Sumner clarified.

"Probably where I done drugged her."

"What?"

There was some confusion.

"Yeah, where I done put her over my back."

"Drugged" was Hembree's way of saying "dragged."

Whenever Hembree talked about blood, clothing, or any detail other than the actual murders, he exhibited a calm, casual demeanor. He even sounded somewhat articulate (if only in his strange Southern brogue). Whenever he went into a murder narrative, however, and talked about the actual moment he took the girls' lives, a sudden mania came over him. His eyes bulged. His speech grew faster and harder to understand. He used his hands to make points, clearly caught up in the exact moment he took their lives.

Finished in the basement, after some time in the kitchen, Hembree asked if he could warm up some tea he had found on the stove.

Hensley said sure.

"That's about it, huh?" Hensley observed as Hembree took his tea out of the microwave.

"I guess . . . y'all are the ones—"

"Well, have you covered everything?"

"Yeah, I suppose."

Hensley was confident they had enough—more than enough, actually. It doesn't get much better for a detective than having an alleged murderer walk you through the crime scenes, pointing out what he did, when, how, and where he left evidence. Not only was Hembree confessing to these crimes, but he was giving the GCPD corroborating evidence with which to prosecute him. All of this, one had to imagine, Hembree did with some kind of deal in mind. Maybe he was betting on getting the death penalty taken off the table for his cooperation?

There had to be a catch to all of this: Serial killers don't do anything without a payoff.

Standing near the cops' Crown Vic, Danny Hembree continued to chain-smoke, knowing that when they locked him up, he wasn't going to be smoking at will. He looked around at the neighbors' homes as he leaned against the back of Matt Hensley's unmarked cruiser. He seemed lost in the memories of the house and the neighborhood. There was a moment where it felt as if Hembree was taking it all in, realizing this would be the last time he ever saw the old place.

Michel Sumner walked over.

And here was where Sumner's background in sales came into play.

"I believe it's called the 'soft sell,'" Sumner explained. "Once you've got somebody wanting to buy one thing, that's when you try to get them to buy something else." The add-ons. "At that time, once I knew that he had spilled so much, I walked over there with the intention of wanting to get more information out of him."

Once a suspect gives up the "big stuff," admitting to the "smaller stuff," lesser crimes, can come easy. Throughout the entire interview process, in the back of their minds, Sumner and Hensley had unsolved rapes and robberies and violent attacks they liked Hembree for. Now was the time, Sumner knew, to move in stealthily and get Hembree to talk about those crimes.

Sumner first mentioned a recent rape case Hembree had been fingered for, but had never been convicted. The case was still open. It involved a girl, Ashley Campfield (pseudonym), who had been brutalized in a wooded area not far from Momma's house. There was no doubt Hembree was involved on some level.

Hensley stood nearby, listening.

The girl had reported that Hembree—she knew him—forced her, using a knife, from that familiar abandoned trailer and then drove her to Crowders Creek Road, not far from where he'd tossed Heather's clothing. He then walked her deep into the woods.

The report of the rape was graphic and violent. Hembree had allegedly threatened to kill her by placing a plastic bag over her head. Scared for her life while under Hembree's control, she allowed him to rape her brutally.

"Part of that's true . . . ," Hembree said as he took pull after pull from a cigarette, again using his hands to articulate his points. "I used a knife to force her out of the trailer, but I done never raped her. She got out there, where we agreed to go in the woods, and she done agreed to have sex with me.

We had made a deal and she wanted to back out of it. I couldn't let her back out of no deal she done made."

Interesting way to spin what was a savage, sexually motivated assault.

"Again," Sumner commented later, "he was very flat, the way he explained this."

By 10:06 A.M., Hensley said it was time to go. There was still one more task ahead.

Hensley and Sumner drove Hembree to each location so he could point out for them where he had placed Heather's clothing after dumping her body. Sumner documented the trip on video from the backseat. Hembree sat in the front. Hensley drove.

By now, Hembree was showing signs of fatigue: His five o'clock shadow had turned into a gray stubble; his hair was disheveled; he smelled foul; his shoulders drooped more than they had all night.

Hembree confirmed where he had thrown Heather's clothes by the bridge, her sneakers down the street. Hensley pulled up and stopped. It was a hasty dump-and-run situation, Hembree explained. He never got out of the vehicle. He did it all from the window while driving by.

From Crowders Creek Road, Hembree took them to several additional locations: where he picked Randi up and where they partied that night at Shorty's. Along the way, he pointed out a known drug dealer's house, to whom, Hembree said, he had sold some stolen property on the night before his arrest. Then he took them to the gas station, where he claimed to have purchased the fuel to burn Randi's body. He pointed to a house where he bought most of his dope. As he admitted to murder, Hembree was giving up as many people as he could from the circle in which he ran.

"I mean, I got me no reason to be lying," Hembree said after being asked to go into more detail about the alleged conspiracy to murder Randi, which he said Stella, her sister, and Shorty had dreamt up. "I done told y'all the truth. . . . It was Stella that had asked me, mainly. I mean, she'd sell her soul. . . ."

After Sumner asked what Shorty said exactly, Hembree backtracked, offering, "I don't know. . . . 'Kill the bitch. Kill the whore.' Whatever. Shorty was just the payout man—not the mastermind. . . . Hell, I was killing two birds with one stone."

"How's that again? You were helping the family out, you said, right?" Hensley asked as they drove by the house where he picked Randi up as she walked down the block.

"Shit, I was helping them out and paying Randi back for what she done did to Heather."

Hensley wanted to know what he was talking about.

"Pimping her out," Hembree had the audacity to claim. He was saying that Randi had been acting as one of Heather's pimps. It was a preposterous accusation.

As they headed back to the GCPD, Hensley asked about the girl in the cemetery from the early 1990s, whom Hembree had mentioned back in the box.

Deb Ratchford.

He didn't say much about it, giving them only enough to want more.

Then Sumner asked about the Florida girls Hembree claimed to have murdered.

"I don't want to talk about that," Hembree said at first. Then: "I want a deal." He described the situation with his car again and the money he had and where he wanted it sent, concluding, "Raleigh. I want to go to safekeeping in Raleigh. And then we's can talk about them girls in Florida."

As Hensley pulled into the GCPD parking lot, Hembree said, "Is that the media or something?"

"No, no, no . . . ," both Hensley and Sumner answered simultaneously. "That's a fire truck."

Hensley parked. They sat in the car and continued to talk.

"Anything else you want to tell us about, Danny?"

"Yup, there's some old stuff."

Hensley and Sumner got out. Hembree was escorted by a uniformed officer.

Hembree stopped and asked if he could have a smoke before they went in.

Hensley leaned against a railing outside the door into the DU as Hembree rested against a redbrick wall.

"Y'all need to go and lock Stella up!" Hembree said angrily. He hated this woman. It was obvious he had a vendetta against Stella and wanted to see her go down in flames. "There's already a warrant out for her."

Sumner was behind the camera, still rolling. He asked the question both he and Hensley had been holding off on until now, the end of the interview: "Let me ask you, Danny, what made you come clean at this point?"

Hembree stared straight ahead. He tipped back on his feet, rocked on his heels. "Well, I'm gonna be honest with y'all. . . . I wanted to kill Shorty today. . . . And then on Monday, I was going to do a bank robbery and shoot it out with the cops—with a plastic gun. And when they caught me last night, I just took it as a sign it wasn't supposed [to] come out like that."

Hensley asked Hembree about that "old stuff" he had made reference to inside the car.

There were crimes, Hembree explained, he had committed in the late 1970s with a partner, a guy named Bobby Johnson (pseudonym). There were several major crimes for which he and Bobby had never been caught. These were brutal, vicious offenses. Hembree gave scant details, but enough to make Hensley wonder, as he listened, if he could investigate and find out more.

"We's robbed a store together in Bessemer City back in 1979," Hembree explained. "Bobby kidnapped the clerk at knifepoint."

They took the woman out to Lincoln Academy Road, raped and beat her, leaving her for dead somewhere inside Crowders Mountain State Park.

"But she didn't die," Hembree added. "We saw it the next day in the papers."

Hensley knew they would approach these topics again. But Gastonia Police detectives were waiting for Hembree downstairs in the box to talk to him about another murder. Hensley and Sumner escorted Hembree into the building.

The GCPD wanted Hembree's account of killing Deborah Ratchford in 1992. He'd talked about it a few times. Now was the time to get this murder on record. The idea was to get as much as they could out of Hembree. Once he went before a magistrate, was arraigned, and then locked up, questioning him was over.

Deb Ratchford, an African American from Gastonia, was thirty years old when her brutally assaulted and sexually violated body was found in a densely wooded area on August 4, 1992, near the Oakland Street Cemetery, on North Oakland Street, a twenty-minute drive from Momma's house. She'd been stabbed and slashed multiple times in the upper chest and neck.

Inside the box, Hembree told Gastonia detectives that he, along with a cohort, James Swanson, murdered Ratchford. He didn't say much more than that.

When Gastonia PD took Swanson into custody some time later (the same day they served Hembree with a murder warrant for the Ratchford case), Swanson denied taking part in Ratchford's murder. He protested, "That man is telling a bare-faced lie about me. I'm innocent."

CHAPTER 66

Now twelve hours into his confession, Hembree had stirred up talk around Gastonia as he fingered old friends and crime associates, people he hated, drug buddies, and dealers. He was seemingly on a quest to close cold cases for law enforcement from as far back as 1979, as far away as Florida. The guy would not stop talking and, in the process, burying himself deeper and deeper—that is, if all of what Danny Hembree spouted off turned out to be true.

As Hembree spoke to Gastonia Police investigators, Hensley worked at getting Hembree's car impounded. It was parked at Nick's. Yet, before they towed the vehicle away, Hensley wanted to check on something to see how honest Hembree had been.

The young detective snapped on a pair of latex gloves and opened Hembree's car as it sat in Nick's driveway. Hensley thought back to Hembree telling him how he had hidden "a few beaded bracelets or necklaces" of Randi's inside the glove compartment for the purpose of proving he killed Randi if ever questioned.

After opening the glove compartment and conducting a

cursory search, Hensley came up with five "multicolored beaded bracelets."

Hembree was telling the truth.

When Hensley got back from Nick's on the afternoon of December 5, 2009, he asked Hembree if he'd like to have a smoke. Hensley's offer was by design. Hembree's car had been impounded and towed back to the GCPD, and there it was, on the bed of a tow truck, as Hembree and Hensley came out the back door.

"I wanted him to see that we were listening to him, trying to take care of all the demands he was making. This was important."

Power and control. Hembree had to think he continually maintained it.

As far as those cases in Florida were concerned, Hensley wasn't telling anyone at the moment, but he questioned whether Hembree committed any of them. In Hensley's mind, he believed Hembree was stacking the deck to have more to barter with down the road.

"You kill a few people and you are going to remember that," Hensley said later. What concerned Hensley was the lack of detail Hembree offered. Yes, he said he didn't want to talk about it until he got a deal, but he wasn't clear on anything regarding Florida. All of the information he gave was vague; whereas, when he discussed Randi and Heather, he pinpointed specific details about each murder, without having to think about it.

"Guy like Hembree," Hensley continued, "he'd remember details because of the high or thrill he is getting from the crime at the time."

Sumner felt a bit different about Florida. He said, "We have no evidence to believe he committed the murders he mentioned in Florida. But I have no reason to underestimate his intelligence and his ability to manipulate and conning nature—because Danny Hembree is not going to tell you until it benefits him."

At the time Hembree confessed to Randi and Heather, making slight mention of Florida and Deb Ratchford, he was, Sumner pointed out, "coming off of a crack cocaine binge. That's why we wanted to keep him talking. Hembree was down, depressed. . . . I recall him saying again and again, 'I'm just ready to die, man. I'm just ready to die. Let's just get this over with.' So those two confessions benefited him because he was ready to die. He was tired, physically exhausted. God knows how long he had been on a crack binge. But all that other stuff, Florida and Deb Ratchford, he wanted something for it."

Thus far, Hembree hadn't displayed much in the form of comprehensive facts surrounding Florida. And even a quick call down to the areas Hembree had mentioned led Hensley to consider it all as just a ruse. The county had no record of any murders near the time Hembree had said.

After the GCPD finished interviewing Hembree about the Ratchford case, Sumner and Hensley sat with him inside the box again.

"We need you to look at a statement we've compiled for you," Hensley explained, sliding the pages across the table. The statement detailed everything they had talked about the previous night.

By 3:00 P.M., Hembree had a statement detailing his crimes in front of him. Hembree took his time listening as Hensley read through the statement, word for word. And after making a few corrections, Hembree said he was happy with it, placing his John Hancock in the appropriate spaces.

Hensley asked Hembree if it was okay for them to fetch him the following day or the day after to "talk about some other things."

"Yeah . . . yeah," Hembree said. "Sure."

After signing the statement, Hembree rubbed his hands together for warmth; then he asked if they had done everything he had requested.

Hensley said they were working on it.

Hembree seemed satisfied.

Back in 1997, when Hembree was questioned again about the murder of Deb Ratchford, he admitted to it. But then shortly afterward, Hembree did something he had done his entire criminal career: recant the confession.

"Somewhere in the back of his mind," Sumner explained, "as we finished up with him and he had given [us] . . . Heather and Randi's murders, he knew he could always recant those confessions if he needed to. He is a pathological liar. And to underestimate his abilities in this regard would be foolish."

CHAPTER 67

Some states use a magistrate system. In North Carolina, magistrates are viewed as judges. They are not elected, however. Magistrates are appointed by the court clerk and are not required to have law degrees. Magistrates swear officers to both search and arrest warrants. But they also set bond after police serve those arrest warrants. Magistrates are set up in the local jails and there is generally no attorney present when a suspect is brought before them. Magistrates, it could be said, take some of the burden off judges.

There was not going to be a bond set in Danny Hembree's case. Whether he realized it or not, Hembree faced the most serious charges the state had on its books. There was no chance of Hembree enjoying freedom while he awaited the iron fist of the justice system.

That being said, if a defendant cannot make bond or, in Hembree's case, is not given the opportunity to bond out, he must be brought in front of a district court judge on the following day, where he is then given the opportunity to apply for appointed counsel.

Hembree was slated to go in front of a superior court judge, but Hensley and Sumner had to first get him in to see a magistrate. The magistrate was the first step along what would be, if Hembree chose that route, a tedious legal process toward justice. Of course, Hembree could plead his cases, if a deal was later offered.

"No media, right?" Hembree said as they made their way to the magistrate's office.

"Yeah, Danny."

Word had spread that Hembree had been brought in for the murders and was being questioned. The town was bustling with rumor and allegation. The local media was salivating at the prospect of covering a story with such broad implications and the potential for a nationwide media feeding frenzy.

Television media loved the words "serial killer."

As they escorted Hembree to the magistrate's office, coming around a corner in the building, Matt Hensley was shocked to see them all waiting: reporters whom Danny Hembree had purposely said he did not want to face.

"We had no idea," Hensley said to Hembree.

There were cameras rolling, reporters waiting. A photograph would emerge in the days to come displaying the sheer shock on Hensley's face when they came around that corner and were surprised by the media.

"I'm done. Finished talking," Hembree said.

"Danny, come on. We had no idea."

"Get them out of here now or I will recant everything I said to you," Hembree announced. His demeanor had changed. He became someone else.

All Hensley could think about now was the idea of approaching Hembree again in the future as they began to investigate all the crimes he had admitted to. If Hembree shut them down, they were on their own. If they had him to bounce facts off, it would make the cases go much smoother.

Hensley pulled the magistrate aside and explained what was going on, relaying the promises they'd made to their suspect, adding, "Can you see Mr. Hembree without the media breathing down our backs?"

The magistrate thought about it.

"Yes."

The media was shut out.

It's funny how some people react to the sudden notion that a neighbor or friend could possibly be a vicious serial killer there in front of them, right under their nose the entire time. Perhaps it's denial. Maybe we don't want to admit we've missed a sign. Or possibly it's just that realizing a psychopath committed murder and hid corpses within a stone's throw of your house would unnerve us so much, we block out the reality of the situation.

Whatever the case, it's inevitable that the neighbor ends up on the nightly news, that deer-in-the-headlights gaze, uttering those pedestrian comments we always hear in such a situation.

Thus, "He just didn't strike me as that type of guy," one of Hembree's neighbors said when reporters caught up to the case and went trolling for quotes in Hembree's neighborhood after being shut out by the magistrate.

CHAPTER 68

On December 7, Monday, a pair of detectives from Brevard County, Florida, arrived to speak with Danny Hembree about murders he had supposedly committed in Florida. Hembree had family in Brevard County. He had spent copious amounts of time there. The opportunity existed for Hembree to have committed murders in Florida and, for that matter, at any point along the way, to and fro.

Brevard County is north of Fort Pierce, in the middle of the state, on the east coast. Two Brevard County Sheriff's Department (BCSD) detectives sat down with Hembree, who was being held at the jail across the street from the Gastonia Police Department, downtown. Hembree had made it clear he wanted to be transferred to Raleigh; he wasn't going to be saying much of anything specific to Florida until that demand was met. Hensley had contacted the DA's office to ask about the request and was informed that some sort of arrangement would be made—not necessarily what Hembree wanted, but he was soon going to be transported to the DOC and out of the Gastonia local jail.

Hembree explained to Brevard County detectives, without going into detail, that he and Bobby Johnson had killed two women back in the early 1990s while in Florida. They showed Hembree a mug shot of Johnson, who was serving life for a 2003 first-degree burglary in South Carolina. Johnson was the same age as Hembree, forty-eight.

"That's him," Hembree said, pointing to the photo.

With Hembree not willing to tell much more before he was transferred to a prison of his liking, the next stop for the Florida detectives, they explained to Hensley and Sumner on their way out, was South Carolina and a visit to Bobby Johnson.

"Right now, we have no record of any homicides in the areas Hembree explained during those periods he talked about," one of the detectives told Hensley.

CHAPTER 69

Hembree made his first official appearance in the Gaston County Courthouse on North Marietta Street late in the day, December 7. The DA, Locke Bell, was ready to prosecute Danny Hembree to the full extent, and already was talking about exploring the death penalty.

For a true narcissist, there can be no better stage on which to perform than the structured atmosphere of a United States courtroom, with the media, judge, lawyers, and cops all watching. He is given the opportunity to run the show, so to speak, and control some of what happens from day to day. Hembree would waste no time in exploiting this part of his character to the fullest extent.

When DA Bell announced that his office would seek the death penalty, the alleged killer responded in kind. As proceedings got under way, Hembree indicated he was going to be representing himself for the duration of his case. And since his incarceration inside the local Gaston County Jail, he said, "I'm receiving death threats. I haven't been tried. I haven't been convicted."

Bell stated that security was not an issue inside the jail and Hembree would be staying put. He would not be moved or placed in a safer space. He was fine where he was, until charges had been worked out and a new court date set.

During the short appearance, Hembree was charged with the two murders: Heather Catterton's and Randi Saldana's. Bell implied that Hembree would be charged within a day or two with a third murder, Deb Ratchford's.

As the session ended, Hembree made eye contact with Heather's and Randi's family members who were present in the courtroom, making them aware he was going to be an open wound as the cases went forward. Stella's sister showed up to represent Heather. As Hembree, dressed in a pumpkin-colored jumper, got up to be removed from the courtroom, he smiled at Stella's sister, no doubt thinking back to the accusations he'd made against her, Stella, and Shorty.

Stella's sister stared back at him. It was a gesture, she later told reporters, with the message: Not "all of Heather's family members are . . . going to be your friends and lovers."

Another important factor coming from the day's events became that while Danny Hembree had been incarcerated for lengthier periods of time twice in his lifetime, he had escaped from prison on two occasions. Within his near forty-page criminal record, it was made public that Hembree scaled a wall in 1998 while serving eleven years for burglary, escaped, and was on the run for three days before he was caught. Then a second time, just two years prior, in 2007, Hembree was on work release duty when he took off. He had been working off a five-year bid for robbery. He was caught not long after that escape.

CHAPTER 70

Twenty-three-year-old Nicole Catterton took off after her boyfriend Danny Hembree's arrest. Word on the street was that Nicole was missing. The family was, of course, worried about her. Why take off? Was Nicole concerned enough about Hembree's arrest and her possible role in the crimes? Had she been involved—willingly or not—in covering up for Hembree?

It turned out Nicole was upset with herself for not realizing she had been sleeping with a monster. The guilt became overwhelming. It was not easy to deal with the pain. Nicole was worried that she had inadvertently and unknowingly been a party to Hembree's crimes. That thought alone made her sick: She could have participated, without realizing it, in her own sister's demise.

Nicole had not run off, as it turned out. She was staying at a friend's house, and Nick knew where she was the entire time.

Hensley went to see Nick. He wanted to know what was going on. The rumor mill was churning with word that Nicole had left town. Hensley wanted to know why she would do this. For Hensley, he'd always had a feeling that Nicole, out of all the other players, knew a lot more than she was letting on.

"No," Nick said. "She wasn't reported missing." He picked up the phone and dialed a number.

"I'm fine," Nicole explained to Hensley. "I just cannot be home right now."

Hensley said there was going to come a time when he needed to sit down with her and talk about things.

Nicole said she understood. Just say when.

CHAPTER 71

As they worked to try and back up—or tear apart—what Hembree had admitted to during his interviews, Sumner and Hensley found the store where Hembree claimed to have purchased the gasoline. It wasn't the same store, however, that Hembree had pointed out during that tour of the town while exploring his murder memories. It was another gas station/convenience store down the block.

This was where Hembree and his tales diminished in integrity: the details.

For example, earlier that same day, Hensley had found that girl whom Hembree said he had picked up after leaving Shorty's (the one he said he had gotten oral sex from). However, it turned out Hembree had a few facts wrong. The girl said he'd picked her up, all right, but she had not given him oral sex, not on that day. It was a month prior when she had done it; she remembered distinctly because Hembree had taken her to the abandoned trailer. As they were driving later, "Danny wanted me to go out and make some money (prostitute herself), but I didn't want to." So Hembree pulled over and told her to get out.

Hensley and Sumner walked into the gas station under

the impression that all of the surveillance tape from that time period was gone by now, because those types of establishments don't hold on to tapes that long. But maybe, they hoped, there was a receipt. Hembree said he purchased the fuel on that Sunday morning when he burned Randi's body: November 15, 2009. Yet, after discussing the situation with the manager, she pulled out a receipt from the prior day, Saturday, November 14.

"I remember the purchase," one of the clerks told Hensley over the phone after the manager called. She remembered because the purchase was for a single dollar.

Hensley asked her to explain.

"Nicole Catterton came in to purchase the gas—one dollar's worth."

The receipt matched the story.

They searched the tapes to see if the cameras picked Nicole up inside the store. But that day, for some reason, had been erased.

Hensley wondered how the clerk was so certain she had spoken to Nicole. Hensley couldn't get the thought out of his mind: *How could Nicole buy a gallon of gas, Randi's body show up burned in the woods, and Nicole not know what was going on? Or, at least, put two and two together?*

"I do remember that day," the clerk explained. "She came in and purchased one dollar of gas. While she was in the store paying, she started talking about her sister's death."

"You see the car she came in?" Hensley asked.

"I looked out at the pump and saw the car, but I cannot recall what it was. I didn't see [anyone else], because I didn't really pay much attention."

"We will contact you at a later period," Hensley said.

"No problem."

Nicole! Hensley thought, shaking his head as they drove away from the station. *Did she know? Did she willingly participate in covering up Randi's murder?*

CHAPTER 72

It was the "demons" that "finally got control," Hembree wrote to his mother, Jacqueline Hembree, and sister, Kathy Ledbetter. The dark side, apparently, had taken him down such an immoral path that he'd finally succumbed to its evil forces. Yet, none of that mattered to Hembree now, he explained, because he "hated this life" and all of "its injustice." While sitting in front of Hensley and Sumner on December 9, Hembree penned a letter, warning his mother and sister that it would likely be the last time the three of them communicated in this manner. He was "sorry for the shame" he had cast upon the Hembree family name. He said he hoped that when he saw God on the other side, he could "find peace." In fact, Hembree offered, he had "confessed to God and the police" and hoped that it was enough for God to forgive him and allow him a place in the Kingdom.

In this same letter, Danny Robbie Hembree wanted to "explain" why he had killed the girls. He needed his family to appreciate his mind-set. He wasn't so sure his mother "would understand" his sordid rationale, but he needed to give her some sort of justification—he believed she deserved it—in knowing that the girls were murdered for a *purpose.* He wasn't some nut out in the world killing for no good reason.

Here was Hembree bashing his victims. Undermining their lives and playing the role of God. Hembree was saying that because he had made the decision that their lives weren't worth anything, it was okay to kill them, and take them away from their families, thus never giving them the opportunity to take control of their lives. Hembree claimed Heather needed to be released "from the torture" that she "endured daily," while desperately feeding her drug addiction. He said Heather was sleeping with men as much as twenty times a day for dope. He said as "crazy" as it might sound, he "loved" Heather and "felt sorry for her."

Such a bizarre comment. In his missive, which read as a self-serving script, Hembree wanted people to believe he cared about Heather so much that he strangled and asphyxiated the seventeen-year-old, stomped his bare foot into her throat, tossed her dead body into a closet after dragging it over inverted rug nails, went upstairs, watched TV, made a sandwich, and then days later pitched her body into a culvert between three sewer pipes so it could be eaten up by maggots and wildlife.

As for Randi, Hembree explained in his letter, he had killed her for the things that "she done to Heather." He then broke into the old story of Shorty, Stella, and her sister putting him up to the murder and paying him to do it.

Hembree said he was ready to "stand before" God.

Flip-flopping, he said he didn't kill Deb Ratchford, but he knew who did and was trying to "straighten that out" best he could.

He claimed his life was the "end result of drugs."

He wanted to be cremated and have his ashes "spread on the family plot."

He signed the letter as Danny Boy.

CHAPTER 73

Hensley and a colleague picked up Nicole at the local jail, where she was spending a few days under a revoked bond. There was some concern that Nicole might have seen the news reports that day of what had become a breaking story highlighting Nicole possibly purchasing the gasoline. (Someone at the gas station ran his or her mouth to the press right after Hensley and Sumner left.) It was a big story this early in the judicial process. If Hembree had accomplices, one being the sister of one of his victims, the implications in the media were going to be huge. Many pictured Nancy Grace getting hold of the story and that night on her Headline News nightly show, trashing Nicole in her Southern speak. They envisioned the rambunctious, seething blond lawyer ranting and raving, calling Nicole every name in the book.

"You guys have the televisions on in here today?" Hensley asked a corrections officer (CO) as he and Sumner walked in.

"Yeah . . . but it wasn't on a news channel."

Good thing.

They waited in a small room as the CO fetched Nicole.

"Nicole, we'd like to talk to you about Danny. He's been charged, as you know. Would you come down to the station with us and discuss some things?"

Nicole said she would.

A female officer transported Nicole from the jail to the GCPD. Hensley read Nicole her rights and she signed a waiver, indicating her desire to speak without an attorney.

So far, so good: no resistance.

The main question was if Nicole had any knowledge of the crimes before or after.

"I had no idea of anything at any time," Nicole said. And as she talked through her version of the events, Nicole mentioned how she'd had a hard time remembering things lately. Being hit so many times by cars, she said, she'd developed memory loss and didn't always recall certain events. Hensley later agreed that Nicole seemed willing to remember, but she just couldn't dredge up all she wanted, due to severe head injuries.

Hensley asked Nicole questions that the GCPD had asked everyone else.

Nicole said everyone believed Hembree killed Heather. She'd heard it from her mother, her father, and many people on the street. Yet, she didn't believe it. She said she never saw that side of Hembree, if it even existed.

They wondered if maybe Hembree had some sort of hold on Nicole, even now, after being arrested and charged with murder. Was she protecting him? Was she scared?

Nicole said no.

Then Hensley asked about that specific day, November 14, 2009, if Nicole could recall what she did.

"I spent the night before . . . at Gavin Compton's trailer." This was the trailer next to the abandoned trailer, where Hembree took his women. "I remember going over to Danny's mother's house. I remember talking to Danny's mother. I was drinking that day. We went to Jacob's Food Mart . . . to pick up alcohol. We spent the night at Gavin's."

She didn't mention anything about a gallon of fuel.

"You don't recall going to Kingsway?" Hensley asked.

"Oh yeah! We went to the Kingsway store."

"Why'd you go to the store?"

"We went there to get Gavin's son a blunt, but we didn't buy it. I went inside the store to get a drink."

"I know that you went inside that store to buy a gallon of gas."

"Oh . . . yes. Yes. I did." Nicole said this without any reservation. It came out as though she had forgotten and suddenly remembered—like she had nothing to hide.

"And?"

"Danny sent me in to get it. I used my own money, loose change I had."

Hensley asked if she thought it was odd that he needed just one gallon of gas in a can?

Nicole said she never thought about it until that moment. "I didn't know if Danny put the gas into his car or in a container." She was inside the store the entire time. She didn't actually fill the container. She just paid for it.

"Did you ever see a container of gas?"

"No."

They went through the following morning, that Sunday—the day Hembree said he left his friend's trailer around eight to go and pick up Randi's body and burn it.

"I saw Danny at the kitchen table when I got up. He was drinking a beer." She said it was early. "I didn't see him leave that night or that morning, but he could have, because I slept in."

Nicole explained how they took off to Florida the next day, a Monday. She mentioned how Hembree filled up his car with gas. For Hensley and Sumner, this confirmed Hembree's story of tossing Randi's purse, clothes, and some of her jewelry into a Dumpster behind a store as they drove out of town.

While they were in Florida, Nicole said, she took a call from home, and that was how she found out Randi had been murdered and her body recovered. She said Nick and Stella were worried about her and told her to get home. They said Hembree was responsible for the murders. When Nicole got off the phone with her parents, she said she approached Hembree, saying, "There must be a killer out there."

He didn't respond, so she got drunk. Later on, after the booze hit her hard, Nicole said, she accused Danny of killing her sister.

"I did it," Hembree told Nicole that day in Florida, admitting to murdering Heather.

"So I smashed his windshield," Nicole said. "He called the cops. We left for home the next night."

Nicole never gave a reason why she didn't report what Hembree had said in Florida, but she denied, time and again, having had any knowledge whatsoever of Randi or her sister's murders, either before or after. Additionally, she wasn't scared to drive back home with Hembree after he had admitted killing her sister.

Hensley couldn't shake his original suspicion: Who purchases one gallon of gas (and winds up with a dead girl's jewelry) and doesn't fit it all into what happened? It seemed remarkable that Nicole did not see the writing.

"Nicole held true the entire time, though," Hensley commented. "She said she traded jewelry with Randi and had no idea about Heather or Randi's deaths."

Hensley presented some evidence against Hembree to Nicole and asked her what she thought about it. "Look, you're living with the guy in your father's house. Your sister's been murdered. . . ."

Nicole seemed to understand the logic, but she said she didn't want to walk away from the guy.

It seemed to investigators that Danny was giving Nicole the kind of attention she craved. Perhaps he was good to her.

He likely supported any habits she had. And so it was easy for her to stand by him.

Hensley knew Hembree was just staying close to the Catterton family, telling them what they wanted to hear, and keeping an eye on the case.

"He was a manipulator, a sociopath."

Yet, as time would soon tell, it didn't mean he was stupid.

CHAPTER 74

Those additional cases Hembree mentioned gnawed at Hensley as he watched the tapes of the interviews over the course of a few days. Still sitting in the local jail, Hembree said he and Bobby Johnson had beaten and shot two people and left them for dead in the woods near Kings Mountain. The way they learned both had not died was through the newspapers.

Hensley thought, *What if I head down to the library and conduct a microfiche search?*

As Hensley considered the idea, he took a call from a Brevard County detective.

"We spoke to Bobby Johnson."

"What did he say?"

"Said he didn't know anything about any murders in Florida and wasn't involved."

"That all?" Hensley asked.

"He did confess to those attempted murders Hembree talked to you about, that store clerk in Bessemer City and the man they kidnapped from a hotel in Kings Mountain."

More reason to conduct that archival search, Hensley told

himself. Maybe he could locate those victims and interview them.

As Hensley watched the interview tapes, another important piece of information emerged. During the interview Hembree had given the YCSO before Hensley and Sumner interviewed him, he claimed on two separate occasions that "no one knew he killed Randi and Heather." Yet, when he spoke to Hensley and Sumner, Hembree fingered Stella, her sister, and Shorty in conspiring to have Randi killed.

He was caught in a quandary if he wanted to pin Randi's murder on them. He was lying. It was clear by his own admission.

CHAPTER 75

Danny Hembree had a reputation among law enforcement for confessing to crimes. Inside the box, Hembree liked to run his mouth. As far back as 1993, Hembree was known to be a suspect who liked to talk. As a thirty-five-year-old, Hembree was picked up by the GCPD in 1997 as a suspect in a forgery case. While questioned, Hembree confessed to several armed robberies—serious crimes. They asked him why he did this.

"I want to go to prison," Hembree said. "I want to kick my cocaine addiction and live a normal life."

The checks Hembree was being questioned about were his father's. Hembree had swiped several checks, forged the old man's signature, and cashed them. During the interrogation, not only did Hembree talk about the armed robberies, but he also mentioned "a rape, beating and kidnapping of a Bessemer City convenience-store clerk." It was the same case that Matt Hensley was looking into.

Interviewed by the *Charlotte Observer* at the time of his arrest in 1997, having already done eight-plus years for various offenses, Hembree said: "I wanted to make sure I either never got back out or got help with my addiction. . . ." He explained that the pending armed-robbery charge could put him away for life, but, he told reporter Jeff Diamant, "I believe if people see I genuinely want some help, and I'm willing to put my life on the line to get this help, somewhere along the line I'll get help." If he couldn't get the help he needed, or if it did not work, "I might as well be locked down like an animal the rest of my life."

In total Hembree fashion, even back when he was, arguably, honing his craft of justifying his crimes, he told that same reporter he "always used a BB gun or a blank pistol, and that the stolen money supported his drug addiction." And this, in his mind, made it okay, a nonviolent crime. "I never used a real weapon in any of my robberies. The only person that ever could've got hurt in any of the robberies was me. . . ."

He failed to say, however, that back in 1980, using one of those "fake" weapons, he forced a woman out of a store and into a waiting truck, where he and Bobby Johnson then took her into the woods at three-thirty in the morning. Both men repeatedly raped the woman, according to one account of the crime. Then they beat her and slashed her with a knife several times before dumping her body out of a moving vehicle. She was unconscious. She only survived because she awoke at 5:00 A.M. and managed to find her way to a nearby house and asked for help.

In that same 1997 article, Hembree said he "had information about that particular crime," and claimed to have had nothing "to do with it—but I can sure solve it."

He later admitted to Sumner, though, and then to Hensley, that he took part in this crime. It was 1980—the same year Hembree was married. Furthermore, Hembree, who had pleaded with cops in 1997 for help with his addictions—claiming that locking him up was the only way to solve his problem—would escape two times from custody after being incarcerated on the armed-robbery and forgery charges.

CHAPTER 76

On December 8, 2009, Hembree was charged with the murder of Deborah Ratchford. An accomplice, whom Hembree had fingered during interviews, was also charged. James Swanson denied any part in the murder, however, saying Hembree was making it all up.

This new charge produced a theory that cold-case murders in the area would have to be checked out thoroughly under the pretense that Hembree had committed them. There was no telling how many girls Hembree had murdered. A serial killer such as Hembree doesn't kill one girl in 1992—Ratchford—and then cool off for seventeen years and kill two more within a few weeks. Serials with the mind-set and psychology Hembree displayed need to fulfill their fantasies continually—murder becomes another addiction. If he killed Ratchford, Hembree could have a dozen more bodies to his name.

In court, Hembree did not respond to the charges as Locke Bell stated emphatically that his office would seek the death penalty.

The judge said Hembree could plead against the charges at a later date. This was a formal court date to charge him and enter into the record the fact that the state was seeking to execute Hembree. Hembree's run of crime, apparently, had come to an end. He was staring down the barrel of death himself now, perhaps feeling the hands of the state around *his* throat.

Yet, what nobody knew—and couldn't, really—was that Danny Hembree was working on a plan to make a mockery of the system designed to adjudicate him. And the things he was going to do in the coming months would shock the state of North Carolina and make national, and even international, headlines. It seemed Danny Hembree wasn't quite finished with his game of control. For him, as he smiled out of the corner of his mouth and blew kisses to his sister and mother during this recent court appearance, Hembree was laughing on the inside, preparing to stage the show of his life.

PART FOUR

THE "SUCKERS"

CHAPTER 77

Hensley sat in the tranquility of the local Gaston County Public Library and scrolled through articles, in search of those cases Hembree had mentioned. There had to be something written about both, Hensley believed.

The image Matt Hensley couldn't get out of his mind was Hembree standing, smoking a cigarette outside the GCPD in back of the building, talking about this "old stuff," as Hembree labeled it, in a tone reminiscent of a man describing a cookout he had gone to with his family.

No feeling.

No emotion.

Certainly, no remorse.

It was the Crowders Creek crime, specifically, that alarmed Hensley most—where Hembree talked about abducting a woman from a convenience store. The details Hembree offered were disturbing and shocking enough, and this was banking on the theory that he was likely holding back and glossing the crime over by at least half.

"We're standing there on the back-porch area of the police department," Hensley recalled, "and he's telling us what he did to this woman."

Hembree described how he and Bobby Johnson took the girl out into the woods after forcing her into a truck and then violently raped her. That crime was evil enough. But then Hembree told Hensley how he had taken the woman up to the mountaintop with the intention of killing her. He brought a shovel along.

Confused, Hensley thought maybe Hembree was planning on burying her alive.

"I was going to cut her head off with the spade of the shovel," Hembree said.

Hembree described how he had told her to stand and face the opposite way. He took the shovel and swung it like a baseball bat, hoping the spade portion of the tool would slice off her head.

"But he missed . . . ," Hensley said. "He told me he missed her neck."

The woman let out a terrible, shrieking scream. It scared Hembree and Johnson enough that they took off.

Both figured because Hembree had sliced her with the shovel on the back or side, she'd fall down and bleed to death. Hembree said he was certain he'd seen something in the newspapers after the crime that told him she survived.

So now, Hensley was wading through rolls of microfiche, hoping to come up with a name. If she had survived, he could possibly pay a visit to the woman to get her side of the story. And maybe she could even testify—or at least give the GCPD a statement to put into Danny Hembree's file.

After hours of searching on that first day, Hensley found nothing.

CHAPTER 78

District 27A, which is the Gaston County District Attorney's Office, was busy preparing a case for what both sides believed would be a fall 2010 trial. The DA's office was charging Hembree with one first-degree count in the murder of Heather Catterton. His other alleged victims, Randi Saldana and Deborah Ratchford, would be tried as separate cases. Being a death penalty case, it was going to consume the DA's office, and Locke Bell relied on his assistant district attorney Stephanie Hamlin to dig her heels in for a serious fight. As February 2010 approached, ADA Hamlin was on the case full-time.

Danny Hembree wasn't about to lie down, roll over, and plead; neither was the DA's office. There was not going to be a deal. The DA's office believed Hembree was a vicious predator, career criminal, repeat, serial violent offender, and, at the least, three-time murderer (which made him a serial killer). Danny Hembree was not going to talk his way out of prison.

Hembree was a different guy these days from that admitted murderer showing cops around his mother's house, taking them on a tour of his madness. Hembree was using every resource available to mount what the DA's office assumed would be an insanity defense. On paper, it seemed to be the only card Hembree could play. The evidence against him—in the murders of Heather and Randi—was overwhelming.

Hembree had other plans, however.

Defense attorneys Brent Ratchford (no relation to Deb Ratchford, the woman Hembree was charged with killing) and Richard Beam lodged a full-scale investigation into Hembree's psychological and medical history, looking for a kernel to latch on to and use as a springboard to fight the death penalty and an assumed guilty verdict. Juries do not like to put defendants to sleep if there's the chance they could be insane or mentally handicapped/challenged. It goes against the natural order of morality. You add religious beliefs to that pie and you have a juror (or several, possibly) who would never vote for death. Defense attorneys, the good ones, know this.

According to a request filed by Ratchford and Beam, one of the most pressing issues surrounding Hembree was having their client psychologically evaluated, especially his "propensity to provide false confessions." It appeared Hembree had set a precedent long ago for admitting to crimes he did not commit. If Beam and Ratchford could prove this theory with clinical research and then bear it out with professional and expert testimony, they might have a shot. Furthermore, Hembree had apparently given up on the notion (and come to his senses) of representing himself, since he'd recently agreed to allow Ratchford and Beam to defend him.

In one of the reports written about Hembree's psychological, mental, and physical state, licensed psychologist Claudia Coleman found that Hembree had an enlarged spleen, cirrhosis of the liver, and hepatitis C, among many other medical issues. Most of this stemmed from intravenous drug use, although with Hembree's sexual history of prostitutes and bedding drug users, there was no telling how he had contracted the disease. Hembree had also been whacked with a baseball bat in the head during the late summer of 2009. But a CT scan of his brain had produced nothing in the form of results proving the injury had affected him much more than a terribly bad headache.

Hembree was complaining of shortness of breath and a slow heart rate. The Raleigh prison, where he was being housed—he got his original wish, after all—had ordered a medical evaluation based on those complaints. That evaluation did not produce any life-threatening results. Hembree was not a picture of perfect health, but he was not ready to start sizing up caskets, either.

One particular finding of Coleman's that explained how Hembree truly felt inside focused on his passive-aggressive behavior, the doctor diagnosed. Hembree was paranoid, sure, but he was also a "narcissist" who anticipated "being disillusioned by others." Because of that expectation, he would behave "contrarily" and in "self-destructive ways." Moreover, Coleman said Hembree was "socially unpredictable." He felt "misunderstood" and "unappreciated." He feared that displaying "any weakness" was a "concession" to an "inner feeling of insecurity and ineffectiveness."

Despite these conclusions, Coleman could not give an opinion, she wrote, *with regard to mental status at the time of alleged offense . . . [in reference] to insanity or diminished capacity.*

Why?

[Hembree had] recanted his statements to authorities, she wrote.

(To be clear, though, Hembree "never, *ever* recanted his admissions about Heather and Randi—only Deb Ratchford and the Florida cases," ADA Stephanie Hamlin clarified.)

Coleman addressed the possibility of Hembree giving authorities a "voluntary false confession" under the pretense of him being a guy who liked to play games with cops for the sake of the thrill and the ego stimulation. She made a point to write, *Many false confessions . . . occur in highly publicized sensational crimes.*

But that scenario barely fit here: Hembree's case had not become a national story until after Hembree confessed and began the process of poking at the DA's office and making a mockery of the justice system.

No opinion could be made, Coleman wrote in her report of Hembree giving a voluntary false confession. She warned she was well aware of Hembree having said he made false confessions in the past and even additional false confessions about other crimes in 2009, when he spoke to the YCSO and GCPD.

There was one aspect of a false confession Coleman agreed with. She wrote that it concerned *[Hembree's] desire for attention and the thrill and excitement of duping others.* After speaking with him, she was convinced that all of her observations *[were] factors . . . consistent with aspects of Mr. Hembree's personality disorder.*

Bottom line: The DA's office didn't know it yet, but Hembree was going to lodge an argument that he had made it all up. He had confessed to the murders because that's what Danny Hembree liked to do: He lied in order to bolster his ego and feel like he mattered.

"Laughable," said one law enforcement official. "That's what Hembree's sudden plea of making it all up sounded like."

A freakin' joke.

CHAPTER 79

From a bird's-eye view, the road surrounding Perry Correctional Institution, where Hembree's criminal cohort Bobby Johnson was serving a life sentence, is in the shape of a heart, which encircles a large concrete building and barbed-wire fence. Must be a sardonic metaphor for the love that the South Carolina corrections system has for each and every inmate it checks into its popular, level-3 facility in Pelzer, South Carolina.

On February 26, 2010, Matt Hensley and Michel Sumner took that heart-shaped road into the prison for a sit-down with Johnson. They wanted to hear from Johnson what he and Hembree had done. Get a complete picture of Hembree. In turn, it would tell them how much of what Hembree had admitted to could be corroborated by other sources.

Johnson had a hard look to him. He kept a thick Tony Orlando–style mustache against his pockmarked face. He had the most chilling beady eyes a guy could have. It was obvious that behind those lenses was a man who liked to wreak havoc any chance he could, and prison was probably the only way of stopping him from doing it.

After Johnson waived his rights, he talked about robbing

that convenience store in Bessemer City in such fine detail it sounded as though they'd hit the establishment the previous night. It drove home a point Hensley had made that criminals remember their crimes, especially the violent ones. They become pivotal moments in their lives, like having children or celebrating birthdays.

"We were in a blue Chevy," Johnson explained with his Southern inflection. "We parked at a car wash near the store, on the side. We robbed the clerk, kidnapped her, and then took her with us to Lincoln Academy, where we both raped her."

Within his explanation, Johnson took the opportunity to bash the victim, a common trait serial offenders routinely display (blame their victims in some way for having been victimized) by calling her a "chubby white female, with big glasses."

His memory was fresh. He recalled the color of the "smock" she wore: "Red."

Hensley listened intently to Johnson's scratchy voice. The detective knew a "red smock" had been entered into evidence in a case he had looked at with similar watermarks, and the smock was actually sitting in a property room. This was important: Johnson was being truthful, and the evidence, scant as it was, backed up his statements.

Then Johnson talked about the moment they decided to kill the woman. He said as they were up on Crowders Mountain, "Danny got a shovel from the truck. . . . He took the shovel and hit her across the head." When the blow didn't do what Johnson and Hembree assumed it would, Hembree hauled off and struck her again. That was when, Johnson said, she screamed, frightened them, and they took off.

Hensley asked Johnson about the hotel incident that Hembree had mentioned, without giving many details.

Johnson said he recalled that night, too.

"We robbed a Holiday Inn at Kings Mountain."

"Weapon?"

"Yeah, we had a gun with one bullet in it," Johnson said, going against Hembree's proud admission of never having used a "real" gun during a robbery.

The way Hembree had described this crime differed. Hembree claimed it took place in 1981, or possibly 1982. Hembree couldn't recall the exact year. He said he and Johnson kidnapped, as Hembree labeled the guy, "a nigger" from the Holiday Inn. Hembree gave no reason why they kidnapped the guy after robbing the hotel; but they took the guy out into the woods off Crowders Creek Road and Hembree shot him in the back.

"I was gonna shoot him in the front, but my gun jammed and he done run away," Hembree admitted.

Hembree thought he'd killed the guy, anyway.

"But we's saw it in the papers the next day that he was shot in the shoulder and he done lived," Hembree had told Hensley.

Johnson told the story in somewhat similar detail, but he added more information.

"We put him in the trunk of Danny's blue Ford Escort. We took him out to Henry's Knob in South Carolina." Henry's Knob is a mountain in York County. It's located in Clover, a popular stomping ground of Hembree's. It was a kyanite mineral mine at one time, now deserted. It is a good place to bring someone if you don't want him to return. "We was gonna toss him in a tavern with red water," Johnson said. By "tavern," he meant an actual watering hole. But as they approached it, they thought they'd heard someone in the woods. So they took him to an area near Old Crowders Creek Road. "We made him lie on his stomach. I pointed the gun toward his head and pulled the trigger." It was dark. They couldn't see. "He got up and started running. We jumped in the car and took off. The next night, I set Danny's car on fire."

CHAPTER 80

Hensley needed to go back to the library. He had plenty of information to track down regarding this latest tale of madness from one of Hembree's criminal cohorts. He still wanted to find out about the woman they had raped and attempted to murder. Justice doesn't have an expiration date. Hensley wanted these victims to have their day. Even if the statute of limitations came into play and nothing could be done, Hensley could look each victim in the eyes and say their attackers were in prison on other charges. They would not have to worry or fear them again.

Hensley had YCSO and GCPD records search the archives for reports relating to both cases, but they did not turn up anything. His only chance was the library.

Searching for a second time, Hensley came upon the front page of the local *Gaston Gazette* and the headline he had been looking for jumped out at him: STORE CLERK ALLEGES RAPE, ROBBERY.

September 10, 1980.

"The article outlined the event almost exactly the way Danny Hembree told me it happened," Hensley later said.

The woman's name was never mentioned, making it more

difficult to find her. However, there were two investigators quoted in the article. Hensley had an idea.

He left the library that afternoon and contacted one of the GCPD property officers. The officer found a name logged into an old records book near the date of the incident.

Had to be her.

Hensley then found one of the detectives quoted in the article. She was working for a local sheriff's department and remembered the case well—confirming for Hensley that the name he had been given by the property officer was indeed the name of the victim.

The way police work sometimes comes together is that when one domino falls, the others begin a downward trek. As it turned out, Hensley found the second detective quoted in the article. That cop said he not only remembered the incident, but he had gone to high school with the victim. He even thought he knew where she lived today.

This gave Hensley a maiden name to go along with her married name at the time of the crime. Hensley found her date of birth.

Then an address.

It was exciting to walk up to the door of the woman with the news that they had caught the animals that had brutally raped, beat, and left her for dead in the woods. Of course, there was no way the woman could have forgotten the incident. Hensley was thrilled to be able to bring this news to her.

Hensley and another investigator approached the woman's front door. They knocked. But their air of excitement quickly deflated. Turned out it was the wrong address. The woman no longer lived there.

CHAPTER 81

Hensley could not let it go. He had to find this woman. That second incident involving an African-American man was going to be harder for Hensley to nail down. They did not have a name in that case, and Hensley could not find anything in the local newspapers about it. But the woman— he had a name and date of birth.

So Hensley did a LexisNexis search, a widely used background checking service that, according to its website, *provides an extensive collection of industry-specific background check solutions for organizations such as law enforcement & government agencies.*

Hensley came up with two names.

On March 19, 2010, Hensley knocked on an apartment door near Kings Mountain, North Carolina, and there she was—finally—standing before him.

The victim was eager to talk about her ordeal. She gave details nobody had heard thus far. Some were awfully graphic and equally as disturbing as anything Hensley had heard about the case. According to the victim, Hembree walked into the store about two-thirty in the morning. He went back to a cooler and grabbed a can of beer and then presented it and a sandwich at the counter. It was then that the woman dropped something on the floor. When she bent down to pick it up, Hembree walked up behind her, grabbed her by the throat, and brandished a knife. It had happened so fast, she said. One moment, she was preparing to ring up his purchases; the next, he had his hands around her throat.

"Open the fucking drawer," Hembree ordered through clenched teeth.

"Please don't hurt me," the woman pleaded. "Please—"

"Open. The. Drawer."

She hit the button and the drawer popped open. "I've already done the drop for the night."

Hembree took the $11 inside the drawer.

"You're going with me," Hembree said, not giving her a reason why.

He dragged her out the door and across the street to a car wash, where Johnson was waiting in the truck. She sat in the middle between Hembree and Johnson. They placed a shirt over her head, but she could somewhat see through it. She feared the worst.

"They were not saying anything much," the woman explained. "They were mad because of the eleven dollars. They wanted more money."

When they got to the location near Lincoln Academy Road, deep into the forest, Hembree initiated the rape. He pushed her down on her back after pulling her out of the truck and dragging her out onto a golf course. She was terrified they were going to kill her. Hembree pulled her pants down and "lifted my legs up. . . . He put his penis in my vagina and raped me. He ejaculated inside me. Then the driver put his penis in my vagina and raped me." Johnson "quit" at one point, she explained, telling Hembree, "I'm nervous. . . . I cannot do anything." Johnson couldn't stay erect, so he stopped.

"They got me up and I pulled up my pants and buttoned my shirt—they had my hands tied with my bra [behind my back] as they raped me."

Throughout the entire ordeal, she pleaded with them not to hurt her.

"Please let me go."

Then they took her to a second location. Now up on Crowders Mountain, Hembree dragged her out of the truck again and told her to lie down on the ground. He then took out a shovel from the back of the truck.

"That's when the beating started," she told Hensley. "They hit me in my head, my chest, and neck with the shovel. They stabbed me with it. I prayed for the Lord Jesus to help me. And that's when I went out."

She fell unconscious.

As she talked through this portion of her statement, the woman showed Hensley the enormous scars she had from the crime: They "reminded" her "of what happened . . . every day."

When she "came to" in the woods on Crowders Mountain, Hembree and his partner were gone. So she started walking.

Down near the bottom of the mountain, the woman heard dogs barking. As she walked closer to the barking, she thought, *The dogs cannot hurt me worse than what I have already been through.*

She found a house and knocked on the door. The police came.

"I believe they were trying to kill me," she concluded. "I heard them talking about killing me."

Hensley asked if she wanted to press charges.

"Yes," she said.

CHAPTER 82

Hensley was not giving up on the second victim, a man Johnson and Hembree said they shot. Hensley and another investigator dug in and searched for any reports resembling what Hembree and Johnson had described.

Nothing.

Yet, just as they were about to abandon the search, a name popped out.

The guy, an African American, lived an hour's drive south, in South Carolina.

After the guy answered the door, Hensley explained why they were there, adding, "I'm interested in charging Mr. Hembree for the incident that occurred with you in 1981, if you're willing to prosecute."

"Sure," the man said. "Come in."

Hensley didn't know it then, but charging Hembree was going to be a problem. Hembree had admitted to the crime during a 1997 interview with police while being questioned about another crime. The victim in the case agreed then with the prosecutor not to prosecute because Hembree was facing a long sentence on other charges. So for his admission, Hembree got a break on this particular case.

The crime still resonated with the victim, however. It was a brutal attack, much more violent and racially motivated than Hembree or Johnson had admitted.

The guy was working as a night auditor at the Holiday Inn. Two guys walked into the hotel and asked him to make change. As soon as he opened the cash register, one of the men drew a (real) weapon and demanded all the cash.

After he handed them the money, they "then ordered me to climb over the counter and come with them."

They tied his arms around his back with his belt. Then they stuffed him into the trunk.

"They even made him sing old slave and gospel songs," one law enforcement official later recalled. Hembree and Johnson denigrated his heritage and his ancestors, calling him the n-word the entire time.

As they drove down the road, the man recalled, he was locked up inside the dark trunk, bouncing around, thinking they were going to kill him. He began to pray out loud.

"Then I heard one of them shout, 'Shut up back there, nigger.' " And the man instantly knew that what they had in mind was probably torturing him simply because of his skin color—that it was a racially motivated hate crime of the worst type.

"What are you going to do with me?" the man yelled.

"We're taking you somewhere and leaving you," one of them shouted back.

When they got to the woods, they took him out of the trunk and blindfolded him with a shirt. The man listened as they discussed what to do next.

One of them said, "Put him back in the trunk."

"What's wrong?" the man asked when he heard this.

"It's too busy around here. . . . We'll have to take you somewhere else."

After arriving at that second location, they took him out of the trunk and walked him deep into the forest. Then Hembree took off the guy's blindfold while stating: "Lay on the ground."

"I recall him telling us, too," Hensley noted, "that they, at first, were looking for a cliff to toss him off, but couldn't find one."

While on the ground, the man heard a shot fired and jumped up. As he did this, he realized the gun was now pointed in his face. He didn't know it right away, but he had been hit in the shoulder.

So he turned and ran away into the darkness of the woods as fast as he could.

"I don't know if they tripped over each other [as they chased] me, because I heard one of [them] tell the other to 'get up and get him!' "

The man soon found a house. And the "friendly" neighbor made him wait outside as the cops were called in.

Matt Hensley presented both cases to Locke Bell. Hensley wanted Hembree and Johnson charged. This was serious violence. Justice needed to be meted out. The victims deserved their day in court.

"Put it in the [Hembree] file," Bell said. If nothing more, they would fight to get both cases presented as evidence of Hembree's absolute thirst for violence.

CHAPTER 83

In April 2010, Hembree, dressed in an orange jumpsuit, shackled at the wrists and legs, his lawyers flanking him, officially pleaded not guilty to charges of murdering Randi Saldana and Heather Catterton. The proceeding was a formality; it was brief and all business. Trial dates were discussed. It would be a year, likely, before Hembree's first trial began.

The previous week, Heather's family gathered at her grave site. March 29, 2010, would have been Heather's eighteenth birthday. Nicole was taking her little sister's death especially hard these days. As she thought about their lives, which seemed so long ago now, Nicole couldn't reconcile a time she thought she would ever be standing at Heather's grave celebrating her little sis's entry into adulthood. It just didn't register. Heather's death was crushing to her family as they reminisced and thought about how things could have been different, what they could have done. Was there a sign Danny Hembree had given? Could they have seen his violent side and stopped it?

Hindsight—the ultimate reality check.

CHAPTER 84

Preparing for trial, now scheduled to begin in October 2011, Hembree's attorney Richard Beam received a letter dated September 18, 2011, from Dr. Donald Jason, a private-practicing forensic professional specializing in pathology, licensed in the state of North Carolina. Dr. Jason's credentials were impressive. He was an associate professor at the Wake Forest School of Medicine in Winston-Salem in the pathology department on the autopsy service, and a county medical examiner in Forsyth County, as well as a designated forensic pathologist in North Carolina. Having earned a bachelor's in chemistry, he attended the New York University School of Medicine. He went to St. John's University School of Law.

"Before law school, I had done internship and residency in pathology and then served two years in the United States Navy as chief of pathology at several naval hospitals in New England," he said in court, "and then after I left the Navy, I went to law school on the GI Bill and also went to work for the Office of the Chief Medical Examiner in New York City on their staff."

Jason's letter focused on the "cause" of Heather's death specifically. Here was Hembree's specialist giving his opinion regarding how Heather had died. After all, if she wasn't murdered, how could the state argue that in front of a jury?

It seemed to be a reach, considering that Hembree had admitted to strangling Heather and suffocating her with a plastic bag.

Dr. Jason reviewed all of the reports surrounding Heather's death, some thirty pages of documents, on top of 118 photographs. He read through Hembree's "discussion," as he put it in his letter, with police on December 5, 2009.

How "discussion" was spun from "admission" or "confession," the doctor never said.

Beam was most interested in a paragraph halfway down page one: *Cause of Death,* it read. It was Jason's professional opinion with "reasonable medical certainty" that Heather's death *[could not] be determined scientifically from the findings of the autopsy, including toxicological analysis.*

So the doctor was saying there was no way, based on the autopsy results from the state pathologist, to determine how Heather had died. He was putting into question the findings of the state and taking them to task for determining that Heather was murdered when the results of the autopsy did not, in his opinion, back up that assumption.

Jason went on to note the "basis" for such a contrary opinion. He used the state's pathologist's own words in her original autopsy report against her, noting how he "agreed" with the state's contention that the cause and manner of death are "undetermined." In Jason's view, the "only positive finding at autopsy," which was related to "the cause of death," was the existence of cocaine in Heather's bloodstream. He was certain the level of cocaine in Heather's blood at the time of her death was actually higher than the original autopsy had reported.

Why?

There is no definite lethal level of cocaine in the blood at autopsy due to chemical transformation, Dr. Jason claimed. It all depended, the doctor explained, *[on the] manner in which the drug is taken, the worst being smoking crack cocaine.*

He pulled back on the reins before actually blaming Heather's death on her cocaine use, stopping just short of saying she died from an overdose: *It is not possible to state with certainty that the cause of death . . . was cocaine toxicity [and it is] also not possible to rule it out with certainty.*

The doctor concluded that Heather could have died from a "variety of other means." He described Heather's "scrapes and bruises" as "minimal." He was sure none of them could *either account for the death or indicate the mechanism of the death.*

Dr. Jason said he'd studied everything. Given the "absence" of any major injuries or traumas to her body, the only conclusion he could draw was "cocaine toxicity" as the "most likely cause." As a well-established pathologist, with an impressive résumé, he told Hembree's lawyers it was his opinion that Heather, at age seventeen, overdosed on crack cocaine.

The idea that Hembree's defense team had found a doctor to claim Heather died of a drug overdose did not surprise investigators.

"You know, this was the only case that they had," Michel Sumner commented, "and, well, it was not a bad one. The fact that Mr. Hembree is a pathological liar—what is a lie and what isn't a lie?—and you have some doctor-for-hire telling them what they want to hear. . . . I thought it was a good defense." However, "We felt we had a great case with the evidence. But, of course, when you get to court, that is another thing entirely—a whole 'nother ball game."

Indeed.

CHAPTER 85

With a death penalty case, jury selection was going to take forever and become the key to get what each side wanted out of the trial. Every detail and motion and argument surrounding a capital case is drawn out. Lawyers and judges always err on the side of caution, which takes time. Many lawyers say the voir dire process is the most important part of any murder trial: choosing the right group of people to hear the case.

On October 3, 2011, that process began in the *State of North Carolina* v. *Danny Robbie Hembree Jr.* The Honorable Judge Beverly "Bev" Beal presided; Locke Bell and Stephanie Hamlin argued for the state; Richard Beam and Brent Ratchford were there to try and save Hembree's life.

At exactly 10:00 A.M. in Courtroom 4D, things got going. It was set to be a battle royale—what, with both sides not even agreeing Heather had been murdered. The most volatile creature in it all, of course, was sitting and enjoying this moment—*his* moment in the spotlight. Hembree had been waiting for this day. This was where Hembree was not necessarily in his element, as the cliché might reckon, but was ready and willing to use any means necessary to disrupt, manipulate, strong-arm, and make a mockery of the proceedings. He was game to turn Lady Justice's stage into a jester's court. As he sat, Hembree was plotting and planning one hell of a ride for everyone, making sure to turn the spotlight on him and keep it there.

There were 124 jury candidates present on the first day. In addition, the media presence in the courtroom was intense, all of whom were ready to report every tick of the clock. Everyone was under the impression that the trial was going to last longer than your average murder case. Death penalty cases were intricate, lengthy processes with more sidebars and arguments than most other felony trials. If Danny Hembree was found guilty, there would be the equivalent to a second trial for sentencing as witnesses were presented, arguing for and against death. The days would be long, exhausting, and emotionally taxing. Testimony was going to be graphic and technical.

Thus, after a long speech by Judge Beal to the jury candidates, it was off and running with questions. Those questions took ten business days, with a few breaks and a weekend in between, in order to whittle down that pool to fifteen jurors whom everyone was happy with: seven males, five females, with two additional females and one male as alternates.

On October 18 (two years to the day Heather was never seen alive again), a calm and pleasant fall Tuesday morning in Gaston County (the temperature would actually hit 80 degrees Fahrenheit by midday), opening statements began with DA Locke Bell attacking Hembree's character, letting jurors know what type of cold human being he was.

"February 2009!" Bell shouted, pacing the room in front of the jury. "Danny Hembree met Heather Catterton's mother at a local hotel. The mother brought along her sixteen-year-old daughter, Heather Catterton. . . . You will *hear* that that night he *bought* her . . . and had sex with her in that motel room. That was in February. . . ."

Hembree sat, content. His hair, now mostly dark gray

with patches of white, was well groomed and cut, fluffed up nicely as though he'd been to a salon. He wore a button-down tan dress shirt and Buddy Holly–style wired-rimmed glasses. He paid careful attention to everything going on around him.

Locke Bell spent the next few moments describing the night Hembree convinced Heather and Sommer to party. He talked about how Hembree manipulated the situation so that he could get rid of Sommer and her boyfriend, leaving him all alone with Heather.

"And you will hear how he got her to go down into the basement . . . dressed in a pair of socks and a little sweater that she put over her because she was cold." He paused, leaving jurors momentarily with that image of a teenager, cold, young, naïve, walking into a dark, musty basement toward her death. "You will hear that as she went into the basement, holding a flashlight, the defendant took a piece of wire . . . and wrapped it around her *neck* and pulled her to the floor. And then you will hear how he took his hand with a plastic . . . bag"—here Bell mimed Hembree's kill method—"and she fought for . . . fifteen minutes before she was dead."

It went quiet in the courtroom. These chilling words caused everyone present to listen with rapt attention.

The seasoned DA turned his focus toward Randi next. He spoke of the fight Hembree initiated with Nicole so he could get Randi alone. As he outlined this situation with Randi, so close to explaining how Hembree had managed to get rid of Sommer and her boyfriend just two weeks prior, it was clear this was one of Hembree's key MOs. He wasn't the type of killer to sneak up on a stranger and force her into an alley. He wasn't the type to stalk prostitutes—although he loved paying for sex—along rainy, slick downtown streets under the cloak of darkness, trolling along like the Green River Killer. He wasn't the type to follow a woman home from her job and attack her in a parking garage, or manipulate college girls by feigning injury. Hembree was a killer who found a situation he felt comfortable in, a victim he felt comfortable with, and then used the situation to his advantage. He would get his chosen victim alone, thus giving him the opportunity to act out whatever twisted and perverted fantasy he had on that day. When it came down to it, Danny Hembree was a killer without a conscience—a predator who thought about, planned, and plotted each murder with meticulous attention to his sickening needs.

Then, after a bit of detail regarding how Randi was murdered and her body set afire, Bell said, "You will hear from a lot of witnesses. You will see photographs. And you will get to see on video and hear Danny Hembree talking about it. At the end of this case, we will come back and ask you to find the defendant guilty of first-degree murder of Heather Catterton."

The DA spent exactly ten minutes outlining the state's case because the nuts and bolts of this prosecution were simple: Hembree *admitted* killing Heather. The evidence backed up his claims. And the state of North Carolina had that evidence ready to lay out, piece by piece, witness by witness. DA Bell standing, bantering on and on in some long-winded opening, making promises and pointing out pieces of evidence, would not convince a jury of anything. The case the state had made, Bell knew, would.

CHAPTER 86

Richard Beam took no time giving away Danny Hembree's case. And in retrospect, it was the only chance Hembree had: "Ladies and gentlemen, a lot of what Mr. Bell said is absolutely true." Beam had one of those clean-shaven, shiny Kojak-style heads. He was well respected in Gaston County. "The only issue is . . . what killed Heather Catterton? . . . There is going to be described for you the *injuries* that resulted from this violent assault—but . . . not *one,* will you hear the pathologist say. *No* problems! *No* contusions to the face! *No* bruises! She will tell you that the toxicology screen for Miss Catterton . . . had various items in it that could possibly be a cause of death." Beam had a way about him. He was able to convey his theories and thoughts with a delicate emphasis. He was passionate for his client's well-being.

"It's their burden"—he pointed at the prosecutors—"to prove to you what caused Ms. Catterton's death." Then, knowing he was facing what was an Everest-sized mountain to climb in getting around Hembree's confessions, the appointed lead defense attorney said: "You will have to determine the credibility of Mr. Hembree based upon everything you're going to hear. And, ladies and gentlemen, by the time this is over"—he took a brilliant pause for effect—"you wouldn't believe him if he said the sky was blue."

CHAPTER 87

Very much a woman who was not about to take any bull from anyone without speaking her mind, thirty-six-year-old ADA Stephanie Hamlin, a mother of two, did not have aspirations of becoming a prosecutor when she first considered law school. Hamlin's goal was to become a defense attorney and fight for the rights of defendants. That would all change after a traumatic event in her life. However, when she started, Hamlin said later, she was all about fulfilling her deep-seated liberal roots, which she had embraced and perfected while in college.

"My mom always said that early on, as a child, I talked about becoming a lawyer because I said I wanted to help people," Hamlin commented.

Young and pretty, sporting an athlete's body at five feet five inches tall, with brown hair and hazel-blue eyes, ADA Stephanie Hamlin was born and raised outside Boston. Her mother divorced Stephanie's father and moved them to Georgia. Stephanie attended law school at the University of Georgia, Athens. It was on that campus that she fell in love with "trial work" and became part of a team that produced mock trials in a tournament setting. They'd travel to different states to compete. Pretty soon, Hamlin found herself running the tournaments within the university, part of a group that decided who would be on the team. And it was during this period, between her second and third year of law school, when Hamlin's vocational aspirations—that switch from defense to prosecutor—took place.

She was in South Charlotte one afternoon at a family member's office. Hamlin would borrow the space two or three Sundays prior to a trial competition. She was alone one particular weekend and noticed someone "lurking" about. She had seen him before and thought he was a maintenance worker. But on this day, the man violently assaulted her.

"From that point forward," the ADA said, "I realized I no longer wanted to become a defense attorney—I just couldn't do it."

More than the crime committed against her, Stephanie Hamlin recognized through the experience of becoming a crime victim that there was a desperate need to educate first responders to crime scenes. She saw a hole in the system and hoped with her type A personality, work ethic, and determination—not to mention a desire and firsthand experience—she could fill it.

Late into the morning of October 18, 2011, the state's first witness, YCSO investigator Alex Wallace, was questioned by Stephanie Hamlin regarding his role in the investigation. Wallace walked jurors through coming upon Heather's body. This was the best place for the prosecution to begin: the call to go out and initiate the death investigation of a teenager. Through Wallace's testimony, ADA Hamlin was able to enter into evidence crime scene photos, including Heather's clothing, and the area where her body was found. This gave the crime scene context. It made it real. Heather's killer tried to hide her body. He'd tossed her clothes on the side of the roadway, hoping no one would find them. It wasn't as if she was walking along, fell, hit her head, and suddenly lost her pants, undergarments, and shoes, and then suffocated to death. Heather was stripped naked from the waist down and placed in the brush between two sewer pipes so nobody would find her. Just the fact that her clothes were found down the road indicated her killer did not want her or her clothing to be found.

The state required attorneys to sit behind their tables when questioning witnesses. The only time they could get up and do the traditional *Law & Order* walk in front of the jury box and judge's bench was during opening and closing arguments. This boded well for the prosecution and its concern for Stephanie Hamlin. Many on the state's side, including Detective Matt Hensley (who sat with the state every day), believed Hembree despised Hamlin with an intensity so deep he was going to lash out. Maybe Hembree hated all women—but it was clear to Bell and Hensley, who warned Stephanie on occasion, that if he could, Hembree would attack the ADA.

"Be careful when you're walking over near Hembree's table," Hensley warned Hamlin once. "Don't go near him. He could jump up and stab you in the neck with a pen."

"There were times when Hembree looked over at our table and appeared frustrated and, at times, confident, with a snake-like grin," Hensley explained. "Stephanie was sure he was going to lunge our way. . . . I guess I felt like that could have happened. . . . Hembree wanted to intimidate and make everyone feel uneasy. He's just a bully."

CHAPTER 88

Alex Wallace's testimony was cut and paste: a narrative from law enforcement perfectly placed, giving jurors an idea of how the case began.

After Wallace, the state called Walter Pettingill, a North Carolina State Bureau of Investigation (NCSBI) forensic examiner, who had provided the state with fingerprint cards, ultimately identifying both Randi and Heather. Pettingill's testimony was direct. He fingerprinted both girls, ran those prints through the system, and was able to obtain positive identification.

When Pettingill left the courtroom, Randy Clinton, the YCSO investigator who found Heather's clothes, walked in, raised his right hand, sat down, and told his tale of searching the road and coming upon that piece of red clothing near the bridge. Down the embankment, Clinton explained, they found additional clothing items that the YCSO later proved belonged to Heather Catterton. A ways more, Clinton said, there was a single tennis shoe. The way Clinton explained all of this, it sounded as though Heather's clothing had been dismembered and then spread about the woods and along the roadside on the border of South and North Carolina to throw investigators off. It was a graphic, ideal metaphor—one that the state could not have planned. The explanation of law enforcement finding her clothing humanized Heather.

It didn't take but a few minutes, but when Hembree's defense finished with its unremarkable cross-examination of Randy Clinton, Stephanie Hamlin indicated how late it was getting to begin questioning her next witness. Hamlin said she didn't want to fight the clock and be stopped midway, adding how "we do have another witness, but it's a witness that's going to take far longer [than the previous two] . . . and just for the purposes of interruption, we'd ask that that witness be called first thing in the morning."

"Very well," Judge Beal said.

CHAPTER 89

Stephanie Hamlin's first superior-court trial as a new SADA took place during the second week of September 2001. On 9/11, that now dark day in American history, there she was in the middle of her first jury trial and it was cut short, obviously, after the world changed and the word "Al-Qaeda"—rightly so—became a household cussword. Hamlin had just entered into her supporting role of ADA for the 27A Prosecutorial District. When Danny Hembree's name came across her desk, she had been with the office a little over a decade, yet the Hembree trial became the first time she tried a capital felony murder case.

Locke Bell was an elected DA. He had run unopposed, and had been at the desk four years. What made Locke Bell such an asset to the state was his background: a long, affluent career as a defense attorney. This gave Bell the advantage of looking at things from both sides. He knew what it was like to sit on the opposite side of the courtroom and, at times, defend the indefensible.

Hamlin called her boss a "big picture" type of DA, while she stayed focused on details. They didn't always agree; but in that regard, they worked well together.

"Locke is very smart," said one colleague. "He has very good ideas. A lot of people expect prosecutors to be very calm, but because he had been a defense attorney for so many years, Locke has that flare and flamboyancy about him—he's aggressive. He's straightforward. No joking around."

With Hamlin calling Detective Brian Bagwell at 9:29 A.M. on October 19, the second day of trial testimony, it was clear where the state was taking its case. Bagwell, a CSI with the YCSO, had attended Randi's autopsy. He could bring jurors into the autopsy suite without the glitz, glam, technicality, and often taxing detail a pathologist sometimes overdoes. Bagwell collected evidence from the autopsy, so he was there also to affirm the evidence chain of custody. And, as an added bonus, he had collected Heather's clothing evidence from the side of the road—bagged and tagged it.

Through Bagwell, Hamlin was able to introduce another round of photographs depicting Heather's clothing: how it was found, where, and what condition it was in.

Richard Beam had just a few inconsequential questions for the detective. Then, with Bagwell gone, Hamlin announced: "Your Honor, the state is going to call Sommer Heffner."

Here was the trial's first taste of a witness who could potentially hurt Danny Hembree, depending on which way the testimony went. Each witness for the state, of course, was offering his or her shovelful of dirt to drop atop Hembree's casket, but Sommer had that personal story of being with Hembree on the night Heather went missing. Besides Hembree, Sommer and her boyfriend were the last to see Heather Catterton alive. Hamlin and Bell knew Sommer's testimony had the potential to go either way, however.

As Sommer walked toward the jury box, Hembree stared at her. Sommer was a bit beaten and battered by her addictions. She wore a blue hoodie. Her brunette hair was streaked with blond highlights. She looked tired, but determined. Throughout the entire ordeal of dealing with the DA's office, Sommer had no trouble admitting her faults. She was well prepared to be brutally honest.

Sommer was twenty years old. She told jurors her story of meeting up with Heather on that day, bringing her boyfriend along, and then taking off with Hembree, Heather, and her boyfriend for a night of partying.

"Crack cocaine?" Stephanie Hamlin asked, referring to the drug of choice that night. "Do you—and I'm not going to ask who you got that from—but were you the actual person that got the crack cocaine?"

"No."

"Who was?"

"Danny."

"And what, if anything, happened at that point?" the ADA said, asking Sommer what Hembree's intent, by providing them with crack, had been. He wasn't paying for the drugs because he was a nice guy. They both knew "free" crack came with a price. In fact, before they could even smoke any of it, Heather had been expected to pay up.

"Heather and Danny went into a bedroom, and I'm guessing they did a date," Sommer explained. "And afterward, after they were done, we all got high."

"So at some point Danny and Heather were left alone together."

"Yeah."

"Did they remain in this trailer?"

"Yeah."

"And then after—how long did that last until they came back out? Do you remember?"

"About ten . . . fifteen minutes."

"And you described this as a 'date.' What do you mean, 'did a date'?"

"Had sex."

"And then you indicated that at that point, when they finished, you got high."

"Yeah."

"Did you have any crack cocaine with you?"

"No."

"Did you have any other drugs with you?"

"No."

"How did you get high?"

"I smoked the crack he bought."

Sommer established one of Hembree's core MOs when he was with Gastonia females: dangling crack cocaine in front of them as a lure to do what he wanted. He'd done this for years. He was known for it.

As her testimony continued throughout much of the day, Sommer explained how they arrived back at Hembree's mother's house after going to the Bi-Lo to exchange the coins for cash, and how the argument between Hembree and her boyfriend led to her boyfriend's ejection from Momma's house.

"And what happened?" Hamlin asked.

"We smoked some more," Sommer testified, "and then we ransacked his mother's house because he told me and Heather and [my boyfriend] that there was at least [two hundred] or three hundred dollars stashed somewhere, and we never did find the money. But he become real, real violent. Real mean."

"Okay. Now, you were going to trade partners and be with Danny. Was this something that you wanted to do?"

"No," Sommer admitted. "I was wanting to do it to get more crack." She had been bitten by the bug and was now in a position where she would do anything, within reason, to get more. Hembree was the man with the money and the means.

"You were going to do it to get more crack?"

"Yes."

"And you indicated that after you ransacked the house—well, did you find any money?"

"No. . . ."

"And what do you mean by 'he became agitated'? Who are you referring to?"

"Danny."

"And describe that."

"He was just threatening to shoot [my boyfriend] and kill him, and he ended up locking him out of the house. And I had to persuade, or beg him, actually, to let him back in because it was freezing cold outside. . . ."

Sommer explained the effect crack has on the body and the mind. Then she described how the night got late and Hembree left her boyfriend out in the cold again at the liquor store—this time, leaving him behind for good. This gave Hamlin the opportunity to walk Sommer into how Hembree was the last person to be with Heather before she went missing. Sommer explained how she'd begged Heather to get out of Hembree's car that night.

Through Sommer's believable testimony, the jury now had an image of Hembree and the victim driving off into the night alone.

The only impeachable part of Sommer's testimony was her reputation. The rest of it was the facts as she had recalled them. Sommer's boyfriend had backed her up and given police the same story.

Before the end of her direct examination, Hamlin asked Sommer if she recalled what Heather was wearing.

"She had on blue jeans, white tennis shoes, a gray hoodie, toe socks. I don't remember what color shirt she had on."

Hamlin showed Sommer photos of the clothing items and Sommer verified the photos.

* * *

Richard Beam cleared his throat and asked Sommer, as his first cross-examination question, how many times she spoke to the police throughout their investigation.

"Two or three times," she answered.

He asked the same question, substituting the DA's office for the police.

Sommer gave the same answer.

The big revelation Beam was working up to came down to Sommer, apparently, once telling police that her boyfriend had not smoked crack on that night, while on another occasion telling them he had. It was, in the scope of the facts Sommer had testified to, insignificant. The bottom line was that Sommer had given the police different facts at different times. This happens routinely. Cops interview sources. They recall various facts and different times. What Sommer didn't do, however, was change those facts, which would have been a red flag indicating possible deception. Sommer had stuck to the same story, time after time.

Beam kept his focus on this item as Hamlin objected. Through those objections and an eventual discussion without the jury present, Beam said he wanted to offer that Sommer Heffner was meeting Heather on that day to celebrate Heather's release from prison. However, Hamlin staunchly objected on the basis that their reason for meeting was irrelevant, and the prison comment would, of course, paint the victim in a bad light.

They battled it out. The judge finally said he was not going to allow it. It didn't matter that Heather had just gotten out of prison. In the judge's ruling, it was the object of cross-examination in a court of law to bring into account a witness's credibility. The victim had to be protected at all costs.

The jury returned. Beam got Sommer to admit she smoked a lot of crack that night and also drank a lot of booze. Then Beam was able to work into a question how Sommer had possibly taken some of Hembree's money that night, which was the reason why Hembree became angry.

Sommer did not respond to it.

As they went back and forth, it became apparent that all the defense had here was the possibility of bashing Sommer's reputation and magnifying her addictions, which she had admitted to readily.

As the morning drew to a close, Beam had Sommer focus on the things Heather had done to feed her own addictions, which Sommer had explained. This had all been said already—there was nothing groundbreaking about Sommer's descriptions of Heather trading sex for drugs.

A tactic many defense attorneys choose is bouncing around a lot. They skip from the beginning of a narrative to the end, back to the middle, and then back to the beginning, thus confusing the witness so she has a hard time recalling certain facts. If you're lying, this can work to catch you. But it didn't work here. Sommer was speaking her truth. It didn't make a difference how it was packaged: That night was a moment in her life she was never going to forget. Her best friend went missing and wound up dead.

As the lunch recess came, jurors were given their instructions not to discuss the case among themselves. They would all return, Beal explained, at two in the afternoon promptly. As the jury was excused, the judge indicated that the lawyers needed to hash out yet another issue Beam wanted to approach with Sommer.

Beam explained his concern about not being able to ask Sommer certain questions about Heather because, in the truth of the matter, Beam explained, "Our defense is that she (Heather) ingested huge amounts of cocaine and it killed her. The fact that she has a continuing cocaine habit is relevant to that issue. Not only that, I was under the impression the whole theory of the state's motive for my client was that he killed this lady because of her engaging in sex with black men. Unless I've missed that somewhere . . ."

The judge seemed a bit agitated. He explained that the state did not need to prove motive. Motive was not a legal requirement. The judge called it "rule number one!"

As the judge explained, Beam piped in, standing to his feet, tipping his head to the side, stating, "Well . . ."

"Have a seat, Mr. Beam," the judge snapped.

Beam said all he wanted was "parameters" regarding bringing in Heather's reputation.

Judge Beal said he understood, but it was up to the state to set those parameters with their objections.

That settled—however confusing it sounded—they broke for lunch.

After the recess, Sommer was back on the stand. Beam asked a few more questions; Hamlin a few follow-ups; then Sommer was cut loose.

In the end, despite all of the arguing back and forth about what she could and could not testify to, Sommer Heffner held her ground, kept her composure, and gave jurors her truth—as best she could recall it. And that was all, Sommer later said, she had wanted to do for a best friend who was never going to "get to meet my children."

CHAPTER 90

Among the questions prosecutors were asked when they headed into the first trial were these main concerns: Why not try Hembree for both murders at the same time? Why stage two trials when the state could have tried both cases together? Why put everyone through a trial all over again, once the first case was fully adjudicated?

ADA Stephanie Hamlin explained: "We did want to join Heather and Randi. We asked to do that, but the judge would not allow it."

The DA's office had "all these arguments set up with case law" setting a precedent. But as the law reads, cases tried together must show enough similarities to match up to each other.

"I still think we should have been able to do it," Hamlin commented.

One of the problems the judge faced was the scrutiny capital felony cases were given if a guilty verdict came in. The automatic appeal process begins right away. Judge Beal did not want anything to tip the balance and send the cases back to trial. He routinely erred on the side of caution— "And always ruled on the side of the defense, which is normal for a capital case . . . ," said one court official. It was a smart move. All the DA needed was one death penalty sentence. And with the judge allowing testimony and evidence of Randi's murder as part of Heather's case, it was as though Randi was having her day in court, too.

Shellie Nations did not mind when the DA spoke to her about this. As long as Randi ultimately saw justice, that was all that mattered.

The defense, strangely enough, did not want the cases to be tried together. That was something the DA's office found bizarre. Thus, in being able to try both separately, the DA had two chances at convincing a jury of guilt and death. Why wouldn't Danny Hembree argue against that?

When it came time to discuss which of the girls' cases should be tried first, Hamlin and Bell disagreed.

"For me, Randi's case was a slam dunk," Stephanie Hamlin explained with all due respect to her boss. "We had a cause of death. We had injuries. A punch to the nose. Blood evidence. . . . To me, it was a winner."

Bell felt extremely sympathetic toward Heather. He wanted to try her case immediately. The problem Hamlin saw was that they didn't have an official cause of death in Heather's case and it could be argued. Suffocation doesn't always show up on the body. It's a clean way to kill someone. This posed a problem.

The one thing they did have, however, was a defendant saying—and explaining on video in graphic detail—how and where he had killed the victim. Down in the basement of Momma's house, Hembree had given Hensley and Sumner a description, holding little back, regarding how he had killed Heather and she had struggled to her last breath. That alone was compelling evidence.

CHAPTER 91

The next two witnesses came and went quickly, setting the scene of Randi Saldana's murder. First up was Katherine "Kat" Sturgell, the unlucky horseback rider who stumbled upon Randi's corpse. Then YCSO captain Jerry Hoffman, who responded to the crime scene and secured it.

After Hoffman, the state put up Sabrina Gast, who had testified briefly the previous day. Gast was brought back in to finish the technical side of the pathologist's role in death investigations. Gast focused on Randi's autopsy and what the medical examiner's office had uncovered. The photos that came out of Gast's testimony were the most brutal and graphic yet. They depicted what fire does to the human body when it is only partially consumed. Randi was unrecognizable, of course, save for her tattoos and several sections of her body that did not burn. Yet the most chilling photo turned out to be how Randi had been bound by that severed lamp cord Hembree had admitted to using on her legs. One photo showed this in all of its indisputable horror: her burned, blackened feet; her red legs, bound midway by a piece of copper with the plastic coating melted off. When one looked at this, it was clear that Randi's killer took his time to bind her legs, took his time to drag her from the basement of Momma's house to his car, took his time to package her body up in a blanket, took his time to drag her from the car to the woods, took his time to pour gasoline over her body and ignite it—but not, as the photos explicitly revealed, to stand by and watch her burn into ash.

Shellie Nations was sick to her stomach. The tears. The gut-wrenching emotional distress. Shellie had been shown photos of Randi's jewelry during the investigation. Some of those (used here, too) were of Randi's charred corpse, her jewelry still strapped on her body. The DA's office had chosen to use 12 X 8 photographs that the jury could pass around and actually handle. This strategy worked twofold: One, to give jurors a close-up look at the carnage Hembree was responsible for; and two, so the gallery (family members of the victims, especially) did not have to be put through the often agonizing showing of graphic images on a large computer/video screen.

Bell took up questioning Gast. And for the most part, her testimony was clean and coherent, devoid of technical terms that few understood. Gast had a way of simplifying the most difficult aspects of medical evidence collection during autopsy and the coroner's role at a crime scene.

Another important feature of Gast's testimony was introducing the photos of Randi's tattoos.

Within about twenty minutes, Gast was finished, Hembree's defense not asking her one cross-examination question.

Then Eowyn Corcrain took the stand. Corcrain had an interesting job at the Medical University of South Carolina. Explaining her credentials, Corcrain said, "Well, I did a bachelor's degree in biology and then a master's degree in medical parasitology. . . ."

Parasitology is a subsection of pathology that involves field training and intense research "focused on identification of different sorts of blowflies. . . ." Blowflies are generally present in corpses left out in the elements for a period of time; yet, some will attach to a dead body minutes after it expires. Blowflies, within the cycle of life, are maggots. Blowflies, which generally feed on rotting flesh and meat, can smell a dead body from a mile away. They have a reputable purpose: cleaning the world of dead carcasses. But some see the irritating, metallic-colored, mechanical/futuristic-looking insects as a menace. After all, it is the "sheep blowfly" that reportedly causes the Australian sheep industry more than $150 million per year in losses.

"I did a postgraduate clinical certification in histopathology (examining tissue at a microscopic level) at the Medical University of South Carolina," Corcrain explained. "I completed the Medicolegal Death Investigator Training Program at St. Louis University in St. Louis, and then I did about a year-and-a-half on-the-job training before I took my current position."

Corcrain was the lead technician present at Randi's autopsy. She took a sample of Randi's blood. She then took that vial of blood and gave it to Brian Bagwell.

After that, Hamlin handed Corcrain over to Richard Beam, who promptly said, "We don't have any questions, Your Honor."

Ending the day, the DA's office called another evidence witness, whose testimony was once again left unimpeached by Hembree's defense team.

CHAPTER 92

In order to win a case one feels might be slipping away, one must find a beat and go with it. An attorney must consistently remind the judge that he doesn't like where a certain aspect of the opposition's case is headed; and he must, gradually, without being overbearing or irritating, beat that drum again and again. The repetitious nature of it says he is not happy with what's going on in front of him, which might ultimately be one of his issues on appeal.

For Richard Beam, as the October 20 morning session began without the jury present, his point of contention was the state's theory of motive. He felt the state was continually changing its position regarding why Danny Hembree murdered the women. He felt the state should stick to its original theory of hating the behaviors of the women. He felt the state should not bounce around and bring in witnesses reflecting a different viewpoint from that original notion Hembree had given law enforcement during interviews.

"Just briefly, Your Honor, to clarify some issues we had yesterday so we know when we're asking questions," Beam said first thing.

Stephanie Hamlin, while getting her things together for

the day and arranging them on the table, was struck by this comment. She stared at Beam. *This again?* she thought.

"We thought we understood the theory of the state's case being . . . what their allegations of motive were, and, obviously, we'll want to delve into those issues during cross-examination and things of that nature. Yesterday, there seemed to be some—I heard two *different* things from the state concerning their theory of motive. . . . We want to clarify that so we know the perfect questions to ask."

Beam wasn't challenging the state on its supposed motive flip-flop, necessarily; instead, he wanted to know where they stood so he could defend against it.

Hamlin was baffled: "Clarify what?"

"Is their contention this motive was . . . racially motivated or not? . . . We just simply want to *know* . . . how to frame our questions and ask them. We thought we understood that."

The judge thought it was a reasonable argument. "What says the state?"

Locke Bell stepped in, stating rather tersely: "The state says Danny Hembree murdered Heather Catterton in this first-degree murder. *That* is our position in this case!"

"Is the state going to contend that they are not going to argue the racial motivation of this?" Beam wondered. "They seemed to say that yesterday to this court."

Judge Beal had heard enough. Locke Bell had stated quite clearly the state's case against Hembree, who had sat rather quietly and almost invisibly during the past few days. His only actions seemed to be to lean over every once in a while to whisper something in Beam's ear, or to turn and blow Momma and his sister a kiss.

"Counsel," the judge said, "I don't see that this is a question for a judicial determination. I don't understand. Can you cite me some law that says I can compel the state to reveal its theory of the case?"

Beam didn't approve. "Well, Your Honor, when they're objecting to questions we ask, the court is called upon to make evidentiary rulings, correct? Now, yesterday, Miss Hamlin told this court they were *not* contending this was a racially motivated killing when we were talking about questions to ask Miss Heffner. Then two hours later, Mr. Bell stands up and says they *were*! In order for us to *effectively* cross-examine witnesses and frame questions *appropriately* and ask questions that are *legal* under the rules of evidence, which the court has to rule upon, if their motive is that . . . we should be allowed to ask questions about *that*."

Bell countered: "Your Honor, I believe Mr. Beam is wrong. Motive, as Your Honor stated, is not an element we have to prove. Mr. Hembree gives several reasons why he killed these two ladies, and he gives several reasons why he killed Miss Catterton—and there is *no* duty under the law"—Bell shook his head back and forth—"for us to pick which of Mr. Hembree's numerous—well, he says, 'motives' . . . but we don't have to prove motive."

Beam considered continuing, but he caved: "That's fine."

They picked up the argument again for several more minutes as Beam could not let the issue go, but eventually they agreed to disagree.

The state called GCPD detective Chris McAuley, who talked about the search conducted at Nick's house on the same night that Hembree was there. This allowed the state to enter photographs of Randi's jewelry taken from Nicole's possession.

As Beam began his cross, there was another break in the action so the judge could send the jury out and the lawyers could haggle over yet another inconsequential legal issue regarding potential future testimony.

When they returned to testimony before the jury, Beam

brought up a point through his cross-examination of McAuley that the jewelry had been found in possession of Heather's sister, Nicole, not Hembree, even though Hembree was present. Beam wanted this fact to be clear for jurors.

McAuley said it was.

After that, McAuley was done.

CHAPTER 93

By far, the most sympathetic witness to date came next. Shellie Nations was an innocent murder victim's family member. She walked slowly; her shoulders were slumped, and her head slightly bowed. It was hard for Shellie to be in the same room with Hembree—even worse, sitting in front of him, speaking about her sister's life and final days. Shellie didn't need a jury to confirm for her that Danny Hembree had killed her sister. She *knew*. By looking at the man, Shellie later said, she felt him gloating, taking joy in the process— and that alone told her he was guilty.

Within a few questions by ADA Hamlin, Shellie brought the trial back to the reason why they were all sitting there. What this trial was about, Shellie implied with her gentle tone and motherly demeanor, was how two women had been brutally murdered. These were not women who did not care about their lives. These women did not grow up with the dream of becoming addicted to drugs. Heather and Randi were sisters and daughters; they were considerate human beings who got caught up in the street life. They did not deserve their fate. No one had the right to play God in their lives and decide what was best for them.

"Okay," Hamlin said, "you indicated that [Randi] was charismatic and had a heart of gold."

"Yeah. Randi, she was the type of person if you asked her for something and you needed it, the way we were raised is you gave it, you know, and you gave it with good intentions." Shellie was sincere. She was her sister's voice now. "She never really wanted to hurt anyone with the intentions of hurting them," Shellie added, explaining how Randi was "the type of person if she knew . . . she hurt your feelings, she would come back and she would freely apologize and admit to her wrong in that." Furthermore, Shellie said, she and Randi had been raised together their "whole lives" and she could not "count on one hand the arguments my sister and I had."

Shellie talked about Randi's love for jewelry, and how there was hardly a time in Randi's life when Shellie could recall Randi not wearing jewelry.

After this introduction into Randi's love of bracelets, necklaces, and rings (especially), Hamlin handed Shellie photos of Randi's jewelry and asked her to verify the items.

There was one ring among other pieces of jewelry Shellie claimed "without a doubt" Randi owned "for fifteen years."

They moved on to Randi's tattoos.

As the first break of the new day came, the judge and lawyers discussed the idea of jurors writing things down, taking notes. This discussion went on and on. The judge even brought jurors in and questioned them.

When they were finished (not agreeing on anything specific), Shellie was asked to take the stand again and conclude her direct questioning. Over the next several minutes, Hamlin had Shellie identify several additional pieces of Randi's jewelry and point them out in photographs.

As Beam opened his cross-examination, he asked Shellie how often it was she saw her sister.

"Not every day," Shellie clarified. "Sometimes it may be once or twice a week. . . ."

"You knew her real well?"

"I knew her very well."

"You knew about the problems she had?"

"I did."

Then, being sure to get it on record, Beam said: "She had a drug problem?"

"Yes, she did."

Bell and Hamlin listened carefully, waiting for the opportunity to pounce, paying close attention to how far Beam was going to take this. There was, of course, a difference between mentioning a victim's lifestyle as it pertained to the case and bashing a victim for the sake of trying to make it appear as though her lifestyle had killed her.

Beam asked how long Randi's drug problem existed. It was a fair question.

"I know it started early, at least in her twenties. . . . We had put Randi . . . I, myself, had put Randi in rehab, and it's something she really wanted control of."

"She never managed to get control of it—did she?"

"She tried."

"I understand that she tried."

"Yes, she did."

"But she didn't manage to get control of it—did she?"

"As far as the drugs? No. She never got a hold on the drugs."

No sooner did the state wonder where Beam was headed than he asked Shellie if she ever went over to Shorty's house with Randi.

Not only had she never gone to Shorty's, Shellie said, but she didn't even know to whom Beam was referring.

Then Beam asked a stupid question: "You knew she had two children?"

"She had three."

"She had three?" Beam asked, shocked by this. He wanted to know where the children lived.

Shellie explained.

Beam said, "That's because of the problems Miss Saldana had?"

"Yes."

Beam used that as a bridge into the jewelry, but he realized Shellie couldn't give him what he wanted, which was apparently that some of the jewelry did not belong to Randi. So after a brief discussion, Beam looked down at his notes and said: "I don't think I have any further questions at this point."

CHAPTER 94

After a much-needed weekend break, on Monday, October 24, they were back at it. Before the end of that previous Friday, Locke Bell and Stephanie Hamlin had introduced what might be considered the apex of the state's case: Eddie Strait, the YCSO investigator who had interviewed Danny Hembree after he was arrested in December 2009 for those IHOP burglaries. It was that arrest and the interviews that followed—wherein Hembree admitted to murdering "those girls"—that the state had on videotape/DVD, which became the beginning of the end for Danny Robbie Hembree.

Through Strait's testimony, the state was able to enter those DVDs, on which Hembree had admitted to both crimes. The key witness for the state in explaining all of this was going to be GCPD detective Matt Hensley. Hensley was slated to give a detailed account of the admissions, thus setting up that walk-through video of Momma's house and the interviews Hensley and Sumner conducted with Hembree after the YCSO handed him over.

Before Hensley could do that, however, Strait concluded his testimony and the state called Rob Probst, the man behind the camera recording the walk-through interview. After Probst, Kimberly Miller, a scientist who received blood from the body of Randi's burned corpse and compared it to the blood found inside Momma's house—which was Randi Saldana's—was called.

As murder trials go, all of this testimony was brief and to the point, with very little contention or cross-examination from Hembree's attorneys. For the defense, the best it could do here was to allow the experts to speak their truth and get them off the stand as quickly as possible. All of this evidence was unimpeachable, scientific, nonexculpatory forensics, which, for the most part, was unchallengeable.

Tuesday morning began with more of the same: experts and blood evidence. All of it was based on the blood found inside Momma's house as compared to Randi Saldana's DNA. There was a discussion regarding Hembree's DNA being mixed with some of the samples taken. In pithy, unblemished, and easy-to-understand testimony by several experts, it was clear the science in this case backed up the videotaped admission/confession Hembree had made to not one investigator, but a total of five.

Watching this, one could say the state's case against Hembree had gone past overdrive and was now headed into hyperspeed toward the finish line.

CHAPTER 95

Matt Hensley wanted to see Hembree pay for his crimes ever since a few years back when Hembree, in such a cold and callous manner, admitted to killing the women as if they deserved to die. To Hensley, Danny Hembree was a sociopath without the possibility of redemption—a violent, bloodthirsty killer at the core of his being. Nothing was going to stop Hembree from killing again, Hensley was certain—that is, except life behind bars or a death sentence.

"I was well prepared for testifying in this trial and felt like I knew this case better than anyone," Hensley said later. "I was prepared to present the evidence and handle any questions the defense had to throw at me."

Despite all of his preparation, however, Hensley was "a little nervous upon taking the stand."

There were cameras in the courtroom, recording the trial for the nightly newscasts. All the local media was present, as well as a few national writers and producers. For Hensley, it seemed like the world was watching. He'd never been involved in a case with this much interest.

"This was the first trial I had been involved in with this magnitude of media attention," Hensley recalled.

Walking from the prosecution's table to the stand, Hensley told himself: *Just don't trip and fall or do something embarrassing like that.*

Funny what runs through your mind at pivotal moments.

And because he had prepped so well, once the questions came, he found that his "nervousness quickly subsided and everything went smoothly."

Hensley talked about how he had initially become involved in the case as a sideline investigator, playing off the YCSO's work, watching in the background as a case against Hembree materialized. Yet, no sooner did Hamlin and Hensley get a solid back-and-forth rhythm going than the judge stopped proceedings—at 11:31 A.M.—to take up a matter, he explained to jurors, he "need[ed] to . . . understand and determine before we can go forward with evidence in your presence."

Matt Hensley wanted to testify about something Hembree had said in his presence. The judge wasn't sure the comment fell under the guidelines of evidence. So out the jury went, once again, to wait for the lawyers to hash it out.

The argument was over what Hembree had said while they were serving the search warrant at Nick's house. The judge wanted to make sure it was not going to be prejudicial toward Hembree. So he implored Hensley, without the jury present, to tell him what Hembree had actually said.

"I heard Danny Hembree tell Nicole Catterton that she doesn't have to let us search her room or take any of her jewelry without a paper," Hensley clarified.

Beam thought a moment. He wanted to know what relevance that statement had in Hembree's case. Because what it sounded like to him, Beam insisted, was his client advising his girlfriend of her legal rights.

Nothing more.

Hamlin contended the statement showed how Hembree

did not want Nicole to cooperate with the search. Then, further along, the ADA said it also gave the impression Hembree didn't want cops to find Randi's jewelry, which they were searching for under the warrant.

They went back and forth before the judge overruled Beam's objection and asked that the jury be brought back in.

Hensley continued answering questions and was able to tell the jury what Hembree had said. With that now on record, Hamlin asked Hensley about the night of December 5, 2009—how Eddie Strait woke Hensley from a deep sleep and they realized the case was now in the hands of the GCPD.

What Hamlin wanted Hensley to point out before they viewed the interview in open court was the fact that Danny Hembree was "alert" and coherent. He could talk about things fluidly (which jurors would see for themselves once the video played). And he understood completely what was happening. Hembree wasn't some junkie coming down off a binge of heroin, scratching his legs, sweating, seeing invisible spiders crawling along the walls, begging for some sort of replacement narcotic. Hembree was a crack addict who had stopped smoking the drug many hours before. He was a man who had taken a nap, gotten himself something to eat, had several cups of coffee, and smoked several cigarettes. In addition, Hensley noted, Hembree waived his rights to an attorney. He wanted this confession to take place as much as they did.

The DVDs were introduced. What was important about the DVDs became a significant ruling by the judge regarding what the jury was going to hear on the DVDs. A painstaking process took place of editing and redacting (muting) portions of the DVDs to take out anything Hembree had discussed other than the two murders. None of the other crimes Hembree admitted to—the savage rape attack in the woods with his partner in crime, Bobby Johnson, the abduction and violent attack of the man from the hotel, the Deb Ratchford murder, and the Florida cases. None of those were part of the DVDs. The jury would not hear of Hembree's penchant for violence and his history of attacking and/or raping and/or attempting to kill people.

With all of that discussed, the state played the first DVD.

A break followed the screening of the first DVD. After a lunch recess and several arguments without the jury present, it wasn't until three o'clock that they were ready to begin hearing testimony again.

Although he'd be back the next day, Hensley was done for now. The state indicated it was close to resting its case, and called forensic pathologist Dr. Cynthia Schandl. Schandl had conducted Heather's autopsy. She was going to be an important witness for both sides. If Hembree's team didn't believe Heather was murdered, Schandl was the witness they'd want to begin broaching that argumentative theory with on cross-examination.

CHAPTER 96

Locke Bell took the bridles and questioned the state's pathologist. Bell knew Dr. Schandl could have a major impact on the state's case. So, about five minutes into his direct, Bell handed the pathologist a graphic image of Heather's neck.

"Do you recognize that photograph?"

"This is a photograph fairly close-up when Heather Catterton still has her sweatshirt around her neck," Schandl explained. "And you can see the necklace around her neck, and there's still some plant debris on her body, and so it's basically a close-up of her neck."

"Does that show some of the external—if I use the wrong words, please correct me—external trauma to the neck area?"

Stopping just short of giving Bell what he wanted, she said, "Well, what it shows is discoloration around the neck area. . . ."

That discoloration, of course, would fit neatly into an argument—backed up by Hembree's own words—that Heather's killer had carefully placed his foot on her neck to hold her down so the bag over her head could finish a job he'd started.

For the next few minutes, they discussed the clothing Heather wore and the clothing found down the road from her body.

Bell asked the pathologist to explain what suffocation is and how it is viewed on the body by a pathologist during autopsy, following up with, "The defendant stated he placed a plastic bag over Miss Catterton's mouth to suffocate her, putting a hand on her, and just held her and held her nose. Is there *anything* about the autopsy you did that would be inconsistent with what he said?"

"No, sir."

"Did you find *anything* in the autopsy that would show that she was not suffocated?"

"No, sir."

"Is suffocation something you can always . . . Is there always physical evidence of it? Or sometimes there's no evidence? How does that work?"

Dr. Schandl cleared her throat, shifted a bit to get comfortable, and leaned into the microphone. "Sometimes there is no evidence and sometimes there is some evidence." Giving an example of what she meant, she talked about how, in some cases, there "is a way to commit suicide by suffocation that won't leave any marks where you're using a plastic bag and, you know, this elaborate contraption. . . . The bag doesn't fall down on your face."

It was an important clarification. Why? The pathologist had put context into her argument. She illuminated that by seeing suicides of this nature come through her autopsy suite throughout the years, the research proved that not all suffocation deaths showed clear signs of trauma. "And basically," she concluded her thought, "you're just excluding oxygen. There's no trauma to anything. So you're not going to see anything on the body."

Beam took notes.

"Now," Schandl continued, "if somebody is smothering somebody with something, then you *may* expect to have some trauma, maybe, you know. It just depends on the situation—how much resistance there is, how much trauma you might get. But, again, there is the whole continuum between seeing absolutely nothing on one side and seeing all kinds of trauma on the other side. . . ."

Bell knew he had given the jury a reasonable explanation as to why they might not see Hollywood *CSI*-like trauma in Heather's autopsy: those purple, yellow, and red bruises that television crime shows play up.

Still, the DA needed to take it one step further. "Mr. Hembree stated . . . that he used a cord around her neck to bring her to the floor and then released it. Would the defendant's using a cord around her neck to bring her to the floor and then releasing it be inconsistent with your findings?"

"No, sir."

"At one point, the defendant said, he stepped on her throat. Would that automatically cause damage to the throat, which would be found in an autopsy?"

"Not necessarily. It would depend on many different factors. . . . There's a very popular form of massage where people walk around on people's backs and you're not leaving bruises. So, I mean, it really depends upon the level of force that was used so that you can step on someone and *not* cause bruising."

"The defendant stated he had given cocaine to Miss Catterton that night. Would that be consistent with your findings?"

"Yes, sir."

Bell introduced the autopsy report.

Schandl talked about how homicide is sometimes not always immediately visible in an autopsy, but a pathologist with concerns about a death might report the death as "pending." That term—"pending"—was designed to figure into an ongoing investigation law enforcement was conducting. If a pathologist, for example, was given a police report months after an autopsy she had conducted where the cause of death was still in question—and in that report a suspect confessed to the murder and admitted suffocating the victim—the pathologist would then amend her report, simply because she now had all of the facts in front of her.

The next point of contention Bell had to address was the amount of cocaine in Heather's system. Bell had to make sure the jury knew it wasn't a lethal amount, which Hembree's team was certain to argue.

One of the problems with proving an overdose is that there is no textbook lethal amount of cocaine available for experts. For each user, the amount she uses daily determines the amount that can kill her. It's different for every user.

"That's true," Schandl said to Bell's mention of this. "It can be very low, or it can be very high."

Users develop tolerances.

"If you were suspecting or looking to see if someone died of a cocaine overdose," Bell asked, "are there specific things you would look for in an autopsy?"

"Not necessarily. Because, again, the level can be anywhere. Now, if you have someone who is a chronic user or somebody who has heart disease, they're going to be at an increased risk for a sudden death from cocaine because they already have something wrong with the heart. . . ." Further, she said how cocaine, especially, "puts an increased stress on the heart by increasing your heart rate, making your vessels constrict and get smaller. . . ." The combination of an underlying heart condition and cocaine was a recipe for a sudden heart attack. "So, I mean, it's more likely that you have a cocaine-related death when you have a preexisting heart condition of some sort."

After a pause, the doctor added: "But, again, it's not reliable as far as the level goes, and there's nothing specific to look for. If someone takes cocaine over their whole lifetime or other stimulants of that sort, you can see chronic changes in the heart. . . ."

Switching gears, Bell said: "Let me ask you . . . did you

see any—in autopsy, looking at Randi—did you see any signs that she had a stroke?"

There was the concern that Hembree would claim Randi died at his house of an overdose or she had a sudden reaction to smoking dope and he panicked and hid her death by burning her corpse. Bell had to make it clear he was referring to both girls here.

"No, sir."

"How about any signs of a heart attack?"

"No, sir."

"So, did you see any of these signs that you say are sometimes there if someone has died of a cocaine overdose?"

"No. There was nothing to point to that. No, sir."

Bell asked a few more questions and handed Schandl to Beam.

CHAPTER 97

Richard Beam began his cross-examination by asking Dr. Schandl about the injuries Heather sustained around her neck and how the doctor had conducted a "layer-by-layer neck dissection" of tissue in that area. Then Beam handed the doctor a photograph depicting the procedure.

She studied it.

"And in the case of Heather Catterton, I did not see any hemorrhage to the strap muscles or the deep structures of the neck, and that is what this picture depicts," Schandl explained, further stating that the discoloration she found around Heather's neck could have been anything, and she could not "tell you what that's the result of."

What she had testified to under direct was that at the time of the dissection, Schandl did not have all of the information she needed to make an expert opinion regarding what had caused the discoloration, however. That came later, when the reports were in and she found out Hembree had admitted to placing his foot on Heather's neck. Then what had happened made sense to the doctor.

Beam asked Schandl if she had read a transcript of the Hembree DVD interview or watched the DVD.

She said she had not done either.

"And talking about the toxicology, I take it what you're saying is, any amount of cocaine is potentially lethal?" Beam asked.

"That is correct."

"And the scientific review of the evidence you determined from the pathological examination of Heather Catterton is that you still don't know what the cause of death was?"

"That is correct."

Dr. Schandl had never expressed an exact cause of death. In her opinion, after reviewing all of the evidence, she agreed with the defendant's version of suffocation.

Beam insisted, "I believe at one point . . . you told me that you exclude things, and there are several causes of death that are potential for Miss Catterton in this case. Is that correct?"

"Yes, sir."

"And that's simply because the physical evidence doesn't allow you to exclude everything."

"That is correct."

"And as part of your suspicions concerning possible strangulation, you spent a great deal of time examining that potential cause of death?"

"Yes, sir."

"Found nothing physically to support that as a cause of death?"

"Nothing conclusive. No, sir."

"Just as you can't conclusively determine whether she died of a cocaine overdose."

"I cannot."

Beam went into Schandl's education and experience. The doctor said she'd conducted over two thousand autopsies.

"And you teach other pathologists how to do the procedure, correct?"

"Yes, sir."

Beam was done.

Bell indicated he did not have any redirect questions.

They discussed putting Hensley back up to conclude his testimony, but Hamlin was concerned there were only fifteen minutes left to the day and Hensley's testimony would exceed that time. So, at 4:48 P.M., the trial was recessed until nine-thirty the following morning.

CHAPTER 98

"What helped us," Stephanie Hamlin later explained, "was the 404B evidence we were allowed to bring in." Despite not being able to come out and explicitly link the two cases of Randi and Heather, or add the Deb Ratchford case and make a claim Hembree was a bona fide serial killer, the state was allowed to present evidence of Randi's death to the jury through the testimony of witnesses (404B). This gave them the opportunity to show a pattern: Heather and Randi died in similar ways, by the same hand. So if a juror didn't buy into the cause of death for one of the girls, he or she could look to the other and maybe realize how Hembree had used the same modus operandi to lure and then murder, which might allow that juror to take a leap on the other case.

"They (both murders) were close in time and proximity," Hamlin explained. "So although we didn't show a pattern necessarily, we did show his motives . . . and that right there was huge. If we had only been able to use Heather's case and not Randi's, it might have been more of an issue for us."

Beside the normal, built-in trepidation all prosecutors face going into trial, obtaining a guilty verdict was not a concern for the DA's office. What they were most apprehensive about was the "capital" aspect of the trial.

"It's very rare in North Carolina right now," Hamlin added. "People just don't want to give [a death] sentence that often anymore. So we were worried about that. But altogether, capital cases are just so, so long. . . ."

There had been moments during the voir dire process, while picking a jury, when Hamlin questioned a potential juror and the questions she asked had made some jurors cry.

"And I'd wonder, 'What am I doing to make them cry?' "

It was the seriousness of a capital case: A juror is judging someone for taking a life and placing death in his hands, and then that juror is placed in the same position. For some, the emotional weight of making that decision is extreme.

Proving the cause of death in Heather's case caused Stephanie Hamlin some stress; as did the fact that it was a capital case, with the hours she'd spend away from her husband and children. It was a lot to take on.

"In retrospect, I should not have worried about the cause of death," Hamlin commented. "It was like a day-to-day thing. With a regular murder trial, you present evidence and you wait for a verdict. With a capital case, you have to pace yourself because it's *so* long. You have to be on all the time."

Hamlin had prosecuted many trials involving blood and trace evidence, so it was second nature for her to put on a witness and enter those same types of exhibits through the witness's testimony. And in Danny Hembree's case—as Hamlin considered how the state's side of presenting evidence and witnesses was coming to a close during the second week of trial—the number of exhibits had run into the dozens.

CHAPTER 99

In a moment of rare courtroom solidarity, surely a rarity in capital cases, after the judge asked if Hembree and his team had viewed the DVDs Hensley was going to be referring to during his resumed testimony on October 26, Beam responded, "Your Honor, as much as I hate to admit it, I think Miss Hamlin is correct about what she's done. It does look like they have redacted everything that either was not corroborative or impeachment."

To make sure, Judge Beal asked: "Is there anything that has been redacted that the defense wishes was not redacted?"

"No. Honestly, Your Honor, it was appropriate."

After a brief discussion about his upcoming testimony, Hensley was asked to sit and complete his direct.

As they got going, they discussed the transcript of the first interview Hensley and Sumner had conducted with Hembree.

Hensley agreed the transcribed interview was a good reference and the transcript reflected the content of the interview.

Then Hamlin had Hensley tell the jury how he had un-

covered additional evidence in Hembree's vehicle: those bracelets that Hembree had told Hensley would be there to "prove"
he killed Randi.

Hensley concurred that he found Randi's boots exactly
where Hembree said they'd be inside Momma's house. Hembree had even pointed to them on the video.

They spent some time talking about the location of
Randi's boots and how the boots were packaged as evidence.

Hamlin entered a transcript of the Hembree interview
into evidence.

From there, they talked about the ride-along Hembree
did with Sumner and Hensley. It was all there, straight from
Hembree's own tongue:

Crowders Creek Road.

That bridge on the border.

Heather's clothing.

The gas station where he said he purchased the fuel to
burn Randi's body.

Where he saw Randi walking along the road and picked
her up.

Where he dumped Heather's body.

The abandoned trailer.

Apple Road—Kings Mountain State Park.

Momma's house.

Some words spoken can never be taken back. This evidence, despite any argument Danny Hembree now lodged,
was one of those moments.

Late in the day, after several arguments, without the jury
present, regarding what could and could not be said,
Stephanie Hamlin concluded her direct and handed Hensley
over to Beam.

Richard Beam began at the moment Hensley received
the call from Eddie Strait.

After that, and a brief discussion about times, Beam

asked Hensley about Randi's death and if Hembree first indicated to him it was "the result of a conspiracy."

"Yes, that's what he told us . . . ," Matt Hensley agreed.

"He told you that Stella Funderburk . . . Heather's mother, [Stella's sister], who was Heather Catterton's aunt, and Bobby Mercer. That is the right name, correct?"

"Yes, sir."

"[His] nickname is Shorty. He said he had paid him to kill Miss Saldana. Correct?"

"That's what—yeah, that's what—I think both paid him. They conspired to have her killed."

"He told you how they had paid him roughly an eight ball of cocaine to kill Miss Saldana, correct?"

"Yes."

"I believe he told you half up front from Shorty, correct?"

"That's what I recall him saying, yes."

It seemed Beam was on a slight roll here, bouncing along, maybe not knocking on the door of doubt, but heading toward the neighborhood where it might exist. Momentum. Every lawyer likes to establish a push and then drop whatever bomb he has in his arsenal.

"This was information you were interested in, correct?" Beam asked.

"Yes. We listened to everything he had to tell us."

After discussing how Hensley interviewed each of the so-called conspirators separately during the GCPD's investigation, Hensley said he and the DA's office did not see any evidence of a conspiracy. Just wasn't there. In his opinion, Hensley explained, after studying all of the information they collected about a possible conspiracy, he and Sumner "felt like [Hembree] was just trying to take them down with him."

Not being able to rattle Hensley about a potential conspiracy the GCPD might have missed, Beam moved on. And for the next twenty minutes, he attacked minor things that had already been established as uncontaminated evidence against Hembree:

Randi's boots.

The jewelry.

Hembree saying he "stood on Heather's neck for five minutes."

How they collected blood from Momma's house.

How Hensley and Sumner wanted to "keep" Hembree talking for as long as they could.

Hembree's requests for a Raleigh prison and impounding his car.

How many interviews they conducted with Hembree.

If Hensley had ever seen a copy of Heather's autopsy before December 5, 2009. (He hadn't.)

Back to the conspiracy for a few beats.

How long Hensley spent going through the transcript to make sure "it was right"—which brought them to the end of the workday.

In all, Beam made zero progress. He simply went over what jurors already knew and would never question, anyway. These were routine matters for a cop of Hensley's caliber.

Matt Hensley came across as a clean-cut, young, eager, straight-laced cop who, if nothing else, dotted every *i* and crossed every *t* meticulously. Hensley was a cop who followed the book. Left no stone unturned. This was clear as he talked through the case he, Sumner, and the GCPD had built against a guy who had admitted killing two girls.

Hembree had given them a map of his madness. Their job was to follow it and make sure he was telling the truth. And in the end, when all was said and done, Hensley said repeatedly, Danny Hembree's admissions checked out.

CHAPTER 100

First thing the following morning, October 27, Hensley was slated to take the stand again and answer more of Beam's questions. There was an early argument, without the jury present, over a reference to "the Florida girls," as Beam labeled it, within the transcript and DVD. That mention in the DVD and transcript had been redacted. There was a feeling from Hembree's camp that they wanted to, for some unspecified reason, bring this out in questioning. It was dangerous territory for Hembree, the judge warned. What was he getting at? Why offer up what could potentially be more damning evidence? Why give the jury precedence? It didn't make much strategic sense to anyone, it seemed, except to Hembree and his team.

Throughout the two weeks of trial, quite shockingly to everyone on the law enforcement side, Hembree had not made a spectacle of himself or the trial. Many thought he would. Sure, he had given dirty looks to witnesses and law enforcement, and had given the impression he wanted to jump out of his skin and attack someone. But he was rather quiet and behaved himself.

No one knew what Hembree was planning, obviously, but he would live up to his reputation—and exceed it—of being a meddler in the coming days.

Beam was wondering if he could use this Florida evidence to Hembree's advantage. The judge questioned Hembree himself about it, asking if the defendant understood the implications of bringing Florida in and the impact it might have on his case. The judge called the move "a great risk."

Hembree said he knew of the dangers, but he wanted to move forward.

"Do you understand this could all go against you? It could be a mistake in strategy. Do you understand that?" the judge reiterated.

"I understand that."

The judge asked again.

Hembree gave the same answer.

The other problem the judge had was time: It was now 11:20 A.M. The jury had been waiting patiently since coming into court almost two hours ago now. The judge said he was going to "seek forgiveness" from jurors for keeping them locked in a room for so long.

By 11:27 A.M., the jury was back. Just in time for lunch.

"I beg your forgiveness" were the first words out of the judge's mouth before explaining the reason for the delay.

Matt Hensley, who had gone off to wait, was back on the stand.

Beam brought Hensley up to that Florida moment of the interview that was conducted on December 5, 2009, which allowed the defense to enter into a discussion with Hensley about it.

"And one of the things that York County detectives told you about . . . was that [Mr. Hembree] had mentioned killing two people in Florida."

"Yes, sir," Hensley answered.

"And you, of course, asked Mr. Hembree about that, right?"

"Yes, sir."

"And you continued to ask Mr. Hembree about that pretty much throughout the whole time that you had him for the interview and in the car and things of that nature, right?"

"Yes. It was brought up several times."

"And your purpose for that was you were trying to gather details from Mr. Hembree about that to relay them to other law enforcement officers, correct?"

"Yeah, we wanted to know about two bodies—dead bodies—in Florida."

"Okay. And you had asked him—and, at first, he told you he didn't want to talk about it, right? Or he gave you a little bit of information?"

"Yes, I believe so—"

The judge interrupted. "Let me ask you to pause just a second. Now, members of the jury, I need to give you some instructions in regard to another one of our rules. . . ."

Judge Beal explained.

With the go-ahead from the judge, Beam asked Hensley about a timeline and location for the murders in Florida.

Gender of the "alleged victims."

How Hembree's admissions of Florida were mixed with his confessions about Randi and Heather.

How Hensley and Sumner got Florida law enforcement involved and how they came up to North Carolina to speak about the cases.

How it was also part of the conversation about Shorty and the conspiracy to kill Randi.

How Hembree had talked about ending his own life during that time period.

Then Beam's motive became clear: They brought in this information so Beam could prove—by example—that Hembree was prone to giving false confessions. He enjoyed making up stuff.

Again, Beam seemed to develop some momentum, but it ran out of gas as he had no climax, no big reveal, no finale of any sort to prove Hembree was lying. The implication was that Hembree told law enforcement lots of things. Yet, the truth of the matter remained: Hembree's claims were either backed by evidence or not.

Beam concluded his cross by asking Hensley how many additional murders he had investigated based on what Hembree told them.

"About seven or eight," Hensley said. This sounded big. The obvious follow-up would have to be: "How many murders did you prove Danny Hembree had committed beyond Heather's and Randi's?"

But Beam didn't ask that question and, in fact, indicated he had nothing further for Hensley.

Hamlin had a few redirect questions.

Beam had no recross questions.

Hamlin had a mini-conference with Bell. Then: "That's the evidence for the state, Your Honor."

They rested.

The judge called a recess.

It was near three o'clock in the afternoon when the defense called its first witness.

Stella Funderburk—Heather's mother, Hembree's old flame—walked into the courtroom.

CHAPTER 101

It was obvious that fifty-one-year-old Stella Funderburk had been a striking woman once. However, time and life had taken its toll. Stella appeared tired. She came across as a witness who did not want to be there. Not long after Heather was found, Stella told a local-television news station how she'd cried "every day. . . . I wake up, crying, and [go] to bed, crying." Some saw this as too little, too late. After all, Stella had invited this monster into her daughter's life.

Stella spoke in a near whisper and had to be told repeatedly to speak up and move closer to the microphone.

She said she had known Danny Hembree for thirty years.

"Do you have an addiction to controlled substances, ma'am?" Beam asked.

"No. I wouldn't say I had an addiction."

"Do you use controlled substances?"

"I have."

Beam asked what kind.

"Crack cocaine, alcohol," Stella admitted.

As they talked, Stella claimed Heather had been "in a relationship" with Shorty and that Shorty was supplying Heather with drugs.

"Were you aware of how she supported her drug habit?"

"Well, she was living with [Shorty], yeah. I knew he was going to give [her] drugs."

"Did she engage in dating other men?"

"No, not that I know of."

"You didn't know anything about her dating other men?"

"No."

"Did you engage in a conspiracy to hire Mr. Hembree to kill Randi Saldana?"

"No, I didn't."

They went on to talk about Sommer Heffner, her daughter Nicole's issues, how Hembree dated Nicole and often stayed at Nick's during the time Heather and Randi went missing, and how Hembree gave Nick and Stella rides.

Then, as quickly as they got started, Beam had nothing further.

It was unclear why Stella had even been called.

Bell took on Stella's cross-examination. Stella had an immediate distaste and bitterness in her tone as the DA asked when Hembree first met Heather. This was that alleged encounter Hembree had said he had with Stella and Heather inside a motel, when he supposedly purchased Heather from Stella.

Stella didn't see it that way: "She went down there (meaning to someone's house). . . . All of us went down there. Nicole wasn't with us, and Heather had told me she had been with Danny. . . . And so, anyway, I went to use the phone to call somebody to come and get me and Heather. When I come out, her and Danny had done left."

"And you and Danny were dating or seeing each other at that time?"

"No! We weren't dating."

"When was the last time y'all dated?"

"We never really dated."

After this, Stella had nothing to share that amounted to what would become important for jurors deciding Hembree's guilt or innocence.

Bell asked at one point: "And you told the police on November twenty-third that it was about six to eight months prior [to Heather's disappearance] that you knew that Danny had sex with Heather?"

"Yes."

"And that she would have been sixteen at the time!"

"She was seventeen in March. I don't know if she was . . . I don't know if she was . . . I thought she was seventeen, but she might have been sixteen."

Bell seemed frustrated. He'd ask a question and it seemed Stella answered a different one, so he ended his cross.

Beam had a few additional questions, one of which seemed to attack Stella's and Heather's characters: "Did you engage in sexual activity for cocaine?"

"No."

"Did you know that Heather engaged in sexual activity for cocaine?"

"Heather told me afterward, yeah."

"You say she told you 'afterward.' Was that [with] Danny or was that with someone else?"

"Excuse me, what?"

"When you said Heather told you afterward she engaged in sexual activity for cocaine, are you referring to with Danny, or are you referring to somebody else?"

"Yeah, with Danny."

CHAPTER 102

Over the next two days, Richard Beam called several witnesses who did little to put a shine on whatever swampland in Florida he was trying to sell jurors. There was no clear indication as to what Danny Hembree's defense was getting at with the questions Beam asked or the witnesses he called.

Near the end of the day, October 28, Beam put up Bobby Mercer.

Fifty-two-year-old Mercer said just about everyone he personally knew called him by his nickname, Shorty.

Then there was a little issue of the clothes Shorty wore on this day: prison scrubs. Beam asked and Shorty made it clear he was serving time at the Gaston Correctional Center in Dallas, North Carolina, for possession of cocaine.

Shorty called Heather "a friend." He said she stayed at his house "every now and again" and he provided her with cocaine "every now and again."

"Was she engaged in, to your knowledge, was she engaged in the activity of trading sex for cocaine?" Beam asked several questions later.

"Well, when I met her, that's how the rumor was in the street—that when I met her, she were like that."

"When you met her, that was the rumor in the street?"

"Yes, sir."

"Did you ever give her cocaine?"

"Yes, I did."

"Did you ever trade with her cocaine for sex?"

"No! I didn't treat her that way."

There was an odd intensity about Shorty. He spoke with a strange authority that was hard to put a finger on. He came across as a guy with secrets; yet, someone speaking his truth, no matter how it affected people. This was the way Shorty lived his life. He had no trouble admitting his faults, crimes, talking about his lifestyle. Sure, there were things Shorty held back—criminals always downplayed their role in things, to a certain extent—but there was also a profound sense of "I don't care" in his voice, "You can't hurt me."

One interesting fact that came out of this conversation was how street-smart and desperate Heather was, this for a sixteen-year-old. Here she was hanging around with a fifty-year-old man (at the time), even living with him on occasion. Shorty said Heather would hide out at his house a lot, dodging authorities and people she didn't want to see. To Shorty, Heather was a lost soul—a kid whom people used and abused.

After all was said and done, Beam only managed to prove with Shorty's testimony that Shorty had given Heather cocaine—a fact that had been established on day one of the trial.

Smartly, Bell got right into Randi's case with Shorty, asking questions that led Shorty to place Hembree in Randi's presence on the day Randi went missing. Shorty tried stopping Randi from leaving his house that day, he explained, but she wouldn't listen. He also talked about the fight Hembree and Nicole had—the impetus for Hembree taking off after Randi left.

The jury was getting a picture of Hembree's MO: Two women went missing; Hembree was with both; and both wound up dead.

After a series of questions about that fight Hembree had with Nicole, Bell asked: "And you accused him of killing [Randi and Heather]—didn't you?"

"Yes, I did."

"And I believe you told the police that when you did, you had a knife in [your] pocket in case he tried anything."

"Yes, I did."

"He wouldn't look you in the eye, would he?"

"No, sir."

Beam objected. Sustained.

After a few more questions, Shorty was excused by both attorneys.

CHAPTER 103

There was the underlying tension of whether Danny Hembree would testify. Would he be able to stifle his hubris enough to make a sound choice for himself in this regard?

Most narcissists would jump at the opportunity to sit and take control of the stage. They believe what they have to say has the power to change minds, to sway jurors, to control the situation and the outcome. They think their truth is the only truth; and they are, beyond a doubt, smarter than anyone else. The Mayo Clinic, in a brief, plain description, defines narcissistic personality disorder (NPD) in its simplest form, noting how the narcissist *[enjoys] an inflated sense of [his] own importance . . . Those with [NPD] believe that they're superior to others and have little regard for other people's feelings. But behind this mask of ultra-confidence lies a fragile self-esteem, vulnerable to the slightest criticism.*[1]

Indeed, a clinical description that seemed written on the basis of Danny Hembree's life.

[1]See http://www.mayoclinic.com/health/narcissistic-personality-disorder/DS00652, where this quote is derived from, for additional information about NPD.

Still, could Hembree walk away from this courtroom without speaking? Was he actually capable of it?

When Hembree's defense announced its decision, ADA Hamlin was not the least bit surprised.

Hensley, on the other hand, wondered what in the name of justice Hembree was doing?

"First of all, I was shocked to hear he was going to testify. . . . The news came just before the lunch break, so we had some time to process it. I was excited. I couldn't wait to hear what he was going to say, because I couldn't imagine what he could say that would assist him in his effort to convince the jury he was not guilty."

CHAPTER 104

Danny Hembree wore a button-down, striped dress shirt and thick-framed glasses. He walked toward the stand with that incredibly pompous, cocky stride he'd become known for by anyone spending even the slightest amount of time with him. With all of the local media attention the case garnered, with everyone in the room focused on him, Hembree enjoyed this moment in the spotlight more than he had, perhaps, any other since his arrest. Many wondered what he had to gain by opening himself up to cross-examination. But here he was, in all of his inflated glory, waiting to be sworn in.

In all fairness, actually, this was Hembree's only chance. By this point in the trial, Hembree was looking at a guilty verdict as his best-case scenario, and a death sentence as the worst. He would need to begin to mount some sort of lifeline and hope to reach one juror.

"All right, sir," the judge said. "Now, have you talked about this decision to testify with your attorneys?"

"For the last two years," Hembree said defiantly.

"Do you understand that if you do testify, you can be asked questions on cross-examination?"

"I understand that."

"And do you understand those questions can include questions about your prior convictions for a period of ten years in the past for crimes for which the punishment is more than sixty days in jail or prison?"

"Yes, sir. Intend to open the door for that!"

"All right. Now, after thinking about this matter and talking about this matter with your attorneys, is it your decision to testify on your own behalf in this case?"

"It is."

Hembree was told to stand and wait for the jury to walk in and follow the clerk's instructions.

"Do you wish to swear on the Bible or be affirmed?" the judge asked.

"It don't make no difference. The Bible will be aw-right."

Hembree had an odd way of speaking, making motions with his mouth and lower jaw as if he had dentures and they were loose. It was distracting.

"All right. Sheriff, let's bring in the jury."

Several additional instructions were given by the judge as the gallery stirred. With Hembree, this part of the trial could go two ways: smoothly or out of control. There was no middle gray area in the world where Hembree lived.

The judge asked if he was perfectly clear that in agreeing to testify on his own behalf, his testimony could "arise questions about matters you said to the police officers other than what's already come into evidence?"

"Your Honor," Hembree explained, seemingly frustrated, "the way I understand it is, that's the only way the truth can get out." He paused. "So I welcome it."

Stephanie Hamlin sighed.

Danny Hembree started at the beginning: his birth, his marriage, his divorce, his kids, where everyone lived, where

he had worked, his substance abuse issues. He said he did
not discriminate when it came to using drugs: "Just about
anything you could get high on or drunk. . . ."

Beam worked his way into:

Hembree's lifetime dependency on prescribed medications (some for back pain, others for his various psychiatric
ailments).

How many doctors he'd seen.

The prescriptions he'd been given.

How much booze he drank every day.

Who his friends were.

How he met Nicole.

How long he had known Stella.

That trailer park and the abandoned trailer he frequented.

When given the opportunity, Hembree trashed Nicole,
airing all of her issues. There was a clear "I'm better than all
of these people" tone to Hembree's posture and voice. The
implication was that yes, he hung around with Stella, Nick,
Heather, Nicole, and some of the others. He even liked some
of them, sure. But he was much smarter, far superior, and
they should count their blessings he allowed them into his
life.

Beam asked about Heather and how they wound up together in October 2009.

"I was stock sober," Hembree said for some strange reason. "I done seen Heather in October, because October the
eleventh—the reason I know is because Heather was in
prison in Raleigh, and she was scheduled to get out the seventeenth."

He explained how Nick was ill then, so Stella "made
some phone calls" and wound up making "arrangements
where [Heather] could be released a week early" to go see
Nick. "But prior to that . . . I was scheduled to go pick Heather up on the seventeenth. . . . It didn't pan out."

"Well, did you . . . After she was released on the eleventh,
did you see her during that week?"

"Yeah."

"Where did you see her at?"

"Well, I had talked to her on the phone. She called me when she got home. . . . She was there with Nicole at her daddy's house, and she wanted to know if I was going to come over. I was at my mom's house, and . . . I told her no. I had something else to do and I would catch up with her later on during the week. . . . And I didn't see her again until the seventeenth. . . . Heather was over at [Shorty's] house. I had never met [Shorty] or been over to his house at that time."

Hembree then explained how he, Stella, and Nicole drove to Shorty's "and picked Heather up, and from there we went to West Gastonia and picked up [some other friends]."

At some point that day, he took everyone to see Nick in rehab. Stella drove, Hembree said, because he was too drunk.

"Now, what happened when you got back to Nick's [house]?"

"We was just messing around. Me and Nicole was sitting in the bedroom where Nick usually slept . . . and Stella [and her boyfriend] were in the living room . . . and Heather was there doing something . . . [and] I got into a fuss with Nicole about something. She wanted me to buy her [something], and I told her . . . I probably would have bought her some. . . . But when she would take a lot of [them], she would get pissed off and start smacking me around, you know, beating on me. . . . She's kind of got a violent temper . . . so I didn't. . . ." When he refused, Nicole left.

Beam and Hembree talked back and forth. Hembree was playing up his role as leader of a group of people that, by his view, was going nowhere in life. Hembree made it sound as though he was their only hope, as if they all looked to him to make decisions and give advice as to how to lead their lives. He took pleasure in being the Svengali—someone they turned to for everything.

Then Beam asked about that night with Sommer, Heather, and Sommer's boyfriend. How had it started?

Hamlin and Bell listened, took notes, shook their heads, clearly disgusted by most of what Hembree had to say. There was an agenda here within Hembree's testimony. It was heading somewhere. He had an end game up his sleeve.

"Well, I went into the bathroom with Heather," Hembree explained, totally contradicting what he had said on several previous occasions, and also what Sommer had testified to. "I talked to her on the phone, and I wanted to be with her, so I told her, 'Do you want to go hang out? Let's party.' And she said something to the effect that, well, she didn't want to leave Sommer, because Sommer was her friend, and they just . . . they hadn't seen each other in a while." He did not recall Sommer being inside the bathroom with him and Heather, as both Sommer and Nicole had reported. "And I said, 'I don't have a problem with that. Sommer can go with us.' And Sommer said, 'Well, I can't leave my boyfriend because, you know, I just can't do that, you know.' So I said, 'Well, hell, he can go, too.' "

The way Hembree made it sound was like they were talking about going bowling. He described the conversation like a cordial, general discussion. He did not recall all of it taking place in the bathroom as Heather sat in the tub.

Hembree said the Marlboro Man pulled up to Heather's house and blew his horn. So he went out and asked him what he wanted. Hembree had never seen the Marlboro Man before.

The Marlboro Man said he wanted Heather.

Hembree told him to leave and call Heather later.

Beam then digressed. He asked Hembree how and when he first met Heather.

"It was Valentine's Day . . . 2009. And the reason I remember that is because I got paid fifteen hundred dollars that day for a roofing job, and it was Stella's birthday, and I was dating Stella at the time. Matter of fact, I done give

Stella fifty dollars for her birthday to buy some boots with, which she later spent on [something else]." He stopped talking. "Okay. I've lost my train of thought here."

They moved on.

Hembree mentioned driving to a hotel on that day he first met Heather.

"Did you go in?" Beam asked.

"I did."

"What did you do once you went in?"

"I looked around," Hembree testified. "There was a big bed sitting there, and Heather was sitting on this side and some blond-headed girl sitting on this side." He used his hands to elaborate. "And they were in . . . They wasn't naked, but they, you know, they was putting their clothes back on. And there was, like, four or five old men sitting in chairs down beside this bed." Hembree claimed Heather and the other girl, by his best guess, were "putting on a show. I guess they (the old men) was paying to see it. . . ."

Bell didn't like where this was heading and objected.

"Objection sustained. Question?"

"Anyway, once you observed the gentlemen sitting in the chairs and the girls . . . putting their clothes on, what did you do at that point?"

Hembree recognized someone in the room as a drug dealer he knew. So he decided to purchase some dope and "made a deal . . . and I bought, like, a quarter ounce. And I asked him about the girls. I said . . . 'I want a girl.' And he said, 'Well, I ain't got nothing to do with those girls. They can do whatever they want to do.' So I went to the bathroom, and the blond-headed girl, she done come back out. I talked to her for a few minutes, and I just really didn't like her. And so when Heather came back there and I seen her in the light real good, she looked like she was about twelve years old with a lot of makeup on, and I asked her how old she was. She said, 'I'm nineteen.' And I said, 'You're not nineteen.' "

Hembree asked Heather for identification, he said. "You

know, I was just kind of kidding around, right? And she basically told me to go fuck myself, and she walked out of the bathroom. So I left without either one of them."

It was sometime later when he met Heather again, inside another motel room. She was with Stella. Playing it down on the stand, Hembree testified he hadn't actually tried to purchase Heather from Stella, but asked Stella if he could have sex with her daughter. He said Stella was shocked by this statement, but she ultimately said what Heather did was her own business.

Beam led Hembree back onto that night when Hembree left with Sommer and Heather and Sommer's boyfriend, George. Up to a certain point, Hembree stuck pretty much to the script he had written with Hensley and Sumner—a script, mind you, Sommer's version of the same events backed up.

When it came time to explain the "show" Sommer and Heather put on for Hembree and Sommer's boyfriend inside the abandoned trailer, however, Hembree wanted to clarify something. He wanted the jury to know he was not some guy who went around dangling crack in front of the neighborhood girls, hoping they would trade sex for it. That was not how he operated. He was not that type of person.

"Did you give it (crack) to them?" Beam asked.

"Yeah, I did. I gave it to them," Hembree said.

"Was that before or after they engaged in their show?"

"Let me see if I understand your question. I want to elaborate. At *no* time was the cocaine in exchange for sex. There wasn't no deals made like that. The cocaine—originally, I bought it for Heather and me, but Heather wanted her friend to come, so I shared my cocaine with them."

"Everybody understood there was going to be cocaine and sex involved, right?"

"Obviously, I mean . . . yeah."

Hembree talked about going back to Momma's. She wasn't

home, so they partied inside the house. And then, after they started looking for the money, Sommer's boyfriend had swiped some or all of it, Hembree believed. He got pissed and threw the boyfriend out. Hembree said the boyfriend handed him a twenty-dollar bill at one point and apologized for stealing it.

Then Hembree bought more dope before he "got rid of" Sommer's boyfriend by ditching him at the liquor store.

After scoring the drugs, Hembree told Sommer either to come alone and get high, or go back with her boyfriend, but he and Heather were going back to Momma's house.

Sommer, of course, chose the former.

"And once you got back to your mother's house, what did you do at that point?"

"We went back to my den and watched porn and smoked crack and had sex."

"And then what did you do?"

"Well, like I said, we smoked dope and had sex till probably until two-thirty or three o'clock in the morning. Then we . . . left the den and went to my room and got into bed."

"What did you do once you got to your room?"

"Well, went to sleep. But it took, you know, hour, hour and a half. I was drinking, you know, while I was in there. I usually went to bed with alcohol and woke up with alcohol."

"What was Heather doing?"

"She was laying beside me."

Up until this point, Hembree's story of the night was somewhat probable and could line up with the evidence that law enforcement had and what Hembree told the YCSO, Hensley, and Sumner.

Hembree, however, proclaimed a new revelation after Beam asked him: "Now you indicate you were laying there in bed and went to sleep. When was it that you woke up?"

"Ten, eleven o'clock the next day."

"Anybody else there in the residence at that time?"

"No."

"When you woke up, where was Heather Catterton?"

"She was still laying beside me."

"What did you do when you woke up?"

"I slipped out of bed, went into the kitchen, got me a beer, and came back to the room. Attempted to wake Heather up."

"When you attempted to wake Heather up, what, if anything, did you discover at that point?"

"Well, I touched her and she was cold. She wasn't stiff or nothing, but she was kind of heading that way. I knew she was dead."

It's important to note here that in Hembree's new version, Heather would have been dead for up to seven or even eight hours. It takes, generally, only three hours for rigor mortis to begin setting in. The peak of rigor takes place at around the twelve-hour mark. If Heather was cold, as Hembree had testified, she had been dead for at least six hours. (Under a conditional room temperature of 70 degrees Fahrenheit, a body does not become cold in fewer than six hours.) Rigor would have been firmly set. Heather's body would have been unmistakably stiff to the touch. There is no way one could say "she was kind of heading that way" with regard to rigor in this situation.

Danny Hembree was clearly lying.

"Once you saw that, what did you do?"

"Drank my beer, tried to figure out what I was going to do, kind of freaked out, weighed my options, and made a selfish decision."

"What did you decide to do?"

"I decided to hide her body and not tell anybody that she died in my bed."

"Why did you do that?"

"Well, I can't think of any circumstance or anything that would make me call the police and tell them that I've got a dead female in my bed that died probably from drugs that I had given her, with my criminal background." He repeated how "selfish" it was to think of storing Heather's corpse in the closet before dumping her body in the woods. "But it was a no-brainer for me."

"Why did you tell the police on these DVDs—that the jury has seen—that you killed her?"

"I was picked up for armed robbery in Gastonia. . . ."

With that answer, Hembree broke into an elaborate, illogical story about how he faced years behinds bars for several armed robberies he had recently committed after being picked up. So he thought, *What the hell. I might as well admit to murdering the girls, and the heat will be taken off the robberies.*

The obstacle in telling this lie was getting around the notion that burglary and robbery were more severe crimes than first-degree murder. If what Hembree was saying was to be believed, this had to be his thought process. It didn't make sense. It almost seemed—as it rolled off Hembree's Southern tongue—as though the questions Beam fed him to arrive at these answers made Beam look naïve and gullible. The theory was so preposterous and implausible that it had to insult the jury's intelligence.

Yet, in Beam's defense, he had to cater to his client's wants. This was Hembree's story. Beam had to go with it, regardless of what he believed personally.

"Well, you're doing what's best for you to tell the police that you killed Heather Catterton—how is that the best for you?"

"Well, here's the way it is, and this is what went down. When I confessed to the police there, I confessed to *multiple* murders and other multiple felonies. As I started telling Detective Hensley about my crimes, the stories started getting bigger and bigger and bigger, and I was just saying stuff as I went along. But the reason for that was . . . to gain leverage and bargaining power with the district attorney's office in Charlotte. Because when I went back over there, I knew that I was going to have to deal with these armed-robbery charges." He explained the robbery charges, adding, "By me confessing to all this other stuff, it took the light off of the armed robberies, and they was willing to negotiate with me. . . . I successfully negotiated them down to . . . two of the armed robberies into one charge, run it consecutive with the other charge, and got an additional forty months added to my time."

In Hembree's crooked way of thinking, he thought he could sell to jurors that he "wasn't worried about these confessions, or none of that stuff," as he put it, "because when all the evidence came out and everybody looked at everything, and I explained and they got a chance to see the whole truth, and not the practiced and polished, edited version that the state has presented with stuff blacked out and muted and all that stuff—"

Bell objected. Hembree was trying to use what the jury could not hear to his advantage. He couldn't have it both ways.

The judge overruled the objection.

CHAPTER 105

When she heard Hembree spew his latest version of why he had confessed to a murder he did not commit, Stephanie Hamlin thought: *Well, this is par for the course.* "At that point in the trial," she added, "nothing Danny Hembree did surprised me. His explanation as to . . . [the murders] was so absurd to me. I could not believe it."

Bell and Hamlin would have their chance to challenge all of this nonsense soon enough; but for now, this was still "The Danny Hembree Show."

As he continued, Hembree stated that the walk-through with Hensley and Sumner throughout Momma's house was a "performance."

Hembree explained further by saying, "I mean, I was selling Hensley a car." He played down those moments in the video when he described killing Randi and Heather and showed them where he hid their bodies. "This was a big feather for [Hensley's] cap, the biggest case of his entire career—with enough media attention to share with Locke Bell, there, to give him the spotlight. It was a big case. They were under pressure from the media to solve these cases."

Beam asked: "Did you use a plastic bag to suffocate Heather Catterton?"

"No, I did not."

"Did you use a cord to take her to the ground?"

"No, I did not."

"Did you stand on her throat in your mother's laundry room in the basement?"

Hembree laughed under his breath. "That's ridiculous. Absolutely not. Did not."

"Did you kill Heather Catterton?"

"I did not."

After several more questions, the judge requested a lunch recess.

Even if Hembree was now saying he did not kill Heather, he still had that one little problem of how Randi died (a second dead woman in his presence). One woman addicted to drugs who overdosed in his house was slightly plausible—if one tossed out the three separate confessions Hembree had made, on top of all the evidence. However, a second woman whose body was torched by Hembree, and whose blood was found inside Momma's house, was something else entirely.

"It was clear they were going to harp on the toxicity level of cocaine in Heather's system," Hensley recalled. "I didn't think the jury would believe it. But I remember sitting there thinking, 'Okay, Danny, how are you going to explain Randi's death?'"

That was the question.

After a lunch break, Beam set up Hembree's explanation of Randi's death by asking Hembree to go back to that night he met up with Randi.

As Hembree talked his way through, he made sure to trash Nicole and Stella whenever the opportunity arose. And when it came time for Hembree to explain how he had taken off with Randi, he said the argument he had with Nicole was part of a plan to get Nicole out of there so he could be alone with Randi.

"I decided just to pick a fuss with Nicole," he testified. "It was real easy to do. The least little thing would piss her off, so that's what I did. After Randi had left, pretending like she was going to meet her ride—[but] to meet me down at the end of [the street]—I picked a fuss with Nicole, and then I just walked out of the house, got in the car, went up to the end of the street, made a U-turn, and came back down."

"When you came back down, what did you do?"

"I stopped and let Randi in the car."

"And when you let Randi in the car, what was your purpose in doing that? Why did you do that?"

"I was going to go have sex and party."

Beam asked: "What happened when you got to that trailer?"

"We went in the bathroom and lit a candle, and we did a couple hits." The way he made it sound was as if he and Randi were on a date. "I remember it was kind of cold. It wasn't, like, freezing, but it was cold. . . . She asked me, if she stayed all night, would I take her to drop her off at her baby daddy's house the next day?"

"After she said that, what happened then?"

"Well . . . we was going to go down to . . . where it was warm out. Like I said, it was kind of chilly. The bed that was in the trailer, there weren't no covers in that trailer. We went down to [a friend's house] and then I realized . . . it was a weeknight. . . . [But my friend] has a son . . . and when he's there, [my friend] don't have nobody over. No drugs, no alcohol, except for him. . . . So I told Randi, we can go to my momma's house, but I would have to sneak her in because, you know, Momma just wouldn't . . . let me bring women to the house. . . ."

Hembree said he drove around "to the back and pulled up under the sundeck, next to the swimming pool, and told Randi to wait." He went up the steps onto the sundeck, and through the sliding glass door. Hembree could see Momma "sitting at the bar, reading—the same place she's been reading for thirty years, the same time every night."

Hembree knocked on the door and Momma let him in.

He sat down.

"We talked for a few minutes, and I smoked a cigarette, and I got up and went down to my den down the hallway and unlocked the window and pushed it up."

Then he told Momma good night.

"And I went back, but instead of going to the den, I went out . . . the front door. I left it open and I told Randi to come on. And my intention was to bring Randi in the front door and down the hallway. But then I thought better of it, you know, because if Momma was to come through the door to use the bathroom or something, I mean, it was right there. She would see, and, you know, that would be the end of that plan. . . ."

"And did you get her into the house through the window?" Beam asked.

In Hembree's version, he and Randi had made a fun time out of getting Randi into the house through the window because they were both high and drunk. It was difficult, he said, because the window was so high off the ground.

"But finally," he continued, "when I got her up there, she started in the window and she hit the . . . bridge of her nose" on the metal portion, cutting herself. "It was hardly bleeding. I think, you know, just a little bit. When I done that, she said, 'Son of a bitch'—I mean, not cussing me, but just that was what she said. So she goes on in, and I went back around to the front door, went in, shut the door, went down to the den, put in a porno, and we sit there, started smoking and partying, waiting on Momma to go to bed."

Hembree said they spent "three or four hours watching porn, having sex, and smoking."

Hembree claimed they smoked a lot of crack. "When I smoke cocaine, I like to have sex—and I like to smoke and then have sex, and I like to smoke and then have sex . . . and that makes the crack last—the cocaine lasts a lot longer, instead of just sitting around, smoking it all up, and then, you know, have sex."

"And you said this went on for three or four hours?"

Hembree agreed.

"Well . . . did you finish smoking the crack cocaine that you had, or what caused you to stop that activity?"

"When Randi . . . ," Hembree started to say, but he trailed off and paused. Then, without Beam prompting him, he said: "When I killed Randi."

Hensley, sitting, watching, listening to every word roll off Hembree's tongue, was shocked by this statement: "When I killed Randi." After all of that buildup by Hembree, all of those careful explanations of the night. What was he now trying to say?

"I was confused initially," Hensley recalled. "I couldn't understand where he was going with it."

"Well," Beam said, seeing that Hembree had brought it up and maybe tripped on his own words, "how did you kill Randi?"

Hembree said Randi was sitting on the couch. Once again, he mentioned (just in case anyone had forgotten) how they had "been having sex and we were watching pornos. . . ." But then, with very little fanfare, Hembree made this incredible statement: "I was performing oral sex on Randi while she was sitting on the couch—and I had her leg up over this shoulder, and I had my right hand up around her throat . . . and I just killed her, man."

So he had strangled Randi by accident, without trying, without realizing it—all while performing oral sex on her.

"I wasn't trying to kill her," Hembree stated. "I was just trying to increase her orgasm. I mean, we had done it earlier."

Ah, Hensley thought, *here we go.* This was the Hembree that Hensley knew all too well. "When Hembree told the absurd story about the sex act he and Randi were engaged in that resulted in Randi's death, I thought it was a joke. I couldn't believe what I was hearing, and this was actually happening in front of me. I thought it was a mockery. I recall putting forth an effort to control my expression as I looked around the courtroom to see the expression of others after hearing this story. Unbelievable!"

"Laughable" was perhaps a better way to describe what many sitting, listening to this absurd story, felt as Hembree embarked on a maddening fantasy of strangling Randi while having sex with her. But on and on, he went, telling this incredible tale as though jurors were going to buy it simply because he was telling it.

"When you said you 'had done it earlier,' what do you mean?" Beam asked, setting Hembree up.

"Well, we was having sex. Randi was riding, like, cowgirl style on top, and I was back, and she had put her hands around my throat. She had been massaging my chest and put her hands around my throat. And while we was having sex, she just squeezed off the air. And when I had an orgasm, it was euphoric. I mean, it was just fantastic. . . ."

Hembree now claimed Randi died while he was performing autoerotic asphyxiation (AEA). This practice is generally associated with cutting off the blood supply to the brain while masturbating. The lack of oxygen to the brain is said to cause sensations increasingly intensified as the airflow to the brain decreases. Accidental death is sometimes attributed to AEA because a person's judgment at the time is impaired by the act itself. Hembree was saying Randi had introduced him to it that night by performing it on him, and so he was reciprocating by doing it to her while he performed cunnilingus.

"Well, how did you discover that Randi was actually dead?" Beam asked.

With a straight face, Hembree gave his most ridiculous answer of the day: "During the time that I was performing oral sex on Randi and choking her, I was masturbating at the same time." He went on to say they climaxed "at the same time, and then I just laid my head down on her lap to rest and catch my breath. . . ." And when he "looked up," Randi's head was "leaned over like this, right here, and her eyes were just glazed over."

He actually felt the need to act this moment out for jurors.

So, in a panic, after realizing something was wrong, Hembree checked for a pulse, didn't find one, and then "pulled her down on the floor." He was "going to give her CPR, but as soon as I got her down on the floor, her bowels moved, and I knew she was dead."

This was the second time Hembree had mentioned that one of the dark spots on the carpet in the den was feces attributed to Randi. He'd explained it during that walk-through with Hensley and Sumner. The problem with the story, however, was that it did not hold up to forensics.

"It was never proven," Hamlin said of that supposed fecal matter stain on the carpet, which Hembree pointed out. "And we never found her clothes. There was a spot on the floor, but it was blood."

CHAPTER 106

Danny Hembree went on to discuss how he hid Randi's body in the basement of Momma's house and then decided to transport her out to the woods so he could burn her corpse. He told jurors he employed Nicole to purchase the gasoline. Why he did this, Hembree said, was out of necessity.

"To cover up the evidence . . . like I said . . . self-preservation kicked in. . . . I cut across the state line because that would be in . . . two jurisdictions, and anytime you get two agencies from different jurisdictions—especially from, like, two different states—you know they're not going to share everything and it kind of confuses the investigation. And to be honest with you, I know this sounds sick and cruel and cold, but I was pissed off at Randi for dying, and, I mean, that's just being honest."

When Hembree took Randi out into the woods and lit her body on fire, he said he knew the end was near and he would eventually be caught. So he decided to embark on a two-week bender to end all benders and then commit suicide by cop somewhere at the conclusion of his run.

"What did you do for the next couple weeks?"

"I couldn't really tell you, exactly. I just stayed stoned. It was surreal. It was just like walking underwater. I mean, I was just mind fucked. I mean, I don't know. I can't tell you, man."

The remainder of Hembree's direct examination was, above all, a man now saying he had lied about nearly everything he had told police. He even came up with an excuse for lying about killing both girls, saying he felt admitting the murders was better than going down for the robberies. Yet, when it came time to talk about those robberies, Hembree stressed through Beam's questioning how he had used a toy gun, as if it made the crimes less threatening and less fearful for those on the receiving end.

Hembree said he did not kill anyone in Florida. He made it up because he believed it would give him more "leverage" when cutting deals with the DA's office.

Then he and Beam broke into a conversation about how many medications Hembree had been on throughout his life. They discussed how many psychiatric hospitals he had been admitted into—and how often he lied to police throughout his life.

And then Richard Beam was done.

CHAPTER 107

After a much-needed break, ADA Stephanie Hamlin, at first a bit nervous about questioning Hembree, got right into it with the admitted killer: "So your story since this morning is, up until a few minutes ago, that you got caught for some robberies with a plastic gun, and when you got caught for those, you thought it would be a good idea to confess to *two* capital murders to help you with your robbery sentence?"

"That's *your* interpretation. I disagree with about half of what you said," Hembree snapped back.

Hamlin knew right then how easy it was going to be to rattle Danny Hembree. Any nervousness she might have had going in had now subsided. Just that one response told Hamlin how "much of a jerk" Hembree sounded like. He was going to alienate jurors. He'd already disrespected jurors repeatedly by cussing on direct.

"But that's what you testified to?" Hamlin said.

"No!"

"You said you were playing the system, so you decided to confess to those two murders because you knew it would help you with the robbery charges in Charlotte."

"Um . . . that's pretty close. Yeah."

Hamlin made her point again: Hembree's answer sounded as stupid as it was. The guy confessed to two murders (punishable by the death penalty if found guilty) in lieu of confessing to several robberies? It was preposterous. Did Hembree think jurors were ignorant?

"And then you said you kept the story going because you wanted to put a feather in Detective Hensley's cap?" Hamlin asked.

"No," Hembree stated. "You've misunderstood what I said. Would you like me to clarify that?"

What did the prosecutor have to lose? Hembree was digging his own hole. "Sure," she said.

"Actually, what I said was, Detective Hensley, being young and overzealous, this case would have been a big feather in his cap with enough room and glory to go around for the DA to get some media attention, who everybody knows is a media hound, anyway. . . ."

Hamlin asked the obvious next question: "So you told Detective Hensley you killed Heather Catterton and Randi Saldana so that Mr. Bell could get some media attention?"

"No. That's not what I told him. That's just a spin-off of what I told him. The reason I told him was to protect myself."

Hamlin knew one of her greatest assets in questioning Hembree was going to be asking the same questions twice.

"Protect yourself from these robbery charges in Charlotte?"

"Absolutely," Hembree said. "I was looking at life without parole. I'm no worse off now than I was then, before I confessed."

"You're no worse off confessing to *two* capital murders?"

Hembree said: "That's exactly right."

"So, from what you just told this jury, within a three-week time period, you were smoking crack and having sex with two women, and they just by chance died at your momma's house with you."

"I don't think it was by chance."

They discussed Randi's death. Hamlin questioned Hembree about the blood in the den and wanted to know if he was telling jurors it was all from a nick on the bridge of Randi's nose, which she had acquired while climbing into the house through the window. Was this what he wanted jurors to accept?

He said it was. And the reason why there was blood in the den, Hembree said, "When I choked her, it forced the blood out. . . ."

After being asked, Hembree denied there was any blood found on the couch.

Hamlin reminded the defendant that forensic testing, which several experts had testified to, proved it was Randi's blood on the couch.

Hembree still wouldn't agree.

They moved on.

Hamlin wanted to know how Hembree choked Randi.

"We were having sex. I was performing oral sex on her. She was sitting on the couch. I choked her with this hand, right here," Hembree said, sticking it out.

"So you were performing oral sex on her, and you were doing *what* to yourself?"

"Masturbating."

"And you took one hand while you're performing oral sex and you reached all the way up while she's sitting on the couch?"

"It wasn't that big of a reach."

"And you killed her with your one hand while you're performing oral sex *and* playing with yourself?"

"I believe that's my testimony," Hembree said with a modicum of sarcasm. "But I don't recall saying, 'playing with myself.' I believe I said, 'masturbating.' "

The hatred he had for this woman questioning him revealed itself in his tone and demeanor. ("He was very demeaning on the witness stand toward me, and the jurors picked up on it . . . ," Hamlin said later.)

"Masturbating?" Hamlin asked again.

"Yes."

"And then all of a sudden," she added, raising her voice, "you notice that she's dead and that she's bleeding?"

"Yeah."

Then came the thunderous denouement Stephanie Hamlin had been leading up to: "And [the blood] got somewhere on the couch *and* down in the closet?"

Realizing he'd been tripped up by his own words, Hembree said: "Uh-huh."

Stephanie Hamlin asked Hembree about a confession he claimed to have made to police about a murder in Buncombe County, North Carolina. It was a confession Hembree had thought he had given to the police. It was a good indication that Hembree had forgotten how many women he had murdered throughout the years.

They traded barbs, back and forth. Each time, the ADA added one more shovel filled with dirt atop Hembree as he fell deeper into what was becoming a bottomless pit. Every time Hembree thought he was one-upping the prosecutor with his snarky, snappy remarks and weak explanations, Hamlin came back with a fact that shut him down. Take those Florida cases, for example. Hamlin pointed out that the first time Hembree had ever mentioned making up those confessions was during his direct examination. He had never said anything about a false confession where Florida or Heather or Randi had been concerned until he sat on the stand to pronounce his innocence.

Hembree balked at that accusation. He said it wasn't true.

But all the jury had to do was look at the record and see that it was.

At one point, Hamlin asked Hembree about the detail he had gone into when discussing the murders of Heather and Randi with law enforcement.

"Yeah, I'm pretty good at that," Hembree responded.

"Pretty consistent detail," Hamlin pointed out.

"Yeah. I mean, if you're going to tell a lie, you want to stick to it."

"And, in fact," Hamlin added, making a direct point, "when there were times that Detective Hensley would ask you questions, he may have gotten [things] wrong, but you actually corrected him to make sure he was getting this true story right."

Hembree said, "Yeah."

Hembree denied every violent crime he had admitted to police, including those attacks in the 1980s with his crime partner Bobby Johnson. Through this line of questioning, which became nothing short of a verbal-sparring match, Hembree's hubris got the best of him. He had a tough time controlling his anger and what was a growing hatred for the ADA.

"Why did you confess to those [other crimes]?" Hamlin wanted to know. Why bring in additional crimes? If you're making up confessions to throw off the DA on some robberies, why make matters worse by bringing in more violent crimes?

"Well, this last time I just throwed it all in: four, five, six murders, couple kidnappings. I mean, they were eating it up. I was laying it down. They was picking it up."

"So you were doing this for fun?"

"No!" Hembree raged. Hamlin had poked him one too many times. "I've already explained why I'm doing it, to you. Are you dense, lady?"

She laughed.

Hembree continued: "I told you I done it because I needed to use the leverage to beat those robbery charges. . . ."

"So you admitted to two capital murders, a rape, a robbery, another beating, to help you out on some robbery charges you had with a plastic gun?"

"Among other things, yes."

"How did confessing to the 1981 and 1980 rapes and robberies and assaults, how did that help you with your . . . robberies?"

"It was just more crimes. . . . It was just the story got bigger and bigger as it went along."

Hamlin cleared something up by stating how Hembree had escaped from custody on five separate occasions, not three, as had been originally reported.

Hembree agreed, almost to the point of bragging about his expertise in that area, saying, "It's not my fault that they're dumb enough to go for my bullshit."

This led to a long-winded description by Hembree of how he had outsmarted and roughed up prison guards in order to make the escapes.

The intensity of the questioning grew as it continued. In a very smart, veteran move, Hamlin asked Hembree about his aggression, which seemed to be pouring out of him as he spoke, along with the aggressive behavior he had displayed throughout his life. She queried how it related to the confessions he had made and what he had explained to a psychiatrist during one of his evaluations.

"No, lady," he said, referring to her insistence that he had told his psychiatrist he was aggressive and had a propensity for violence. "I'm talking about the confessions and all the false information that I give to authorities to play the game with them. It's documented. It's a thirty-year history."

"Thirty-year history of you talking to doctors about your impulse—that you can't keep your impulses under control!"

"I don't know what you're talking about!" Hembree shouted.

"You don't remember that . . . thirty-year history back?"

"I was speaking of the thirty-year history of my thoughts, confessions, and saying just whatever is convenient, playing the game with the police. I would have to see the documents. In fact, I have probably three thousand mental-health documents in my cell down there, and there's no way possible that I can understand or remember all of them. . . ."

Hembree went on to say he could recall only being charged with one assault in all of his fifty years, adding he's "never been combative or anything with the authorities"—this after admitting to fighting with guards in order to break out of jail. "Now, if you take all the mental-health stuff that's there, and all the statements that I made and stuff that's written down, a lot of it is true, and I was actually probably seeking some kind of help, but basically it was bullshit, too, to get certain types of medication in prison."

Wanting clarification, Hamlin asked, "So, what you're saying is, you say bullshit when it's benefiting you—like when you're facing two murder charges—you're going to come up with bullshit and say it from that stand?"

"I don't understand that. Are you making a statement and asking me to agree with it, or are you asking a question?"

"That was a question."

"I don't understand."

As evidence, Hamlin offered several reports from Hembree's doctors proving he had discussed being aggressive and violent, behaviors he had denied.

Still, with his own words in black and white in front of him, Hembree would not admit to any of it.

Hamlin asked Hembree about one specific report detailing how in 2009 he checked himself into the hospital because of "homicidal ideation or wanting to kill your [former] in-laws."

With the statement put in front of him, Hembree said he recalled the incident.

"And is this the same time you talked about how you had beat up one of your psychiatrists that tended to you in the jail?"

"I don't remember making that statement . . . ," Hembree answered.

"So you want this jury to believe that everything you've ever said in the past is not true, and that two women died in your presence within a three-week time period and both were accidental? You want this jury to believe *that*?"

"Objection," Hembree's attorney shouted. "Asked and answered at least four times."

"Objection sustained."

Hamlin was on a roll. The ADA asked Hembree about several armed robberies he had committed and pleaded to over the years, pointing out for jurors, without shoving it down their throats, that Hembree had not recanted any of those charges.

Hembree countered by saying he did that so he could "consolidate" the charges into one, bartering a twenty-month sentence.

To which, Hamlin responded, "You manipulated the system?"

"Well, I mean, I choose to call it 'working the system.' 'Manipulation' is, you know, in the eye of the beholder. I don't know. I just work the system. I do whatever is best for *me*. If you want to call it 'manipulation,' then that's fine, I guess."

This was all the prosecutor needed to hear. Her follow-up was terse and piercing: "You do whatever is best for you?"

"Most of the time," Hembree answered.

Hembree had just closed the lid, burying himself.

Hamlin paused. Then: "Nothing further."

"Further examination?" Judge Beal asked Hembree's lawyers.

They were good, too.

It was 4:00 P.M. Beam admitted he had been caught off guard and thought Hembree's cross-examination would go until the end of the day, so he had not prepared another witness.

They agreed to resume at nine-thirty the following morning.

CHAPTER 108

Juries are unpredictable. Just when lawyers think they've got a jury figured out, they come back and surprise the attorneys. Most lawyers, as a rule of thumb, try not to make predictions or consider how a jury might be keeping score: those looks each juror might offer on his or her way into the courtroom, or reactions to evidence and testimony. Add a capital case to the mix and it intensifies all those feelings. One cannot help trying to gauge what jurors are thinking. Part of a jury's unpredictability, it is widely believed throughout the legal system, is that jurors rely—as much as we say they don't or shouldn't—on personal beliefs, intimate biases, intuition, and core human values. Part of what goes into a jury's decision is how each juror responds to the evidence, obviously; but an even greater part, according to a paper published in the *DePaul Law Review*,[2] is how jurors react to witness testimony. Evidence is expected. How a witness tells his or her story is what ultimately convinces most jurors which way to vote.

[2] "The Predictability of Juries," by Valerie Hans and Theodore Eisenberg (1/1/2011: http://scholarship.law.cornell.edu/cgi/viewcontent.cgi?article=1201&context=facpub)

Danny Hembree and his team could have put up ten experts to talk about his proclivity for falsifying confessions and making up stories. They could have questioned investigators on every aspect of the investigation, digging and searching for that one mistake law enforcement inevitably and unintentionally made. They could have entered into evidence reports by psychiatrists and psychologists that explained how much Hembree had lied. Yet, none of it would have negated the bitter, abrasive, and combative testimony that Hembree offered himself on cross-examination: how he went after ADA Hamlin at times and demeaned her; how he attacked her personally; how he denied every serious fact she threw at him. Not a thing any additional witness from this point on could say would wash that nasty taste out of jurors' mouths that they undoubtedly had from listening to Danny Hembree spew his vitriol.

"I think I was just so tired after that cross-examination," Hamlin later said after being asked how Hembree's coarse attitude and condescending nature affected her. "I was glad it was over. I do remember I had fun cross-examining him. It is very rare as a prosecutor to be able to cross-examine a murderer."

After listening to Hembree's rants, all jurors had to do, if they felt inclined, was put themselves in the position of Heather or Randi at the receiving end of a drug-drunk maniac who didn't like what was said to him. Hembree had shown jurors who he was. He gave himself away.

Beam had to try to redeem his witness. And so over the course of the next several days, that's what Hembree's attorneys set out to do. Beam called a Brevard County sheriff to explain how he had looked into those homicides Hembree admitted to in Florida, but the witness said he could not find any victims matching the time frame associated with Hembree's admissions.

After the sheriff, Beam called another law enforcement officer, Detective Michel Sumner, who offered nothing of any significance to bolster Hembree's new story of making false confessions. Yet, through Sumner's cross-examination by ADA Hamlin, something happened.

Something Hamlin and Bell had discussed with Sumner before his testimony was what he should say regarding Hembree's psychological condition. Sumner was told repeatedly, Hamlin said, not to analyze Hembree psychologically. Don't go down that road of saying he's a sociopath, a psychopath, and, especially, a pathological liar. That wasn't Sumner's job, Hamlin stressed. The detective was there to discuss what Hembree had said and verify those facts.

"Do you think Hembree was lying when he talked about killing Randi and Heather?" Hamlin asked Sumner before court began that day.

"No," Sumner said, adding that he believed Hembree 100 percent.

"So he's not a pathological liar, then. He does tell some truths. But if you go up there and say he's a pathological liar, you're saying he lied about killing these women," the ADA outlined.

The impression Hamlin had left with her brilliant cross-examination of Hembree was that he, in fact, picked and chose what he lied about. It was a conscious decision; it wasn't something he couldn't control. He intentionally selected when to tell the truth and when to fabricate.

Sumner, however, got up on the stand and called Hembree a "liar."

Really? Hamlin said to herself as Sumner went on with Beam to talk about Hembree not always telling the truth.

Beam saw an opening as Hamlin sat, frustrated.

"Do you remember telling me that Mr. Hembree . . . couldn't tell the truth consistently?" Beam asked Sumner.

"Yes, I do remember telling you that."

"That was your opinion, right? And that's how you phrased it, correct?"

"That was my opinion, without clarifying the answer. I wasn't able to clarify my answer after making that statement."

"But your opinion is still, and was, that he can't tell the truth consistently?"

"That is true of certain matters, certain individuals, um, certain people he stated he killed."

Stephanie Hamlin wanted to pull out her hair.

"As far as you know?" Beam asked.

"Of course."

"That's your opinion, right?"

"Based on the evidence, that is my opinion."

"Okay," Beam concluded. "I don't have any further questions."

During a recess, Hamlin found Sumner and cornered him. "How *dare* you go up there," she said angrily, "and say that after having what? One meeting with him? And all of a sudden, *you* become this expert on how much Danny Hembree lies or doesn't lie, when obviously he has told the truth on numerous occasions."

Sumner felt bad. He didn't know what to say. The prosecutor had a point.

Hamlin was livid. They had been sailing along; Hembree's defense was falling down. Now this bump! Sometimes, that's all it takes for that one juror on the fence—a reason to disagree with the state and—boom—a hung jury. A problem juror—a mistrial.

Any number of possibilities.

The point was, Hamlin said later, "Hembree doesn't always lie. And here was one of our own saying that Hembree was a liar. Sumner was agreeing with the defense. . . . I mean, look, I don't know Detective Sumner that well, and I somewhat understand what he was trying to do. But we told him not to analyze Hembree. I guess our personalities just don't match up. I was really pissed at him."

"That's what I thought about Danny Hembree," Sumner said later.

Sumner's analysis of Hembree was "totally objectionable, and we did object to it repeatedly," Hamlin explained.

After that hiccup, Hembree's hired clinical psychologist, Dr. Claudia Coleman, under the direction of Beam, told jurors she had done an evaluation of Hembree after being contacted by his attorneys. And through Coleman's testimony, Beam was able to get the psychologist to say exactly what he needed: Hembree had a history of making up confessions. She believed he could be lying here, too, and that his answers to her during their sessions were truthful.

Coleman said Hembree suffered from "major depression since adolescence." She had reviewed "thousands of pages" of documents pertaining to his mental-health history. That research, combined with her personal meetings with Hembree while he was in prison, contributed to her opinion.

Coleman's testimony went on far too long. Her answers, although quite professional and believable, were far too long-winded. Juries want sound bites, not graduate-school-level textbook descriptions of disorders they have no interest in learning about. They want "yes" or "no," with a little bit of context. As this type of expert testimony carried on, it came across as a hired doctor bolstering a defendant's argument. It became so obvious it was almost embarrassing to listen to at times.

After a lengthy discussion among the lawyers, without the jury present, there was one point when the judge allowed Coleman to talk about what Hembree's lawyers referred to as a "brain injury" Hembree had. Coleman said it was her opinion that "he has a brain impairment, my testing shows, and it's consistent with several things in his history. . . ."

One could almost hear the gallery collectively think: *So what?* The guy might have a brain injury. Yes, he abused drugs and alcohol. He probably had been whacked in the head during fights on a number of occasions. Sure, he had lied about things in the past and had confessed to things he did not do. Yes, he sat with countless psychologists and was even treated in psychiatric hospitals for mental disorders. And, of course, Hembree, like Coleman said, was your classic narcissist.

True, Coleman had testified in court over two hundred times throughout a thirty-year career and made, just in the past five years alone, over $500,000 doing it. But none of this mattered in the end: Danny Hembree had admitted killing these two women, and the science and evidence backed up his statements. There was no spinning those facts. These were truths Hembree was now trying to take back.

As Locke Bell tore apart Coleman's testimony on cross-examination, bringing into question all that money she had made testifying in court for various defendants, he brought up one pivotal, nearly forgotten point regarding Hembree's "false confessions." Bell was able to sketch out for jurors through his questioning of the psychologist—with Coleman consistently agreeing—that Hembree, within that DVD of him traveling around with Sumner and Hensley, knew all of the facts of Heather's and Randi's deaths he had talked about during his interrogations: where they were dumped, how they were brought out to each location, where Heather's clothes were located, how he murdered both women, etc. None of what he said during that car ride or inside the box was ever recanted, at any time, to law enforcement. He had told this story to police and never went back on it. Even after he cut those deals with the DA and got placement in the prison he had wanted, Hembree stuck to his admissions.

Coleman could do no more than repeatedly agree with Bell that Hembree knew detail after detail surrounding the girls' murders, the dumping of their bodies, it all panned out through the evidence, and was backed up—without question—by his own (unrecanted) statements to law enforcement.

Late into Halloween, Dr. Donald Jason, Forsyth County medical examiner and pathologist, sat in the witness stand and told his story of reading through the autopsy reports, examining the autopsy photos, and reviewing a transcript of the interviews Hembree conducted with Hensley and Sumner. It took all of about five minutes into his direct testimony, after being asked about Heather's cause of death, for Dr. Jason to give Beam the goods: "In my opinion, it's not possible to scientifically determine what the cause of death of Heather Marie Catterton was based on the autopsy and where she was found and the autopsy including the toxicology report. There are indications that the most probable cause of death is cocaine toxicity."

Bell objected to that response.

Beam continued and Dr. Jason furthered their argument of Heather dying by overdose. He stated how much cocaine was in Heather's system and testified that Heather's body did not display "any trauma that would be consistent with being cause of death."

No fractures.

No brain injuries.

No bruises of any significance.

No signs of strangulation.

Mostly just small, insignificant "abrasions," said the doctor.

Heather, the doctor testified, most likely died of a cocaine overdose.

* * *

When Bell got hold of him, the DA latched on to Dr. Jason's disregard for how Randi died and how his opinion was based solely on Heather's case. Then Bell got the doctor to admit that within one of his own reports, he had written, *It cannot be determined scientifically from the autopsy and the toxicology report [how Heather had died]*—and that his testimony and his report differed in viewpoints.

As a final cross-examination question, Bell asked: "Did you see where Danny Hembree said he took a plastic . . . bag and held it over her mouth and suffocated her that way? Did you see that?"

And the doctor responded: "Perhaps. I don't really remember."

Jurors had to ask themselves: *How could you do a thorough re-examination of the cause of death and miss that one, seemingly all-important fact?*

The Hembree team brought in its forensic scientist, a toxicology expert, to testify that Heather had large amounts of cocaine in her system—a fact that had been well established by this point in the trial. It was redundant testimony. They were beating a drum too loudly and far too repetitively. The jury was either going to buy that Heather died of an overdose or they were not. Most likely, they were going to toss all of the testimony associated with her blood and cocaine toxicity levels and rely on what Hembree had said, plus the fact that Heather, sad as it sounded, was a chronic crack cocaine user and used to high levels of the drug.

Next up was a licensed psychologist to talk about Hembree's brain injury and its effect on him making up stories. Redundant testimony once again, offering nothing in the form of explaining how Hembree, a career criminal with violent offenses all over his record, wound up being in the presence of two dead girls in fewer than three weeks.

* * *

On November 1, Beam called a physician to counter the state's claim—and the admission Hembree had made several times to law enforcement—that Hembree punched Randi in the face. The doctor, in the end, said he could find no evidence that Randi's body showed those kinds of injuries. On her nose, or anywhere.

An issue came up; Beam asked that the jury be excused. He had a serious matter to discuss. It involved something unorthodox, and perhaps a bit costly and even dangerous. But he felt it needed to be done in order for his client to get a fair shake, especially in the face of the death penalty.

The judge was curious, as was everyone else in the courtroom.

Hamlin and Bell could only look at each other in bewilderment.

What now?

CHAPTER 109

Richard Beam had the floor.

The passionate defense attorney began his argument with the DVD videos. He said the state's videos were the only source for jurors to get a clear picture of the Hembree residence. That was a little bit unfair. Yet, what would be equally unfair was for his defense team to go out and make its own video. Even if the defense attorneys did that, it still wouldn't give jurors a good depiction of Momma's house and how "tight it is in reality" inside the residence. There was a "marked difference" in stepping into the home and seeing it on video, Beam suggested.

In addition, Beam suggested the same could be said for the trailers.

Thus, Beam motioned for the opportunity to allow the judge and jury to take a bus trip to both locales and view them in person. It was imperative to his defense and for the explanations he was going to be giving jurors surrounding those residences.

Bell had several problems with this. On the top of the state's list was the simple fact that two years had gone by and there was "no guarantee things are the same way [inside either place]. Mr. Hembree says to the police, 'I want to get all this resolved so Momma can clean the house up.' We have no guarantee that the furniture is still in there. We have no guarantee that the basement . . . [or] anything looks like it did before."

Next, Bell argued, the crimes that took place inside the trailers "happened at night" and Hembree's defense had "not shown any reason why" going out there during the daytime would be beneficial. This thought led Bell to bring up a point he had wanted to make for some time.

"I think we need to take this into tremendous consideration. . . . [It's] from the Gaston County tax office. It's the footprint of this house with the measurements. Your Honor, if you look at that, you will see the bedroom—if you take the twenty-nine feet that the house is in width, subtract out four feet for a hallway, which has been testified to, and the stud walls in between it, you have about twenty-five and a half feet. You have rooms on either side. You have—what you end up with, Judge, is a bedroom of about twelve by twelve." The size of the room, Bell added, worried him; there wasn't enough room in the house for everyone to fit. He listed how many people would be walking through those tight spaces. "We have fifteen jurors. We have the defendant, sixteen. Your Honor is seventeen. Court reporter is eighteen. Nineteen and twenty for the lawyers. . . . That is *before* we bring in the sheriff. . . . From a security standpoint, we're talking about twenty-one people, plus the deputies, shoved into this room, with the court reporter trying to write and take it all down. The jury cannot be protected."

What if Hembree tried something? Bell proposed. What if Hembree had made this suggestion to go out there so he could hurt somebody?

"I thought it was ridiculous and it proved nothing," ADA Hamlin said later. "Being in that basement [again] would be so creepy. I truly believe Hembree just wanted to see his house one last time before he went back to prison, and that is the *only* reason he wanted to argue this motion."

"Mr. Hembree would have to be in restraints," Bell continued, trying to convince the judge this was not going to be as easy as shuffling everyone into buses. Precautions had to be taken into account. "If he is in an area the size of that, with all the jurors and everybody else, Your Honor included, he would have to be in very, very secure restraints, which as Your Honor knows, you're not supposed to show the defendant in that kind of situation. So even in those restraints, if he volunteered to have shackles on, still the jury would *not* be safe."

Beam argued that the photos were not an accurate portrayal of these pivotal locations and the jury deserved to see them in person. "It's a different spatial relationship when you're there in person versus the photographs," Beam said. "I'm not saying the photograph isn't accurate. It is. It just doesn't convey the spatial relationships of the rooms, and there's no way to do that with a video or photos. It requires going in person."

The judge thought about the possibilities as he talked through it with both sides, leaning toward a visit. First, though, he wanted to head out to each place himself, which he would do during the lunch recess. He worried about the media reporting from the scene. Was that a violation of Momma's privacy? Would any of the jurors' identities be compromised?

"The paramount rule is," Beal advised, sending a message to any media present, "at no time shall the jurors be videotaped or photographed . . . so that's where we stand. We won't know any more until . . ." Beal paused. "I really . . . have trepidation about this process, but the first step is, I have to go see it. . . ."

Just after giving a clear warning to the media, fifteen

hours later, when court resumed on November 2, Judge Beal said he had been informed that one of the local news stations aired footage of a juror entering the jury box. Thus, the judge suspended all coverage of cameras inside the courtroom, announcing he would make a final decision on the matter when he had a moment to review the footage. The question everyone was asking, however, would that one mishap by the media destroy Danny Hembree's chances of getting the jury out to Momma's house and the trailer?

CHAPTER 110

When the trial resumed, the same expert testimony Hembree's defense had been trying to sell to jurors regarding how the girls had died continued. There was a bit of testimony surrounding an idea that Randi did not have a broken nose, despite Hembree's confession of having punched her in the nose while inside his den, thus the reason for all the blood that forensics had uncovered. Bell had put up an expert who testified there was broken cartilage on Randi's nose. Hembree's expert said he didn't find that to be true.

Before the end of the day, Beam called a retired Gaston County Police Department detective. He had interviewed Hembree in the late 1970s and early 1980s. Beam asked the detective about a statement he had taken from Hembree.

Yet, no sooner had he been called than Beam concluded: "Other than those documents (reports) that you have in front of you, you don't have an independent—away from those documents—recollection of actually speaking to Danny Hembree?"

"No, I don't."

Many wondered why the cop had been called, to begin with.

The rest of the day was essentially eaten up by arguments without the jury present. The state wasn't sold on the idea that going out to both places was prudent. It was a dangerous hassle for everyone and did not move proceedings forward— and maybe even a way for Hembree to flex that control he so desperately craved.

ADA Hamlin argued with Beal about the differences in the properties then and now. There was no comparison. It might even confuse jurors more than help them.

The state's arguments did no good, however. Judge Beal explained, "I've already addressed the fact that I realize there are some differences, but I think the value of seeing the property is of value [and] is substantial to the jury. In my discretion, I'm going to order that there shall be a jury view to take place [tomorrow]."

Beal explained the rules for the visits.

Everyone was going: Hembree, his lawyers, the state, judge, court reporter, and several sheriffs.

Decision made, the judge ordered jurors back into the courtroom and explained what was happening. He gave specific instructions for what they could and could not do during the outing, banged his gavel, and told everyone to get a good night's rest.

CHAPTER 111

When they returned the following morning from what was an uneventful trip out to the locales, the judge called a longer than usual recess so jurors could have a break, eat lunch, and be ready to resume testimony. The trial was beginning to weigh on those involved. It had become a long, tedious process of watching a runaway cart careen down a rocky slope toward a cliff. It was almost a given, anyone sitting in the courtroom felt, that Danny Hembree was going down. There was nothing that could save Hembree from a guilty verdict, anyone involved in the day-to-day business of the trial agreed. The only question left surrounded the death penalty: Would this jury put the value of the two victims' lives, regardless of what types of lives they had led, over Hembree's? There was no doubt in the minds of most court watchers that Hembree deserved it. He had played God and taken lives for his own twisted reasoning. He wasn't mentally challenged, insane, or incompetent. He wasn't acting out on voices inside his head. There had not been a shred of evidence to prove these were two accidental deaths.

And so, by the end of the day, November 3, 2011, after a bus trip, several instructions from the judge, and arguments by attorneys that each side had met its burden of proof, the defense rested.

Very soon Hembree's fate would be in the hands of this jury, which had been paraded countless times in and out of the courtroom so the attorneys could argue their points.

At 3:26 P.M., the judge brought the jury in and announced that the "evidence portion" of the case had concluded.

One could *almost* hear a united, silent sigh from the jury: *Thank goodness.*

The judge indicated he was giving jurors the following day off. This was so that each juror could "refresh" him- or herself and take Friday through the weekend to relax. They would be back on Monday, well rested for closing arguments, which the judge warned were "quite likely to be lengthy."

Deliberations would begin after that.

CHAPTER 112

On Monday morning, November 7, the law allowed for both of Hembree's attorneys to give a closing argument.

Brent Ratchford, who had worked doggedly for Hembree behind the scenes, spoke to jurors first. A point Ratchford banged about first was that Heather and Randi lived sordid lives within an underground, dodgy Gastonia drug culture that not many people in the courtroom would comprehend. He said the girls had "passed on"—a strange term that Ratchford had chosen, one that is generally used to describe the end of a sick aunt or granddad's life, instead of "murdered" or "died"—because of their chosen lifestyles. Same as his client, he stopped short of blaming the girls for their own deaths.

Ratchford quoted their experts and explained how—all of them—believed Heather died from a cocaine overdose: "Because [Heather's] levels [of cocaine] . . . fall within impaired driving, people who go to the emergency room having distress because of toxicity, and also fatalities—people who die of a cocaine toxicity or overdose. Her levels fell in all three of those categories, so that's extremely important evidence. That's why [our experts] put it in the report."

The word "cocaine" came up again and again in Ratchford's closing.

He leaned heavily on it: cocaine, cocaine, cocaine.

Ratchford pushed the notion of convicting Hembree on lesser charges, explaining, "[The judge is] going to break down first-degree murder, second-degree murder, and . . . involuntary manslaughter. . . . Danny didn't choke Heather Catterton to death." He said Hembree didn't suffocate Heather, either. He did, however, give her cocaine . . . "and she died as a result." And that, defense attorney Ratchford contended, was "not first-degree murder" or "second-degree murder. . . . It's involuntary manslaughter!"

Near the end of what became an argument built around the idea of feeling sorry for Hembree and looking at Heather as desperate and strung out, Ratchford got caught up in his own narrative, pleading: "Can you imagine what it feels like to be hopeless? Let your mind wander on that just a second. Hopeless. Without any hope." He called it "a dark hole" for a guy like Hembree to "be in." Then the attorney asked what anyone else would do. "You take cocaine and alcohol to make yourself feel better . . . ," he said, adding how the drug made Hembree "feel normal." Why? "Because you are abnormal and you don't know why—"

The judge interrupted. "Mr. Ratchford, I'll . . . ask you to pause for a second." Then Judge Beal spoke to the jury. "At no time should you put yourselves in the position of anyone involved in the case. To the extent that it's part of argument, it's intended to be a rhetorical device, but it's not proper to put yourselves in the position of someone—you should apply the rules of law I give. . . ."

For the next half hour, Ratchford talked about the dangers of cocaine and how "any amount" could "kill" and "be lethal."

He closed by imploring jurors to "pay attention" and "listen for what you don't hear," saying how what we don't hear is sometimes "the most telling fact, and the one thing you're going to not hear with certainty is what caused Heather Catterton's death."

Strange ending. It was clear throughout this trial, and jurors would be able to view the DVDs again if they chose, that Hembree explained perfectly well how Heather Catterton had died. Her killer had gone into great detail, in fact.

Richard Beam began with the burden of proof argument and morphed into a discussion about a Robert Redford, Daryl Hannah, and Debra Winger film, *Legal Eagles,* and how the judge and Redford's lawyer character in that film got into a little tiff as Redford's character made the point that his case was more complicated than the prosecution wanted jurors to believe. That same argument was relevant in Hembree's case, Beam insisted.

Further along, Beam brought up Randi: "I want you to listen to what [the state] talked about. They're going to talk about all the evidence about Randi Saldana because they don't have much evidence of what caused the death of Heather Catterton."

After that, Beam mentioned the drug lifestyle and the effect smoking crack cocaine had on the human body. As he went on and on, Beam's theme came into focus with one word he routinely leaned on: "abnormal." He said over and over that everything in Hembree's case was abnormal: Hembree asked for coffee while being interrogated; he jumped around from crime to crime during his interrogation; he readily admitted to several murders; he had no trouble confessing to crimes that police could not later prove.

This sort of "dodge the real issue" argument did not come across as patently salable. Hembree was a liar, absolutely. He was a lifelong convicted felon, yes. He was a repeat violent offender, certainly. One could talk around that all he wanted; but when the facts of the case were there to look at, there was no choice but to believe Hembree was exactly who he had said he was: a serial murderer.

Then Beam brought in an age-old defense tactic: reasonable doubt. He said, "Mr. Hembree told you on the stand [Heather] passed away in her sleep on the bed. That actually does appear to be consistent with the condition of the body. As I said, abnormal is normal in this case."

It was clear Beam could have gone on all day, arguing each point as if back at university debating a classmate.

"There [are] a lot of things in this case, ladies and gentlemen, a lot of evidence, much of it dealing with Miss Saldana. But the real question still remains—What killed Heather Catterton?"

Beam went on so long, in fact, the judge called a recess.

When they came back, Beam bantered on about the differences between Randi's and Heather's deaths. Finally he concluded, "When you view Mr. Hembree, you have to view in context, and when you do that, you'll understand he would say anything that he thought would benefit him then." In this case, "it did," he added. Yet that didn't "mean he did it." What it meant, the lawyer said, was that Hembree wanted "to benefit" from it.

And that was "the reason the appropriate verdict is involuntary manslaughter."

CHAPTER 113

Stephanie Hamlin took on the state's task of wrapping up its evidence in a bow and presenting it to jurors. While sitting and listening to Beam and Ratchford, Hamlin considered two things. Thus, she started off on a reproachful note, totally dismantling Ratchford's and Beam's arguments, bringing the state's case back to ground level: "I hope at this point you've had a couple of minutes for the smoke to clear," she said, standing up. "The smoke that the defense just kind of put up there and tried to confuse you. This is reality. This is not *Shawshank Redemption* or *Legal Eagles.* . . . There are two women dead, and that man right there"—Hamlin pointed at Hembree—"killed them. Danny Hembree, who has been sitting in front of you for approximately four, five weeks of evidence, he has been manipulating the system his *entire* adult life."

Hamlin next smartly warned jurors not to allow Hembree to manipulate them, too. Then, after some difficulty getting a PowerPoint presentation up and running, the ADA read from a statement Hembree had given the YCSO when he admitted killing both girls. The quote Hamlin focused on, of which she played a recording for jurors, came out clear and chilling: "I killed them at Momma's. . . . I killed Heather downstairs in the laundry room, and I killed Randi in my den. You'll find her blood all over the couch. . . ."

"I killed. . . . I killed. . . . I killed"—.

Words of a guilty man uttered from his own mouth—now an admission that reverberated in everyone's minds.

Hembree was an admitted killer. Didn't matter what he said now.

Why not believe him? He was broken when he confessed. He was tired. He was finished. Given two years to come up with a way out of those confessions, here they were now, arguing whether a killer admitted to murdering two women—possibly several others—or made it all up to catch a break on a few robberies.

"Everything Danny Hembree said back on December 5, 2009," Hamlin said, "he confessed to two capital murders to get a deal on robbery charges? That makes no sense. That makes no sense at all."

The way the ADA put it, Hembree's new version was so weak, so half-baked and desperate, could there be any other scenario possible besides what he had confessed to?

She went through all of the state's evidence. She played pieces of video/audio to hammer key points home, again and again using Hembree's own words to bury him.

Hitting her stride, Hamlin made an important observation: "First of all, Danny and Heather were not boyfriend-girlfriend." She added how they "were not in a relationship." She explained how Heather was sleeping with him, sure—and she was "having sex with him," absolutely—but it was all "for crack."

"When the crack is gone, she is gone. . . . She didn't spend the night at his house to have breakfast in the morning. . . ."

So true. The way Hembree played up his relationship with Heather, it was as if they had been in a romance and he was spending the night with her as a normal course. But that wasn't the case. By all accounts, Heather despised her sister's boyfriend. She hated him. She could not stand to be around him.

Unless, that is, he had drugs.

For thirty more minutes, Hamlin described the differences between a cause of death and what science proves, making sure to note that the science in Heather's case backed up her being strangled with a cut lamp cord and suffocated.

The signs were subtle, but they were there.

After talking for a time about Randi's death and how Hembree's autoerotic asphyxiation story could not be true, Hamlin moved on to how the jury should view the case under the law, pointing to how the state had to prove only Hembree's "intent." They did not have to prove how he did it, only that he intended to do it.

As Hamlin spoke, Hembree stared. He wrote something down on a scrap of paper.

Hamlin made sure jurors heard the word "manipulation" in relation to Hembree and his entire criminal career. She said there was no reasonable doubt in this case. Like a lot of things, the defense was tossing it out there, hoping it would stick.

In a concluding, passionate plea, with commitment to what she was saying, ADA Hamlin brought it all back to day one, fleshing out more of Hembree's lies: "So he took his time, he got advice, and he tried the best he could to make his elaborate tale fit the evidence. Think back to December fifth. . . . When he knew nothing, when he had no legal advice—consistently, voluntarily, he told the police everything, and it was consistent with what the evidence showed." She then pointed at Hembree, saying, "This man—and this is rare—*confessed* to murder." She pointed out how for "hours" jurors had watched Hembree "confess to killing Heather and Randi." But now, of course, "after . . . two years, the defense . . . put up smoke screens," she added, saying how they had tried to confuse jurors any way they could get away with it.

"This is not 'The Danny Hembree Show,' " Hamlin said. "This is not some bad episode of *CSI*. This is real life! We've got two women dead—and he killed them."

She then asked that jurors find the defendant guilty of first-degree murder in the death of Heather Catterton. Then ADA Hamlin thanked them and sat down.

The judge read his instructions and recessed until the following morning.

A deputy called Stephanie Hamlin over as the day wound down and the attorneys gathered their things to leave.

"I found this," the deputy said, handing the prosecutor a piece of paper.

Hamlin took it. "Thanks."

Hembree had written it while Hamlin was giving her closing and handed it to one of his defense attorneys. It must have gotten dropped on the floor.

The paper said: *I wish this bitch would shut up.*

CHAPTER 114

The next morning, the jury began deliberating and re-turned a verdict after lunch, likely taking that much time to make it look good.

On the way into court, Hembree spoke to one of the deputies. "If I get the death penalty," he said, nodding toward ADA Hamlin, who was just then walking in, "it's because of *that* bitch."

The judge addressed the jury foreperson. "Ma'am . . . has the jury reached a unanimous verdict?"

"Yes, sir."

The judge took the envelope and handed it to the clerk.

"Members of the jury . . . you have found . . . Danny Hembree guilty of first-degree murder. Is this your verdict, so say you all?"

There was some noise in the courtroom. The gallery buzzed. People whispered and talked loudly. Some left, run-ning to go make calls to editors and producers.

"Quiet," Judge Beal said.

"Yes," the jury said in unison.

ADA Hamlin, who had spent a year preparing for this case, dropped her head and took a deep breath. The trial had been exhausting—emotionally and physically. Part of it had to do with a family member of Hembree's subtly alerting her that they knew more about Stephanie Hamlin's personal life than the prosecutor felt comfortable with.

"It always scared me that [this person] knew a lot about me," Hamlin said later. "About my family, my husband, where he went to school, where he used to work."

Hembree smiled a cocky smirk after the verdict.

Tears came for the families of his victims.

Hembree's mother and sister sat unsurprised, but in obvious shock.

The trial was far from over, however. Now it would shift to the penalty phase as Hembree's team argued to save his life. They'd present testimony and evidence they believed could help get Hembree a life sentence. It was going to be emotional and tense. There were lots of people in the courtroom thirsty for Hembree's blood. And with the jury coming back so quick on first-degree murder—essentially saying Hembree was a double murderer and maybe even a serial killer—it was going to be a war.

The judge asked everyone to be ready for the penalty phase. It was set to begin on the following morning, November 8.

CHAPTER 115

As they got started the following day, the judge asked Danny Hembree to stand.

"I understood that there is some recommendation that you have a psychiatric evaluation. What's your approach to that?" Beal asked.

Hembree responded with his signature swagger: "You want to do the mental thing, that's fine. But like I said, I just want to be left alone. Let these people go ahead and have their show, sign the paper, and get me the hell back up to Raleigh, and I'll be calm, cool, and cooperative."

The judge said he wanted to be sure the process was fair.

The rest of that day was taken up by motions and mechanics.

When they returned after a weekend break, Hembree spoke again. This time, he lashed out at his defense team: "My attorneys have advised the state . . . [and] court numerous times that they couldn't adequately prepare a defense for me. They have told me point-blank they have been ineffective in assisting me. Now . . . for the last six weeks . . . I have assisted constantly in my defense. I have been called upon to make decisions, competent decisions, or I should say they should be competent decisions based on information that I get. Now I found out yesterday there's documents I haven't gotten. . . . I may need [more time] in defense of my life. . . . I ask you to set aside the verdict based on ineffective assistance of counsel, and let's start this thing over and do it right! That's all I have."

Locke Bell stood and defended Rick Beam, noting, "Mr. Beam and I were first involved in a capital murder case in 1993. . . . Beam was with the district attorney's office. . . . Since 1993, Mr. Beam and I have continued to try murder cases all over the western part of North Carolina. Mr. Beam, I know, has tried them in numerous counties and has done very well with them. . . . Mr. Beam, after leaving the DA's office, defended many, many, many people charged with first-degree murder, capital cases. He has worked in federal court . . . [and] has always done a very professional job, as he has done here today."

Hembree expressed how unimpressed he was, adding, "I'm only concerned about this case!" He said he wanted more time and there were documents he said he had not seen. "Like I said, I don't care nothing about what Mr. Bell has done with Mr. Beam in the past. I only care about what is done in my case. I don't care if he has to work every night for the rest of the year, but I want to be treated fairly. And that's what I'm asking the court to do, and I respectfully request that you set this verdict aside."

The judge said no.

As the penalty phase moved forward, the state presented evidence first, putting up witness after witness describing how violent Hembree had been throughout his life. Each had his or her own story to tell regarding being beaten up or robbed by Hembree. The guy was ruthless and uncaring—a true sociopath, with no feeling or remorse. Over the years, he had robbed and beaten people, forced himself on females, raped and pillaged. There didn't seem to be a time in his life when he had done anything good for anyone. He had no redeeming qualities. He had no sense of compassion for anyone. The burden on the state was to prove aggravating circumstances—and if there was ever a life modeling the epitome of that burden, Hembree's was it. Witness after witness talked about being victimized by this man. He'd hurt people when he didn't have to. He'd hurt people for fun. He'd hurt people for money and drugs and sex. Over two days, the state presented witnesses bolstering its claim that Danny Hembree was a repeat offender who committed the act of murder maliciously and deserved death. There was no doubt when the state finished that Hembree, if the death penalty is to be a punishment the state doled out for capital murder, was its poster child.

On November 14, Hembree's defense began presenting witnesses to the contrary, many of whom came in and talked about how Hembree was mentally unstable, had issues all his life with depression and perhaps even brain damage. They testified to how he had been on a host of psychiatric medications throughout his life and was addicted to booze and drugs and should not be held responsible for his actions. He was a bad boy—very bad, indeed—but he did not deserve to die for impulses he had no control over. And no witness brought this home more than Hembree's mother, Jacqueline Hembree.

Momma.

To maybe everyone else in the courtroom, Danny Hembree was a killer, a bastard, a rapist, a violent offender, a crack addict, and a drunkard. But to this woman, who had raised him, he was her son. No matter what he did, whom he killed, whom he hurt, despite his guilt or innocence, Danny Hembree was Momma's boy. Nothing anybody said could take away the love she felt for her Danny Boy. She had given him life—and here she was now, trying to give him life once again.

Jurors got a firsthand account of Hembree's father. Momma said they had lived in California and even Berlin, Germany, near the time of "the wall and everything." It was chaotic. She was pregnant with Danny. Their lives revolved around where Mr. Hembree was stationed. Hembree's father had been trained in infantry, but he worked in a tank unit.

All of this led up to a problem Momma had with her pregnancy. She was three months pregnant. Before they left South Carolina to embark on a new tour, she was told her "uterus was too low for the baby to develop and that I was going to lose him either with or without [an] operation."

So Momma went into surgery while three months pregnant.

No one explained there could be side effects, because it was thought there would be no child.

Hembree survived, obviously, and the first year of his life was incredibly rough for Momma as she dealt with the boy's issues: "Well, I'd say the first three months of his life, he cried all the time, and they just said it was colic."

As he grew, Danny's problems, Momma said, also grew: "He was [a] nervous child, and once he started school, we were told he was very intelligent, but he would disrupt the class sometimes, not by being mean or doing bad things, just he would get bored. . . . And then when he was about twelve, we took him to his pediatrician because he was very nervous and he would chew the skin around his fingernails, and we were very concerned about that. And we were told by his pediatrician to leave him alone—that he was going through this depression because he was the smallest child in his class and he hadn't grown enough and caught up with the rest of the kids."

Momma said that as Danny got older, the shaking and nervousness spun out of control.

"He could sit somewhere and his leg would shake and it

would just constantly tremble. And we didn't know why that
was. And I had a doctor later to tell me that his insides shook
like that—even his tongue."

Hembree was fourteen when his behavioral problems
started. Part of it was based on the hard life he and his
brother had been put through with a military dad ruling the
house with an iron fist.

"Well . . . my husband, he was very hard on those boys
because that's the way he was raised. He was raised in a family of seven children, and his father was a very strict disciplinarian. And had he known about Danny and [his brother's]
problems mentally at the time, I don't think he would've reacted the way he did all the time."

Momma said Danny and his brother developed severe
mental issues based on how much their daddy drank and
how badly he treated them. But there was also, she claimed,
a strange dynamic between Danny and his sibling she had a
hard time coming to terms with.

"[Danny's brother] had a complete mental breakdown a
few months shy of his eighteenth birthday. And . . . we had
noticed . . . he had always followed Danny. He had never
quite developed his own personality and Danny was his idol.
He looked up to Danny. And it was after Danny got into
trouble the first time is when [his brother] had the mental
breakdown months later. And we found out that he—well, at
first, he was diagnosed as schizophrenic and it was a misdi-
agnosis. Once we changed doctors and . . . they changed it
to the fact that he was a manic-depressive, with a bipolar
disorder."

It was after the diagnosis that Danny met with doctors,
Momma testified, and they said he had a chemical imbal-
ance. All of it was the result of the operation she'd had while
Danny was three months in her womb.

"[His doctor] told us that not only did Danny have a
chemical imbalance in the brain, that he also had brain dam-

age. And then he started asking me about his medical background. And then I told him about the surgery I had when I was three months pregnant. And he seemed to think that the anesthesia at the time could possibly have caused the brain damage."

She talked about the medications Hembree was put on after the diagnosis, how he became an introvert, staying home a lot, afraid to go outside. Soon Danny stopped taking his meds, because he didn't like how they made him feel.

One of the things Hembree enjoyed as he grew into a young adult was going to jail. He thrived in that environment, because it was structured and decisions were made for him, Momma explained. He was told what to do and when to do it. He needed that. When Momma visited him, she noticed Danny was "quieter, calmer, more caring for our feelings, more interested in his family and what we felt, and how we were getting along, versus when he was out. [Then] it was like we became secondary to him versus his pleasures. When he was incarcerated, he cared deeply about his children."

When Hembree was released in January 2009, Momma recalled, he got out of jail and lived with her, but his life had changed.

"He came home to be with me because, you know, I'm by myself now. And he stayed there with me a couple of months constantly. And then he started meeting up with these people that were into drugs and alcohol and sex. And he more or less moved out. . . . I think it was in like August, or the latter part of July, he went to stay with the Cattertons."

Momma said that she could tell he was not taking his medication during this period. This led her to tell a story about little Danny, as a baby, getting a diaper stuck to his face. He couldn't breathe for a period of time. Momma believed the lack of oxygen to his brain exacerbated his problems further.

In the end, calling Momma was a good play by the defense to try and humanize a man who had been looked at and seen as a monster.

The next day, Hembree's son and sister testified, reinforcing Momma's claims that Hembree was severely incapacitated and inhibited by his mental difficulties and had taken medications all his life for psychiatric issues. It was solid, serious testimony from people who knew Hembree personally, aside from his street life of drugs.

Did any of this testimony negate the fact that Hembree knew what he was doing when he killed both women?

The jury was going to have to decide.

Closing arguments came and went, and the judge gave his instructions.

CHAPTER 116

On November 18, after a day of deliberations, the jury came back. After a series of questions, the judge addressed the jury foreperson regarding Hembree's mental state and relationships with his family and the aggravating factors surrounding the murder of Heather Catterton. The jury's decision was announced in the form of a question to the foreperson: "Is it the recommendation of the jury . . . [to] recommend that the defendant, Danny Robbie Hembree Jr., be sentenced to death—is that the unanimous decision of the jury?"

"Yes, sir," the foreperson said.

Danny Hembree's hubris and narcissism were never more evident than after being asked at the end of the death penalty proceedings if he had anything to say.

"Yes, sir, there is," Hembree insisted. "This verdict here is what the Catterton family was asking for, and I hope that it can bring some closure and start the healing process for them. . . . And I would like to read these four verses. It's the lyrics of a [Johnny Cash] song that I modified into a poem. . . .

It says everything that I'd like to say." And with that, Hembree talked about how prison had been "a living hell" for him and how he hated "every inch" of a system that had "cut me and have scarred me through and through." He said after every bid, he walked out "a wiser, weaker man." He blamed politicians for the conditions and how no prisoner is rehabilitated. He said prison had "bent" his "heart and mind " and the "stone walls turn my blood a little cold." He asked for Prison (as a proper noun) to "rot and burn in hell," repeating how the four-wall institution he had lived in throughout much of his life was "a living hell."

Perhaps it was the power of suggestion, but moving back into that Hollywood metaphor Hembree's attorneys had brought up earlier, the judge's final words seemed to have been pulled straight from the script of one of those blockbuster legal thrillers: "The prisoner, Danny Robbie Hembree Jr., having been convicted of murder in the first degree by unanimous verdict of the jury . . . having unanimously recommended the punishment of death, is therefore ordered and . . . sentenced to death. And the sheriff of Gaston County, North Carolina, in whose custody the said defendant now is, should forthwith deliver said prisoner . . . to the warden of the state's penitentiary . . . and the said warden shall cause the said prisoner . . . to be put to death as by law provided." Judge Beal paused a moment, taking a breath before delivering his final words: "May God have mercy on his soul."

Danny Hembree, who did not react in any way to the verdict, was on his way to death row, where he would mount one of his most revolting manipulative moves ever.

CHAPTER 117

It took Hembree two months to stir up controversy and piss off everyone. It was almost humorous how much noise a guy facing death, locked up for basically twenty-three hours a day, could make from that space. But Hembree managed to rattle the media and public's cage from the confines of death row.

This latest outburst of disrespect came in the form of a letter addressed to the local Gastonia newspaper, the *Gaston Gazette*. It was taunting and sarcastic and shocking. In the one-page missive, Hembree called himself a "gentleman of leisure" while on death row, enjoying "color TV" with air-conditioning, while taking "naps at will." He bragged about eating "three well-balanced, hot meals" a day and being housed in a building with a "55 million dollar hospital," providing him with "round the clock free medical care."

The quote that stirred the most public outrage as the letter went viral had Hembree taunting his death sentence: *Kill me if you can, suckers!*

Hembree knew there hadn't been an execution in North Carolina since 2006 and asked the public if *[it was] aware that the chances of my lawful murder taking place in the next twenty years if ever are very slim?*

"He's sitting down there, looking at the law and laughing," Locke Bell told the same newspaper. "He's been sentenced to death. He shouldn't be watching color TV."

Nick Catterton was in tears as he read the letter. He felt Hembree was spitting on his daughter's grave.

Kathy Ledbetter, Hembree's sister, came out and apologized the following day, saying she was sorry. The letter, Kathy suggested, was just another sign that her brother was mentally unstable.

Others said Hembree was out of control.

The discussion turned global as the *Daily Mail* and other British media covered it.

People were outraged.

CHAPTER 118

In March 2012, just before jury selection began on the second trial, Danny Hembree wrote Stephanie Hamlin a letter. He said he was "concerned" about her "health," because in his view she had gained some weight recently (she hadn't). He told the ADA she should get herself a gym membership and start working out.

Hamlin laughed at Hembree's stupid, desperate attempt to get to her.

By March 13, both sides were at it again. Bell, Hamlin, Judge Beal, Beam, and Ratchford tried the same case, mostly, with the same witnesses. It had a déjà vu feel to it. The only difference for the state was they presented Randi's murder first and backed it up with Heather's. The reason they went forward with prosecuting Hembree for Randi's murder, a source in law enforcement explained, was as an insurance policy ("a backup sentence") should anything happen with the automatic appeal initiated in the first death penalty verdict. The state wanted a second guilty verdict to fall back on, should Hembree find a way out of the first.

One of the more dramatic moments for the state during the second trial came when Shellie Nations, Randi's sister, testified. When Shellie saw Randi's boots, which had been placed on the stand before her, she lost it, saying later that all she could think of while staring at her sister's shoes was "the final steps my sister took. . . . It really broke me down."

"This case was a slam dunk," Hamlin said. "It was a stress-free trial for us because we knew the evidence so well. We knew what to expect."

Cruise control.

That is, until Hembree took the stand.

The defense put up Hembree first, after the state concluded its case. It was a tactical move. In order to prove Hembree was a liar and had made false confessions, his lawyers needed him to explain it.

So Hembree sat and told that same tale he had back during the first trial.

When it came time for cross-examination, however, Locke Bell told ADA Hamlin, "You had a crack at him already—I want my shot."

"No problem," Hamlin said.

Which was when Danny Robbie Hembree decided to cause mayhem.

CHAPTER 119

Prior to Hembree's defense presenting its case, ADA Hamlin shared with the court that she had received a letter from the attorney general's (AG's) office regarding Danny Hembree. It was serious stuff. The AG informed Hamlin that an anonymous, typed letter had been sent to its office indicating she and Hembree had had an affair. The letter writer knew things about Hamlin and her husband's personal lives. Details not many others could have known. Things only someone close to them would know. The letter explained that prior to Heather's death, Hamlin and Hembree had had sex; after Hembree hooked up with Nicole, and Heather wound up dead, Hamlin decided to prosecute Hembree because she was jealous.

"The AG's office didn't take it seriously enough to open an official inquiry," a source told me. "They laughed it off, apparently. I guess they checked it out, but nothing came of it, basically."

The judge called a hearing to discuss the matter and figure out if the court needed to conduct its own investigation and remove ADA Hamlin from the case.

The jury was sent out. There was talk among the lawyers and judge whether everyone should be heard on the record and allowed to argue each side of the matter. Beam and Ratchford took a moment and spoke to Hembree privately about it.

When they returned, Beam explained there was no reason to be heard. He said he couldn't discuss their reasoning because of attorney-client privilege, but the bottom line was that none of them deemed the letter valid.

"In the end, either Hembree typed the letter himself or had someone else do it," a source close to both sides told me. "But he knew it to be a false document."

The judge was convinced the letter was bogus. He warned the courtroom that nobody was to mention the letter—in any way—during the trial.

So Hembree sat on the stand once again. The trial had been going on for two weeks by then. Hembree was being buried by the prosecution.

On April 2, 2012, while Locke Bell was cross-examining Hembree, he approached the convicted killer with a question about that letter he had written to the local newspaper while on death row—the letter in which Hembree mocked the system.

Hembree said, "What I'm wondering about, are you gonna show the letter about the sexual relationship between me and Stephanie that the attorney general sent in here the other day . . . ?"

With his arms folded, standing in front of the witness, Locke Bell dropped his head and smiled. He knew what Hembree had just done.

"Laugh!" Hembree said to Bell, who had turned his back to the convicted killer and walked away. "But the truth's the truth!"

Jurors looked at each other: *What just happened?*

That was it. The judge called a recess.

Hembree's defense team asked to withdraw from the case. The judge approved the request.

The state objected, arguing that Hembree should represent himself because he had caused the entire problem. The trial should go on. The state should not be punished.

Standing now behind his table, both lawyers flanking him, Hembree went on a rant, shouting, "No matter what the state says, I got a conflict with these two guys!"

As he said that, Shellie Nations, who had sat and listened to Hembree's antics and long-winded outbursts long enough, stood, pointed at Hembree, and shouted: "I got a conflict with *you,* too! You killed my sister! Did you not say you killed my sister? You son of a bitch!"

Hembree turned around in utter shock, his upper lip quivering. He seemed startled, rattled, surprised by Shellie's eruption.

Shellie was immediately taken into custody by sheriffs.

In the end, the judge declared a mistrial.

Which was maybe what Danny Hembree had planned all along.

CHAPTER 120

One of the problems for ADA Hamlin arising out of this latest fiasco, something she wanted to clear up, was how the media reported what took place inside the courtroom that day. Some of the reporting had brought Stephanie to tears that night when she saw it.

Reading and watching some of the reporting, if one didn't know better, one would come out of it thinking Stephanie Hamlin and Danny Hembree had had sex. That's what many locals thought. The thread of the story surrounding the bogus letter to the AG's office was not a part of the reporting. Stephanie would go to her local supermarket and people would stop her and say, "Aren't you the prosecutor that had sex with that killer? You were the reason why it was mistried!"

No one in the media focused on the fact that Hembree's statement on the stand was untrue. The way it was reported made it seem as though Hembree had testified to having sex with the prosecutor. No media outlet reported how, in a hearing earlier in the trial, it had been discussed that the letter

was a false document and everyone—including the judge
and Hembree's lawyers—agreed.

"What hurt me so bad is that I am friends with a lot of
them (reporters) who covered the trial," Hamlin told me
later.

CHAPTER 121

As the days and months went on, ADA Hamlin and DA Bell wondered what in the heck Hembree was going to do next. How could they try him for Randi's murder and assure that he not make a spectacle of the court? He was sure to cause problems if they went back to trial. Hembree was having fun, exploring all layers of his narcissism.

There was also the issue of Hembree "becoming obsessed" with Hamlin and her family, ADA Hamlin had heard from a source.

Hembree knew "way more" than anyone should have known about the prosecutor. It seemed he wanted to destroy her.

After long discussions with Hembree and his attorneys, Shellie Nations, and others involved in the case, the state decided to offer Hembree a plea.

On Tuesday, February 5, 2013, surprising everyone, Danny Hembree took that plea, which resulted in a twenty-six-year sentence for murdering Randi Saldana.

Part of the plea, however, was that the state would dismiss Hembree's potential connection to the murder of Deborah Ratchford.

Shellie Nations recalled being there to hear the plea: "I think he finally realized he had been defeated. He took my sister's life. You see, the only prayer I have for his life is that when he meets his Maker, those two girls, Randi and Heather, are standing, side by side, and they take a piece of him like he took a piece of them."

CHAPTER 122

It was a year after Randi's murder. By then Shellie Nations had explained to Randi's son—the boy Shellie had custody of—who his mother was. It was a graceful, tragic moment in many ways. Shellie had fulfilled her sister's wish. Shellie was alone in the car with the boy. It was just the two of them. The moment she finished explaining the situation to the child, Shellie couldn't believe it, but she heard three knocks on the back windshield of her car. They were driving down the road at the time.

"Did you hear that?" Shellie asked Randi's son.

He looked over at his aunt. His "eyes were big" and bulged, Shellie recalled. It was an OMG moment.

"Did you *hear* that?" Shellie asked again.

"Them three knocks?" the boy asked.

"I had never told him about the knocks or how many," Shellie explained. "He came out with it. I felt like it was Randi sitting right behind us in the car, telling me it was all okay now. And I knew. I *knew,*" Shellie added through tears, "Randi was telling me it was all okay now."

EPILOGUE

I wrote to Danny Hembree as I began this project in late 2011. It was a short letter introducing myself. I promised to give him the space he needed to tell his story.

Hembree wrote back immediately. He opened his missive by saying he didn't "need" me to tell his story, and the "cleverly disguised wording" of my letter to him had "fallen on deaf ears." He explained how we lived in America and I could "write what the fuck" I wanted "to write." He said I hadn't done my research, because he would never agree to interviews with me through letter writing. Only in person.

Then came the feelings of inadequacy many narcissists cannot hide from. Hembree said "just because" he was a "convicted killer" did not mean he was "stupid."

He didn't know if I was a "crock pot or what." (Hembree actually meant "crackpot.") He bragged that his "story" was about a "hell of a lot more than 3 murders."

After that, he wrote one of his more interesting comments. Saying how crime fans would "eat up" his life story of crime and the things he had not yet talked about, Hembree added, *Not to mention the other bodies that haven't been found yet.*

He said if I was serious about interviewing him, I would make the trip to the North Carolina prison where he resided and interview him in person. Once there, if he liked what I had to say, *I'll participate,* he wrote.

Power and control. Hembree's two most prevalent traits at play. He was baiting me.

There was not a chance I was going to waste my time. I could see him sitting behind the glass (or refusing to see me at all) and laughing at my appearance.

So I wrote back.

I told him he needed to begin writing to me if he wanted his voice heard. I would not be visiting him without first having a commitment in writing and him beginning to tell me his story vis-à-vis letters and/or phone conversations. We could do those interviews quite easily. Then, after I was comfortable he was not playing me, I would visit him.

Never heard from Danny Hembree again.

I contacted Hembree's sister, Kathy Ledbetter, and we had several conversations and exchanged several e-mails. Kathy wanted to help; I know she did. But in the end, she refused and told me to stop contacting her.

I conducted over one hundred interviews for this book and reviewed thousands of pages of documents. I want to thank everyone for their honesty, integrity, and willingness to tell their stories.

Don't miss the next exciting real-life thriller
by M. William Phelps

TO LOVE AND TO KILL

Coming from Kensington Publishing Corp. in September!

Keep reading for a preview excerpt . . .

CHAPTER 1

Footsteps. The soft, spongy slap of rubber work shoes against the scratched, unwaxed, filthy surface of a tile floor. One after the other.

Pitter-patter.

Squeak, squeak, squeak.

Waitresses take perhaps thousands of steps during a shift. Always coming and going, while certain obnoxious patrons bark orders, make crass comments and groundless, tasteless judgments, before getting up and leaving squat for a tip.

The South is full of roadside diners serving up high cholesterol and diabetes—all you have to do is walk in, sit down in a booth, sporting ripped, waxy seats and grimy checkered tablecloths, and the journey into the greasy-spoon experience has begun.

Heather Strong had been a waitress at one of these places for nearly ten years, though she mainly worked the register as a cashier these days. She took to the job because it suited her character—outgoing, loud, always on the move—and put food on the table for her children. In February 2009, Heather, a beautiful, blue-eyed, brown-haired, twenty-six-year-old mother and soon-to-be divorcée, was working at the

Petro Truck Stop out on Highway 318 in Reddick, Florida. The Iron Skillet restaurant inside the Petro was a busy joint. It was one of those just-off-the-freeway pit stops filled with tired, hungry, dirty, foul-mouthed, penny-pinching, smelly men coming in off the road, piling out of their musty Mack trucks, looking for cheap fast-food meals saturated in grease. Heather drew the eyes of most of these men because she was so stunningly gorgeous in a simple American-girl kind of way. She had the figure of a swimsuit model, sure; but that exterior beauty was juxtaposed against an inner abundance of innocence and purity, a warm heart. Still, for anyone who knew Heather, there was no mistaking the fact that this young woman could take care of herself if necessary.

There was also a hidden vulnerability there within Heather's forced smile: You could tell she had struggled in life somewhat. But with the right man by her side (whom she had found just the previous year, but had let go of after getting back with her husband), Heather could find that picket-fence happiness all young women in her shoes longed for.

"What's a hot little thang like you doing in a place like this?" was a common remark Heather endured more times than she could count. She hated it every time. Paid no mind to men who spoke to her disrespectfully like that. She had a job to do. Kids to feed. She was making ends meet. It didn't mean she had to take insults and sexually aggressive comments.

"Give me your check and let's get y'all cashed out?" Heather would snap back. "I ain't got all day."

Heather seemed tired on this day. She'd been having a rough go of things lately, to say the least. Most of those problems stemmed from the relationship with her children's father, her husband, twenty-seven-year-old Joshua "Josh" Fulgham, a rather complicated and volatile man with a past she had recently separated from. Since the breakup, Heather had been living with another man, more out of convenience than love. But that leash Josh had around his wife had not been severed completely. Josh wanted his kids and was afraid Heather would one day take off with them; he promised a nasty custody battle coming down the road. He was also enraged at the fact that Heather was living with a man Josh saw as a danger to his children.

"You seen Heather around?" Heather's boss asked a coworker a day after Valentine's Day, February 15, 2009. It had been a normal day at the Petro: regulars, new customers, broken coffee machine, same dirty dishes coming from the kitchen, stains on the silverware. 'Bout the only thing different was that Heather had not come to work. It was so unlike her not to show up. If there was one thing about Heather Strong, work was first and foremost. She needed the money to support her kids—and that darn husband of hers, he rarely gave her anything to help out, yet always seemed to have the cash to buy "party goods" or go out and have a good time.

"She always called," Heather's boss later explained.

"I haven't seen her," Heather's coworker said.

"Huh," Heather's boss responded. "If you do, tell her to call me."

Heather generally worked the morning shift, although she did sometimes take on a double. On most days, she'd come in and set up the salad bar and then go about her ordinary duties.

She should have been in by now, thought Heather's boss, looking at the clock in her small office, trying to shake a bad feeling that something was terribly wrong.

CHAPTER 2

Heather's first cousin, Misty Strong, was at home in Columbus, Mississippi, where Heather grew up and had lived most of her life. Misty, equally as beautiful as Heather, could pass for Heather's identical twin—the two girls looked so much alike.

"Heather was like a sister to me," Misty later said.

A few weeks had gone by and Misty had not heard from her cousin. This was odd. Heather and Misty kept in touch. However streetwise Heather had become over the years, especially while living in Florida, she was green in many ways of the world, Misty knew. It seemed that Heather had only one man most of her life and he had taken her to Florida: Joshua Fulgham. Josh and Heather met in Starkville, Mississippi. Heather was sixteen, waitressing after school at a local restaurant; Joshua, one year older, was a customer. Josh was that tough, rugged, overprotective and overly jealous type. He was well known in the Mississippi town where he grew up as a bruiser and tough, troubled kid. Josh was five feet eight inches tall and weighed about 175 pounds—one of those physiques people might say he was born with, a guy who could eat anything and never gain an ounce. Josh generally wore his hair shortly cropped, but had turned to an entirely shaved head later in life. For Heather, Josh fit the image of a badass she liked so much. Heather felt comfortable around Josh. She felt protected. The two of them hit it off right away on that day inside the restaurant.

From the start, Misty Strong later observed, Josh and Heather had issues. He was rough with her. He liked to manhandle Heather a lot when he wanted his way. The cops were often involved. After meeting, dating and then living together as teens, Heather having a child, with another on the way, Mississippi didn't seem to entice them as it once had. So Josh and Heather made the decision to move to Florida. It was 2004. Josh had potential job prospects in Florida—or so he said. He had family down there. The move felt like a step up. Heather wasn't thrilled at going, moving away from her family in Mississippi, but she thought what the hell, why not give it a try. They could always move back if things didn't work out.

Misty knew with Heather moving away, there was little she could do. Once Heather was gone, in fact, Misty had lost touch with her for a time, and Misty believed it was Josh holding her down, keeping Heather from contacting her family. One more way for Josh to govern over Heather and keep her tied down.

"He was just too controlling," Misty explained. "He didn't want her around any family or anybody that cared about her."

Heather didn't even have her own cell phone or computer back then, during their early days in Florida. She had been totally cut off from everyone back home.

Just the way Josh liked it.

Then, in early 2008, after nearly four years of living with Josh, raising two kids and going through hell and back, Heather showed up in Columbus one day.

"I've finally left him," she told Misty.

"Thank God."

Misty and Heather's grandmother was sick at the time. She was actually dying. So they bonded over that family crisis. The two women picked up their "sister" relationship from back in the day and stayed in touch daily. Misty kept telling her cousin it was all going to be okay. There was no need to worry about anything. She'd help with the kids. She'd help Heather start over. The key to it was for Heather to stay the hell away from Josh, who was still in Florida. If Heather could do that, she had a chance. Everyone in her family believed this.

There was one day when Misty went to see their grandmother, who was on her last days. When Misty returned, Heather was gone.

And so were her bags.

Damn.

"Josh had . . . brought her back to Florida," Misty later recalled. No one knew it, but he snuck into town, convinced Heather she needed him and drove her back.

Heather had gone willingly, apparently. She wanted to work things out for the kids' sake. That was Heather—always yearning to find that pristine image of the American family unit on the other side of a dark rainbow. What mother, after all, doesn't want her children's father to be a part of their lives? Maybe Josh was changing. He was angry and sometimes violent; but when he was good, he was a nice guy. They got along and loved each other.

Or was Heather locked in that same fantasy that many abused women see in their dreams?

I'll give him just one more chance. He'll change. You'll see.

Things didn't work out for Heather. Josh *didn't* change. So Heather moved out and found someone else to live with in Florida, thinking it would be better for the kids if she stayed in the state this time. The place she found had a computer. Heather now had a cell phone. She and Misty were in contact just about every day, sometimes several times a day.

"Myspace, cell phone, e-mail," Misty said.

But then, suddenly, it stopped. *Boom!* One day Heather wasn't communicating anymore. Misty and Heather had been talking for months. Heather was saying that Josh had a girlfriend now. He was letting go. Heather had someone new, too. There had been some issues between Heather and Josh's new girlfriend, and Josh sometimes seemed to want to reconcile with Heather, but Heather was saying things were beginning to settle down. They finally had figured out that maybe they just weren't meant to be together. Josh seemed to accept this.

Now Misty was concerned, however. It was late in the day on February 25, 2009, and she had not heard from Heather in well over a week. Misty knew damn well that something was up. It was so unlike Heather not to call or e-mail for this long a period.

So Misty called Heather's brother, Jacob, and asked if he had heard from her.

"No," Jacob said.

"Any idea where she is?"

Jacob responded, "I got a call from [Heather's friend]. She was concerned."

"Concerned? How so?"

"Well, Heather had all her belongings over there at her friend's. Now all of her stuff is gone and she is missing."

"Missing?" Misty answered. She felt her stomach turn. Her body now felt numb. Then that life-will-never-be-the-same-after-today feeling came on all at once. Misty felt it.

"Missing"—the word that no one wants to hear. It sounded so final.

So dangerous.

So deadly.

"Your book stirred me to tears and drove me to prayer! Please send me more information about your ministry to native missionaries. May God continue to bless you and use you."

—Miss J. S.
Towson, Maryland

"I have just finished reading your book, and I have been deeply stirred by it. I am eligible for Social Security this year, and my husband is going to let me use all of my monthly check for missions. We will live on his Social Security and pension. It is amazing how the Lord stretches our funds. But our life-style is simple, and giving is our greatest joy."

—Mrs. D. F.
Binghamton, New York

"I read your book and think it is one of the most dynamic, down-to-earth books that I have ever read. I want to give a copy to our pastor, each board member and selected other people at our church."

—Mr. P. W.
Santa Margarita, California

"I just finished reading *Revolution in World Missions* by K.P. Yohannan. The thought that for the cost of supporting one missionary from Canada as many as ten local Asian missionaries could be supported continues to astound me."

—Mr. S. D.
Calgary, Alberta

"We both read K.P.'s book and were very moved to change part of our life-style to further the gospel. I hope we can do more as we get braver!"

—Mr. and Mrs. D. F.
Los Alamos, New Mexico

"I saw myself too many times in your book, K.P. Although we are going through a financial trial right now, I realize how very blessed we are compared to most of the rest of the world. I have caught sight of your vision."

—*Mrs. S. S.*
Chesapeake, Virginia

"After finishing your book, our family is now deciding how we can be a part of God's plan for His church in Asia. If you have any suggestions, we would enjoy your input — especially from the experience you have acquired."

—*Mr. P. P.*
Fort Atkinson, Wisconsin

"We have been challenged and convicted by *Revolution in World Missions*. We believe that our Lord Jesus is offering us the chance to share in His work in Asia — a chance we don't want to miss!"

—*Mr. and Mrs. M. D.*
Pacifica, California

"After reading *Revolution in World Missions* I am convinced our small amount of money can do more good in this mission than many others we participate in."

—*Mrs. I. T.*
Houston, Texas

Revolution in World Missions

To open their eyes, and
to turn them from darkness to light,
and from the power of Satan to God,
that they may receive forgiveness
of sins, and inheritance among
them that are sanctified by faith.

— Acts 26:18

Creation House
Strang Communications Company
600 Rinehart Road
Lake Mary, FL 32746
(407) 333-3132

Unless otherwise noted, all Scripture quotations are from the
King James Version of the Bible.

Scripture quotations marked NIV are from the Holy Bible,
New International Version. Copyright © 1973, 1978, 1984,
International Bible Society. Used by permission.

Paperback:
First printing, July 1986
Second printing, November 1986
Third printing, May 1987
Fourth printing, December 1987
Revised edition, July 1989
Pocket-size:
First printing, May 1991
Second printing, January 1992
Third printing, June 1992
Fourth printing, August 1993
Fifth printing, March 1994
Sixth printing, June 1994
Seventh printing, March 1995

*This book is dedicated to George Verwer,
founder and international director
of Operation Mobilization,
whom the Lord used to call me into
the ministry and whose life and example
have influenced me more
than any other single individual's.*

Acknowledgments

There are hundreds of people who have had an impact on this volume — from those who have made suggestions, to those who have given encouragement, to those who have influenced my life and ministry. To all of them — all of you — I want to thank you and thank the Lord for placing you in my path.

Of those especially close to me during the long writing, editing and review of this manuscript, I would like to thank William T. Bray, David and Karen Mains, Gayle Erwin, Dave Hicks and Martin Bennett for their honest criticism and unwavering support of this entire project.

Special thanks also are due Margaret Jordan, Heidi Chupp and Jenifer George, who typed the manuscript, and to Larry Jerden for his contributions to the introduction and for his overall management of its production.

Most of all, of course, my greatest debt is to my wife, Gisela, for her careful reading of all that was written and for her suggestions that made the critical difference in several passages. Most of all, her emotional and spiritual support made the writing of this book possible. Without her standing beside me and encouraging me during these eventful years, this book — and the message it proclaims — would not have been possible.

K.P. Yohannan

Contents

Part III: The Way

Foreword

by David and Karen Mains

We all are skeptical of Christians with big dreams. We don't know why exactly — perhaps we have met too many who pursued visions but whose personal lives were nightmares.

The first time we remember meeting K.P. Yohannan we brought him home for dinner, and our family dragged this slight Indian along with us to a high school gymnasium to sit through an American rite of passage — an all-school spaghetti supper. Across the paper tablecloth, the garlic bread and the centerpieces — shellacked lunch sacks filled with an assortment of dried weeds and pasta (created by members of the Mains family!) — we heard of a dream to win not only India but all of Asia for Christ.

Since that evening in the noisy gymnasium in West Chicago, Illinois, there have been many more shared experiences — phone calls from Dallas; trips to the cities and backwaters of India; pastors' conferences in open thatched-roofed, bamboo-sided pavilions;

laughter; travel on Third World roads; and times of prayer.

Very simply said, we have come to believe in K.P.

And we believe in his plan for evangelization which, with the profundity of simplicity, bypasses the complexity of technology and challenges Asians to give up their lives to win their fellow countrymen to Christ.

This book, *Revolution in World Missions*, reveals one of God's master plans to reach the world before the end of time. With absolute confidence we know we can endorse the integrity of its author, a man of God, and we are thrilled with the work of Gospel for Asia.

You can read knowing that those evangelists traveling into the unreached villages of Asia have more heart, more fervor, more passion to spread the gospel of Christ than most of us who are surrounded by the comforts and conveniences of our Western world.

We know because we have seen them and talked with them, and they have put us to shame.

It is the internationals who are the wave of the missionary effort of the future. K.P. Yohannan's book paints the picture of how that dream can become reality.

This is one dreamer of whom we are no longer skeptical. We think you will find reason to believe as well.

Introduction

Revised Edition, 1992

B efore the second half of the 1980s rolled around, most evangelical Christians in Western countries tended to view mission history in terms of only two great waves of activity.

The first wave broke over the New Testament world in the first century as the apostles obeyed the Great Commission. It swept through the Jewish and pagan communities of the Roman Empire, bringing the message of salvation to all of the Mediterranean world, much of Southern Europe and even some parts of Asia.

The second wave was most often dated from William Carey's pioneer work in eighteenth-century India. It began a flood of nineteenth- and twentieth-century missions to the colonies of the great European powers. Although World War II marked the end of this colonial era, it still frequently defines the image of missions for many Western Christians.

But around the world today, this definition is fast

13

disappearing as the Holy Spirit is breaking over Asian and African nations, raising up a new army of missionaries. These humble, obscure pioneers of the gospel are taking up the banner of the cross where colonial-era missions left off.

This third wave is the native missionary movement. Thousands of dedicated men and women are bringing the salvation story to their own people — millions of lost souls in closed countries who would probably never learn about the love of God by any other means.

As Christians in the West gradually develop a greater understanding of what this third wave means to world evangelism, it becomes a potent challenge to our attitudes and life-styles. Thousands of individuals and churches are becoming senders of native missionaries, praying and supporting them on the frontiers of faith.

Revolution in World Missions has undergone various revisions over the past eight years. I have sought to clarify basic areas of misunderstanding surrounding the native missionary movement, such as the changing role of Western missionaries and standards of accountability in native missions. By printing a pocket-sized edition at a much lower cost, we have also made it more available to the public.

The impact this book has made continues to grow. Pastors have written us, testifying of the dramatic changes their church's mission programs have had. Fathers and mothers — and their children — are learning to live more simply and creatively in order to support native missionaries. Young adults, faced with eternal matters, are choosing to make their lives count for the kingdom rather than succumb to the climb up the ladder.

I believe we will see this generation reached for Christ as this exciting third wave of mission leadership unites with concerned Christians and churches around the world. As we draw nearer to Christ in unity, feeling His heartbeat for lost and dying souls, we realize that we are all serving one King and one kingdom. May this book serve to bring greater unity and cooperation among all God's people, as we seek to obey His will together.

K.P. Yohannan

Part I

THE VISION

1

How Many Would Be Beaten and Go Hungry?

The silence of the great hall in Cochin was broken only by soft choking sobs. The Spirit of God was moving over the room with awesome power — convicting of sin and calling men and women into His service. Before the meeting ended, 120 of the 1,200 pastors and Christian leaders present made their way to the altar, responding to the "call of the North."

They were not saying, "I'm willing to go," but "I am going."

They made the choice to leave home, village and family, business or career and go where they would be hated and feared. Meanwhile, another six hundred pastors pledged to return to their congregations and raise up more missionaries who would leave South India and go to the North.

I stood silently in the holy hush, praying for the army of God crowded around the altar. I was humbled by the presence of God.

As I prayed, my heart ached for these men who

came to the altar. How many would be beaten and go hungry or be cold and lonely in the years ahead? How many would sit in jails for their faith? I prayed for the blessing and protection of God on them — and for more sponsors across the seas to stand with them.

They were leaving many material comforts, family ties and personal ambitions. Ahead lay a new life among strangers. But also I knew there would be spiritual victory as they would witness many thousands turn to Christ and help to form new congregations in the unreached villages of North India.

How different were my tears now from those on that fateful day of decision back in 1973. Then I sat on a Punjabi curbstone blinded by the bitter tears of frustration and failure. Today tears of joy trickled down my cheeks as I realized how God had turned my despair into victory. Out of that crisis of discouragement, the God of Abraham had answered prayers. Here before my eyes was proof He is creating a third wave in missions — calling native believers to the harvest field.

With me in the meeting was U.S. Christian radio broadcaster David Mains, a serious student of revival. He had joined us in Cochin as one of the conference speakers. He later testified how the Lord had taken over the meeting in a most unusual way.

"It would hardly have been different," he wrote later, "had Jesus Himself been bodily among us. The spirit of worship filled the hall. The singing was electrifying. The power of the Holy Spirit came upon the audience. Men actually groaned aloud. I have read of such conviction in early American history during the times like the two Great Awakenings, but I had never anticipated experiencing it firsthand."

But the Lord isn't simply calling out a huge army of native workers. God is at work saving people from sin in numbers we never before dreamed possible. People are coming to Christ all across Asia at an accelerated rate wherever salvation is being proclaimed. In some areas — like India, Indonesia, the Philippines and Thailand — it is not uncommon now for the Christian community to grow as much in only one month as it formerly did in a whole year.

If anything, I have found reports of mass conversion and church growth are being underplayed in the Western press. The exciting truth about God's working in Asia has yet to be told. This dearth of information about what is happening in most countries is partly because the press has limited access. Except for in a few countries, like Korea and the Philippines, the real story is not getting out.

A remarkable movement to Christ is developing in the North Indian state of Rajasthan, known as the "land of kings." We started work in this area with a team of South Indian native evangelists in 1965. At that time it was known in our language as the "wilderness of the gospel." For hundreds of years, British and American missionaries had carried on educational and medical work in this area. However, there was never any true indigenous church movement. But now, in just three months, we have seen new churches planted in twenty-one villages. In a major provincial capital, over one thousand came to Christ in one week alone! In my opinion, this is a miraculous movement of the Holy Spirit similar to accounts in the book of Acts or in early church history.

When you think of the past record, the progress is staggering. The people of this state have resisted the gospel for centuries. Many Christians have been seriously injured in riots caused by angry mobs who oppose the preaching of Christ. Some have even died for their faith.

These new church growth movements are being led by unknown bands of native evangelists who have never had one line of publicity in the Western press.

Typical of the many native missionary movements that have sprung up overnight is the work in the Punjab of a native brother from Kerala. A former military officer who gave up a commission and army career to help start a gospel team, he now leads more than four hundred full-time missionaries. Recently I received a request from him asking us to sponsor another one hundred helpers. Ten years ago we would have been happy to see three or four workers raised up. But now, thanks to the support that has been coming through Gospel for Asia, he has been able to accept a steady stream of new staff from South India.

Like other native mission leaders, he has discipled ten "Timothys" who are directing the work in almost military precision. Each of them in turn will be able to lead hundreds of additional workers who will have their own disciples.

As I sat down to write this chapter, I opened a letter from him telling of the missionary trip he just completed in Maharashtra state. Forty-two new churches were established there in twelve days. In another area populated by Mang tribals, fifty additional villages need full-time native evangelists to come and establish their new churches.

With his wife he set an apostolic pattern for their workers similar to that of the apostle Paul. On one evangelistic tour that lasted fifty-three days, he and his family traveled by bullock cart and foot into some of the most backward areas of the tribal districts of Orissa state. There, working in the intense heat among people whose life-style is so primitive that it can be described only as animalistic, he saw hundreds converted. Throughout the journey, demons were cast out, and miraculous physical healings took place daily. Thousands of the tribals, who are enslaved to idols and spirit-worship, heard the gospel eagerly.

In just one month he formed fifteen groups of converts into new churches and assigned native missionaries to stay behind and build them up in the faith.

Similar miraculous movements are starting in almost every state of India and throughout other nations of Asia.

In one area of India hundreds of villagers turned to the Lord when four of their pagan priests were miraculously saved.

Native missionary Jesu Das was horrified when he first visited the village and found no believers there. The people were all worshipping hundreds of different gods, and the four pagan priests controlled them through their witchcraft.

Stories were told of how these priests could kill people's cattle with witchcraft and destroy their crops. People were suddenly taken ill and died without explanation.

The destruction and bondage these people were living in is hard to imagine. Scars, decay and death were portrayed on their faces, because they were totally controlled by the powers of darkness.

When Jesu Das told them about Christ, it was the first time they ever heard that there was a God who did not require sacrifices and offerings to appease His anger.

As Jesu Das continued to preach in the market-place, many people came to know the Lord.

But the priests were outraged. They warned Jesu Das that if he did not leave the village, they would call on their gods to kill him, his wife and their children.

But Jesu Das did not leave. He continued to preach, and villagers continued to be saved.

Finally, after a few weeks, the witch doctors came to Jesu Das and asked him the secret of his power.

"This is the first time our power did not work," they told him. "After doing the 'pujas,' we asked the spirits to go and kill your family. But the spirits came back and told us they could not approach you or your family because you were always surrounded by fire.

"Then we called more powerful spirits to come after you — but they too returned, saying not only were you surrounded by fire, but angels were also around you all the time."

Jesu Das told them about Christ. The Holy Spirit convicted each of them of their sin of following demons and of the judgment to come.

With tears, they repented — renouncing their gods and idols — and received Jesus Christ as Lord.

As a result of their pagan priests following the Lord, hundreds of other villagers also were set free from sin and bondage.

In Thailand, where more than two hundred native missionaries with the Thai Ezra Team are pioneering village evangelism, one group personally shared their faith with 10,463 in two months. Of these, 171 gave their lives to Christ, and six new churches were formed.

Over one thousand came to Christ in the same reporting period. Remember, this great harvest is happening in a Buddhist nation that never has seen such results.

In the Philippines, where a native evangelistic team recently spent fifteen weeks reaching ten villages in Bataan, more than seventeen thousand were counseled for salvation. Another team with a traveling film ministry reported 44,548 conversions in 1983.

Documented reports like these come to us daily from native teams in almost every Asian nation. But I am convinced these are only the first few drops of revival rain. In order to make the necessary impact, we must send out hundreds of thousands more workers. We're no longer praying for the proverbial "showers of blessings" — we must see cloudbursts. I'm believing God for virtual thunderstorms of blessings in the days ahead.

How I became a part of this astonishing spiritual renewal in Asia is what this book is all about. And it all began with the prayers of a simple village mother.

2

O God,
Let One of My Boys Preach

Achiamma's eyes stung with salty tears. But they weren't from the cooking fire or the hot spices that wafted up from the pan. She realized time was short. Her six sons were growing beyond her influence. Yet not one showed signs of going into the gospel ministry.

Except for the youngest — little "Yohannachan" as I was known — every one of her children seemed destined for secular work. My brothers seemed content to live and work around our native village of Niranam in Kerala, South India.

"O God," she prayed in despair, "let just one of my boys preach!"

Like Hannah and so many other saintly mothers in the Bible, she had dedicated her children to the Lord. That morning, while preparing breakfast, she vowed to fast secretly until God called one of her sons into His service. Every Friday for the next three and a half years, she fasted. Her prayer was always the same.

But nothing happened. Finally, only I, scrawny and little — the baby of the family — was left. But there seemed little chance I would preach. I was so shy and timid I trembled when asked to recite in class. Although I had stood up in an evangelistic meeting at age eight, I kept my faith mostly to myself.

In fact, I had turned into the village's youngest recluse — a nonperson who avoided sports and school functions. I showed no leadership skills. I was comfortable on the edge of village and family life, a shadowy figure who moved in and out of the scene almost unnoticed.

Then, when I was sixteen, my mother's prayers were answered. A visiting gospel team from Operation Mobilization came to our church to present the challenge of faraway North India. My ninety-pound frame strained to catch every word as the team spoke and showed slides of the North.

They told of stonings and beatings they received while preaching Christ in the non-Christian villages of Rajasthan and Bihar. It stretched my imagination to visualize the hot arid plains of North India. Sheltered from contact with the rest of India by the high peaks of the Western Ghats, the lush coastal jungles of Kerala were all I knew of my homeland. The rest of India seemed an ocean away to the Malayalam-speaking people of the southwest coast, and I was no exception.

Besides the wildlife and fish that thrived in the surrounding rivers and tropical rain forests, the Malabar Coast had long nourished India's oldest Christian community. Christianity was one of India's oldest religions, because the flourishing sea trade with the Persian Gulf made it possible for St. Thomas to introduce Jesus Christ at nearby Cranagore in A.D. 52. Other Jews already were there, having arrived two hundred years earlier.

As the gospel team portrayed the desperately lost condition of the rest of the country — 500,000 villages without a gospel witness — I felt a strange sorrow for the lost. That day in my heart I vowed to help bring the good news of Jesus Christ to those strange and mysterious states to the North. At the challenge to "forsake all and follow Christ" I somewhat rashly took the leap, agreeing to join the student group for a short summer crusade in unreached parts of North India.

So my decision to go into the ministry was largely because of my mother's faithful prayers. Although I still hadn't received what I later understood to be my real call from the Lord, my mother encouraged me to follow my heart in the matter. When I announced my decision, she wordlessly handed over twenty-five rupees — enough for my train ticket. I set off to apply to the mission's headquarters in Trivandrum.

There I got my first rebuff. Since I was underage, they at first refused to let me join the teams going north. But I was permitted to attend the annual training conference to be held in Bangalore, Karnataka.

At the conference I heard missionary statesman

George Verwer for the first time. He challenged me as never before to commit myself to a life of breathtaking, radical discipleship. I was impressed how Verwer himself put the will of God for the lost world before career, family and self.

Alone that night in my bed, I argued with both God and my own conscience. By two o'clock in the morning, my pillow was wet with sweat and tears. I shook with fear. What if God would ask me to preach in the streets? How would I ever be able to stand up in public and speak? What if I were stoned and beaten?

I knew myself only too well. I could hardly bear to look a friend in the eye during a conversation, let alone speak publicly to hostile crowds on behalf of God. As I spoke the words, I realized that I was behaving as Moses did when he was called.

Suddenly, I felt that I was not alone in the room. A great sense of love and of my being loved filled the place. I felt the presence of God and fell on my knees beside the bed.

"Lord God," I gasped in surrender to His presence and will, "I'll give myself to speak for You — but help me to know that You're with me."

Then it was morning. I awoke to a world and people suddenly different. Walking outside, the Indian street scenes were the same as before: children running between the legs of people and cows, pigs and chickens wandering about, vendors with baskets of bright fruit and flowers on their heads. I loved them all with a supernatural unconditional love I'd never felt before. It was just as if God had removed my eyes and replaced them with His.

For the first time I was seeing people as the heavenly Father sees them — lost and needy but with potential to glorify and reflect Him.

I walked to the bus station. My eyes filled with tears of love. I knew that these people were all going to hell — and I knew that God didn't want them to go there. Suddenly I had such a burden for these masses that I had to stop and lean against a wall just to keep my balance.

So this was it. I knew I was feeling the burden of love God feels for the lost multitudes of India. His loving heart was pounding within mine, and I could hardly breathe. The tension was great. I paced back and forth restlessly to keep my knees from knocking in fright.

"Lord!" I cried. "If You want me to do something, say it, and give me courage."

Looking up from my prayer I saw a huge stone. I knew immediately I had to climb that stone and preach to the crowds in the bus station. Scrambling up, I felt a force like ten thousand volts of electricity shooting through my body.

I began by singing a simple children's chorus. It was all I knew. By the time I finished, a crowd stood at the foot of the rock. I had not prepared myself to speak, but all at once God took over and filled my mouth with words of His love. I preached the gospel to the poor as Jesus commanded His disciples to do.

I saw myself fulfilling His mission in His power.

Suddenly I had superhuman boldness. As the authority and power of God flowed through me, words came out I never knew I had — and with a power clearly from above.

Others from the gospel teams stopped to listen. The question of my age and calling never came up again. That was 1966, and I continued moving with mobile evangelistic teams for the next seven years.

We traveled all over North India, never staying very long in any one village. Everywhere I would preach in the streets, while others distributed books and tracts. Occasionally, in smaller villages, we would witness from house to house.

Although I often would witness and join in the ministry, my real heart was with open-air preaching. I knew that most people were illiterate and enjoyed listening to me passionately proclaim the Lord.

Using a "wordless flag" stitched together from cloth strips, I explained the gospel easily to illiterate villagers. The flag had four bars of color and in itself attracted many people to learn its meaning. The black bar of cloth represented our sinful hearts before Christ entered. The red bar, His cleansing blood. The white, our new hearts. And the yellow, our hope of walking the golden streets of heaven. From the back of diesel vans, beside bicycles and on foot, this simple banner made the good news of Christ clear to thousands.

And with the flag we often would sing the children's chorus:

"My heart was black with sin,
    until the Savior came in.
His precious blood I know,
    has washed me white as snow.
And in His word I'm told
    I'll walk the streets of gold.
Oh wonderful, wonderful day,
    He washed my sins away."

My urgent, overpowering love for the village people of India and the poor masses grew with the years. People even began to nickname me "Gandhi Man" after the father of modern India, Mahatma Gandhi. Like him, I realized without being told that if India was to be won, it would be by brown-skinned natives who loved the village people.

Even as I studied the Gospels, it became clear to me that Jesus understood the principle well. He avoided the major cities, the rich, the famous and the powerful. Rather than go to the elite centers of influence, He concentrated His ministry on the poor laboring class. To reach India and the other nations of Asia, all we have to do is reach the poor.

As I traveled, viewing the effects of pagan religions on India, I realized that the masses of India are starving because they are slaves to sin. The battle against hunger and poverty is really a spiritual battle, not a physical or social one as secularists would have us believe.

The only weapon that will ever effectively win the

war against disease, hunger, injustice and poverty in Asia is the gospel of Jesus Christ. To look into the sad eyes of a hungry child or see the wasted life of a drug addict is to see only the evidence of Satan's hold on this world. All bad things are his handiwork. He is the ultimate enemy of mankind, and he will do everything within his considerable power to kill and destroy human beings. Fighting this powerful enemy with physical weapons is like fighting an armored tank with stones.

I can never forget one of the more dramatic encounters we had with these demonic powers. It was a hot and unusually humid day in 1970. We were preaching in the northwestern state of Rajasthan — the "desert of kings."

As was our practice before a street meeting, my seven co-workers and I stood in a circle to sing and clap hands to the rhythm of Christian folk songs. A sizeable crowd gathered, and I began to speak in Hindi, the local language. Many heard the gospel for the first time and eagerly took our Gospels and tracts to read.

One young man came up to me and asked for a book to read. As I talked to him, I sensed in my spirit that this was a person hungry to know God. As we got ready to climb aboard our gospel van, he asked to join us.

As the van lurched forward, he cried and wailed. "I am a terrible sinner," he shrieked. "How can I sit among you?" With that he started to jump from the moving van. We held on to him and forced him to the floor to prevent injury.

That night he stayed at our base and the next morning joined us for the prayer meeting. While we were praising and interceding, we heard a sudden scream. Then we saw the young man lying on the ground, tongue lolling out of his mouth, his eyes rolled back.

As Christians in a pagan land, we knew immediately he was demon-possessed. We gathered around him and began taking authority over the forces of hell as they spoke through his mouth.

"We are seventy-four of us....For the past seven years we have made him walk barefoot all over India....He is ours...." They spoke on, blaspheming and cursing, challenging us and our authority.

But as three of us prayed, the demons could not keep their hold on the young man. They came out when we commanded them to leave in the name of Jesus.

Sundar John was delivered. He gave his life to Jesus and was baptized. Later, he went to Bible school for two years. Since then the Lord has enabled him to teach and preach to thousands of people about Christ. Several native Indian churches have started as a result of his remarkable ministry — all this from a man many people would have locked up in an insane asylum.

Today, Sundar John is continuing in fellowship with us as a native missionary evangelist. But there are literally millions of people like him in India — deceived by demons and enslaved to their horrible passions and lusts.

This is the kind of miracle that kept me going from village to village for those seven years of itinerant preaching. Our lives read like pages from the book of Acts. Most nights we slept between villages in roadside ditches, where we were relatively safe. Sleeping in non-Christian villages would expose us to many dangers. Our team always created a stir, and at times we even faced stonings and beatings.

We were persecuted, hated and despised. Yet we kept going, knowing that we were blazing a trail for the gospel in districts that never before had experienced an encounter with Christ.

One such village was Bhundi in Rajasthan. This was the first place I was beaten and stoned for preaching the gospel. Often literature was destroyed. It seemed that mobs always were on the watch for us, and six times our street meetings were broken up. Our team leaders began to work elsewhere, avoiding Bhundi as much as possible. Three years later, a new team of native missionaries moved into the area under different leadership and preached again at this busy crossroads town.

Almost as soon as they arrived, one man began tearing up literature and grabbed a nineteen-year-old missionary, Alex Sam, by the throat. Although beaten severely, Sam knelt in the street and prayed for the salvation of souls in that hateful city.

"Lord," he prayed, "I want to come back here and serve You in Bhundi. I'm willing to die here, but I want to come back and serve You in this place."

Many older Christian leaders advised him against his decision, but being determined, he went back and rented a small room. Shipments of literature arrived, and he preached in the face of many difficulties. Today fifty people meet in a small church there. Those who persecuted us at one time now worship the Lord Jesus, as was the case with the apostle Paul.

This is the kind of commitment and faith it takes to win North Indian villages to the Lord Jesus.

At another time we arrived in a town at daybreak to preach. But word already had gone ahead from the nearby village where we had preached the day before.

As we had morning tea in a roadside stall, the local militant leader approached me politely. In a low voice that betrayed little emotion, he spoke:

"Get on your truck and get out of town in five minutes or we'll burn it and you with it."

I knew he was serious. He was backed by a menacing crowd.

Although we did "shake the dust from our feet" that day, there is a church meeting in that same village today. In order to plant the gospel, risks must be taken.

For months at a time I traveled the dusty roads in the heat of the day and shivered through cold nights — suffering just as thousands of native missionaries are suffering today to bring the gospel to the lost.

In future years I would look back on those seven years of village evangelism as one of the greatest learning experiences of my life. We walked in Jesus' steps, incarnating and representing Him to masses of people who had never heard the gospel before.

If Only She Were an Indian

I was living a frenetic, busy life — too busy and thrilled with the work of the gospel to think much about the future. There always was another campaign just ahead. The mobile gospel teams I worked with — and often led — were just like family to me. I came almost to enjoy the gypsy life-style we lived, and the total abandonment to the cause of Christ that is demanded of an itinerant evangelist.

But I was about to reach a turning point. In 1971 I was invited to spend one month in Singapore at a new institute which had been started by John Haggai. It was still in the formative stages then — a place where Asian church leaders would be trained and challenged to witness for Christ.

With Haggai was another of the great men of our times, Bob Pierce, founder of World Vision. My encounters with these men would eventually change the direction of my life, and their words were to haunt me for years to come.

When I met Haggai, I knew he believed in me instantly. I sensed he was not afraid for me to reach my full potential — that he wanted me to dream great dreams and accomplish God's very best for my life. Unlike so many Christian leaders from the West, there was nothing in Haggai that tried to hold me back or keep me in "my place."

He was the first person who made me believe that nothing is impossible with God. He was full of stories. In them all, Christians were overcomers and giants — men and women who received a vision from God and refused to let go of it. Diligence to your calling was a virtue to be highly prized.

In both Pierce and Haggai I found men who refused to accept impossibilities. The normal boundaries accepted by others didn't exist for them. Here were men who saw everything in global terms and from God's perspective. I was walking on dizzying heights, dreaming dreams and thinking thoughts I'd never allowed myself to entertain in the past.

These were men who refused to accept sin. If the world was not evangelized, why not? If people were hungry, what could we do about it? These men didn't think like Hindus; they refused to accept the world as it was. And I discovered they were willing to accept personal responsibility to become change agents.

Pierce prayed like no man I had ever met. One of his prayers is still a regular part of my devotional life: "O loving God, break my heart with the things that break the heart of Jesus."

He told a story once that I have never forgotten. Early in his ministry he had been a part of the Billy Graham Evangelistic Team. Unlike the others, he seemed to have no outstanding public gift, and that troubled him. Finally, he prayed a prayer that eventually led him to Korea and the founding of World Vision:

> O living God, I cannot preach like Billy Graham. I cannot sing like Cliff Barrows. But, Lord — if there's something You want someone to do and they won't do it — then tell me. I promise I'll do it with all my heart, with everything I have in my power and in the best way I know how. Amen.

It was that servant spirit which led Bob Pierce to start World Vision on every continent and in every nation of Asia. Millions were touched in the two decades of his Asian ministry.

Toward the end of my month with them, John Haggai challenged me into the most painful introspection I have ever experienced. I know now it implanted a restlessness in me that would last for years.

It eventually would cause me to leave India to search abroad for God's ultimate will in my life.

Haggai's challenge seemed simple at first. He wanted me to go to my room and write down — in one sentence — the single most important thing I was going to do with the rest of my life.

He stipulated that it could not be self-centered or worldly in nature. And one more thing — it had to bring glory to God.

I went to my room to write that one sentence. But the paper remained blank for hours and days. I left the conference with the question still ringing in my ears.

For years I would hear the words of John Haggai, "One thing...by God's grace you have to do one thing." Disturbed that I might not be reaching my full potential in Christ, I began at that conference to re-evaluate every part of my life-style and ministry. Nothing changed right away, but I started asking, seeking and knocking in prayer. I knew I had to find and submit to the specific will of God for my life.

I left Singapore newly liberated to think of myself in terms of an individual for the first time. Up until that time — like most Asians — I always had viewed myself as part of a group, either my family or a gospel team. Although I had no idea what special work God would have for me as an individual, I began thinking of doing my "personal best" for Him.

The seeds for future change had been planted, and nothing could stop the approaching storms in my life.

While my greatest passion was still for the un-reached villages of the North, I now was traveling all over India.

On one of these speaking trips in 1973, I was

invited to teach at the spring Operation Mobilization training conference in Madras. That was where I first saw the attractive German girl.

As a student in one of my classes, she impressed me with the simplicity of her faith. Soon I found myself thinking that if she were an Indian, she would be the kind of woman I would like to marry some day.

Once, when our eyes met, we held each other's gaze for a brief, extra moment, until I self-consciously broke the spell and quickly fled the room. I was uncomfortable in such male-female encounters. In our culture, single people seldom speak to each other. Even in church and on gospel teams, the sexes are kept strictly separate.

Certain that I would never again see her, I pushed the thought of the attractive German girl from my mind. But marriage was on my mind. I had made a list of the six qualities I most wanted in a wife and frequently prayed for the right choice to be made for me.

Of course, in India, all marriages are arranged by the parents, and I would have to rely on their judgment in selecting the right person for my life partner. I wondered where my parents would find a wife who was willing to share my mobile life-style and commitment to the work of the gospel. But as the conference ended, plans for the summer outreach soon crowded out these thoughts.

That summer, along with a few co-workers, I returned to all the places we had visited during the last few years in the state of Punjab. I had been in and out of the state many times and was eager to see the fruit of our evangelism there.

The breadbasket of India, the Punjab is one of the richest agricultural areas in the world. Just as the flat plains of Kansas supply most of America's wheat, the Punjab produces most of the wheat and other grains of India. Its population of fifteen million is dominated by turbaned Sikhs, a fiercely independent and hard-working people who have always been a caste of warriors.

Before the partition of India and Pakistan, the state also had a huge Muslim population. It remains one of the least evangelized and most neglected areas of the world.

We had trucked and street-preached our way through hundreds of towns and villages in this state over the previous two years. Although British missionaries had founded many hospitals and schools in the state, very few congregations of believers now existed. The intensely nationalistic Sikhs stubbornly refused to consider Christianity, since they closely associated it with British colonialism.

I traveled with a good-sized team of men. A separate women's team also was assigned to the state, working out of Jullundur.

On my way north to link up with the men's team I would lead, I stopped in at the North India headquarters in New Delhi.

To my surprise there she was again — the German

girl. This time she was dressed in a sari, one of the most popular forms of our national dress. I learned she also had been assigned to work in Punjab for the summer with the women's team.

The local director asked me to escort her northward as far as Jullundur, and so we rode in the same van. I learned her name was Gisela, and the more I saw of her the more enchanted I became.

She ate the food and drank the water and unconsciously followed all the rules of our culture.

The little conversation we had focused on spiritual things and the lost villages of India. I soon realized I had finally found a soul mate who shared my vision and calling.

Romantic love, for most Indians, is something you read about only in storybooks. Daring cinema films, while they frequently deal with the concept, are careful to end the film in a proper Indian manner.

So I was faced with the big problem of communicating my forbidden and impossible love. I said nothing to Gisela, of course. But something in her eyes told me we both understood. Could God be bringing us together?

In a few hours we would be separated again, and I reminded myself I had other things to do. Besides, I thought, at the end of the summer she'll be flying to Germany, and I'll probably never see her again.

Throughout the summer, surprisingly, our paths did cross again. Each time I felt my love grow stronger. Then I tentatively took a chance at expressing my love with a letter.

Meanwhile, the Punjab survey broke my heart. In village after village I found that our literature and preaching appeared to have little lasting impact. I still hadn't learned the secret of making disciples and planting churches. So the fruit had not remained. Most of the villages we visited appeared just as illiterate, idolatrous and demon-controlled as ever. The people still were locked in disease, poverty and suffering. The gospel, it seemed to me, hadn't taken root.

Finally, in one town I felt such deep despair I literally sat down on a curb and sobbed. I wept the bitter tears that only a child can cry.

"Your work is for nothing," taunted a demon in my ear. "Your words are rolling off these people like water off a duck's back!"

Without realizing I was burning out — or what was happening to me spiritually — I fell into listlessness. Like Jonah and Elijah, I was too tired to go on. I could see only one thing. The fruit of my work wasn't remaining. More than ever before, I needed time to reassess my ministry.

My co-leaders, alarmed at my personal crisis and aware that something was deeply wrong, insisted I take a month off to recoup. I went to Bombay for that month.

While there, I corresponded with Gisela. She had, in the meantime, returned to Germany. I finally decided I would take two years off from the work to study and make some life choices about my ministry and possible marriage.

I began writing letters abroad and became interested in the possibility of attending a Bible school in England. I also had invitations to speak in churches in Germany.

In December I bought an air ticket out of India. I would be in Europe for Christmas with Gisela's family.

During the next month I got the first tremors of what soon would become an earthquake-size case of culture shock.

As the snow fell, it was obvious to everyone I soon would have to buy a winter coat and boots — obvious, that is, to everyone except me. One look at the price tags sent me into deep trauma. For the cost of my coat and boots in Germany, I could have lived comfortably for months back in India.

And living by faith was hard for my future in-laws to accept. Here was this penniless street preacher from India, without a single dollar of his own, insisting he was going to school but he didn't know where, and asking to marry their daughter.

One by one the miracles occurred, though, and God met every need.

First, a letter arrived from E.A. Gresham, a total stranger from Dallas, Texas, who was then regional director of the Fellowship of Christian Athletes. He had heard about me from a Scottish friend and invited me to come to the United States for two years of study at what was then the Criswell Bible Institute in Dallas. I replied positively and booked myself on a low-cost charter flight to New York with the last money I had. This flight, it turned out, also was to become a miracle.

Not knowing I needed a special student visa, I bought the ticket without the chance for refund. If I missed the flight, I would lose both my seat and the ticket.

Praying with my last ounce of faith, I asked God to intervene and somehow get the paperwork for the visa. As I prayed, a friend in Dallas, Texas, was strangely moved to get out of his car, go back to the office and complete the paperwork. Later, he testified of a strange urge from God compelling him to complete the paperwork and personally take it to the post office. In a continuous series of divinely arranged "coincidences," the forms arrived within hours of the deadline.

Before leaving for America, Gisela and I became engaged. I would go on to seminary alone, however. We had no idea when we would see each other again.

4

I Walked
in a Daze

As I changed planes for Dallas at JFK International in New York, I was overcome at the sights and sounds around me. Overseas you hear stories about the affluence and prosperity of America, but until you see it with your own eyes, the stories seem like fairy tales.

But Americans are more than just unaware of their affluence — they almost seem to despise it at times. Finding a lounge chair, I stared in amazement at how they treated their beautiful clothes and shoes. The richness of the fabrics and colors was beyond anything I had ever seen. As I would discover again and again, this is a nation that routinely takes its astonishing wealth for granted.

As I would do many times — almost daily — in the weeks ahead, I compared their clothing to that of the native missionary evangelists whom I had left only a few weeks before. Many of them walk barefoot between villages or work in flimsy sandals. Their threadbare cotton clothing would not be acceptable as cleaning rags in the United States. Then I discovered most Americans have closets full of clothing they wear only occasionally — and I remembered the years I traveled and worked with only the clothes on my back. I had lived the normal life-style of most village evangelists.

Economist Robert Heilbroner describes the luxuries a typical American family would have to surrender if they lived among the one billion hungry people in the Third World:

> We begin by invading the house of our imaginary American family to strip it of its furniture. Everything goes: beds, chairs, tables, television sets, lamps. We will leave the family with a few old blankets, a kitchen table, a wooden chair. Along with the bureaus go the clothes. Each member of the family may keep in his 'wardrobe' his oldest suit or dress, a shirt or blouse. We will permit a pair of shoes for the head of the family, but none for the wife or children.
>
> We move to the kitchen. The appliances have already been taken out, so we turn to the cupboards...the box of matches may stay, a small bag of flour, some sugar and salt. A few moldy potatoes, already in the garbage can, must be rescued, for they will

provide much of tonight's meal. We will leave a handful of onions, and a dish of dried beans. All the rest we take away: the meat, the fresh vegetables, the canned goods, the crackers, the candy.

Now we have stripped the house: the bathroom has been dismantled, the running water shut off, the electric wires taken out. Next we take away the house. The family can move to the toolshed.... Communications must go next. No more newspapers, magazines, books — not that they are missed, since we must take away our family's literacy as well. Instead, in our shantytown we will allow one radio....

Now government services must go next. No more postmen, no more firemen. There is a school, but it is three miles away and consists of two classrooms....There are, of course, no hospitals or doctors nearby. The nearest clinic is ten miles away and is tended by a midwife. It can be reached by bicycle, provided the family has a bicycle, which is unlikely....

Finally, money. We will allow our family a cash hoard of five dollars. This will prevent our breadwinner from experiencing the tragedy of an Iranian peasant who went blind because he could not raise the $3.94 which he mistakenly thought he needed to receive admission to a hospital where he could have been cured.[1]

This is an accurate description of the life-style and world from which I came. From the moment I touched foot on American soil, I walked in an unbelieving daze. How can two so different economies co-exist simultaneously on the earth? Everything was so overpowering and confusing to me at first. Not only did I have to learn the simplest procedures — like using the pay telephones and making change — but as a sensitive Christian, I found myself constantly making spiritual evaluations of everything I saw.

As the days passed into weeks, I began with alarm to understand how misplaced are the spiritual values of most Western believers. Sad to say, it appeared to me that for the most part they had absorbed the same humanistic and materialistic values that dominated the secular culture. Almost immediately I sensed an awesome judgment was hanging over the United States — and that I had to warn God's people that He was not going to lavish this abundance on them forever. But the message was still not formed in my heart, and it would be many years before I would feel the anointing and courage to speak out against such sin.

Meanwhile, in Texas, a land that in many ways epitomizes America, I reeled with shock at the most common things. My hosts eagerly pointed out what they considered their greatest achievements. I nodded with politeness as they showed me their huge churches, high-rise buildings and universities. But these didn't impress me very much. After all, I had seen the Golden Temple in Amritsar, the Taj Mahal, the Palaces of Jhans, the university of Baroda in Gujarat.

But what impresses visitors from the Third World are the simple things that Americans take for granted: fresh water available twenty-four hours a day, unlimited electrical power, telephones that work and a most remarkable network of paved roads. In India, the water, electricity, telephones and transportation operate erratically — if at all. Communication is a nightmare. We must wait days for long-distance calls to go through. At the time, we still had no television in India, but my American hosts seemed to have TV sets in every room — and operating day and night. This ever-present blast of media also disturbed me. For some reason, Americans seemed to have a need to surround themselves with noise all the time. Even in their cars, I noticed the radios ran when no one was listening.

Why do they always have to be either entertained or entertaining? I wondered. It was as if they were trying to escape from a guilt they hadn't yet defined or even identified.

Perhaps it was because I still weighed less than 110 pounds, but I was constantly aware of how large — and overweight — most Americans seemed to be. There is a reason why Americans need big cars, big homes and large furniture. They are big people. This came home vividly to me when I went to buy clothes. Like so many other Asian students, I had to go to the youth departments in the stores — adult sizes were just too large.

I was amazed at how important eating, drinking, smoking and even drug use were in the Western life-style. Even among Christians, food was a major part of fellowship events.

This, of course, is not bad in itself. "Love feasts" were an important part of the New Testament church life. But eating can be taken to extremes. One of the ironies of this is the relatively small price North Americans pay for food. One study showed that in the United States only 17 percent of disposable income is spent on food. In India it is 67 percent. When you have $10,000 to spend, that 17 percent works out to a comfortable $1,700. For the Indian family earning $200, 67 percent is $134. This is the kind of reality I had lived with every day, but Americans have real trouble thinking in these terms.

Often I would speak at a church, and the people would apparently be quite moved as I told of the suffering and needs of the native evangelists. They usually would take an offering and present me with a check. At first, this seemed like a great amount of money. Then with their usual hospitality, I would be invited to eat with the leaders following the meeting. To my horror the cost of the food and "fellowship" would frequently be more than the money they had just given to missions. To my amazement I found that American families routinely eat enough meat at one meal to feed an Asian family for a week. No one ever seemed to notice this but me, and slowly I realized they just hadn't heard the meaning of my message. They were simply incapable of understanding the enormous needs overseas.

Even today I sometimes cannot freely order food when traveling in the United States. I look at the costs and realize how far the same amount of money will go in India, Burma or the Philippines. Suddenly I'm not quite as hungry as I was before.

Many native missionaries and their families experience days without food — not because they are fasting voluntarily — but because they don't have money to buy rice. This occurs especially when they start new work in villages where there are no Christians.

Remembering the heartbreaking suffering of the native brethren, I sometimes would refuse to eat the desserts so often served to me. I'm sure this made no difference in supplying food to hungry families, but I couldn't bear to take pleasure in eating while Christian workers in Asia were going hungry. The need became real to me through the ministry of Brother Moses Paulose, who is today one of the native missionaries we sponsor.

There are thousands of islands and endless miles of coastal backwaters in Asia. Millions of poor, uneducated fisherfolk live along these coastlines. Their homes usually are small huts made of leaves and their life-styles are simple — hard work and little pleasure.

These fishermen and their families are some of the most unreached people in the world. Hardly any mission work ever has been done among them. But God called Paulose and his family to take the gospel to the unreached fishing villages of Tamil Nadu on the East Coast of India.

I remember visiting his family. One of the first things he discovered when he began visiting the villages was that the literacy rate was so low he could not use tracts or printed materials effectively. So he decided to use slides. All that stood in his way was the fact that he had no projector or money to purchase one.

In order to buy the projector, he made repeated trips to a hospital where he sold his blood until he had the money he needed.

It was exciting to see the crowds his slide projector attracted. As soon as he began to put up the white sheet which served as a screen, thousands of adults and children gathered along the beach. Mrs. Paulose sang gospel songs over a loudspeaker powered by a car battery, and their five-year-old son quoted Bible verses to passersby.

When the sun had set, Brother Paulose began his slide/preaching presentation. For several hours, thousands sat in the sand, listening to the gospel message while the sea murmured in the background. When we finally packed to leave, I had to walk carefully to avoid stepping on the hundreds of children sleeping on the sand.

But the tragedy behind all this was the secret starvation he and his family faced. Once I heard his long-suffering wife comforting the children and urging them to drink water from a baby bottle in order to hold off the pangs of hunger. There wasn't enough money in the house for milk.

Ashamed to let the non-Christian neighbors know he was without food, he would keep the windows and doors in his one-room rented house closed so they couldn't hear the cries of his four hungry children.

On another occasion, one of his malnourished children fell asleep in school because he was so weak from hunger. "I am ashamed to tell the teacher or our neighbors," he told me. "Only God, our children, and my wife and I know the real story. We have no complaints or even unhappiness. We're joyfully and totally content in our service of the Lord. It is a privilege to be counted worthy to suffer for His sake...."

Even when the teacher punished his children for lack of attention in class, Paulose would not tell his secret suffering and bring shame on the name of Christ. Fortunately, in this case, we were able to send immediate support to him, thanks to the help of generous American Christians. But for too many others, the story does not end as happily.

Is it God's fault that men like Brother Paulose are

going hungry? I don't think so. God has provided more than enough money to meet his needs and all the needs of the Third World. *The needed money is in the highly developed nations of the West.* North American Christians alone, without much sacrifice, can meet all the needs of the churches in the Third World.

A friend in Dallas recently pointed out a new church building costing $37 million. While this thought was still exploding in my mind, he pointed out another $7-million church building going up less than a minute away.

These extravagant buildings are insanity from a Third World perspective. The $37 million spent on one new building here could build nearly seventy-five hundred average-sized churches in India. The same $37 million would be enough to guarantee the evangelization of a whole state — or even some of the smaller countries of Asia.

But I rarely spoke out on these subjects. I realized I was a guest. The Americans who had built these buildings had also built the school I was now attending, and they were paying my tuition to attend. It amazed me, though, that these buildings have been constructed to worship Jesus, who said, "The foxes have holes, and the birds of the air have nests; but the Son of Man hath not where to lay his head" (Matt. 8:20).

In Asia today, Christ is still wandering homeless. He is looking for a place to lay His head, but in temples "not made with human hands." Our newborn Christians usually meet in their homes. In non-Christian communities, it is often impossible to rent church facilities. Instead of hindering church growth and evangelism, I have found this often increases our impact on the community.

There is such an emphasis on church buildings that we sometimes forget that the church is the people — not the place where the people meet.

But God has not called me to fight against church building programs. I think what troubles me much more than the waste is that these efforts represent a worldly mind-set.

Why can't we at least vow to spend a simple tithe of what we use for ourselves in the cause of world evangelism? If churches in the United States alone had made this commitment in 1986, there would have been $4.8 billion available to gospel outreach!

And what's more, if we had used these funds to support native missions, we could have fielded an army of evangelists the size of a major city.

5

A Nation Asleep in Bondage

Religion, I discovered, is a multi-billion dollar business in the United States. Entering churches, I was astonished at the carpeting, furnishings, air conditioning and ornamentation. Many churches have gymnasiums and fellowships that cater to a busy schedule of activities having little or nothing to do with Christ.

The orchestras, choirs, "special" music — and sometimes even the preaching — seemed to me more like entertainment than worship.

Many North American Christians live isolated from reality — not only from the needs of the poor overseas, but even from the poor in their own cities. Amidst all the affluence, there are millions of terribly poor people. But Christians have moved into the suburbs and left these people living in the inner city. I found that believers are ready to get involved in almost any activity which looks spiritual but allows them to escape their responsibility to the gospel.

For example, one morning I picked up a popular Christian magazine. There were many interesting articles, stories and reports from all over the world — most written by famous Christian leaders in the West.

Then I noticed what this magazine offered me as a Christian. There were ads for twenty-one Christian colleges, seminaries and correspondence courses; five different English translations of the Bible; seven conferences and retreats; five new Christian films; nineteen commentaries and devotional books; seven Christian health or diet programs; five fund-raising services.

But that wasn't all. There were many little ads for all kinds of products and services: counseling, chaplaincy services, writing courses, church steeples, choir robes, wall crosses, baptistries and water heaters, T-shirts, records, tapes, adoption agencies, tracts, poems, gifts, book clubs and pen pals.

It was all rather impressive. Probably none of these things is wrong in itself, but it bothered me that one nation should have such spiritual luxury while forty thousand people were dying in my homeland every day without hearing the gospel even once.

In Christian bookstores I found varieties of products beyond my ability to imagine. If the affluence of America impressed me, the affluence of Christians impressed me even more.

The United States has about five thousand Christian book and gift stores — and many secular stores also carry religious books. All this while more than four thousand of the world's nearly six thousand five hundred languages are still without a single portion of the Bible published in their own language. In his book *My Billion Bible Dream*, Rochunga Pudaite says, "Eighty-five percent of all Bibles printed today are in English for the nine percent of the world who read English. Eighty percent of the world's people have never owned a Bible while Americans have an average of four in every household."[1]

Besides books, there are well over a thousand Christian magazines and newspapers. Christian radio and television are heard twenty-four hours a day around the clock in almost every part of the country. Over fifteen hundred Christian radio stations broadcast the gospel full time, while most countries don't even have their first Christian radio station. Nearly two thousand radio and TV programs are produced for Christians in the United States, but fewer than four hundred are produced for use overseas.

The saddest observation I can make about most of the religious communication activity of the Western world is this: *Little, if any, of this media is designed to reach unbelievers. Almost all is entertainment for the saints.*

The United States is blessed with over one million full-time Christian workers, or one full-time religious leader for every 230 people in the nation. What a difference this is from the rest of the world, where 2.7 billion people have still to hear the gospel once.

Among the unreached or "hidden peoples" there is only one missionary working for every 500,000 people. These are the masses for whom Christ wept and died. They have yet to hear the gospel even once.

There are still 16,000 distinct cultural groups in the world without a single church among them to preach the gospel, while America has between 400,000 and 450,000 congregations or groups.[2]

One of the most impressive blessings in America is religious liberty. Not only do Christians have access to radio and television, unheard of in most nations of Asia, but they are also free to hold meetings, convert and evangelize, and print literature. Donations to Christian organizations are tax-exempt. How different this is from many Asian nations where government persecution of Christians is common and often legal.

Such was the case in Nepal, where until recently it was illegal to change one's religion or to influence others to change their religion. According to the law, you were to remain forever in the religion into which you were born. Christians often faced prison there for their faith.

Perhaps the most famous Nepali prisoner is Brother P—, known as the "Apostle to Nepal." This native missionary served time in fourteen different prisons between 1960 and 1975. He spent ten out of those fifteen years suffering torture and ridicule for preaching the gospel to his people.

His ordeal began when he baptized nine new believers and was arrested for doing so. The new converts, five men and four women, also were arrested, and each was sentenced to a year in prison. P— was sentenced to serve six years for influencing them.

Nepali prisons are typically Asian — literally dungeons of death. About twenty-five or thirty people are jammed into one small room with no ventilation or sanitation. The smell is so bad that newcomers often pass out in less than half an hour.

The place was crawling with lice and cockroaches. Prisoners slept on dirt floors. Rats and mice gnawed on fingers and toes during the night. In the winter there was no heat; in summer no ventilation.

For food, the prisoners were allowed one cup of rice each day, but they had to build a fire on the ground to cook it. The room was constantly filled with smoke since there was no chimney. On that inadequate diet, most prisoners became seriously ill, and the stench of vomit was added to the other putrefying odors. Yet, miraculously, none of the Christians was sick for even one day during the entire year.

After serving their one-year sentences, the nine new believers were released. Then the authorities decided to break P — . They took his Bible away from him, chained him hand and foot, then forced him through a low doorway into a tiny cubicle previously used to store bodies of dead prisoners until relatives came to claim them.

In the damp darkness, the jailer predicted his sanity would not last more than a few days. The room was so small he could not stand up or even stretch out on the floor. He could not build a fire to cook, so other prisoners slipped food under the door to keep him alive.

Lice ate away his underwear, but he could not scratch because of the chains, which soon cut his wrists and ankles to the bone. It was winter, and he nearly froze to death several times.

He could not tell day from night, but as he closed his eyes, God let him see the pages of the New Testament. Although his Bible had been taken away, he was still able to read it in total darkness. It sustained him as he endured the terrible torture. For three months he was not allowed to speak to another human being.

P—was transferred to many other prisons. In each, he continually shared his faith with both guards and prisoners.

Although P— is constantly in and out of prisons, he has refused to form secret churches. "How can a Christian keep silent?" he asks. "How can a church go underground? Jesus died openly for us. He did not try to hide on the way to the cross. We also must speak out boldly for Him regardless of the consequences."

Coming from India, where I was beaten and stoned for my faith, I know what it is to be a persecuted minority in my own country. When I set foot on Western soil, I could sense a spirit of religious liberty. North Americans have never known the fear of persecution. Nothing seems impossible to them. Christians here go about their affairs without giving a thought to the possibility of persecution.

With all these blessings, the abundance in both spiritual and material things, affluence unsurpassed by any nation on earth, with a totally unfettered church, I expected to see a much bolder witness. God's grace obviously has been poured out on nation and church in a way no other people ever have experienced.

From India, I always had looked to America as a fortress of Christianity. Instead I found a church in spiritual decline.

American believers are still the leading givers to missions, but this appeared due more to historical accident than the deep-set conviction I expected to find. As I spoke in churches and met average Christians, I discovered they had terrible misconceptions about the missionary mandate of the church. In church meetings — as I listened to the questions of my hosts and heard their comments about the Third World — my heart would almost burst with pain.

These people, I knew, were capable of so much more. They were dying spiritually, but I knew God wanted to give them life again. He wanted His church to recover its moral mandate and sense of mission.

I didn't yet know how. I didn't know when. But I knew one thing: *God did not shower such great blessing on this nation for the Christians to live in extravagance, in self-indulgence and in spiritual weakness.*

By faith, I could see a revival coming — the body of Christ rediscovering the power of the gospel and their obligation to it.

But for the time being, all I could do was sense how wrong the situation was — and pray. God had not given me the words to articulate what I was seeing — or a platform from which to speak. Instead He still had some important lessons to teach me, and I was to learn them in an alien land far from my beloved India.

6

What Are You Doing Here?

The Bible says that "some plant" and "others water." The living God now took me halfway around the world to teach me about watering. Before He could trust me again with the planting, I had to learn the lesson I'd been avoiding in India — *the importance of the local church in God's master plan for world evangelism.*

It really started through one of those strange coincidences — a divine appointment that only a sovereign God could engineer.

By now I was a busy divinity student in Dallas at the Criswell Bible Institute, intently soaking up every one of my classes. Thanks to the scholarship that God had so miraculously provided, I was able to dig into God's Word as never before. For the first time I was doing formal, in-depth study, and the Bible was revealing many of its secrets to me.

After my first term, Gisela and I were married, and she joined me in Dallas at the beginning of the next school term, October 1974. Except for preaching engagements and opportunities to share about Asia on weekends, I was fully absorbed in my studies and establishing our new home.

One weekend a fellow student invited me to fill the pulpit at a little church he was pastoring in Dallas. Although it was an American congregation, there were many native American Indians in fellowship.

Gisela was especially thrilled because through much of her childhood, she had prayed to be a missionary to "Red Indians on the Great Plains of America." While other schoolgirls dreamed of marriage and a Prince Charming, she was praying about doing ministry work among Native Americans. Much to my surprise, I found she had collected and read more than a hundred books about the tribal life and history of American Indians.

Strangely challenged and burdened for this little congregation, I preached my heart out. Never once did I mention my vision and burden for Asia. Instead I expounded Scripture verse by verse. A great love whelmed up in me for these people.

Although I didn't know it, my pastor friend turned in his resignation the same day. The deacons invited me to come back the next week and the next. God gave me a supernatural love for these people, and they loved us back.

Late that month the church board invited me to become the pastor, at the age of twenty-three. When Gisela and I accepted the call, I instantly found myself carrying a burden for these people twenty-four hours a day.

More than once I shamefacedly remembered how I had despised pastors and their problems back in India. Now that I was patching up relationships, healing wounded spirits and holding a group together, I started to see things in a wholly different light.

Some of the problems God's people face are the same worldwide, so I preached against sin and for holy living. Other problems (such as divorce, an epidemic in the West but almost unheard of in India) I was completely unprepared to handle.

Although my weight had increased to 106 pounds, I still nearly collapsed when I attempted to baptize a 250-pound convert! We had regular water baptisms and people came to Christ continually. We were a growing, soul-winning church with a hectic round of meetings that went six nights a week.

Besides preaching twice on Sunday and at the Wednesday night prayer meetings, I taught home Bible studies and the adult Sunday school class.

The days passed quickly into months. When I wasn't in classes, I was with my people. We learned to visit in homes, call on the sick in hospitals, marry and bury. Gisela and I were involved in the lives of our people day and night. I gave myself to them with the same abandonment that characterized my village preaching in North India.

Since we had several Indian tribal groups represented in the congregation as well as "anglos," we soon found we were having much more than a two-way, cross-cultural experience. We actually were ministering to several different cultures simultaneously.

The "staying power" and disciple-making were what my ministry in North India had lacked. I saw why I had failed in the Punjab. It isn't enough to hold evangelistic crusades and bring people to Christ. Someone has to stay behind and nurture the new believers into maturity.

Now God was showing me the answer to my prayers back in the Punjab. When I sat on that curb in Ferozpur and wept out the question, Where is the fruit? I was really asking, Where is the church? Now called to be a pastor, I was experiencing the process of how fruit is preserved. This, I understood at last, is what my work back in India had lacked.

For the first time I began to understand the goal of all mission work. It is the "perfecting" of the saints into sanctified, committed disciples of Christ. Jesus commanded us to go to all the nations, baptizing them and teaching them to obey all the things He had revealed. The gospel-team ministry I had led in India was going, but we weren't staying to do the teaching.

The church — a group of believers — is God's ordained place for the discipleship process to take place. God's Plan A for the redemption of the world is the church, and He has no Plan B. The Bible says that Jesus loved the church. He laid down His life for

71

her — His bride. He is coming back for a community of believers who have been made spotless.

As I went through the process of shepherding a local congregation, the Lord revealed to me that the same qualities are needed in native missionary evangelists. Now I knew what kind of men and women would be needed to reach the hidden peoples of Asia.

In my imagination I saw these same discipleship concepts being implanted in India and throughout Asia. Like the early Methodist circuit riders who planted churches on the American frontier, I could see our evangelists adding church planting to their evangelistic efforts.

But even as the concept captured me, I realized it would take an army of people — an army of God — to accomplish this task. In India alone, 500,000 villages are without a gospel witness. And then there are China, Southeast Asia and the islands. I could see we would easily need a million workers to finish the task.

But this was an idea too big for me to accept, so I pushed these thoughts from my mind. After all, I reasoned to myself, God has called me to this little church here in Dallas. I was getting very comfortable where I was. The church supported us well.

Didn't God miraculously bring us here? I argued with my conscience. God was blessing my ministry. Our first baby was on the way. I had begun to accept the Western way of life as my own, complete with a house, automobile, credit cards, insurance policies and bank accounts.

My formal schooling continued as I prepared to settle into building up the church. But my peace about staying in Dallas was slipping away.

By the end of 1976 and early in 1977, I heard an accusing voice every time I stood in the pulpit: What are you doing here? While you preach to an affluent American congregation, millions are going to hell in Asia. Have you forgotten your people?

A terrible inner conflict developed. I wasn't able to recognize the voice. Was it God? Was it my own conscience? Was it demonic? In desperation, I decided to wait upon God for His plan. I had said we would go anywhere, do anything. But we had to hear definitely from God. I just couldn't go on working with that tormenting voice.

Finally I announced to the church that I was praying, and I asked them to join with me in seeking the will of God for our future ministry.

"I seem to have no peace," I admitted to them, "about either staying in the United States or returning to India." *What is God really trying to say to me?*

As I prayed and fasted, God revealed Himself to me in a vision. It came back several times before I understood the revelation.

Many faces would appear before me — the faces of Asian men and their families. They weren't all Indians. They were from many lands. They were holy men and women, with a look of dedication on their faces. Gradually, I understood who these people were. It was like an image of the army of God that is now being raised up to take the gospel to every part of Asia.

Then the Lord spoke to me: "They cannot speak what you will speak. They will not go where you will go. You are called to be their servant. You must go where I will send you on their behalf. You are called to be their servant."

As lightning floods the sky in a storm, my whole life passed before me in that instant. I had never spoken English until I was sixteen, yet now I was ministering in this strange language. I had never worn shoes before I was seventeen. I was born and raised in a jungle village. Suddenly I realized I had nothing to be proud of; it wasn't my talents or skills that had brought me to America. My coming here was an act of God's sovereign will. He wanted me to cross cultures, to marry a German wife and live in an alien land. All this preparation was to give me the experiences I would need to serve in a new missionary movement.

"I have led you to this point," said God. "Your lifetime call is to be the servant of the unknown brethren — men whom I have called out and scattered among the villages of Asia."

Every Christian needs to know God's calling. We are commanded to know the will of God for our lives (see Eph. 5:17). I was as excited as a child with a new toy.

Knowing that at last I had found my life's work, I eagerly rushed to share my new vision with my church leaders and executives of missionary societies. To my utter bewilderment, God seemed to have forgotten to tell anyone but me.

My friends thought I was crazy. Mission leaders questioned either my integrity or my qualifications — and sometimes both. Church leaders whom I trusted and respected wrapped fatherly arms around my shoulders and counseled me against undue emotionalism.

Suddenly, through a simple announcement, I found myself alone, under attack and forced to defend myself. I was aware that following the call of Jesus always involves some degree of suffering and persecution. Now I knew that had I not waited for such a clear calling, I no doubt would have collapsed under those early storms of unbelief and doubt. But in my heart I remained convinced of my call, certain that God was initiating a new day in world missions. Still no one seemed to catch my enthusiasm.

Secretly I had prided myself on being a good speaker and salesman, but nothing I could do or say seemed to turn the tide of public opinion. While I was arguing that "new wine needed new wineskins," others could only ask, "Where is the new wine?"

My only comfort was Gisela. She had been with me in India, and she accepted the vision without question. In moments of discouragement, when even my faith wavered, she refused to allow us to let go of the vision. Rebuffed, but certain that we had heard God correctly, we planted the first seeds by ourselves.

I wrote to an old friend in India whom I'd known and trusted for years, asking him to help me select some needy native missionaries who already were doing outstanding work. I promised to come and meet them later, and we started planning a survey trip to seek out more qualified workers.

Slowly, from out of my church salary and Gisela's nursing pay, we sent the first few dollars to India.

I became compulsive. Soon I couldn't buy a hamburger or drink a cola without feeling guilty. We quietly sold off everything we could, pulled our savings out of the bank and cashed in my life insurance.

We realized we had fallen into the trap of materialism. In seminary we were required to take courses on practical matters. I still can remember how my professor solemnly instructed his class of young "preacher boys" to lay aside money every month for emergencies, purchase life insurance and build equity in a home.

But I couldn't find any of this in the New Testament commands of Christ. Why was it necessary to save our money in bank accounts when Jesus commanded us not to lay up treasures on this earth? The Lord began to speak to me about all of this.

"Haven't I commanded you to live by faith?" asked the Holy Spirit.

So Gisela and I conformed our lives literally to the New Testament commands of Christ regarding money and material possessions. I even traded in my late model car for a cheaper used one. The difference went straight to India. It was a joy to make these little sacrifices for the native brethren. I knew that it was the only way we could get the mission started.

In those early days, what kept me going was the assurance that there was no other way. Even if people didn't understand that we had to start a native missionary movement, I felt an obligation to the knowledge of God's call.

First, I knew Western missions never could get the job done. Since my own nation and many others were closed to outsiders, we had to turn to the native believers. Even if Western missionaries somehow were permitted back, the cost of sending them would be in the billions each year. Native evangelists could do the same for only a fraction of the cost.

I never told anyone that I eventually would need such huge sums of money. They already thought I was crazy for wanting to support eight or ten missionaries a month out of my own income. What would they think if I said I needed millions of dollars a year to field an army of God?

But I knew it was possible. Several Western missionary societies and charities already were dealing with annual budgets that size. I saw no reason why we couldn't do the same. But as logical as it all was in my mind, I had some bitter lessons to learn.

Giving birth to a new mission society was going to take much more energy and start-up capital than I ever could imagine. I had a lot to learn about America and the way things are done here. But I didn't know anything about that yet. I just knew it had to be done.

With youthful zest, Gisela and I went to India to do our first field survey. We returned a month later, penniless but committed to organizing what eventually would become Gospel for Asia.

Soon after our return, I revealed my decision to the congregation. Reluctantly we cut the cords of fellowship and made plans to move to Eufaula, Oklahoma, where another pastor friend had offered me some free space to open offices for the mission.

On the last day at the church, I tearfully preached my farewell sermon. When the last goodbye was said and the last hand was grasped, I locked the door and paused on the steps. I felt the hands of God lifting the mantle from my shoulders. God was releasing me of the burden for this church and the people of this place. As I strolled across the gravel driveway, the final mystery of Christian service became real to me.

Pastors — like missionary evangelists — are placed in the harvest fields of this world by God. No mission society, denomination, bishop, pope or superintendent calls a person to such service. In Gospel for Asia, I would not presume to ordain and call the native brethren, but simply be a servant to the ones whom God already had chosen for His service.

Seeking counsel from older Christian leaders, I eagerly listened to anyone who would give me advice. Everywhere I went I asked questions.

And I received offers of some strange help from various leaders. One dear man, a Christian executive who had spent a lifetime organizing another mission, just smiled in amusement when I asked for his advice.

"Here," he said, trying to be sensible and helpful, "the best advice I can give is this. Let me take over the support of the men you've committed yourself to in India. Give up this thing and just go back to India. People here will never trust you. In fact, it's impossible for them to do what you're suggesting."

That, of course, wasn't what I was ready to hear. I knew God had called me, and much of the advice I got was similarly suicidal and destructive. I found we had to learn most of our lessons by painful trial and error. The only way I escaped several disastrous decisions was my stubborn refusal to compromise the vision God had given. If something fit in with what God had said to me, then I considered it. If not — no matter how attractive it appeared — I refused. The secret of following God's will, I discovered, usually is wrapped up in rejecting the good for God's best.

One piece of advice did stick, however. Every Christian leader should have this engraved in his subconsciousness: *No matter what you do, never take yourself too seriously.* Paul Smith, founder of Bible Translations on Tape, was the first executive to say that to me, and I think it's one of the best single fragments of wisdom I've received from anyone.

God always chooses the foolish things of this world to confound the wise. He shows His might only on the behalf of those who trust in Him. *Humility is the place where all Christian service begins.*

Beginning to Feel
Like a Beggar

It didn't take long for me to make some early mistakes, and I couldn't afford any of them. We began the mission penniless, and I soon learned that even printing simple prayer letters and postage are a big expense.

We began without any kind of plan for regular involvement, but God soon gave us one. On one of my first trips, I went to Wheaton, Illinois. There I called on almost all the evangelical mission leaders. A few encouraged me — but not one offered the money we then needed desperately to keep going another day. The friend I stayed with, however, suggested we start a sponsorship plan through which North American families and individuals could support a native missionary regularly. It turned out to be just what we needed.

The idea — to lay aside one dollar a day for a native evangelist — gave us an instant handle for a program anyone could understand. I asked everyone

I met if he or she would sponsor a native missionary for one dollar a day. Some said yes, and that's how the mission began to get regular donors.

Today, the "Dollar-a-Day" Pledge Plan is still the heart of our fund-raising efforts. We send the money — one hundred percent of it — to the field. Today we are sponsoring thousands of missionaries each month in this way.

Since I was sending all the pledge money overseas, we still were faced with the need to cover our overhead and living expenses here in the United States. Time and time again — just when we were at our lowest point — God miraculously intervened to keep us and the ministry going.

One Sunday when we were down to our last dollar, I drove our old $125 Nova to a nearby church for worship. I knew no one and sat in the last row. When it came time to take the offering, I quickly made an excuse to God and held on to that last dollar.

"This is my last dollar," I prayed desperately, "and I need to buy gas just to get back home."

But knowing God loves a cheerful giver, I stopped fighting and sacrificed that last dollar to the Lord. The plate came by, and I dropped in the dollar.

As I left the church, an old man came up to me. I had never seen him before and never have since. He shook my hand silently, and I could feel a folded piece of paper in his palm. I knew instinctively that it was money. In the car, I opened my hand to find a neatly folded ten dollar bill.

Another afternoon, I sat grimly sulking on our sofa in Eufaula. Gisela was busy in the kitchen, avoiding my eyes. She said nothing, but both of us knew there wasn't any food in the house.

"So," said a coy voice from the enemy, "this is how you and your God provide for the family, eh?" Up until that moment, I don't think I'd ever felt such helplessness. Here we were, in the middle of Oklahoma. Even if I'd wanted to ask someone for help, I didn't know where to turn. Things had gotten so low I had offered to get a job, but Gisela was the one who refused. She was terrified that I would get into the world of business and not have time to work for the native brethren. For her there was no choice. It was wait on the Lord. He would provide.

As the demonic voice continued to taunt me, I just sat still under the abuse. I'd used up my last bit of faith, declaring a positive confession and praising God. Now I sat numb.

A knock came at the door.

Gisela went to answer it. I was in no mood to meet anyone. Someone brought two boxes of groceries to our doorstep. These friends had no way of knowing our need — but we knew the source was God.

During those days our needs continued to be met on a day-to-day basis, and I never had to borrow from the missionary support funds. I am convinced now that God knew the many trials ahead and wanted to teach us to have faith and trust in Him alone — even when I couldn't see Him.

In some way, which I still don't really understand, the trying of our faith works patience and hope into the fabric of our Christian lives. No one, I am convinced, will follow Jesus very long without tribulation. It is His way of demonstrating His presence.

Sufferings and trials — like persecution — are a normal part of the Christian walk. We must learn to accept them joyfully if we are to grow through them, and I think this is true for ministries as well as individuals.

Gospel for Asia was having its first wilderness experience, and the Oklahoma days were characterized by periods of the most painful waiting I'd ever faced. We were alone in a strange land, utterly at the end of our own strength and desperately dependent on God.

Speaking engagements were hard to come by in the early days, but they were the only way we could grow. Nobody knew my name or the name of Gospel for Asia. I still was having a hard time explaining what we were all about. I knew our mission in my heart, but I hadn't learned to articulate it yet for outsiders. In a few short months, I had used up all the contacts I had.

Setting up a speaking tour took weeks of waiting, writing and calling. By the winter of 1980, however, I was ready to start on my first major tour. I bought a budget air ticket that gave me unlimited travel for twenty-one days — and somehow I managed to make appointments in eighteen cities. My itinerary would take me through the Southwest, from Dallas to Los Angeles.

On the day of my departure, a terrible winter storm hit the region. All the buses — including the one I planned to take from Eufaula, Oklahoma, to Dallas — were cancelled.

We had an old 1969 Nova that had some engine problems, so a neighbor offered to let me use an old pick-up truck without a heater. The vehicle looked as if it couldn't make it to the next town, let alone the six-hour drive to Dallas. But it was either the pick-up or nothing.

If I missed my flight, the tightly packed schedule would be ruined. I just had to go now.

Doing the best I could to stay warm, I put on two pairs of socks and all the clothing I could. But even with the extra protection, I was on U.S. Highway 75 only a few minutes when it appeared I'd made a terrible mistake.

A freezing snow covered the windshield within minutes. Every mile I would have to stop, get out and scrape the windows again. After doing this one or two times, my feet and gloves were soaked and frozen. I realized that the journey, usually only four hours long, was going to take a lot longer than the six hours I had left. If I made it to Dallas, the trip would take twelve hours at this rate.

And the emphasis of that statement should be placed on the "if." In my worst scenario, I saw the newspaper headlines reading "Preacher Freezes to

Death in Winter Storm." My head dropped to the steering wheel, and I cried out to God.

"Lord, if You want me to go — if You believe in this mission and in my helping the native evangelists — please do something."

As I looked up, I saw a miracle on the windshield. The ice was melting rapidly before my eyes. A warmth flooded the truck. I looked at the heater, but nothing was coming out. Some miraculous source of heat was filling the cab. Outside the storm continued to rage. It kept up all the way to Dallas, but the truck was always warm, and the windshield was always clear.

This miraculous start was only the beginning of blessings. For the next eighteen days, I gained new sponsors and donors in every city. The Lord gave me favor in the eyes of all I met.

On the last day of the tour, a man in California came up to the pastor and said God had told him to donate his second car to me.

I cancelled my airline reservation and drove all the way home, rejoicing in the car God had provided — and receiving new inspiration and instruction from God as I drove.

This is the pattern I was to follow for the next few years. I survived from one meeting to the next, living out of the trunk of the car and speaking anywhere I could get an invitation.

All our new donors and sponsors came from one-on-one contacts and through the meetings.

I knew there were faster, more efficient ways to acquire new donors. Many times I would look at the mass mailings and radio/TV broadcasts of other missions. But everything they were doing required large sums of money I didn't have and didn't know how to get.

Eventually, we moved back to Dallas. By now I was traveling full time for the ministry, and the strain was taking a heavy toll both on my family and on me. I was starting to burn out — and I almost hated the work.

Two factors were wearing me down.

First, I felt like a beggar. It is hard on the flesh to be traveling and asking for money day after day and night after night. It was almost becoming a sales operation for me, and I stopped feeling good about myself.

Second, I was discouraged by the poor response — especially from churches and pastors. Many times it seemed to me my presence threatened them. Where, I wondered, was the fraternal fellowship of working together in the extension of the kingdom? Many days I would call on people for hours to get only one or two new sponsors. Pastors and mission committees would listen to me and promise to call back, but I would never hear from them again.

It seemed as though I always was competing against the building fund, new carpets for the fellowship hall or next Saturday night's Jesus rock concert.

Despite the solemn message of death, suffering

and need I was presenting, people still would leave the meetings with laughter and gossip on their lips. I was offended at the spirit of jocularity in the churches. It wounded me. So many times we would go to eat after I had just shared the tragedy of the thousands who starve to death daily or the millions of homeless people living in the streets of Asia.

Because of this, I was becoming angry and judgmental. As I felt uglier and uglier inside, depression settled in.

Early in 1981 — while driving alone between meetings in a borrowed car near Greensboro, North Carolina — all the dark feelings of psychological burn-out crept over me. I was having a full-fledged pity party, feeling sorry for myself and the hard life I was leading.

With a start, I began to tremble with fear. Suddenly I felt the presence of someone else. I realized that the Spirit of the Lord was speaking.

"I am not in any trouble," He chided, "that I need someone to beg for Me or help Me out. I made no promises that I will not keep.

"It is not the largeness of the work that matters, but only doing what I command. All I ask of you is that you be a servant.

"For all who join with you in the work, it will be a privilege — a light burden for them."

The words echoed in my mind. This is His work, I told myself. Why am I making it mine? The burden is light. Why am I making it heavy? The work is a privilege. Why am I making it a chore?

I instantly repented of my sinful attitudes. God was sharing His work with me, and He was speaking of others who would join me. Although I still was doing the work alone, it was exciting to think others would be joining with me and that they too would find the burden to be light.

From that moment until this, I have not been overpowered by the burden of heading Gospel for Asia. I find building this mission an exciting, joyful job. Even my preaching has changed. My posture is different. Today the pressure is off. No more do I feel I have to beg audiences or make them feel guilty.

Since the work of Gospel for Asia — and the whole native missionary movement — is initiated by God, it doesn't need the worries and guidance of man.

Whether our goal is to support ten thousand or ten million missionaries, whether it is working in ten states or a hundred, or whether I must supervise a staff of five or five hundred, I still can approach this work without stress. For this is His work, and our burden is easy.

By now we had rented offices in Dallas, and the mission was growing steadily. I sensed it was time for a big step forward. I waited upon God for a miracle breakthrough. We had hundreds of native missionaries waiting for support by mid-1981, and I realized that we soon would have thousands more. I no longer could communicate personally with every new sponsor. I knew we had to use mass media.

But I didn't know where to begin.

Then it happened. I met Brother Lester Roloff.

Roloff now is with the Lord, but during his life he was a rugged individualist who preached his way across five decades of outstanding Christian service.

Near the end of his life, I approached him for help in our ministry. His staff person, in arranging the interview, said I would have only five minutes. They were astonished when he gave me two hours of his time.

When I told him about the native missionary movement, he invited me to be his guest on the "Family Altar" — his daily radio broadcast. At that time we were helping only one hundred native missionaries, and Roloff announced over the air that he personally was going to sponsor six more. He called me one of the "greatest missionaries he had ever met" and urged his listeners to sponsor native missionaries as well. Soon we were getting letters from all over the country.

As I read the postmarks and the letters, I realized again how huge the United States and Canada are. Roloff was the first Christian leader I'd ever met who already had done what I knew we needed to do. He'd learned how to speak to the whole nation.

For weeks I prayed for him, asking God to show me how I could work with him and learn from his example.

When the answer came, it was quite different from anything I had expected. The Lord gave me an idea which I now realize was unusual, almost bizarre. I would ask Roloff to loan me his mailing list and let me ask his people to sponsor a native missionary.

Trembling, I called his office and asked for another appointment. He saw me again but was very surprised at my request.

He told me that he'd never done anything like that before and had never loaned his list to anyone — even his best friends. Many agencies had asked to rent his list, but he had always said no. I thought my cause was lost, but he said he would pray about it.

The next day he called me back. He said the Lord had told him to give us his list. He also offered to write a letter of endorsement and interview me again on the radio broadcast at the same time the letter went out.

Elated, I praised God. But I soon learned that this was only the beginning of the miracle.

The list was a fairly large one, and to print a brochure, my letter and his letter, together with the mailing, would cost more money than we had.

There seemed to be only one way to get it. I would have to borrow — just once — from the missionary funds. I figured it out again and again. If I worked it just right, I could get the money to the field with only a few weeks' delay. But I had no peace about the plan. I'd always used the funds exactly as designated.

It came time to send the regular monies to the field. I told our bookkeeper to hold the money for one day, and I prayed. Still no peace. The next day I told her to hold the money up for another day, and I went back to prayer and fasting. Still no peace. I delayed it for a third day — and still God wouldn't release me to use the missionary support funds.

I was miserable. Finally I decided that I couldn't break the trust of our donors — even for the Lord's work. I told my secretary to go ahead and send the missionary money.

I now realize we had gone through one of the greatest tests of the ministry. This was it, my first chance to get a major increase in donors and income — but it had to be done with integrity, or not at all.

A half hour after the check had gone off to the field, the phone rang. It was from a couple whom I had met only once before at our annual banquet in Dallas.

They had been praying about helping us, and God had laid me on their hearts. They asked if they could come and talk to me, and they wanted to know what I needed.

After I explained the cost involved for printing and putting out the mailing, they agreed to pick up the entire amount of this project, which was nearly twenty thousand dollars. Then the printer became so moved by the project that he did it for free! Plainly God had been testing me, and He miraculously showed that if we were obedient, He indeed would provide.

The art work went off to the printers and soon printed letters were sitting on skids, ready for the post office. I had prepared a special radio broadcast to coincide with the arrival of the mailing — and the broadcast tapes already had been shipped to the stations in many parts of the nation.

Timing was everything. The mail had to go on Monday. It was Friday, and I didn't have undesignated money in the general fund for the postage. This time there was no question of borrowing the missionary money. It stayed right where it was.

I called a special prayer meeting, and we met that night in the living room of our home. Finally the Lord gave me peace. Our prayers of faith would be answered, I announced. After everyone had gone home, the phone rang.

It was one of our sponsors in Chicago. God had been speaking to her all day about giving a five thousand dollar gift.

"Praise God," I said.

That mailing incident proved to be another turning point in the history of Gospel for Asia. We received many new sponsors — a double increase in the number of evangelists we were able to sponsor.

In later years, other Christian leaders like Bob Walker of Christian Life Missions and David Mains of "Chapel of the Air" would help us in similar ways. Many of the people who joined our ministry through those several early mailings have since helped to expand the ministry even further, giving us a base of contacts from every state in the union. God had given us a clear message for the body of Christ — *a call to recover the church's missionary mandate*.

In every place, I preached this same message — a prophetic cry to my brothers and sisters in Christ on behalf of the lost millions in the Third World. Through it, thousands of believers started to change their life-styles and conform to the demands of the gospel.

8

Missions Are Not Dead; the Leadership Is Changing Hands

Several hundred dedicated believers now were supporting native missionaries. But despite this aura of success, many things broke my heart, especially the condition of American Christians. What had happened to the zeal for missions and outreach that made this nation so great? Night after night I would stand before audiences, trying the best I could to communicate the global realities of our planet. But somehow I wasn't getting through. *I could see their unfulfilled destiny so clearly. Why couldn't they?*

Here were people of great privilege — a nation which is more able, more affluent and more free to act on the Great Commission than any other in all history. Yet my audiences didn't seem to comprehend this. Even more confusing to me was the fact that in personal dealings I found my hosts to be basically fair, often generous, and spiritually gifted. Like the church in first-century Corinth, it appeared to excel in every spiritual blessing.

Why then, I asked the Lord, wasn't I getting through?

If the native missionary movement was really the will of God — and I knew it was — then why were the people so slow to respond?

Something obviously had gone very wrong. Satan had sprung a trap, or perhaps many traps, on the minds of Western Christians. It was plain to see they had lost the gospel mandate. They had abdicated the heritage of missionary outreach, the call of God that still rests on this nation.

In my prayers I began to seek a message from God that would bring a change in life-style to the church. It came over a period of weeks. And that message came loud and clear: *Unless there is repentance among Christians — individually and in concert as a community of believers — an awesome judgment will fall on America.*

I was certain then, and still am today, that God's loving hands of grace and forgiveness remain extended to His people. Two reasons, it appeared to me, were the cause for the current malaise that has fastened like cancer on American believers. The first is historical. The second is the unconfessed sins related to three basic iniquities: pride, unbelief and worldliness.

Historically, the Western church lost its grip on the challenge for world missions at the end of World War II — and ever since that time its moral mandate and vision for global outreach have continued to fade.

Today the average North American believer can hardly pronounce the word "missionary" without having cartoon caricatures of ridiculous little men in pith helmets pop into mind — images of cannibals with spears and huge black pots of boiling water.

Despite a valiant rearguard action by many outstanding evangelical leaders and missions, it has been impossible for the Western missionary movement to keep up with exploding populations and the new political realities of nationalism in the Third World.

Most Christians in North America still conceive of missions in terms of blond-haired, blue-eyed white people going to the dark-skinned Third World nations. In reality, all of that changed at the end of World War II when the Western powers lost political and military control of their former colonies.

When I stand before North American audiences in churches and missions conferences, people are astonished to hear the real facts of missions today. The frontline work of missions in Asia has been taken over almost completely by indigenous missionaries. And the results are outstanding. Believers are shocked to learn that native missionaries are starting hundreds of new churches every week in the Third World, that thousands of people a day are being converted to Christ, and that tens of thousands of well-qualified, spiritually able men and women now are ready to start more mission work if we can raise their support.

In India, which no longer permits Western missionary evangelists, more church growth and out-reach are happening now than at any point in our history.

China is another good example of the new realities. When the communists drove Western missionaries out and closed the churches in 1950, it seemed that Christianity was dead. In fact, most of the known leaders were imprisoned, and a whole generation of Chinese pastors was killed off or disappeared in communist prisons and torture chambers.

But today communication is open again with China, and we find forty thousand to fifty thousand underground churches have sprung up during the communist persecution. The number of Christians now has grown to an estimated fifty million — fifty times the size of the church when Western mission-aries were driven out. All this again has happened under the spiritual direction of the indigenous church movement.

From a historical perspective, it is not difficult to trace how Western thinking has been confused by the march of history. In the early 1950s, the destruction of the colonial missionary establishment was big news. As the doors of China, India, Burma, North Korea, North Vietnam and many other newly inde-pendent nations slammed shut on Western missionar-ies, it was natural for the traditional churches and denominational missions to assume that their day had ended.

That, of course, was in itself untrue, as evidenced

by the growth of evangelical missions in the same period. But many became convinced then that the age of missions had ended forever.

Except for the annual missions appeal in most churches, many North American believers lost hope of seeing the Great Commission of Christ fulfilled on a global scale. Although it was rarely stated, the implication was this: If North American or Western European-based mission boards aren't leading the way, then it can't happen.

Mission monies once used to proclaim the gospel were more and more sidetracked into the charitable social programs toward which the new governments of the former colonies were more sympathetic. A convenient theology of mission developed that today sometimes equates social and political action with evangelism.

Many of the Western missionaries who did stay on in Asia also were deeply affected by the rise of nationalism. They began a steady retreat from evangelism and discipleship, concentrating for the most part on broadcasting, education, medical, publishing, relief and social work. Missionaries, when home in the West, continued to give the impression that indigenization meant not only the pull-out of Western personnel but also the pull-out of financial and other assistance.

The debate among Western leaders about the future of missions has in the meantime raged on, producing whole libraries of books and some valuable research. Regrettably, however, the overall result on the average Christian has been extremely negative. Believers today have no idea that a new day in missions has dawned or that their support of missions is more desperately needed than ever before.

True, in many cases, it no longer is possible, for political reasons, for Western missionaries to go overseas, but American believers still have a vital role in helping us in the Third World finish the task. I praise God for the pioneer work done by Hudson Taylor and others like him who were sent by believers at home in the past. Now, in countries like India, we need instead to send financial and technical support to native evangelists and Bible teachers.

Imagine the implications of being involved in the work of the Great Commission, of getting your church and family to join with you in supporting native missions.

Picture this very possible scene. You finish your life on this earth. You arrive in heaven. There, enthroned in all His glory, is our Lord Jesus Christ. The other saints and martyrs you've so often read about are there: Abraham, Moses, Peter and Paul, plus great leaders from more recent times. Your family and loved ones who obeyed the gospel also are there. They are all welcoming you into heaven.

You walk around in bliss, filled with joy and praises. All the promises of the Bible are true. The streets really are gold, and the glory of God shines brightly, replacing the sun, moon and stars. It is beyond the power of any man to describe.

Then, scores of strangers whom you don't recognize start to gather around with happy smiles and outstretched hands. They embrace you with affection and gratitude.

"Thank you....Thank you....Thank you," they repeat in a chorus. With great surprise you ask, "What did I do? I have never seen you before."

Then they tell you the story of how they came to be in heaven, all because your love and concern reached out to them while they were on earth. You see that these persons come from "every tongue and tribe," just as the Bible says — from India, Bangladesh, Bhutan, Thailand and the Philippines.

"But what exactly did I do?" you ask. Then, like a replay of a videotape, your mind goes back to a day of your life on earth when a local mission coordinator came to your church. He told you about the lost millions of Asia — about the 300 million who have never heard the gospel in India alone. He told you about the desperately poor native missionaries and challenged you to support them.

You were one of those who said yes. The crowd of Asians continue: "As a result of your support, one of our own — a native evangelist — came to us and preached the gospel of the kingdom. He lived simply like us, speaking our language and dressed in our clothing. We were able to accept his message easily.

"We were serving idols and never had the opportunity to hear the gospel until he came and preached to us. We learned for the first time about the love of Jesus, who died on the cross for us, and how His blood redeemed us from sin, Satan and death."

As the crowd finishes, several whole families come up to you. You can see the tenderness and gratefulness on their faces as well. They join the others, taking you in their arms and thanking you again.

"How can we ever express our appreciation for the love and kindness you showed to us on the earth? We were struggling in the service of the Lord. Often we went without food. Our children cried for milk, but we had none to give. Unknown and forsaken by our own people, we sought to witness to our own people who had never heard the gospel. Now they are here in eternity with us.

"In the middle of our suffering, you came into our lives with your prayers and financial support. Your help relieved us so much — making it possible for us to carry on the work of the Lord. We are one of the missionary families you supported in Asia.

"We never had a chance to see you face-to-face in the world. Now we can see you here and spend all eternity rejoicing with you over the victories of the Lord."

Now Jesus Himself appears. You bow as He quotes the familiar Scripture verses to you: "I was an hungered, and ye gave me meat: I was thirsty, and ye gave me drink: I was a stranger, and ye took me in: naked, and ye clothed Me....Verily I say unto you, Inasmuch as ye have done it unto one of the least of these my brethren, ye have done it unto me" (Matt. 25:35-40).

Is this just a fanciful story, or will it be reality for many thousands of North American Christians? I believe it could happen as Christians arrive in heaven and see how they have laid up treasure where moth and rust cannot corrupt.

Every time I stand before an audience, I try to ask two very important questions early in my message:

• Why do you think God has allowed you to be born in North America or Western Europe and to be blessed with such material and spiritual abundance?

• In light of the super-abundance you enjoy here, what do you think is your minimal responsibility to the untold millions of lost and suffering in the Third World?

Every Christian needs to ask himself why God allowed him or her to be born here rather than among the poor masses of Africa and Asia. Did you earn that right?

What does it mean to be born among the privileged elite of this world? Why do you have so much when others have so little? Think a moment about the vast difference between your country and the nations without a Christian heritage.

The material abundance here is staggering. One-fourth of the world lives on an income of less than three dollars a week — most of them in Asia. The gross national product per person in South Asia is only $180 a year. Americans earn an average of fifty-four times more — and Christian Americans, because they tend to live in the upper half of the economy, earn even more.[1]

In most countries where Gospel for Asia is serving the native missionary movement, a good wage is one dollar to three dollars a day. While much of the world is concerned mainly about where its next meal is coming from, affluent North Americans spend most of their wages and waking moments planning unnecessary purchases.

In the United States, Canada and Western Europe, there is freedom of choice. Political freedoms of speech, press and assembly are just part of the picture. There is freedom to worship and organize religious ministries and to choose where and how to live. Citizens are free to organize themselves to correct injustices and problems both at home and abroad.

Moreover, there is leisure time and disposable income. Although these are not written into law, citizens are free from the basic wants that make living so difficult in many other parts of the world.

Also, a large number of service networks are available which make it easy to effect change, such as communications, education, finance, mass media and transportation. Not having these services available is an enormous handicap to people in most other parts of the world.

Finally, few domestic needs exist. While unemployment is a serious problem in some areas, it is many times higher in nearly every country of the

Third World. How many of us can comprehend the suffering of the millions of homeless and starving people in nations like Bangladesh? Overseas the problems are on a grand scale. Some nations struggle to help themselves but still fail woefully.

This list is just illustrative of the many advantages of living in the Western world where benefits have come *largely because of a Christian heritage.*

Part II

THE CALL

9

You Have Destroyed Everything
We Were Trying to Do

If the apostle Paul had not brought the gospel to Europe, the foundation principles of freedom and human dignity would not be part of the American heritage. Because the Holy Spirit instructed him to turn away from Asia and go west, America has been blessed with its systems of law and economics — the principles that made it rich and free.

In addition, America is the only nation in the world founded by believers in Christ who made a covenant with God — dedicating a new nation to God.

Born into affluence, freedom and divine blessings, Americans should be the most thankful people on earth. But along with the privilege comes a responsibility.

The Christian must ask not only why but what should he or she do with these unearned favors?

Throughout Scripture, there is only one correct response to abundance: *sharing*.

God gives some people more than they need so that

they can be channels of blessing to others. God desires equity between His people on a worldwide basis. That is why the early church had no poverty.

"Our desire," wrote the apostle Paul to the rich Christians in Corinth, "is not that others might be relieved while you are hard pressed, but that there might be equality. At the present time your plenty will supply what they need, so that in turn their plenty will supply what you need. Then there will be equality" (2 Cor. 8:13,14, NIV).

The Bible advocates and demands that we show love for the needy brethren. Right now, because of historical and economic factors that none of us can control, the needy brethren are in Asia. The wealthy brethren are in the United States, Canada and a few other nations. The conclusion is obvious: These affluent believers must share with the poorer churches.

"We know we have passed from death to life, because we love our brothers....If anyone has material possessions and sees his brother in need but has no pity on him, how can the love of God be in him? Dear children, let us not love with words or tongue but with actions and in truth" (1 John 3:14-18, NIV).

And, "What doth it profit, my brethren, though a man say he hath faith, and have not works? can faith save him? If a brother or sister be naked and destitute of daily food, and one of you say unto them, Depart in peace, be ye warmed and filled; notwithstanding ye give them not those things which are needful to the body; what doth it profit? Even so faith, if it hath not works, is dead, being alone" (James 2:14-17).

Is missions an option — especially for super-wealthy countries like America? The biblical answer is clear. Every Christian in America has some minimal responsibility to get involved in helping the poor brethren in the church in other countries.

God has not given this superabundance of blessings to American and Canadian Christians so that we only can sit back and enjoy the luxuries of this society — or even in spiritual terms, so that we can gorge ourselves on books, teaching cassettes and deeper-life conferences. He has left us on this earth to be stewards of these spiritual and material blessings. God wants us to become experts on how to share with others.

Believers have a date with destiny. They are to be servants to the expanding churches and movements of God around the world. We need to gain a sense of trusteeship, learning to administer our wealth to accomplish the purposes of God.

What then is the bottom line? God is calling us as Christians to alter our life-styles. We must find ways to give up the non-essentials of our lives so that we can better invest our wealth in the kingdom of God.

To start, I challenge believers to lay aside at least one dollar a day to support a native missionary in the Third World. This, of course, should be over and above our present commitments to the local church and other ministries.

I do not ask Christians to redirect their giving away

from other ministries for native missions — but to expand their giving over and above current levels. Most people can do this.

For many North American and Western European believers — millions of them — this can be accomplished easily simply by giving up cookies, cakes, sweets, coffee and other beverages. Many of these junk foods harm our bodies anyway, and anyone can save enough in this way to sponsor one or even two missionaries a month.

Many are going beyond this and, without affecting health or happiness, are able to sponsor several missionaries every month.

Of course, there are many other ways to get involved. Some cannot give more financially, but they can invest time in prayer and serve as volunteer coordinators to help recruit more sponsors. And a few are called to go overseas to become involved experientially.

The single most important hindrance to world evangelization right now is the lack of total involvement by the body of Christ. I am convinced there are enough potential sponsors to support all the native missionaries needed to evangelize the Third World.

It's true the native missionary movement is relatively new, and many Christians still haven't been challenged to participate, but that is superficial. The real truth is much more basic — and more deadly.

Ask the average person why the Lord destroyed Sodom, and he will cite the city's gross immorality.

However, Ezekiel reveals the real reason in chapter 16, verses 49 and 50: "Behold this was the guilt of your sister Sodom: she and her daughters had pride, surfeit of food, and prosperous ease, but did not aid the poor and needy. They were haughty and did abominable things before me; therefore I removed them, when I saw it."

Sodom refused to aid the needy poor because of pride. We are caught up in a national pride similar to Sodom's. Admittedly, from that pride also come selfishness and perversion, but we need to see that pride is the real root. Deal with that root and you cut off a multitude of sins before they have a chance to grow. One night while speaking at a church missionary conference, I was asked to meet privately with the church council to give my reaction to a new mission program they were considering. This was in a grand old church with a large mission budget.

I already had preached and was very tired. I didn't really want to sit in on a board meeting. By the time everyone arrived, there were twenty-two in the room. The meeting began in the usual way, more like a corporate board meeting at IBM or General Motors than a church board.

The presenter made an impressive, business-like proposal. The scheme involved shifting "third country nationals" from Asia to a mission field in Latin America. It was very futuristic and sounded like a major leap in missions, but warning lights and bells were going off in my mind. To me it sounded like

111

nineteenth-century colonial missionary practice dressed up in a different disguise.

The Lord spoke to me clearly: "Son, tonight you must speak to people who are so self-sufficient they've never asked Me about this plan. They think I'm helpless."

So when the chairman of the church council finally called on me to respond with my opinion of the proposal, I stood and read certain parts of Matthew 28:18-20:

"All power is given unto Me in heaven and in earth. Go ye therefore and teach all nations...to observe all things that I have commanded you: and, lo, I am with you always...."

Then I closed my Bible and paused, looking each one in the eye.

"If He is with you," I said, "then you will represent Him — not just be like Him — but you will exercise His authority. Where is the power of God in this plan?"

I didn't need to say much. The Holy Spirit anointed my words, and everyone seemed to understand.

"How often have you met for prayer?" I asked rhetorically. "How long since you have had an entire day of prayer to seek God's mind about your mission strategy?" From their eyes it was easy to see they had prayed little about their mission budget, which was then in the hundreds of thousands of dollars.

So little of evangelical Christian work is done in total dependence upon the living God. We have devised methods, plans and techniques to "do" God's work. Those involved apparently do not sense a need to pray or be filled with the Holy Spirit to do the work of Jesus.

How far we have drifted from the faith of the apostles and the prophets. What a tragedy that the techniques of the world and its agents are brought into the sanctuary of God.

Only when we are emptied of our own self-sufficiency can God use us. When a church or a mission board spends more time in consultation, planning and committee meetings than in prayer, it is a clear indication the members have lost touch with the supernatural and have ended up, in Watchman Nee's words, "serving the house of God and forgot the Lord Himself."

The discussion went on until 1:30 in the morning, but with a new sense of repentance in the room.

"Brother K.P.," said the leader to me afterward, "you have destroyed everything we were trying to do tonight, but now we're ready to wait on God for His plan." This is the kind of humility that will bring the church back into the center of God's will and global plan. Churches today are not experiencing the power and anointing of God in their ministries because they don't have the humility to wait on Him, and because of that sin, the world remains largely unreached.

Part of this pride is a subtle but very deep racism. In many of my meetings, I will hear innocent-sounding questions such as, How do we know that the native church is ready to handle the funds? or, What kind of training have the native missionaries had?

So long as such questions are based on a sincere desire for good stewardship, they are commendable. But in many cases, I have found the intent of the question is something much less honorable.

Westerners refuse to trust Asians the way they trust their own people. If we're satisfied that a certain native missionary is truly called to the gospel, we have to trust God and turn our stewardship over to him and his elders just as we would to another brother in our own culture. To expect to continue controlling the use of money and the ministry overseas from our foreign-based mission board is an extension of colonialism. It adds an unbiblical element which only humiliates and weakens the native missionary in the long run.

What Christians need to learn is that they're not giving *their money* to native workers, but *God's money* to His work overseas.

Churches need to develop the quiet disciplines they have lost — practices such as contemplation, fasting, listening, meditation, prayer, silence, Scripture memory, submission and reflection.

Instead of glorifying two-fisted fighters in the John Wayne tradition of American folk heroes, Christians would do well to sit still until the power of God is manifested in their Christian activities.

Many Christian leaders are caught up in secondary issues that sap their time and energy.

I'll never forget preaching in one church where the pastor had turned defending the King James translation of the Bible into a crusade. Not only does he spend most of his pulpit time upholding it — but thousands of dollars go to printing books, tracts and pamphlets advocating the exclusive use of this one translation.

In the years I have lived and worked in the United States, I have watched believers and whole congregations get caught up in all kinds of similar crusades and causes which, while not necessarily bad in themselves, end up taking our eyes off obedience to Christ. And in this sense, they become anti-Christ.

Red-hot issues that burn across the horizon — like inerrancy, versions of the Bible, charismatic gifts, the latest revelations of itinerant teachers, secular humanism, or whatever new issue raises its head tomorrow — need to be kept in their proper perspective. There always will be new dragons to slay, but we must not let these side battles keep us from our main task of building and expanding the kingdom of God.

When I go to Asia, I see our churches and theologians there being just as violently divided over a different set of issues, and through this I have come to realize that many times these doctrinal divisions are being used by the evil one to keep us preoccupied with something other than the gospel.

We are driven by powerful egos always to be right. We are often slaves to a strong tendency to "have it our way." All these are manifestations of pride. The opposite of that is the servanthood commanded by Christ.

Making a sacrifice for one of the unknown brethren — supporting his work to a strange people in a strange place, using methods that are a mystery to you — does take humility.

But supporting the native brethren must begin with this kind of commitment to humility and must continue in the same spirit. Sadly, our pride all too often stands in the way of progress.

10

God Is Withholding Judgment

Early in my ministry I learned to beware of boasters. They're usually covering up something. One of the great boasts of many Western born-again, evangelical Christians is their devotion to Scripture. It's hard to find a Christian organization that doesn't at one time or another brag about being "Bible believing." When I first came here, I made the mistake of taking that description at face value.

In reality, I have come to see that many evangelical Christians don't really believe the Word of God. Instead they selectively accept only the portions that allow them to continue living in their current lifestyles.

I'm talking about hell and judgment. These are lost teachings. Believers are willing to accept the concept of heaven, but they look the other way when they come to passages about hell. Very few seem to believe that those who die without Christ are going to a place where they are tormented forever and ever in a bottomless pit where the fire is not quenched; where they are separated from God and His love for all eternity without any chance of return.

Why aren't Christians living in obedience to God? Because of their unbelief.

Why did Eve fall into sin? Because she didn't truly believe in the judgment — that death really would come if she ate what God forbade. This is the same reason many continue in their lives of sin and disobedience.

It's painful to think about hell and judgment. I understand why preachers don't like to talk about it, because I don't either. It's so much easier to preach that "God loves you and has a wonderful plan for your life" or to focus on the many delightful aspects of possibility thinking and the word of faith that brings health, wealth and happiness. The grace and love of God are pleasant subjects, and no one more beautifully demonstrated them than our Lord Jesus. Yet in His earthly ministry, He made more references to hell and judgment than He did to heaven.

Jesus lived with the reality of hell, and He died on Calvary because He knew it was real and coming to everyone who doesn't turn to God in this life.

If we knew the horrors of the potential judgment that hangs over us — if we really believed in what's coming — how differently we would live. The Great Depression and current recessions are only a slap on the wrist compared to the poverty that lies ahead — let alone the bombs, disease and natural calamities.

But God is withholding judgment now to give us time to repent.

Unfortunately, for millions in the Third World, it will be too late unless we can reach them before they slip off the edge into eternal darkness.

For years I have struggled with making this a reality in our meetings. Finally I found a way.

I ask my listeners to hold their wrists and find their pulse. Then I explain that every beat they feel represents the death of someone in Asia who had died and gone to eternal hell without ever hearing the good news of Jesus Christ even once.

"What if one of those beats represented your own mother?" I ask. "Your own father, your spouse, your child...you yourself?"

These millions of Asians who are dying and going to hell are people for whom Christ died. We say we believe it — but what are we doing to act on that faith? Without works, faith is dead.

There's no reason why anyone should go to hell today without hearing about the Lord Jesus. To me this is an atrocity much worse than the death camps of Hitler's Germany or Stalin's Russia. As horrible as the 1.5 million annual abortions are in the United States each year, the eternal loss of multiplied millions of additional souls every year is the greatest preventable tragedy of our times.

If only a small percentage of the fifty million people who claim to be born-again Christians in this country were to sponsor a native missionary, we could have literally hundreds of thousands of evangelists reaching the lost villages of Asia.

When we look at the unfinished Great Commission and compare it to our personal life-styles — or to the activity calendars of our churches and organizations — how can we explain our disobedience? There is only one conclusion — we must see a great repentance from the sin of unbelief.

C.T. Studd, the famous British athlete and founder of Worldwide Evangelization Crusade, was one who gave up all his achievements in this life for Christ's sake. He was challenged to his commitment by an article written by an atheist. That article in part said:

> If I firmly believed, as millions say they do, that the knowledge and practice of religion in this life influences destiny in another, then religion would mean to me everything.
>
> I would cast away earthly enjoyments as dross, earthly cares as follies, and earthly thoughts and feelings as vanity. Religion would be my first waking thought and my last image before sleep sank me into unconsciousness. I should labor in its cause alone.
>
> I would take thought for the morrow of eternity alone. I would esteem one soul gained for heaven worth a life of suffering.
>
> Earthly consequences would never stay

my hand, or seal my lips. Earth, its joys and its griefs, would occupy no moment of my thoughts. I would strive to look upon eternity alone, and on the immortal souls around me, soon to be everlastingly happy or everlastingly miserable.

I would go forth to the world and preach to it in season and out of season, and my text would be:

"For what is a man profited, if he shall gain the whole world, and lose his own soul?"[1]

Another iniquity plaguing the Western church is worldliness.

Once, on a two-thousand-mile auto trip across the American West, I made it a point to listen to Christian radio all along the way. What I heard revealed much about the secret motivations that drive many Christians. Some of the broadcasts would have been hilarious if they weren't exploiting the gullible — hawking health, wealth and success in the name of Christianity.

• Holy oil and lucky charms were offered to those who sent in money and requested them. Instant material blessings were promised.

• Prayer cloths were offered which had blessed believers with $70,000 — $100,000 — new cars — houses — and health.

• Holy soap would be mailed to others who re-

121

quested it. It had been blessed by the speaker. If used with his instructions, it would wash away bad luck, evil friends and sickness. Again he promised "plenty of money" and everything else the user wanted.

While such con games bring a smile to our lips, the same basic package is marketed with more sophistication at every level of this society. Christian magazines, TV shows and church services often put the spotlight on famous athletes, beauty queens, businessmen and politicians who "make it in the world and have Jesus too!"

Affinity group evangelism that targets Christians in athletics, business, politics and media grabs headlines in the Christian press — but where are the stories of those who target welfare mothers, the sick, the divorced and inner-city poor who are dying without Christ?

Today Christian values are defined almost totally by success as it is promoted by Madison Avenue advertising. Even many Christian ministries gauge their effectiveness by the standards of Harvard MBAs.

Jesus said the heart is where the treasures are kept. So what can we say about many evangelical Christians? Getting into debt for cars, homes and furnishings which probably are not needed; sacrificing family, church and health for corporate promotions and career advancement — I believe all this is deception, engineered by the god of this world to ensnare and destroy effective Christians.

"Love not the world," says John in his first epistle, "neither the things that are in the world. If any man love the world, the love of the Father is not in him. For all that is in the world, the lust of the flesh, and the lust of the eyes, and the pride of life, is not of the Father, but is of the world. And the world passeth away, and the lust thereof: but he that doeth the will of God abideth forever" (2:15-17).

The typical media testimony goes something like this: "I was sick and broke, a total failure. Then I met Jesus. Now everything is fine; my business is booming and I am a great success."

It sounds wonderful. Be a Christian and get that bigger house and a boat and vacation in the Holy Land.

But if that were really God's way, it would put some Christians behind the Iron Curtain and in the Third World in a pretty bad light. Their testimonies often go something like this:

"I was happy. I had everything — prestige, recognition, a good job, and a happy wife and children. Then I gave my life to Jesus Christ. Now I am in Siberia, having lost my family, wealth, reputation, job and health.

"Here I live, lonely, deserted by friends. I cannot see the face of my wife and dear children. My crime is that I love Jesus."

What about the heroes of the faith down through the ages? Most of the apostles were martyred. John died in exile. Christian martyrs have written their names on every page of history.

In Russia, Ivan Moiseyev was tortured and killed within two years of meeting Jesus. In China, Watchman Nee spent twenty years in prison and finally died in bondage.

When Sadhu Sundar Singh, born and raised in a rich Sikh's home in the Punjab, became a Christian, his own family tried to poison him and banished him from their home. He lost his inheritance and walked away with one piece of cloth on his body. Yet, following his Master, he made millions truly rich through faith in Christ.

Our native missionaries supported by Gospel for Asia also often suffer for their commitment. Coming from Hindu and Muslim backgrounds, they often are literally thrown out of their homes, lose their jobs and are beaten and chased from their villages when they accept Christ.

They faithfully serve Christ daily, suffering untold hardship because Jesus promised His followers, "In this world ye shall have tribulation, but be of good cheer, I have overcome the world" (John 16:33).

What He promised were trials and tribulations. But we can face them because we know He already has won the battle. God does promise to meet our physical needs. And He does, indeed, bless His children materially. But He blesses us for a purpose — not so we can squander those resources on ourselves, but so we can be good stewards, using our resources wisely to win the lost to God's saving grace.

That is why Gisela and I have maintained a simple life-style over these years. We have not sought to accumulate wealth, but to be good stewards of that which God has given us. Our goal, of course, is to send all we can to help support the work of Asia's native missionaries.

The Scripture tells us, "Whoso hath this world's goods, and seeth his brother have need, and shutteth up his bowels of compassion from him, how dwelleth the love of God in him?" (1 John 3:17).

As A.W. Tozer, noted Christian and Missionary Alliance pastor and author, once said, "There is no doubt that the possessive clinging to things is one of the most harmful habits in life. Because it is so natural, it is rarely recognized for the evil that it is. But its outworkings are tragic. This ancient curse will not go out painlessly. The tough old miser within us will not lie down and die obedient to our command. He must be torn out, torn out of our hearts like a plant from the soil; he must be extracted in blood and agony like a tooth from the jaw. He must be expelled from our souls in violence as Christ expelled the money changers from the temple."

Let's face it, many Western believers are the rich young rulers of our day. Jesus is saying to them, "If thou wilt be perfect, go and sell all that thou hast, and give to the poor, and thou shalt have treasure in heaven: and come and follow me" (Matt. 19:16-24).

11

Why Should I Make Waves?

By the end of 1981 we appeared to be getting a measure of acceptance. People from all over the United States and Canada began to share with us in the ministry of equipping native missionaries to evangelize in their own countries.

But I wasn't satisfied. For some reason I became obsessed, almost neurotic, with a desire to gain greater respect and recognition for our ministry.

We joined the Evangelical Council for Financial Accountability and other associations, but nothing seemed to satisfy me. I didn't realize how insatiable my desire for recognition had become until one night in a little church in Victoria, Texas.

As Gisela and our office staff in Dallas worked to assign our new sponsors to native missionaries, I felt led of the Lord to plan a road tour of fourteen Texas towns to meet with new supporters. Calling ahead, I introduced myself and thanked the people for taking on the sponsorship of a native missionary.

I was stunned by the response. Most of the people had heard me on the radio and appeared thrilled with the idea of meeting me. In every town, someone invited me to stay with his family and made arrangements for me to speak in small house meetings and churches. People were referring to me in a new way — as the president and director of an important missionary organization. Far from being pleased, I was more terrified than ever — afraid that I would fail or be rejected.

Tour plans were completed. The meetings were booked solid, and publicity had gone out, but an unreasonable fear took over. A weariness settled upon me. As the day for my departure came closer, I looked for excuses to cancel or postpone going to meet the people and their pastors.

"My family and the office need me more," I argued. "Besides, I'll be driving alone. It's dangerous and difficult — I should really wait until someone can go with me."

Just when I had almost talked myself out of going, the Lord spoke to me in an unmistakable voice during my personal morning devotion. As on other occasions, it was just as if He were in the room with me. He spoke to me from John 10.

"My sheep hear My voice," said the Lord. "I know My own and My own know Me. My sheep follow Me because they know My voice." I didn't need an interpretation; the message was clear.

The trip, I realized, had been ordained by Him. He

had arranged it and opened the doors for me. My response was to picture myself as a little lamb and follow my Shepherd over the highways and roads. He would go ahead of me to every church and every home in which I was to stay, I assured myself.

The Lord further confirmed my calling and renewed my courage as I prayed. He reminded me I was not speaking on behalf of K.P. Yohannan or Gospel for Asia.

"You will go where I send you," He said, "because you are representing My servants — the unknown brethren — and I am going with you." All I had to do was obey. I did, and it turned out to be a heavenly two weeks. In every home and church I had delightful fellowship with our new friends — and we added a number of additional supporters as a result of those meetings.

The church in Victoria, Texas, was almost my last stop and the Lord had a special surprise waiting for me there. But He had to prepare me first.

As I drove from town to town, I had time alone in the car for the Lord to deal with me on several issues that would have a lot to do with the future of the mission and my own walk with Him.

I had just read a book which told the story of one saint who had prayed for God to "stamp a vision of eternity in both his eyes." I couldn't shake the words of that strange prayer from my mind, and I soon found that I, too, was praying for the same kind of eternal perspective on life.

It was at this time I faced up to one of the most far-reaching policy decisions I ever would make. For some years I had suffered deep pain over the obvious impotence and waste of mission hospitals and schools in India. Now in America I was seeing new forms of the same thing — so many fine churches and Christians seemed to be preoccupied with the things of this world.

There appeared to be massive imbalance between our preoccupation with Christian institutions and the proclamation of the gospel. Both in India and in my travels around Western countries, I constantly uncovered a preoccupation with worldly activities operated by Christian organizations under the guise of "Christian ministry." Often there was little that was distinctively Christian about them — except, of course, that Christian workers operated them or church monies financed them.

One study, for instance, disclosed that nearly 80 percent of all North American missionaries overseas are involved primarily in social work. In contrast, less than a quarter of the American mission force overseas is left to work in evangelism and church planting. Peter Wagner, in his book *On the Crest of the Wave*, says, "I have before me a recent list of openings in a...mission agency which will go unnamed. Of fifty different categories, only two relate to evangelism, both focused on youth. The rest of the categories include, among others, agronomists, music teachers, nurses, automobile mechanics, secretaries, electronics professors, and ecologists."[1]

Although in the early days of our mission I had thought of raising money for orphans and relief operations, I now decided to drop those programs. Others were doing a far better job than we ever could in that area. Besides, it seemed to me the local church, rather than the missionary, should become the center of the outreach.

Social concern *is* a natural fruit of the gospel. But to put it first is to put the cart before the horse; and from experience, we have seen it fail in India for over two hundred years.

So I made a big decision. I decided to get involved only in preaching the gospel and make church planting the central concern of our work. I didn't go this route because I felt other Christian charities and ministries of compassion were wrong in showing the love of Christ, but because I felt we needed to bring the balance back. With so many concentrating on social work, I decided to get involved where there was obviously the greatest need.

But I didn't publicly tell anyone about my decision. I knew this subject would be controversial, and I was afraid others would think I was being judgmental. Most of all, I was afraid people would label me a "fighting fundy" reactionary. I didn't want to appear like a fanatic. All I wanted to do was help the native missionary movement, and I reasoned that getting into an argument over mission strategy wasn't the way to do it.

Then came Victoria, Texas.

The presentation was going nicely. I had shown the GFA slides and was making an impassioned plea for our work. I explained the philosophy of our ministry — giving the biblical reasons why the heathen are lost unless native missionaries go to them.

Suddenly, I felt the Spirit prompting me to talk about the dangers of the humanist social gospel. No one in the audience knew the agony I was going through. I paused for the briefest moment, then went on without saying anything about that subject. I just didn't have the courage to speak about it in public. What would people think? If I spoke out, I'd make enemies everywhere. I knew you couldn't find a church or mission in America which didn't have some kind of social work going. People wouldn't understand. They'd think I didn't care about the hungry, naked, needy and suffering.

Why, I asked myself, should I make waves? People will think I'm an unloving fool — a spoiler of other Christian work. So I managed to get through my presentation, and feeling relieved, I opened up the meeting to questions.

But the Holy Spirit was not about to let me off the hook.

From far in the back of the room a tall man — at least "six foot three," as they say in Texas — came walking steadily up the aisle. He looked bigger and bigger as he came closer to me. I didn't know who he was or what he had to say, but somehow I felt instinctively that God had sent him.

Wrapping a huge arm around my skinny shoulders, he said some words I still can hear ringing today: "This man here, our brother, is fearful and afraid to speak the truth...and he's struggling with it."

I felt my face and neck getting hot with guilt. How did this big cowboy know that? But it got worse, and I was about to see proof that the Spirit of the living God was really using this tall Texan to deliver a powerful confirmation and rebuke to me.

He went on, "The Lord has led you in ways others have not walked and shown you things others have not seen. The souls of millions are at stake. You must speak the truth about the misplaced priority on the mission field. You must call the body of Christ to return to the task of preaching salvation and snatching souls from hell."

I felt like a zero. My worst fears had come upon me, and yet this was undeniably a miraculous prophecy inspired by God — confirming both my disobedience and the very message God had called me to preach fearlessly. But my humiliation and liberation weren't over yet. "The Lord has asked me," he said, "to call the elders up here to pray for you that this fear of man will leave you."

Suddenly I felt like even less than a zero. I had been first introduced, I thought, as a great mission leader. Now I felt like a little lamb. I wanted to defend myself. I didn't feel as if I were being controlled by a spirit of fear; I had felt that I was just acting logically to protect the interests of our mission. But I submitted anyway, feeling a little ridiculous.

Soon the elders of the congregation were crowding around me to pray for an anointing of power on my preaching ministry. And something happened. I felt that power of God envelop me.

A few minutes later I got up from my knees as a changed man. I was released from the bondage of fear that had gripped me. All doubts were gone. I knew God had placed a burden on my life to deliver this message.

Since that day I've insisted we recover the genuine gospel of Jesus — that balanced New Testament message which begins not with the fleshly and worldly needs of people, but with the wisdom of God according to 1 Corinthians 1:30. The plan and wisdom of God are "born again" conversion that leads to righteousness, sanctification and redemption. Any "mission" that springs from "the base things of the world" is a betrayal of Christ and is what the Bible calls "another gospel." It cannot save or redeem people either as individuals or as a society. We preach a gospel, not for the years of time alone, but for eternity.

The only trouble with *half-truths* is that they contain *full lies*. Such is the case with this declaration issued at an international missionary conference: "Our fathers were impressed with the horror that men should die without Christ; we were equally impressed with the horror that they should live without Christ."

Out of such rhetoric — usually delivered passionately by an ever-growing number of sincere humanists within our churches — come myriads of worldly social programs. Such efforts really snatch salvation and true redemption from the poor — condemning them to eternity in hell.

Of course, there is a basic truth to the statement. Living this life without Christ is an existence of horrible emptiness, one which offers no hope or meaning. But the subtle humanist lie it hides places the accent on the welfare of this present physical life.

What few realize is that this teaching grew out of the influence of nineteenth-century humanists, the very same men who gave us modern atheism, communism and the many other modern philosophies that deny God's sovereignty in the affairs of men. They are, as the Bible says, "anti-Christs."

Modern man unconsciously holds highest the humanistic ideals of happiness, freedom, and economic, cultural and social progress for all mankind. This secular view says there is no God, heaven or hell; just one chance at life, so do what makes you most happy. They also teach that "since all men are brothers," we should work for that which contributes toward the welfare of all men.

This teaching, so attractive on the surface, has entered our churches in many ways. It has created a man-centered and man-made gospel based on changing the outside and social status of man by meeting his physical needs. The cost is his eternal soul.

The so-called humanist gospel — which isn't really the "good news" at all — is called by many names. Sometimes it is argued for in familiar biblical and theological terms; sometimes in English it is called the "social gospel" or the "holistic gospel," but the label isn't important.

You can tell the humanist gospel because it refuses to admit that the basic problem of humanity is not physical, but spiritual. *The humanist won't tell you sin is the root cause of all human suffering.* The latest emphasis of the movement starts by arguing that we should operate mission outreach that provides "care for the whole man," but it ends up providing help for only the body and soul — ignoring the spirit.

Because of this teaching, many churches and mission societies are redirecting their limited outreach funds and personnel away from evangelism to something vaguely called "social concern." Today the majority of Christian missionaries find themselves primarily involved in feeding the hungry, caring for the sick through hospitals, housing the homeless, or other kinds of relief and development work.

In extreme cases, the logical direction of this thinking can lead to organizing guerrilla forces, planting terrorist bombs, or less extreme activities like sponsoring dance and aerobic exercise classes. This is done in the name of Jesus and supposedly is based on His command to go into all the world and preach the gospel to every creature. The mission of the church, as defined by these humanists, can be almost anything except winning people to Christ and discipling them.

History already has taught us that this gospel — without the blood of Christ, conversion and the cross — is a total failure. It seldom positively affects the very social condition upon which it primarily focuses. In China and India we have had seven generations of this teaching. It was brought to us by the British missionaries in a slightly different form in the middle of the last century. My people have watched the English hospitals and schools come and go without any noticeable effect on either our churches or society.

Watchman Nee, an early Chinese native missionary, already had put his finger on the problem in a series of lectures delivered in the years before World War II. Listen to some of his comments on such efforts as recorded in the book *Love Not the World*:

> When material things are under spiritual control they fulfill their proper subordinate role. Released from that restraint they manifest very quickly the power that lies behind them. The law of their nature asserts itself, and their worldly character is proved by the course they take.
>
> The spread of missionary enterprise in our present era gives us an opportunity to test this principle in the religious institutions of our day and of our land. Over a century ago the Church set out to establish

in China schools and hospitals with a definite spiritual tone and an evangelistic objective. In those early days not much importance was attached to the buildings, while considerable emphasis was placed on the institutions' role in the proclamation of the Gospel. Ten or fifteen years ago you could go over the same ground and in many places find much larger and finer institutions on those original sites, but compared with the earlier years, far fewer converts. And by today many of those splendid schools and colleges have become purely educational centers, lacking in any truly evangelistic motive at all, while to an almost equal extent, many of the hospitals exist now solely as places merely of physical and no longer spiritual healing. The men who initiated them had, by their close walk with God, held those institutions steadfastly into His purpose; but when they passed away, the institutions themselves quickly gravitated toward worldly standards and goals, and in doing so classified themselves as "things of the world." We should not be surprised that this is so.

Nee continues to expand on the theme, this time addressing the problem of emergency relief efforts for the suffering:

In the early chapters of the Acts we read how a contingency arose which led the Church to institute relief for the poorer saints. That urgent institution of social service was clearly blessed of God, but it was of a temporary nature. Do you exclaim, "How good if it had continued?" Only one who does not know God would say that. Had those relief measures been prolonged indefinitely they would certainly have veered in the direction of the world, once the spiritual influence at work in their inception was removed. It is inevitable.

For there is a distinction between the Church of God's building, on the one hand, and on the other, those valuable social and charitable by-products that are thrown off by it from time to time through the faith and vision of its members. The latter, for all their origin in spiritual vision, possess in themselves a power of independent survival which the Church of God does not have. They are works which the faith of God's children may initiate and pioneer, but which once the way has been shown and the professional standard set, can be readily sustained or imitated by men of the world quite apart from that faith.

The Church of God, let me repeat, never ceases to be dependent upon the life of God for its maintenance.[2]

The trouble with the social gospel, even when it is clothed in religious garb and operating within Christian institutions, is that it seeks to fight what is basically a spiritual warfare with weapons of the flesh.

Our battle is not against flesh and blood or symptoms of sin like poverty and sickness. It is against Lucifer and countless demons who struggle day and night to take human souls into a Christless eternity.

As much as we want to see hundreds and thousands of new missionaries go into all the dark places, if they don't know what they are really there for — and what they must do — the result will be fatal. We must send soldiers into battle with the right weapons and understanding of the enemy's tactics.

If we intend to answer man's greatest problem — his separation from the eternal God — with rice handouts, then we are throwing a drowning man a board instead of helping him out of the water.

A spiritual battle fought with spiritual weapons will produce eternal victories. Thus, we insist upon restoring balance to gospel outreach. The accent must first and always be on evangelism and discipleship.

12

A Bowl of Rice No Substitute
for the Holy Spirit

To keep Christian missions off balance, Satan has woven a masterful web of deceit and lies. He has invented a whole system of appealing half-truths to confuse the church and ensure that millions will go to hell without ever receiving the gospel. Here are a few of his more common inventions:

Lie number one: *How can we preach the gospel to a man with an empty stomach?*

The result of this lie is the fact that, during the last hundred years, the majority of the mission money has been invested in social work. Evangelism and church planting have been ignored and neglected. While it appears to be a rational and logical statement, I disagree with it. A man's stomach has nothing to do with his heart's condition of being a rebel against the holy God.

A rich American on Fifth Avenue in New York City or a poor beggar on the streets of Bombay are both rebels against God almighty, according to the Bible.

For all people, the only way to become a child of God and inherit His kingdom is to repent from sin and humble ourselves before the Lord.

Lie number two: *Humanitarian work is mission work.*

This lie is the tragedy of all tragedies. It is one of the most serious misunderstandings of all time. It has caused millions to die and go to hell without hearing the real gospel of Christ. This lie is taught and spread almost daily in TV specials and mail-outs, as Christian organizations ask for funds to meet only the physical needs of man.

The average church member unthinkingly drops a few dollars in the mission offering plate, trusting that the missionaries "out there" are involved in saving the 2.7 billion unreached souls. But in most cases, he or she is being horribly deceived. With all their social efforts, such mission representatives are simply making a doomed man feel a little better before he goes out into an eternity of suffering.

Lie number three: *Social work is not only mission work, but it is equal to preaching.*

Death and the grave are in this statement. Luke 16:9-23 tells us the pitiful story of the rich man and Lazarus. Of what benefit were the possessions of the rich man? He could not pay his way out of hell. His riches could not comfort him. The rich man had lost everything including his soul. What about Lazarus? He didn't have any possessions to lose, but he had made preparations for his soul. What was more important during their time on earth? Was it the care for the "body temple" or the immortal soul? "For what does it profit a man if he shall gain the whole world and lose his own soul?" (Luke 9:25).

It is a crime against lost humanity to go in the name of Christ and missions *just* to do the social work and yet neglect calling men to repent — to give up their idols and rebellion — following Christ with all their heart. Lie number four: *They will not listen to the gospel unless we offer them something else first.*

I have sat on the streets of Bombay with beggars — poor men who very soon would die. In sharing the gospel with many of them, I told them I had no material goods to give them, but I came to offer eternal life. I began to share the love of Jesus who died for their souls, about the many mansions in my Father's house (John 14:1-2) and the fact that they can go there to hunger and thirst no more. The Lord Jesus will wipe away every tear from their eyes, I said. They shall no longer be in any debt. There shall no longer be any mourning, or crying or pain (Rev. 7:16; 21:4).

And what a joy it was to see some of them opening their hearts after hearing about the forgiveness of sin they can find in Jesus. That is exactly what the Bible teaches in Romans 10:17, "Faith cometh by hearing, and hearing by the Word of God."

Many times I have given my clothes, food and money to poor people. But I never gave any of those things away with the hope this was going to make them come to Jesus Christ or give them the desire to repent. And neither did Jesus. He helped the poor because He loved them; but He spent most of His ministry teaching and making disciples.

It is impossible to substitute a bowl of rice for the Holy Spirit and the Word of God and then expect the same results. This never saves a soul and rarely changes the attitude of a man's heart. Anyone who has ever done social work will explain to you what I mean. Even Jesus rebuked the multitude because He knew their hearts. Many followed Him only as long as it looked as if they'd get a free lunch.

I am not saying the rich churches of America shouldn't continue to spend billions of dollars to meet human needs both here and abroad; yet we must realize we won't even begin to make a dent in the kingdom of darkness until we lift up Christ with all the authority, power and revelation that is given to us in the Bible.

I first learned this horrible truth about the ineffectiveness of humanitarian aid in the late 1970s at a North India survey expedition before we first went to preach. Throughout the Indian churches, the various mission hospitals and schools of North India are well-known.

My co-workers and I eagerly looked forward to visiting some of these missionaries and seeing the local churches. We especially wanted to meet the believers in the villages near these famed mission stations.

To our amazement we could not find a living congregation anywhere. There were hardly any believers at all. The surrounding villages were as deep in spiritual darkness as they had been two hundred years ago before the missionaries came. We were shocked to find after eighty to one hundred years of constant mission work, and after an investment of millions of dollars in these areas, few, if any, living, New Testament churches existed.

As I have traveled throughout India and many other Asian nations, I have seen this same scenario repeated over and over.

In few countries is the failure of Christian humanism more apparent than in Thailand. There, after 150 years of showing marvelous social compassion, the church still makes up only one-tenth of one percent of the entire population.

Self-sacrificing missionaries probably have done more to modernize the country than any other single force. They gave the country the core of its civil service, education and medical systems.

Working closely with the royal family, the missionaries played the crucial role in eliminating slavery and keeping the country free of Western control during the colonial era.

Thailand owes to missionaries its widespread literacy, first printing press, first university, first hospital, first doctor and almost every other benefit of education and science. In every area, including trade and diplomacy, Christian missionaries put the needs of the host nation first and helped usher in the twentieth century.

But today virtually all that remains of this is a shell of good works.

Millions have meanwhile slipped into eternity without the Lord. They died more educated, better governed and healthier — but they still died without Christ and are bound for hell.

Many questions about this disaster started to hurt me deeply. I asked myself, What went wrong? Were these missionaries not dedicated enough? Were their doctrines unscriptural? Perhaps they did not believe in eternal hell or eternal heaven. Did they lack Bible training, or did they just not go out to preach to the lost? Did they shift their priorities from being interested in saving souls to relieving human suffering? I know now it was probably a little of all of these things.

While I was seeking answers, I met poor native brothers involved in gospel work in pioneer areas. They had nothing material to offer the people to whom they preached — no agricultural training and no medical relief or school program. In fact, some of them had very little formal education themselves. But I found that hundreds of souls got saved. In a few years, a number of churches were established.

Again I asked myself, What are these brothers doing right to have these kinds of results, while the other groups with many more advantages had failed?

I finally came to the conclusion that the answer lies

in our basic understanding of what mission work is all about. There is nothing wrong with charitable acts — but they are not to be confused with preaching the gospel.

Feeding programs can save a man dying from hunger. Medical aid can prolong life and fight disease. Housing projects can make this temporary life more comfortable — but only the gospel of Jesus Christ can save a soul from a life of sin and an eternity in hell!

Sin is the root cause of the world's suffering. The battle against hunger and poverty is a spiritual battle, not a physical or social one. The only weapon that will ultimately win the fight is the gospel of Jesus Christ.

To look into the sad eyes of a hungry child or see the wasted life of a drug addict is only to see the evidence of Satan's hold on this world. He is the ultimate enemy of mankind, and he will do everything within his considerable power to kill and destroy people. But to try to fight this terrible enemy with physical weapons is like fighting tanks with stones.

When commerce had been established with the Fiji islanders, a merchant who was an atheist and skeptic landed on the island to do business. He was talking to the Fiji chief and noticed a Bible and some other paraphernalia of religion around the house.

"What a shame," he said, "that you have listened to this foolish nonsense of the missionaries."

The chief replied, "Do you see the large white stone over there? That is a stone where just a few years ago we used to smash the heads of our victims to get at their brains. Do you see that large oven over there? That is the oven where just a few years ago we used to bake the bodies of our victims before we feasted upon them. Had we not listened to what you call the nonsense of those missionaries, I assure you that your head would already be smashed on that rock and your body would be baking in that oven."

There's no record of the merchant's response to that explanation of the importance of the gospel of Christ.

When God changes the heart and spirit, then the physical changes also. To anyone who wants to get involved in meeting the needs of the poor in this world, there's no better place to start than by preaching the gospel. It has done more to lift up the downtrodden, the hungry and the needy than all the social programs ever imagined by secular humanists.

Recently the World Bank published a report revealing for the first time that twenty-seven million Chinese starved to death during the "Great Leap Forward" economic development scheme of Mao Tse-Tung in the 1950s. More recently the same thinking led to the deaths of three million Cambodians when the communists took over Kampuchea. Let us never forget that these schemes — plus the actions of all the Hitlers and Stalins in this century — have been the logical extension of secular humanism applied to government. This is the best these social engineers have to offer when they have total control of a nation. We need to ponder long and hard the devastating results this same thinking has had on the church and its mission to a lost world. Could it be that millions are suffering the flames of hell today because we focused on meeting superficial physical needs rather than concentrating on their most basic need?

If the pure gospel had been preached in China and India in the last century — instead of a watered-down version of the Sermon on the Mount — I'm sure that freedom and prosperity would prevail over much of Asia today. Indirectly, the real gospel produces more social change than all the efforts of the world combined. The various humanist gospels are really mankind's pitiful efforts to find a shortcut to heaven while still on this earth.

But we cannot change the past; we must concentrate on preaching the true gospel of Christ to our generation. A.W. Tozer said it well in his book *Of God and Man*: "To spread an effete, degenerate brand of Christianity to pagan lands is not to fulfill the commandment of Christ or discharge our obligation to the heathen."[1]

These terrible words of Jesus should haunt our souls: "Ye compass sea and land to make one proselyte and when he is made, ye make him twofold more the child of hell than yourself" (Matt. 23:15).

We must learn from the past mistakes of missions and not repeat them. Just before China was taken over by the communists, one communist officer, talking to a missionary named John Meadow, made this revealing statement: "You missionaries have been in China for over a hundred years, but you have not won China to your cause. You lament the fact that there are uncounted millions who have never heard the name of your God. Nor do they know anything of your Christianity. But we communists have been in China less than ten years, and there is not a Chinese who does not know...has not heard the name of Stalin...or something of communism.

"What missionaries have failed to do in a hundred years, we communists have done in ten. We have filled China with our doctrine.

"Now let me tell you why you have failed and we have succeeded," the officer continued. "You have tried to win the attention of masses by building churches, missions, mission hospitals, schools and what not. But we communists have printed our message and spread our literature all over China.

"Someday we will drive you missionaries out of our country, and we will do it by the means of the printed page."

Today, of course, John Meadow is out of China. The communists were true to their word. They won China and drove out the missionaries. Indeed, what missionaries failed to do in a hundred years, the communists did in ten. One Christian leader said that if the church had spent as much time on preaching the gospel as it did on hospitals, orphanages, schools and rest homes — needful though they were — the bamboo curtain would not exist today.

The tragedy of China is being repeated today in other countries. When we allow a mission activity to focus on the physical needs of man without the correct spiritual balance, we are participating in a program that ultimately sends people to hell.

13

He Didn't Want Fans
but Disciples

If we could spend only one minute in the flames and torment of hell, we would see how really unloving is the so-called gospel that prevails in much of missions today.

Theology, which is only a fancy word for what we believe, makes all the difference on the mission field. When we go to the book of Acts, we find that these disciples were totally convinced about the lostness of man without Christ. Not even persecution could stop them from calling people everywhere to repent and turn to Christ.

Paul cries out in Romans 10:9-15 for the urgency of preaching Christ. In his day, the social and economic problems in cities like Corinth and Ephesus and other places were the same or worse than those we face today. Yet the apostles did not set out to establish social relief centers, hospitals or educational institutions. Paul declared in 1 Corinthians 2:2, "When I came to you...I determined not to know anything among you save Jesus Christ and him crucified."

Paul recognized that Jesus Christ was the ultimate answer to all man's problems. While he was concerned about the poor saints, you cannot miss the primary emphasis of his life and message.

I have spoken in churches which had millions of dollars invested in buildings — churches with pastors known as excellent Bible teachers with a heart of love for people. Yet I have discovered that many of them have absolutely no missionary program of any kind.

In preaching to one of these churches, I made the following statement: "While you claim to be evangelicals and pour time and life into learning more and more biblical truths, in all honesty, I do not think you believe the Bible."

They were shocked. But I continued.

"If you believed the Bible you say you believe, the very knowledge there is a real place called hell — where millions will go and spend eternity if they die without Christ — would make you the most desperate people in the world to give up everything you have to keep missions and reaching the lost as your top priority."

The problem with this congregation, as with many today, is that they didn't believe in hell. Yet, all through the Bible, there it is. It is mentioned, in fact, more often than heaven. Yet how we Christians struggle with it.

C.S. Lewis, that great British defender of the faith, wrote, "There is no doctrine which I would more willingly remove from Christianity than this (hell). I would pay any price to be able to say truthfully, 'All will be saved.'"

But Lewis, like us, realized that was neither truthful nor within his power to change.

Jesus Himself often spoke of hell and coming judgment. The Bible calls it the place of unquenchable fire, where the worms which eat the flesh don't die — a place of outer darkness where there is eternal weeping and gnashing of teeth.

These and hundreds of other verses tell of a real place where lost man will spend eternity if he dies without Jesus Christ.

Only a very few believers seem to have integrated the reality of hell into their life-style. In fact, it is difficult to feel that our friends who don't know Jesus really are destined to eternal hell.

Many Christians hold within their hearts the idea that, somehow or other, ways of redemption are available to those who have not heard. But the Bible doesn't give us a shred of hope for such a belief. It states clearly that it is "appointed unto men once to die, but after this the judgment" (Heb. 9:27).

There is no way out of death, hell, sin and the grave except Jesus Christ. He said, "I am the way, the truth, and the life: no man cometh unto the Father, but by me" (John 14:6).

How different our churches would be if we started

to live by the true revelation of the Word of God about hell. Instead, missions, both in the West and in the East, have been infected with death and continue to pass out death to the millions of lost souls who surround us.

The church Jesus called out of this world to be separated unto Himself has, to a great extent, forgotten her reason for existence. Her loss of balance is seen in the current absence of holiness, spiritual reality and concern for the lost. Substituted for the life she once knew are teaching and reaching for prosperity, pleasure, politics and social involvement.

"Evangelical Christianity," commented Tozer prophetically before his death, "is now tragically below the New Testament standard. Worldliness is an accepted fact of our way of life. Our religious mood is social instead of spiritual."

The further our leaders wander from the Lord, the more they turn to the ways of the world. One church in Dallas recently spent several million dollars to construct a gymnasium "to keep our young people interested in church." Many churches have become like secular clubs with softball teams, golf lessons, schools and exercise classes to keep people coming to their buildings and giving them their tithes. Some churches have gone so far from the Lord that they sponsor yoga and meditation courses — Western adaptations of Hindu religious exercises.

If this is what is considered mission outreach at home, is it any wonder the same churches fall prey to the seductive philosophy of Christian humanists when planning overseas missionary work?

Real Christian mission always is aware there is eternal hell to shun and heaven to gain. We need to restore the balanced vision General William Booth had when he started the Salvation Army. He had an unbelievable compassion for winning lost souls to Christ. His own words tell the story of what he envisioned for the movement: "Go for souls, and go for the worst."

What would Jesus do if He walked today into our churches?

I am afraid He would not be able to say to us: "You have kept the faith, you have run the race without turning left or right, and you have obeyed My command to reach this world."

I believe He would go out to look for a whip, because we have made His Father's house a den of robbers. If that is so, then we must recognize that the hour is too desperate for us to continue to deceive ourselves. We are past the point of revival or reformation. If this gospel is to be preached in all the world in our lifetime, we must have a Christian, heaven-sent revolution.

But before revolution can come, we must recognize the need for one. We are like a lost man looking at a road map. Before we can choose the right road that takes us to our destination, we must determine where we went wrong, go back to that point and start over. So my cry to the body of Christ is simple: Turn back to the true gospel road. We need to preach again the whole counsel of God. Our priority must again be placed on calling men to repentance and snatching them from hell-fire.

Time is short. If we are not willing to plead in prayer for a mission revolution— and let it start in our own personal lives, homes and churches— we will lose this generation to Satan.

We can go trading souls for bodies, or we can make a difference by sponsoring Bible-believing native missionaries overseas.

In 1983, forty Indian villages, once considered Christian, turned back to Hinduism. Could it be that whole villages which had experienced the liberating gospel of Jesus Christ would turn back into the bondage of Satan?

No. These villages were called "Christian" only because they had been "converted" by missionaries who used hospitals, material goods and other incentives to attract them to Christianity. But when the material rewards were reduced — or when other competing movements offered similar benefits — these converts reverted to their old cultural ways. In missionary terms, they were "rice Christians."

When "rice" was offered, they changed their names and their religions, responding to the "rice." But they never understood the true gospel of the Bible. After all the effort, these people were as lost as ever. But now they were even worse off — they were presented a completely wrong picture of what it means and what it takes to follow Christ.

Could that be what we fear in North America: no gyms — no softball teams — no converts?

The lesson from the mission field is that meeting physical needs alone does not get people to follow God. Whether hungry or full, rich or poor, human beings remain in rebellion against God without the power of the gospel.

Unless we return to the biblical balance — to the gospel of Jesus as He proclaimed it — we'll never be able to put the accent where it rightly belongs in the outreach mission of the church.

Jesus was compassionate to human beings as total persons. He did all He could to help them, but He never forgot the main purpose of His earthly mission: to reconcile men to God, to die for sinners and redeem their souls from hell. Jesus cared for the spiritual side of man first, then the body.

This is illustrated clearly in Matthew 9:2-7 when He first forgave the sins of the paralytic then healed his body.

In John 6:1-13, Jesus miraculously fed five thousand hungry men plus women and children. He fed them *after* he preached, not *before* to attract their attention.

Later, in verse 26, we find that these people followed Jesus not because of His teachings, or who He was, but because He had fed them. They even tried to make Him king for the wrong reason. Seeing the danger of their spiritual misunderstanding, Jesus withdrew from them. He didn't want fans but disciples.

The apostles did not fear to tell the beggar that "silver and gold have I none; but such as I have give I thee" (Acts 3:6). Then they preached the gospel.

I have had similar experiences all across India. I have yet to meet a person who was not willing to hear the wonderful news of Jesus because of his or her physical condition. Those who say otherwise are simply not telling the truth.

As Christians we must follow the example of Jesus. I do believe we must do all we can to relieve the pain and suffering around us. We must love our neighbors as ourselves in all areas of life. But we must keep supreme the priority of sharing the message of salvation to them — and we must never minister to the physical needs at the expense of preaching Christ. This is biblical balance, the true gospel of Jesus.

14

Without Christ
People Serve Demon Spirits

My hosts in the Southern city where I was preaching at a mission conference had thoughtfully booked me into a motel room. It was good to have a few minutes alone, and I looked forward to having some time for prayer and Scripture meditation.

While settling in, I flipped on the big TV set that dominated the room.

What burst on the screen shocked me more than anything I had ever seen in America. There in beautiful color was an attractive woman seated in the lotus position teaching yoga. I watched in horror and amazement as she praised the health benefits of the breathing techniques and other exercises of this Eastern religious practice. What her viewers did not know is that yoga is designed for one purpose only — to open up the mind and body to receive visitations from demon spirits.

Because this American yogi was dressed in a chic

Danskin body suit, claimed a Ph.D. degree and was on educational TV, I assume many of the viewers were deceived into believing this was just another harmless exercise show. But those of us born and raised in nations dominated by the power of darkness know better. Hundreds of Eastern religions are marketing themselves in the United States and Canada under innocuous — even scientific-sounding — brand names.

Few Westerners, when they see news reports of the poverty, suffering and violence in Asia, take time to stop and ask why.

How is it that the East is bound into an endless cycle of suffering while Western nations are so blessed? Secular humanists are quick to reel out many historic and pseudo-scientific reasons for the disparity, because they are unwilling to face the truth. But the real reason is simple: The Judeo-Christian heritage of Europe has brought the favor of God, while false religions have brought the curse of Babylon on all the nations of Asia.

Mature Christians realize the Bible teaches there are only two religions in this world. There is the worship of the one true God, and there is a false system of demonic alternative invented in ancient Iran. From there, Persian armies and priests spread their faith to India where it took root. Hindu missionaries in turn spread it throughout the rest of Asia. Animism, Buddhism and all other Asian religions have a common heritage in this one religious system.

Because many Westerners are unaware of this fact, demonic influences now are able to spread Eastern mysticism in the West through pop culture, rock bands, singers and even university professors. The media have become the new vehicle for the spread of demon worship and idolatry by American gurus.

But it is hard to blame the average Christian for misunderstanding what is happening to them and the Judeo-Christian heritage which has brought such blessings on their land. Most have never taken the time to study and discern the real situation in the Orient. Few pastors or prophets are sounding the alarm.

In Asia the religion of Babylon is woven into every waking minute of the day. Without Christ, people live to serve demon spirits. Religion relates to everything including your name, birth, education, marriage, business deals, contracts, travel and death.

Because Oriental culture and religion are a mystery, many people in the West are fascinated by it without knowing the power of these demons to blind and enslave their followers. What routinely follows the mystery religions of Babylon is degradation, humiliation, poverty and suffering — even death.

Most believers in America, I find, are overwhelmed by the TV and media news reports from Asia. The numbers reported are beyond imagination: people, problems and needs. The injustice, poverty, suffering and violence appear to be unstoppable. All things Oriental appear to be mysterious. Everything, it seems, is measured either on a grand scale or by one so different that it can't be compared to things familiar.

So in all my travels, I have found it is extremely difficult for most people to relate to Asia's needs. Sometimes I wish I could just scoop up my audience and take them on a six-month tour of Asia. But since that's not possible, I must use words, pictures, slides and video films to paint a clearer picture. It is important that we take the time to understand the real need.

Although Asia is admittedly hard to understand, we must not let that be a reason to ignore it. Two out of every three people in the world live there. That's more than the combined populations of all the African and Latin American mission fields combined. (In fact, it's more than the combined populations of Europe, Africa, North America and South America.)

In terms of numbers alone, Asia must be the top priority in Christian evangelism. From the standpoint of Christian missions, these are more than just big numbers. Asia makes up the vast majority of 2.7 billion hidden peoples who are being missed by traditional missionary efforts and mass media evangelism. They are *the most lost of the lost* — trapped in utter spiritual darkness.

But the big question I hear almost daily is, How can we help — is there anything we can do with problems so gigantic?

As I travel all over North America sharing the needs of missions in Asia, I find that Christians are hungry for straight answers. They want to help if they only knew how.

What are the challenges facing native missions today? How real are the needs? How can Christians best help the Asian church and its missionary efforts?

While I am not trying to minimize the social and material needs of the Asian nations, it is important to realize that Asia's basic problem is a spiritual one. This is easy to lose sight of when the Western media focuses almost entirely on our problems of hunger, poverty and violence. It is difficult for Americans to see pictures of all those starving children on TV without getting the false impression that hunger is the biggest problem.

But what causes the hunger? We as Christians know these horrible conditions are only symptoms of the real problem — spiritual bondage to satanic philosophies. The key factor — and the most neglected — in understanding India's hunger problem is the belief of Hinduism and its effect on food production. Most people know of the "sacred cows" that roam free, eating tons of grain while nearby people starve. But a lesser known and more sinister culprit is another animal protected by religious belief — the rat.

According to those who believe in reincarnation, the rat must be protected as a likely recipient for a reincarnated soul on its way up the ladder of spiritual evolution to Nirvana. Though many reject this and seek to poison rats, large scale efforts of extermination have been thwarted by religious outcry. As one of India's statesmen has said, "India's problems will never cease until her religion changes."

Rats eat or spoil 20 percent of India's food grain every year. A study of United Nations statistics by *India Journal*[1] found that food grain losses in hot, moist climates could be as high as 40 percent from loss due to rodents, birds, insects and spoilage resulting from poor storage. The chief culprit is the Bengal bandicoot rat. A recent survey in the wheat-growing district of Hapur in North India revealed there is an average of ten rats per house.

Of the 1982 harvest of cereals in India, including maize, wheat, rice, millet and so on — a total of 134 million metric tons — the 20 percent loss from rats amounted to 26.8 million metric tons.

The picture becomes more comprehensible by imagining a train of boxcars carrying that amount of grain. With each car holding about eighty-two metric tons, the train would contain 327,000 cars and stretch for 3,097 miles. The annual food grain loss in India would fill a train longer than the distance between New York and Los Angeles.

From these statistics it is apparent that India produces enough food to feed its nearly one billion people. Social programs and attempts to meet physical needs will never get to the root of the problem. Preaching of the gospel does.

The devastating effects of the rat in India should make it an object of scorn. Instead, because of the spiritual blindness of the people, the rat is protected and in some places even worshipped.

Thirty miles south of Bikaner in North India is a temple where rats are worshipped, according to an article in the *India Express*.

"Hundreds of rats, called 'kabas' by the devotees, scurry around merrily in the large compound of the temple and sometimes even around the image of the goddess Karni Devi situated in a cave. The rats are fed on prasad offered by the devotee or by the temple management. Legend has it that the fortunes of the community are linked to that of the rats.

"One has to walk cautiously through the temple compound; for if a rat is crushed to death, it is not only considered a bad omen but may also invite severe punishment. One is considered lucky if a rat climbs over one's shoulder. Better still to see a white rat."

Clearly, the agony we see in the faces of those starving children and beggars is actually caused by centuries of religious slavery. The single most important social reform that can be brought to Asia is the gospel of Jesus Christ. My people need the hope and truth that only the Lord Jesus can provide.

In my own beloved homeland of India, thousands of lives and billions of dollars go into social programs every year. Education, medical and relief efforts operate on a massive scale. It's fascinating for me to watch the seriousness with which U.S. politicians dramatically declare certain parts of their nation to be so-called disaster areas in times of natural calamity.

Many of the crisis problems which are considered disasters here would be only normal, everyday living conditions in most of Asia. When we have disasters in the Orient, the death tolls read like Vietnam war body counts. Asian governments struggle with these tremendous social problems and limited resources.

Yet, despite all the massive social programs operating in India and other Asian countries, the problems of hunger, population and poverty continue to grow. The real culprit is not a person, lack of natural resources or a system of government. It is spiritual darkness. It thwarts every effort to make progress. It dooms our people to misery — both in this world and in the world to come.

That's why I declare our biggest need is spiritual. In India over three hundred million people have never heard the name of Jesus Christ mentioned even once.

Recently, for instance, one native missionary, who serves the Lord in Jammu, asked a shopkeeper on the market if he knew Jesus. After thinking a moment, he said, "Sir, I know everyone in our village. There is not one by that name who lives here. Why don't you go to the next village? He may live there."

Frequently native missionary evangelists find people who ask if Jesus is the brand name of a new soap or patent medicine. In India proper, there are nearly one billion people — three times the population of the United States. Only 3.5 percent of these call themselves Christians.* But almost all of the 0.4 percent of the population that is evangelical Christian is located in just two tiny regions. This is typical of all Asia. When there are born-again Christians, they usually are found huddled together in little pockets.

India, with nearly 500,000 unevangelized villages, is undoubtedly one of the greatest evangelistic challenges facing the world Christian community today. If present trends continue, it will soon be the world's most populous nation. While China has a greater need, there still is not the political freedom there that Indians now enjoy.

Many of India's twenty-two states have larger populations than whole nations in Europe and other parts of the world. Not only are our populations huge, but each state is usually as distinctive as if it were another world. Most have completely different cultures, dress, diet and languages. But few nations in Asia are homogenous. Most are like India to some extent; nations that are patchwork quilts of many languages, peoples and tribes. This diversity, in fact, is what makes Asia such a tremendous challenge to missionary work.

India, of course, isn't the only wide-open door for native missionaries. In nearly every nation there is some degree of freedom for evangelists who emerge from the local soil. Some of the most exciting right

---

* Although this figure reflects the official government census, a number of key Christian leaders who understand the situation believe the number of Christians is actually much greater than reported.

now are found in Korea, the Philippines and Thailand.

To give even a brief survey of all the opportunities would be a book in itself, but I would like to take a whirlwind tour of some of the more exciting open doors we are facing in the Third World today. Here is a country-by-country breakdown of just a few.

Afghanistan. Long one of the militantly anti-Christian nations in the world, this Marxist republic has been under martial law since 1978 when the Soviets invaded the country. The population, officially 99.3 percent Muslim, is constantly shifting as wars and civil strife continue. Many refugees have crossed the border into Pakistan, and there appear to be significant new opportunities to witness to them. There still is a death penalty for conversion to Christianity, however, and no Christian church ever has been established successfully inside the national borders. More than fifty-three languages are spoken by the twenty major ethnic groups.[2]

Bangladesh. One of the most densely populated in the world, this officially Muslim nation has been ruled by a military junta since 1975. Bengali, Urdu and English dominate the five major languages although thirty others are spoken. In the wake of the civil war that tore this nation from Pakistan in 1971, there have been several brief "open windows" of religious freedom. Among minority groups there has been considerable openness to Christ.[3]

Bhutan. This tiny Himalayan kingdom only recently experienced the first slight breezes of freedom. Still officially a Buddhist state, it was totally closed to any outside witness until 1965. It is illegal to evangelize, proselytize or worship publicly. Only three hundred Christians are estimated to exist among the 1.4 million population, but Indian believers living along the border or working in the country have many opportunities to share their faith. Landlocked, Bhutan depends totally on India for trade and foreign relations.[4]

Myanmar (formerly Burma). Although officially closed to outsiders since 1966, this intensely xenophobic nation does have a vigorous native missionary movement in the northern tribal areas. About 1.1 percent of the population is evangelical Protestant, one of the largest percentages in Asia. However, very few Burmese are believers. Most of the Christians are confined to tribal minorities such as the Shan and Karen. Buddhism is the semi-official but powerful religious force that seems to have a viselike grip on the Burmese. Politically, the nation is dominated by secular socialists — a totalitarian group controlled by the army. Although 70 percent of the population is Burmese, there are 129 minority people groups, including nearly one hundred tribes.[5]

Hong Kong. Gateway to China, this wealthy city-state has been a British Crown Colony since 1842. Soon to return to the control of China, it probably enjoys as much religious freedom as any nation in Asia. Over one hundred denominations flourish there among the 5.2 million population. Christians make up over 5 percent of the population, and this is the most vitally strategic city for Chinese evangelism.[6]

Indonesia. With one of the fastest-growing Christian communities in the world, this nation continues to be probably the greatest harvest field of Asia. More than 840 languages are spoken by the population of 151 million. Like Japan and the Philippines, it is made up of widely scattered islands. Complex and exciting, they contain scores of unreached people groups. Religious freedom is widespread, and recently there has been a remarkable outpouring of the Holy Spirit. Many are being called into village evangelism, and the three thousand islands promise to become one of the greatest growth areas for the native missionary movement.[7]

Japan. While religious freedom is protected by the government and many Western missionaries have struggled in this difficult field since World War II, the Japanese largely have refused to accept Christianity.

P.J. Johnstone describes the 118 million people of these islands as "...talented, materialistic, unresponsive and hidden in a centuries-old cocoon of culture and bondage to demonic powers and multiplied varieties of Buddhism."

Proud and apparently unable to respond to the gospel when preached by foreigners, the Japanese desperately need a native church and missionary movement. Evangelical believers make up only 0.03 percent of the population, but in spite of their small size, they have thrust out nearly two hundred missionaries to other Asian nations. The Japanese, if converted, could be a major force in carrying the gospel throughout Asia. Japan's legendary cultural, economic and educational achievements have turned it into one of the greatest nations on earth — and one of the greatest challenges to Christian missions in Asia.[8]

Korea. With probably the most dramatically Christian movement in the world, the Koreans have survived terrible persecution from both the communists and Japanese. They recently have experienced revivals and evangelistic movements throughout the church, government and military. Not only are Korean churches mushrooming, but native missionary movements are powerful forces both in the country and throughout Asia. Over six thousand Korean young people have pledged themselves to mission service in other Asian nations.[9]

Malaysia. Fiercely Muslim, the Malays themselves have vigorously and officially resisted the gospel. Missionary efforts by Westerners have practically stopped under rigid government restrictions. However, among the Chinese, Tamil Indians and the 170 tribal groups there has been steady evangelism and occasional revivals. The country's only hope to find Christ is in the raising up of a strong native evangelism movement internally.[10]

Maldives. Another Muslim stronghold, there are no known Christians on these islands located off the west coast of India. Only 155,000 people inhabit about 220 of the two thousand Maldivian Islands, and they represent an important evangelistic challenge to the Indian church. About ten thousand are living abroad in South India and Bombay.[11]

Nepal. Despite persecution, there are a growing number of Nepali Christians. Native missionaries are actively but covertly working in the country. About half the population is Nepali Hindus, the rest being various tribes and a large Indian minority. There are about nineteen ethno-linguistic groups in the nation.[12]

Despite recent changes in Nepal, still officially a Hindu nation, it is constitutionally illegal to change one's religion in this nation. As in many other Asian nations, believers in the Himalayan kingdom just north of India are discriminated against in school, on the job and in nearly every social activity. Two local Christians were recently beaten and imprisoned by government officials. Their crime? To write the word "Christian" on a government form that asked them to name their religion.

Pakistan. One of the most open doors in Asia, this Islamic republic of ninety-three million souls consistently has permitted Christian minorities a great deal of freedom, including the right to proclaim their faith. Ethnically, the country is almost 60 percent Punjabi but has nineteen major people groups. Muslims are more open than ever to listen to the gospel, and many fear the full imposition of Islamic law. Social pressures and the cultural unacceptability of the present Christian community are commonly pointed out as reasons for the lack of church growth. With the growing influx of Afghani refugees, there is even more reason to see a native missionary movement expand in this land.[13]

Philippines. With nearly 80 percent professing Roman Catholics, the Philippines is the only Asian nation that has claimed to be Christian. Over the last several years there has been a great spiritual move both within and outside the church. Many thousands are discovering real life in Jesus Christ, and evangelistic meetings attract large crowds everywhere.

This archipelago of seven thousand islands offers one of the greatest spiritual opportunities in Asia today. Only a few hundred of the islands have a Christian witness. The evangelical population is less than 7 percent overall, and they are concentrated in one or two major cities.

Ten languages and 150 dialects are spoken by the 173 separate people groups which make up this diverse nation of tiny islands.[14]

Singapore. Another city-state with vast potential as a sending base for native missionaries, it has been a secular state since 1965. Protestant evangelicals account for 1.7 percent of the population, considerably larger than in most Asian nations. Located in a group of forty-one small islands off the tip of Malaysia, the population of Singapore is 2.4 million, mostly crowded on the densely packed main island. The population is 75 percent Chinese, the rest being mostly Malay and Indians.[15]

Sri Lanka. A Buddhist, socialist republic off the southern coast of India, Sri Lanka generally is considered to be one of the worst evangelized countries in Asia. A succession of foreign invaders including the Portuguese, Dutch and British artificially imposed Christianity. The result has been deep anti-Christian bias and a revival of Buddhism in recent years. Fewer than fifty foreign missionaries now remain, and in a country torn by years of civil war a strong native missionary movement is absolutely essential if the nation is to be evangelized. The population of more than fifteen million is largely Singhalese with a large Tamil minority.[16]

Taiwan. Located off the coast of China, this island of sixteen million has a larger-than-average number of evangelicals, about 1.8 percent. After a period of great growth due to immigration — and intense evangelism following the communist takeover of mainland China — Taiwan churches have sent several hundred native missionaries throughout Asia. As a sending nation, Taiwan has significant potential.[17]

Thailand. Another hotbed of spiritual activity, this officially Buddhist kingdom of thirty-five million is developing pockets of great response to evangelistic activity. A vigorous native missionary movement is erupting, but church planting is limited mostly to the Northeast. While less than 0.1 percent of the population is evangelical, the current outreach is more fruitful than at any other time in the history of the nation. Although the country is almost 80 percent Siamese Thai, there are thirty-six other major people groups in the country. The major languages are Thai, English, Lao, Chinese, Malay, Khmer, Vietnamese and fifty tribal dialects.[18]

Temples of This New Religion
Are Atomic Reactors

The native missionary movement, the only hope for these Asian nations, is not going unchallenged by either Satan or the world. Revivals of traditional religions such as Islam and Hinduism, the growth of secular materialism including communism, and the traditional cultural and nationalist barriers are all united in opposition to Christian mission activity.

Masih had terrible memories of his home and the persecution he had suffered there when he first turned to Christ while a Hindu priest. For years he had sought spiritual peace through self-discipline, yoga and meditation as required by his Brahmin caste.

He also had memories of rejection by his family because of his new faith and of the physical attacks when he refused to renounce Jesus. But God called, and so Masih returned to his home village in Uttar Pradesh, India.

"I was brought up in an orthodox Hindu home

where we worshipped many gods," he says. "I even became the Hindu priest in our village, but I couldn't find the peace and joy I wanted.

"One day I received a gospel tract and read about the love of Jesus Christ. I answered the offer on the leaflet and enrolled in a correspondence course to learn more about Jesus.

"On January 1, 1978, I gave my life to Jesus Christ. I was baptized three months later and took the Christian name 'Masih' which means 'Christ.' "

For a Hindu, baptism and the taking of a Christian name symbolize a complete break with the pagan past. To avoid the censure which often comes with baptism, some wait years before they are baptized. But Masih didn't wait. The reaction was swift.

When his parents realized their son had rejected their Hindu gods, they began a campaign of persecution. To escape, Masih went to Kota in Rajasthan to search for a job.

For six months he worked in a factory and meanwhile joined a local group of believers. Through their encouragement, he enrolled in a Bible institute and began to master the Scriptures.

During his three years of study, he made his first trip home. "My father sent a telegram asking me to come home," Masih recalls. "He said he was 'terribly ill.' When I arrived, my family and friends asked me to renounce Christ. When I didn't, much persecution followed, and my life was in danger. I had to flee."

When he returned to school, Masih thought God

would lead him to minister to some other part of India. He was shocked at the answer to his prayers.

"As I waited on the Lord, He guided me to go back and work among my own people," he says. "He wanted me to share the love of God through Christ with them, like the healed demoniac of Gadara whom He sent back to his own village."

Today, Ramkumar Masih — a former Hindu priest — is involved in church planting in his home city and surrounding villages. He is working alone among both Hindus and Muslims in a basically hostile environment.

Although Masih has not had to pay the ultimate price to win his people to Christ, every year a number of Christian missionaries and ordinary believers are killed for their faith throughout Asia. The total in this century probably numbers in the hundreds of thousands, undoubtedly more than the total number of Christians killed in the entire history of the church.

Revivals of traditional religions are occurring all over Asia. Although few countries have gone the route of Iran — where a religious revival of Islam actually toppled the state — religious factionalism is a major problem in many countries.

When government, media and educational institutions are taken over by atheistic materialists, there often can be a great backlash in most nations. As traditional religious leaders are finding out, it isn't enough to drive Western nations out. Secular humanists are in firm control of most Asian governments, and many traditional religious leaders miss the power they once exercised.

At the grass-roots level, traditional religion and nationalism often are deliberately confused and exploited by political leaders for short-term gain. In the villages, traditional religions still have a powerful hold on the minds of most people. Almost every village or community has a favorite idol or deity — there are 330 million gods in the Hindu pantheon alone. In addition, various animistic cults which involve the worship of powerful spirits are openly practiced alongside Islam, Hinduism and Buddhism.

In many areas the village temple still is the center of informal education, tourism and civic pride. Religion is big business, and temples take in vast sums of money annually.

Millions of priests and amateur practitioners of the occult arts also are profiteering from the continuation and expansion of traditional religions. Like the silversmiths in Ephesus, they aren't taking the spread of Christianity lightly. Religion, nationalism and economic gain mix as a volatile explosive that Satan uses to blind the eyes of millions.

But God is calling native missionaries to preach the gospel anyway, and many are taking the good news into areas solidly controlled by traditional religions.

But the enemies of the cross include more than just traditional religionists. A new force, even more powerful, is now sweeping across Asia. It is what the

Bible calls the spirit of anti-Christ — the new religion of secular materialism. Often manifested as some form of communism, it has taken control of governments in a number of states including Afghanistan, Burma, Cambodia, China, Laos, North Korea, Tibet and Vietnam.

But in all Asian nations, even those with democracies like India and Japan, it has gained some control of the state in various non-communist forms.

The temples of this new religion are atomic reactors, oil refineries, hospitals and shopping malls. The priests are most often the technicians, scientists and military generals who are impatiently striving to rebuild the nations of Asia in the image of the industrial West.

The shift of political power in most of Asia has gone toward these men and women who promise health, peace and prosperity without a supernatural god — for man himself is their god.

In one sense, secular humanism and materialism correctly diagnose traditional religion as a major source of oppression and poverty throughout Asia. Humanism is a natural enemy of theistic religion because it is a worldly and scientific method to solve the problems of mankind without God.

As a result of this growing, scientific materialism, there are strong secularistic movements in every Asian nation. They unite and seek to eliminate the influence of all religion — including Christianity — from society.

Modern Asia, in the great cities and capitals where secular humanism reigns supreme, is controlled by many of the same drives and desires that have dominated the West for the last hundred years.

If traditional Asian religions represent an attack of the devil on Christianity, then secular humanism is an attack of the flesh. That leaves only one enemy to discuss, the anti-Christian pressure of the world.

This final barrier to Christ, and still probably the strongest of all, is the culture itself.

When Mahatma Gandhi returned to India from years of living in England and South Africa, he quickly realized the "Quit India" movement was failing because its national leadership was not willing to give up European ways. So even though he was Indian, he had to renounce his Western dress and customs or he would not have been able to lead his people out from under the British yoke. He spent the rest of his life relearning how to become an Indian again — in dress, food, culture and life-style. Eventually he gained acceptance by the common people of India. The rest is history. He became the father of my nation, the George Washington of modern India.

The same principle holds true of evangelistic and church planting efforts in all of Asia. We must learn to adapt to the culture. This is why the native evangelist, who comes from the native soil, is so effective. When Americans here in the United States are approached by yellow-robed Krishna worshippers — with their shaved heads and prayer beads — they reject Hinduism immediately. In the same way, Hindus reject Christianity when it comes in Western forms.

Have Asians rejected Christ? Not really. In most cases they have rejected only the trappings of Western culture that have fastened themselves onto the gospel. This is what the apostle Paul was referring to when he said he was willing to become "all things to all men" in order that he might win some.

When Asians share Christ with other Asians in a culturally acceptable way, the results are startling. One of the native missionaries we support in northwest India, for example, now has evangelized sixty villages and established thirty churches in a difficult area of the Punjab.

He has led hundreds to Christ. On a recent trip to India, I went out of my way to visit this man and his wife. I had to see for myself what kind of program he was using.

Imagine my surprise when I found he wasn't using any special technology at all — unless you want to call the motor scooter and tracts that we supplied "technology."

He was living just like the people. He had only a one-room house made of dung and mud. The kitchen was outside, also made of mud — the same stuff with which everything else is constructed in that region. To cook the food, his wife squatted in front of an open fire just like the neighboring women. What was so remarkable about this brother was that everything about him and his wife was so truly Indian. There was absolutely nothing foreign.

I asked Jager what kept him going in the midst of such incredible challenge and suffering. He said, "Waiting upon the Lord, my brother."

I discovered he spent two to three hours daily in prayer, reading, and meditating on the Bible. This is what it takes to win Asia for Christ. This is the kind of missionary for which our nations cry out.

Jager was won to Christ by another native evangelist. This native preacher came and explained the living God to Jager while he was still a devout Hindu. He told him of a God who hates sin and became a man to die for sinners and set them free. This was the first time the gospel ever was preached in his village, and Jager followed the man around for several days.

Finally, he accepted Jesus as his Lord and was disowned by his family. Overjoyed and surprised by his newfound life, he went about distributing tracts from village to village, telling about Jesus. In the end, he sold his two shops. With the money he earned, he conducted evangelistic meetings in local villages.

This is a man of the culture, bringing Christ to his own people in culturally acceptable ways. The support we Asians need from the West, if we're to complete the work Christ has left us, must go to this kind of self-sacrificing missionary worker.

In light of the challenges facing missions in Asia today, what does this show us about the best possible methods to reach our people? I think the answer is obvious. We must recruit, equip and send out an army of native missionary evangelists.

Only native evangelists come prepared to meet the three big challenges we are now facing in the Orient.

First, they already understand the culture, customs and life-style as well as the language. They don't have to spend valuable time in lengthy preparations.

Second, the most effective communication occurs between peers. While there still may be social barriers to overcome, they are much smaller and more easily identified.

Third, it's a wiser investment of our resources because the native missionary works more economically than foreigners can.

One of the most basic laws of creation is that every living thing reproduces after its own kind. This fact applies in evangelism and discipleship, just as it does in other areas. If we are going to see a mass people movement to Christ, it will be done only through fielding many more thousands of native missionaries.

How many are needed? In India alone we still have 500,000 villages to reach. Looking at other nations, we realize thousands more remain without a witness. If we are to reach all the other hamlets open to us right now, Gospel for Asia will need additional native missionary evangelists by the tens of thousands. The cost to support this army will run into the millions annually. But this is only a fraction of the $4.8 billion U.S. churches lavished on their own needs and desires in 1986. The result will be a revolution of love that will bring millions of Asians to Christ.

The challenge of Asia cries out to us. The enemies of the cross abound. There are giants in the land, but none of them can stand against us as we move out in the authority and power of the Lord Jesus.

For the first time in history, by helping native evangelists it now is possible to see all of Asia evangelized in our generation. This is the bright side of the Asian situation. The problems we face are indeed great, but they can be overcome through a peaceful army of native missionary evangelists.

In spite of the opposition from traditional religion, secular materialism and long-standing cultural patterns, I am certain God wants us to unite with Christians around the world to raise up a Christian witness in every dark corner of Asia.

Part III

THE WAY

16

Offering the Water of Life
in a Foreign Cup

When we think about the awesome challenge of Asia, it is not too much to ask for a new army of missionaries to reach these nations for Christ. But we must ask ourselves: From where are we going to recruit them? Should we look for thousands of new Americans, Canadians and Western Europeans who will uproot themselves and their families to go overseas, learn the local languages and adopt an alien culture as their own? How will we get the governments of those lands to change their immigration and visa policies to let Western missionaries come in? Finally, how will we raise the additional billions of dollars that would be needed every year to keep those missionaries on the fields?

The answer is that tens of thousands of native missionaries are being raised up by the Lord in all these Third World nations right now. They are Asians. Many of them already live in the nation they must reach. Or they live in nearby cultures just a few hundred miles from the unevangelized villages to which they will be sent by the Lord.

The situation in world missions is depressing only when you think of it in terms of nineteenth-century Western colonialism.

If the actual task of world evangelization depends on the "sending of the white missionary," obeying the Great Commission truly becomes more impossible every day. But, praise God, the native missionary movement is growing, ready today to complete the task.

We are witnessing a new day in missions. This is the primary message I have for every Christian, pastor and mission leader. Just a few short years ago, no one dreamed the Asian church would be ready to lead the final thrust. But dedicated native evangelists are beginning to go out and reach their own.

And the exciting message I have for every believer is this: God is calling all of us to be part of what He is doing. *You have a role.*

We can make it possible for millions of brown and yellow feet to move out with the liberating gospel of Jesus. With the prayer and financial support of the Western church they can go preach the Word to the lost multitudes. The whole family of God is needed. Thousands of native missionaries will go to the lost if Christians in the West will help by sharing resources with them.

This is why I believe God called me to the United States. The only reason I stay here is to help serve our

Asian brethren by bringing their needs before God's people in the West. A whole new generation of Christians needs to know that this profound shift in the mission task has taken place. North American believers need to know they still are needed as "senders" to pray and to help the native brothers go.

The waters of missions have been muddied. Today many Christians are unable to think clearly about the real issues because Satan has sent a deceiving spirit to blind their eyes. I don't make this statement lightly. Satan knows that to stop world evangelism he must confuse the minds of Western Christians. This he has done quite effectively. The facts speak for themselves.

The average North American Christian gives only one penny a day to global missions. Imagine what that means. Missions are the primary task of the church, our Lord's final command to us before His ascension. Jesus died on the cross to start a missionary movement. He came to show God's love, and we're left here to continue that mission. Yet this most important task of the church is receiving less than one percent of all our finances.

Of the Western missionaries who are sent overseas, the majority are involved in an unbalanced ministry. Digging wells, operating schools and hospitals, or supporting bands of revolutionary guerrillas is not primarily sharing the gospel. As important as compassionate social concern is in the Third World, it must grow out of the local church. It cannot be superimposed on them by outsiders. The preaching of the gospel will redeem people and produce social change naturally as churches are planted in the villages. The local church is God's tool for Christian caring and sharing.

Approximately 85 percent of all missionary finances are being used by Western missionaries who are working among the established churches on the field — not for pioneer evangelism to the lost. From almost every perspective then, it is obvious that mission spending is being done in areas far from the essence of what real Christian missions is about in the biblical context. The powers of darkness have done a devious job of sidetracking and sabotaging the missionary enterprise of the North American church.

Finally, much of what has passed for missions is really neo-colonial expansionism of our denominations and organizations. In the end, most of that one penny a day the average American Christian has given to missions actually was spent on projects or programs other than proclaiming the whole gospel of Christ. But a shift has taken place in the last forty troubled years.

At the end of World War II, just four short decades ago, almost the entire work of the Great Commission was being done by a handful of white foreigners. To these Christian mission leaders, it was impossible even to imagine reaching all the thousands of distinct cultural groups in the colonies. So they focused their attention on the major cultural groups in easy-to-reach centers of trade and government.

In most of the Asian nations, nearly two hundred years of mission work had been accomplished under the watchful gaze of colonial governors when the era finally ended in 1945. During that time, Western missionaries appeared to be a vital part of the fabric of Western colonial government. Even the few churches that were established among the dominant cultural groups appeared weak. Like the local government and economy, they too were directly controlled by foreigners. Few were indigenous or independent of Western missionaries. Not surprisingly, the masses shunned these strange centers of alien religion, much as most Americans avoid "Krishna missions" in the United States today.

In this atmosphere, the thought of going beyond the major cultural groups — reaching out to the unfinished task — was naturally put off. Those masses of people in rural areas, ethnic subcultures, tribal groups and minorities would have to wait. Teaching them was still generations away — unless, of course, more white foreign missionaries could be recruited to go to them.

But this was not to be. When the colonial-era missionaries returned to take control of "their" churches, hospitals and schools, they found the political climate had changed radically. They met a new hostility from Asian governments. Something radical had happened during World War II. The nationalists had organized and were on the march.

Soon political revolution was sweeping the Third World. And with the independence of one nation after another, the missionaries lost their positions of power and privilege. In the twenty-five years following World War II, seventy-one nations broke free of Western domination. And with their new freedom, most decided Western missionaries would be among the first symbols of the West to go. Now 119 nations — with over half of the world's population — forbid or seriously restrict foreign missionaries.[1]

But there is a bright side to the story. The effect of all this on the emerging churches of Asia has been electric. Far from slowing the spread of the gospel, the gospel began to break free from the Western traditions that had been added to it unwittingly by foreign missionaries.

Sadhu Sunder Singh, a pioneer native missionary evangelist, used to tell a little story that illustrates the importance of presenting the gospel in culturally acceptable terms.

A high caste Hindu, he said, had one day fainted from the summer heat while sitting on a train in a railway station. A train employee ran to a water faucet, filled a cup with water and brought it to the man in an attempt to revive him. But in spite of his condition, the Hindu refused. He would rather die than accept water in the cup of someone from another caste.

Then someone else noticed that the high caste passenger had left his own cup on the seat beside him.

So he grabbed it, filled it with water and returned to offer it to the panting victim of the heat. Immediately he accepted the water with gratitude.

Then Sunder Singh would say to his hearers, "This is what I have been trying to say to missionaries from abroad. You have been offering the water of life to the people of India in a foreign cup, and we have been slow to receive it. If you will offer it in our own cup — in an indigenous form — then we are much more likely to accept it."

Today, a whole new generation of Spirit-led young native leaders is mapping strategies to complete the evangelization of our Asian homelands. In almost every country of Asia, I personally know local missionaries who are effectively winning their people to Christ using culturally acceptable methods and styles.

These local missionaries can bridge the cultural gap in their own nations and quite easily go to neighboring countries, taking the gospel for the first time to millions who formerly rejected it as foreign religion.

While there still is persecution in one form or another in most Asian nations, the post-colonial national governments have guaranteed almost unlimited freedom to native missionaries. Just because Westerners have been forbidden, the expansion of the church does not have to cease.

For some diabolical reason, news of this dramatic change has not reached the ears of most believers in our churches. While God by His Holy Spirit has been raising up a new army of missionaries to carry on the work of the Great Commission, most North American believers have sat unmoved. This I have discovered is not because Christians here are lacking in generosity. When they are told the need, they respond quickly. They are not involved only because they don't know the real truth about what is happening in Asia today.

I believe we are being called to be involved by sharing prayerfully and financially in the great work that lies ahead. As we do this, it is possible that together we can see the fulfillment of that awesome prophecy in Revelation 7:9.

> A great number which no man could number, of all nations, and kindreds, and people and tongues, stood before the throne, and before the Lamb, clothed with white robes, and palms in their hands; and cried with a loud voice, saying, "Salvation to our God which sitteth upon the throne, and unto the throne, and unto the Lamb."

This prediction is about to come true. Now, for the first time in history, we can see the final thrust taking place. It is right now happening as God's people everywhere unite to make it possible.

What should intrigue us — especially here in the West — is the way the native missionary movement is flourishing without the help and genius of our Western planning. The Holy Spirit, when we give Him the freedom to work, prompts spontaneous growth and expansion.

Until we can recognize the native missionary movement as the plan of God for this period in history, and until we are willing to become servants to what He is doing, we're in danger of frustrating the will of God.

17

Our Policy Is the Natives

Does what you have read in the previous chapter mean all Western missionaries should pull out of Asia forever? Of course not.

God still sovereignly calls Western missionaries to do unique and special tasks in Asia. But we must understand that the primary role for Westerners now should be to support efforts of indigenous mission works through financial aid and intercessory prayer.

As gently as I can, I have to say anti-American prejudice still is running high in most of Asia. "There are times in history," writes Dennis E. Clark in *The Third World and Mission*, "when however gifted a person may be, he can no longer effectively proclaim the Gospel to those of another culture. A German could not have done so in Britain in 1941 nor could an Indian in Pakistan during the war of 1967, and it will be extremely difficult for Americans to do so in the Third World of the 1980s and 1990s."[1]

Probably the most difficult message I struggle to

proclaim in North America is that Western missionaries are not welcome in most nations of Asia. In fact, this is a section I write with the greatest fear and trembling — but these truths must be said if we are to accomplish the will of God in the Asian mission fields today.

For the sake of Christ — because the love of Jesus constrains us — we need to review the financial and mission policies of our churches and North American missionary sending agencies. Every believer should reconsider his or her own stewardship practices and submit to the Holy Spirit's guidance in how best to support the global outreach of the church.

I'm not calling for an end to denominational mission programs or the closing down of the many hundreds of missions here in North America — but I am asking us to reconsider the missionary policies and practices that have guided us for the last two hundred years. It is time to make some basic changes and launch the biggest missionary movement in history — one that primarily helps send forth native missionary evangelists rather than a Western staff.

The principle I argue for is this: We believe the most effective way now to win Asia for Christ is through prayer and financial support for the native missionary force that God is raising up in the Third World.

As a general rule, for the following reasons I believe it is wiser to support native missionaries in their own lands than to send Western missionaries.

First, it's bad stewardship to send Western missionaries. At present, the average American missionary family on the field is costing $43,000 a year, and inflation is increasing that cost every day. Based on estimates by C. Peter Wagner, it will cost $163,295 to keep that couple on the field by the year 2000. We're then looking at an annual missionary budget of nearly $117 billion. When you realize that America contributes less than $1 billion now, we're talking about an astronomical fund-raising effort. There has to be an alternative.[2]

During a recent consultation on world evangelism in Thailand, Western missionary leaders called for two hundred thousand new missionaries by the year 2000 in order to keep pace with their estimates of population growth. The cost of even that more modest missionary force is a staggering $4 billion a year.

In India, for only the cost of flying an American from New York to Bombay, a native missionary already on the field can minister for years! Unless we take these facts into account, we will lose the opportunity of our age to reach untold millions with the gospel. Today it is outrageously extravagant to send North American missionaries overseas unless there are compelling reasons to do so. From a strictly financial standpoint, sending American missionaries overseas is one of the worst investments we can make today.

Second, the presence of Western missionaries perpetuates the myth that Christianity is the religion of the West. Roland Allen says it better than I in his classic book *The Spontaneous Expansion of the Church*:

> Even if the supply of men and funds from Western sources was unlimited and we could cover the whole globe with an army of millions of foreign missionaries and establish stations thickly all over the world, the method would speedily reveal its weakness, as it is already beginning to reveal it.
>
> The mere fact that Christianity was propagated by such an army, established in foreign stations all over the world, would inevitably alienate the native populations, who would see in it the growth of the denomination of a foreign people. They would see themselves robbed of their religious independence, and would more and more fear the loss of their social independence.
>
> Foreigners can never successfully direct the propagation of any faith throughout a whole country. If the faith does not become naturalized and expand among the people by its own vital power, it exercises an alarming and hateful influence, and men fear and shun it as something alien. It is then obvious that no sound missionary

policy can be based upon multiplication of missionaries and mission stations. A thousand would not suffice; a dozen might be too many.[3]

A friend of mine who heads a missionary organization similar to ours recently told me the story of a conversation he had with some African church leaders.

"We want to evangelize our people," they said, "but we can't do it so long as the white missionaries remain. Our people won't listen to us. The communists and the Moslems tell them all white missionaries are spies sent out by their governments as agents for the capitalistic imperialists. We know it isn't true, but newspaper reports tell of how some missionaries are getting funds from the CIA. We love the American missionaries in the Lord. We wish they could stay, but the only hope for us to evangelize our own country is for all white missionaries to leave."

Untold millions still are being wasted today by our denominations and missions as they erect and protect elaborate organizational frameworks overseas. There was a time when Western missionaries needed to go into these countries where the gospel was not preached. But now a new era has begun, and it is important that we officially acknowledge this. God has raised up indigenous leaders in every nation who are more capable than outsiders to finish the job.

Now we must send the major portion of our funds

to native missionaries and church growth movements. But this doesn't mean we don't appreciate the legacy left to us from Western missionaries. While I believe changes must be made in our missionary methods, we praise God for the tremendous contribution Western missionaries have made in many Third World countries where Christ never was preached before. Through their faithfulness many were won to Jesus, churches were started and the Scriptures were translated. And it is these converts who now are today's native missionaries.

Silas Fox, a Canadian who served in South India, learned to speak the local native language Telegu and preached the Word with such anointing that hundreds of present-day Christian leaders in Andhra Pradesh can trace their spiritual beginnings to his ministry.

I thank God for missionaries like Hudson Taylor, who against all wishes of his foreign mission board became a Chinese in his life-style and won many to Christ. I am not worthy to wipe the dust from the feet of thousands of faithful men and women of our Lord who went overseas during the times of men and women like these.

Jesus set the example. "As my Father hath sent me," He said, "even so send I you" (John 20:21). The Lord became one of us in order to win us to the love of God. He knew He couldn't be an alien from outer space so He became incarnated into our bodies.

For any missionary to be successful he must identify with the people he plans to reach. Because Westerners usually can't do this, they are ineffective. Anyone — Asian or American — who insists on still going out as a representative of Western missions and organizations will be ineffective today. We cannot maintain a Western life-style or outlook and work among the poor of Asia.

Third, with the Western missionaries and the money they bring, the natural growth and independence of the national church is compromised. The economic power of the North American dollar distorts the picture as North American missionaries hire key national leaders to run their organizations.

Recently I met with a missionary executive of one of the major U.S. denominations. He is a loving man whom I deeply respect as a brother in Christ, but he heads the colonial-style extension of his denomination into Asia.

We talked about mutual friends and the exciting growth that is occurring in the national churches of India. We shared much in the Lord. I quickly found he had as much respect as I did for the Indian brothers God is choosing to use in India today. Yet he wouldn't support these men who are so obviously anointed by God.

I asked him why. (His denomination is spending millions of dollars annually to open up their brand of churches in Asia — money I felt could be far better used supporting native missionaries in the churches the Holy Spirit is spontaneously birthing.)

His answer shocked and saddened me.

"Our policy," he admitted without shame, "is to use the nationals only to expand churches with our denominational distinctives."

The words rolled around in my mind, "use the nationals." This is what colonialism was all about, and it is still what neo-colonialism of most Western missions is all about. With their money and technology, many organizations are simply buying people to perpetuate their foreign denominations, ways and beliefs.

In Thailand a group of native missionaries was "bought away" by a powerful American parachurch organization. Once effectively winning their own people to Christ and planting churches in the Thai way, their leaders were given scholarships to train in the United States. The American organization provided them with expense accounts, vehicles and posh offices in Bangkok.

What price did the native missionary leader pay? He must use foreign literature, films and the standard method of this highly technical American organization. No consideration is being made of how effective these tools and methods will be in building the Thai church. They will be used whether they are effective or not because they are written into the training manuals and handbooks of this organization.

After all, the reasoning of this group goes, these programs worked in Los Angeles and Dallas — they must work in Thailand as well!

This kind of thinking is the worst neo-colonialism.

To use God-given money to hire people to perpetuate our ways and theories is a modern method of old-fashioned imperialism. No method could be more unbiblical.

The sad fact is this. God already was doing a wonderful work in Thailand by His Holy Spirit in a culturally acceptable way. Why didn't this American group have the humility to bow before the Holy Spirit and say, "Have Thine own way, Lord." If they wanted to help, I think the best way would have been to support what God already was doing by His Holy Spirit. By the time this group finds out what a mistake it has made, the missionaries who messed up the local church will be going home for furlough — probably never to return.

At their rallies they will tell stories of victories in Thailand as they evangelized the country American-style; but no one will be asking the most important question, Where is the fruit that remains?

Often we become so preoccupied with expanding our own organizations that we do not comprehend the great sweep of the Holy Spirit of God as He has moved upon the peoples of the world. Intent upon building "our" churches, we have failed to see how Christ is building "His" church in every nation. We must stop looking at the lost world through the eyes of our particular denomination. Then we will be able to win the lost souls to Jesus instead of trying to add more numbers to our man-made organizations to please the headquarters that control the funds.

Fourth, Western missionaries cannot go to the countries where most so-called hidden people live. About 2.7 billion of these people exist in our world today. There are the millions upon millions of lost souls who have never heard the gospel. We hear many cries that we should go to them. But who will go? These people are almost all living in countries closed or severely restricted to American and European missionaries. Although half the countries in the world today forbid the Western missionary, now the native missionary can go to the nearest hidden people group. For example, an Indian can go to Nepal with the gospel; North Americans can't.

Of the more than seventy thousand North American missionaries now actively commissioned, only five thousand are working with the totally unreached hidden people who make up 70 percent of all the unevangelized people in the world. Ralph Winter, general director of the U.S. Center for World Mission, estimates 95 percent of all missionaries are working among the existing churches or where the gospel already is preached.

Fifth, Western missionaries seldom are effective. Unlike the Western missionary, the native missionary can preach, teach and evangelize without being blocked by most of the barriers that confront Westerners. As a native of the country or region, he knows the cultural taboos instinctively. Frequently, he already has mastered the language or a related dialect. He moves freely and is accepted in good times and bad as one who belongs.

He does not have to be transported thousands of miles nor does he require special training and language schools.

The truth of the matter is this: *Western missionaries seldom are effective today in reaching Asians and establishing local churches in the villages of Asia.*

I remember an incident — one of many — that illustrates this sad fact.

During my days of preaching in the northwest of India, I met a missionary from New Zealand involved in Christian literature ministry. She had been a missionary in India for twenty-five years; and during her final term, she was assigned to a Christian bookstore. One day as my team and I went to her shop to buy some books, we found the book shop closed. When we went to her missionary quarters — which was in a walled mansion — we asked what was happening. She replied, "I am going back home for good."

I asked what would happen to the ministry of the book shop. She answered, "I have sold all the books at wholesale price, and I have closed down everything."

With deep hurt, I asked her if there wasn't anyone she could have handed the store over to in order to continue the work.

"No, I could not find anyone," she replied. And I wondered why, after twenty-five years of being in India, she was leaving without one person whom she had won to Christ, no disciple to continue her work.

She, along with her missionary colleagues, lived in walled compounds with three or four servants each to look after their life-style. She spent a lifetime and untold amounts of God's precious money which could have been used to preach the gospel. I could not help but think Jesus had called us to become servants — not masters. Had she done so, she would have fulfilled the call of God upon her life and fulfilled the Great Commission.

Unfortunately, this is a sad truth that is being repeated all over the world of colonial-style foreign missions. Regrettably, seldom are Western missionaries being held accountable for the current lack of results, nor is their failure being reported at home in the United States and Canada.

But at the same time, native evangelists are seeing thousands turn to Christ in revival movements on every continent. Hundreds of new churches are being formed every week by native missionaries in the Third World!

18

Not a Mission but a Theological Problem

God obviously is moving mightily among native believers. These are the wonderful, final days of Christian history. Now is the time for the whole family of God to unite and share with one another, as the New Testament church did, the richer churches giving to the poorer.

The body of Christ in the East is looking to the West to link hands with them in this time of harvest and to support the work with the material blessings that God has showered upon them. With the love and support of North American believers, we can help native evangelists and their families march forward and complete the task of world evangelization in this century.

As I sit on platforms and stand in pulpits all across North America, I am speaking on behalf of the native brethren. God has called me to be the servant of the needy brothers who cannot speak up for themselves in North America.

As I wait to speak, I look out over the congregation, and I often pray for some of the missionaries by name. Usually I pray something like this: "Lord Jesus, I am about to stand here on behalf of Thomas John and P.T. Steven tonight. May I represent them faithfully. Help us to meet their needs through this meeting."

Of course, the names of the native missionaries change each time. But I believe the will of God will not be accomplished in our generation unless this audience and many others like it respond to the cry of the lost. Each of us must follow the Lord in the place to which He has called us — the native evangelist in his land and the sponsors here in this land. Some obey by going; others obey by supporting. Even if you cannot go to Asia, you can fulfill the Great Commission by helping send native brothers to the pioneer fields.

This — and many other similar truths about missions — are no longer understood in the West. Preaching and teaching about missions has been lost in most of our churches. The sad result is seen everywhere. Most believers no longer can define what a missionary is, what he or she does, or what the work of the church is as it relates to the Great Commission.

A declining interest in missions is the sure sign that a church and people have left their first love. Nothing is more indicative of the moral decline of the West than Christians who have lost the passion of Christ for a lost and dying world.

The older I become, the more I understand the real reason millions go to hell without hearing the gospel.

Actually, this is not a mission problem. It is a theological problem — a problem of misunderstanding and unbelief. Many churches have slipped so far from biblical teaching that Christians cannot explain why the Lord left us here on earth.

All of us are called for a purpose. Some years ago when I was in North India, a little boy about eight years old watched me as I prepared for my morning meditations. I began to talk to him about Jesus and asked him several questions.

"What are you doing?" I asked the lad.

"I go to school" was the reply.

"Why do you go to school?"

"To study," he said.

"Why do you study?"

"To get smart."

"Why do you want to get smart?"

"So I can get a good job."

"Why do you want to get a good job?"

"So I can make lots of money."

"Why do you want to make lots of money?"

"So I can buy food."

"Why do you want to buy food?"

"So I can eat."

"Why do you want to eat?"

"To live."

"Why do you live?"

At that point, the little boy thought for a minute,

scratched his head, looked me in the face and said, "Sir, why do I live?" He paused a moment in mid-thought, then gave his own sad answer, "To die!"

The question is the same for all of us: Why do we live?

What is the basic purpose of your living in this world, as you claim to be a disciple of the Lord Jesus Christ?

Is it to accumulate wealth? Fame? Popularity? To fulfill the desires of the flesh and of the mind? And to somehow survive and, in the end, to die and hopefully go to heaven?

No. The purpose of your life as a believer must be to obey Jesus when He said, "Go ye into all the world and preach the gospel...."

That is what Paul did when he laid down his arms and said, "Lord, what do You want me to do?"

If all of your concern is about your own life, your job, your clothes, your children's good clothes, healthy bodies, a good education, a good job and marriage, then your concerns are no different from a heathen's in Bhutan, Burma or India.

In recent months I have looked back on those seven years of village evangelism as one of the greatest learning experiences of my life. We walked in Jesus' steps, incarnating and representing Him to masses of people who had never heard the gospel.

When Jesus was here on earth, His goal was to do nothing but the will of His Father. Our commitment must be only His will.

Jesus no longer is walking on earth. We are His body; He is our head. That means our lips are the lips of Jesus. Our hands are His hands; our eyes, His eyes; our hope, His hope.

My wife and children belong to Jesus. My money, my talent, my education — all belong to Jesus.

So what is His will? What are we to do in this world with all of these gifts He has given us?

"As the Father has sent Me, even so send I you" are His instructions. "Go into all the world and make disciples, teaching them to obey all these things, and lo, I am with you even until the end of the age."

Every Christian should know the answers to some basic questions about missions in order to fulfill the call of our Lord to reach the lost world for His name.

First, what is the primary task of the church? Each of the four Gospels — Matthew, Mark, Luke and John — gives us a war cry from our Lord Jesus. This challenge from Christ is the mission statement of the church. Through the years it has become known as the Great Commission and it summarizes the main activity of the church until Jesus returns as King of kings to gather us to Himself.

Essentially it reveals the reason God has left us here in this world. He desires us to be mobilized to go everywhere proclaiming the love of God to a lost world. Exercising His authority and demonstrating His power, we are to preach the gospel, make disciples, baptize and teach people to obey all the commands of Christ.

So this task is a lot more than handing out leaflets, holding street meetings or showing compassionate love to the sick and hungry. These are all involved, of course. But the Lord is expecting much more of us. He wants us to continue as His agents to redeem and transform the lives of people. Disciple-making, as Jesus defined it, obviously involves the long-time process of planting local churches.

And all these references to the Great Commission are accompanied by promises of divine power: Matthew 28:18-20; Mark 16:15-18; Luke 24:47-49; Acts 1:8. The global expansion of the church obviously is a task for a special people who are living intimately enough with God to discern and exercise His authority.

Which brings us to the second question.

Who is a missionary? A missionary is anyone sent out by the Lord to establish a new Christian witness where such a witness still is unknown. As we traditionally define it today, it usually involves leaving our own immediate culture for another. For example, we usually define a missionary as anyone who takes the gospel to people who differ in at least one aspect — such as language, nationality, race or tribe — from his or her own ethnic group.

For some strange reason, many North Americans have come to believe that a missionary is only someone from the West who goes to Asia, Africa or some other foreign land. Not so. When a former Hindu Brahmin crosses the subtle caste lines of India and works among low-caste people, he should be recognized as a missionary just as much as a person who goes from Detroit to Calcutta.

Christians in the West must abandon the totally unscriptural idea that they should support only white missionaries from America. Today it is essential that we support missionaries going from South India to North India, from one island of the Philippines to another, or from Korea to China.

Unless we abandon the racism implied in our unwritten definition of a missionary, we never will see the world reached for Christ. While governments may close the borders of their countries to Western missionaries, they cannot close them to their own people. The Lord is raising up such an army of national missionaries right now, but they cannot go unless North Americans will continue to support the work as they did when white Westerners were allowed.

Finally, where is the mission field? One of the biggest mistakes we make is to define mission fields in terms of nation states. These are only political boundaries established along arbitrary lines through wars or by natural boundaries such as mountain ranges and rivers.

A more biblical definition conforms to the linguistic and tribal groupings. So a mission field is defined as any cultural group which does not have an established group of disciples.

For example, the Arabs of New York City or the

people of the Hopi Indian tribe in Dallas are un-reached people groups in the United States. There are over sixteen thousand such hidden people groups worldwide — and they represent the real pioneer mission fields of our time.

They will be reached only if someone from *outside* their culture is willing to sacrifice his or her own comfortable community to reach them with the gos-pel of Christ. And to go and do so, that person needs some believers at home who will stand behind him with prayers and finances.

The native missionary movement in Asia — be-cause it is close at hand to most of the world's unreached peoples — can most easily send the evan-gelists. But they cannot always raise the needed sup-port among their destitute populations. This is where Christians in the West can come forward, sharing their abundance with God's servants in Asia.

Missionary statesman George Verwer believes most North American Christians are still only playing soldiers. But just as he does, I know here and there across America there are individuals and groups who believe that, at any cost, the sleeping giant in our nation should be aroused. We are capable of support-ing the needed missionaries, and we should not rest until the task is complete.

You may never be called personally to reach the hidden peoples of Asia; but through soldier-like suf-fering at home you can make it possible for millions to hear overseas.

Today I'm calling on Christians to give up their stale Christianity to use the weapons of spiritual warfare and to advance against the enemy. We must stop skipping over the verses which read, "If anyone would come after me, he must deny himself and take up his cross and follow me" and "Any of you who does not give up everything he has cannot be my disciple" (Matt. 16:24; Luke 14:33, NIV).

Were these verses written only for the native missionaries who are on the front lines being stoned and beaten and going hungry for their faith? Or were they written only for North American believers comfortably going through the motions of church, teaching conferences and concerts?

Of course not. These verses apply equally to Christians in Bangkok, Boston and Bombay.

Says Verwer, "Some missionary magazines and books leave one with the impression that worldwide evangelization is only a matter of time. More careful research will show that in densely populated areas the work of evangelism is going backward rather than forward.

"In view of this, our tactics are simply crazy. Perhaps 80 percent of our efforts for Christ — weak as they often are — still are aimed at only 20 percent of the world's population. Literally hundreds of millions of dollars are poured into every kind of Christian project at home, especially buildings, while only a thin trickle goes out to the regions beyond. Half-hearted saints believe by giving just a few hundred dollars they have done their share. We all have measured ourselves so long by the man next to us we barely can see the standard set by men like Paul or by Jesus Himself.

"During the Second World War, the British showed themselves capable of astonishing sacrifices (as did many other nations). They lived on meager, poor rations. They cut down their railings and sent them for weapons manufacture. Yet today, in what is more truly a (spiritual) World War, Christians live as peacetime soldiers. Look at Paul's injunctions to Timothy in 2 Timothy 2:3-4: 'Endure hardship with us like a good soldier of Christ Jesus. No one serving as a soldier gets involved with civilian affairs — he wants to please his commanding officer.' We seem to have a strange idea of Christian service. We will buy books, travel miles to hear a speaker on blessings, pay large sums to listen to a group singing the latest Christian songs — but we forget that we are soldiers."[1]

Day after day I continue with this one message: Hungry, hurting, native missionaries are waiting to go on to the next village with the gospel, but they need your prayer and financial support. We're facing a new day in missions, but it requires the cooperation of Christians in both the East and West.

19

Lord, Help Us
Remain True to You

Yes, today God is working in a miraculous way. Without all the trappings of high-powered promotion, an increasing number of believers are catching the vision of God's third wave in missions. We already have seen thousands of individuals raised up to share in the work. But I believe this is also only a foretaste of the millions more who will respond in the days ahead. Many pastors, church leaders, former missionaries, and Christian broadcasters in North America are also unselfishly lending their support.

In addition to these sponsors and donors, volunteers are organizing local prayer bands and coordinating united efforts at the grass-roots level throughout Canada and the United States. Without this network of local workers to help provide the needed support, there is no human way the missionary task of the church will be completed. Local GFA coordinators, who work without payment, help represent the work of Gospel for Asia by distributing

SEND newspapers free through Christian bookstores, churches, women's groups and prayer meetings.

They are also helping organize home meetings, speaking at churches or small groups, and explaining the sponsorship program. They do whatever else is necessary to minister and share the message in the supporting nations.

These sponsors, like the poor widow Jesus commended for giving all she had, make great sacrifices.

I'll never forget one dear retired widow whom I met on a speaking tour. Excited about how much she still could do even though she wasn't working, she pledged to sponsor a missionary out of her tiny Social Security check.

After six months I received a very sad letter from her. "Brother K.P.," she wrote, "I am so privileged to be supporting a missionary. I'm living all alone now on only a fixed income. I know when I get to heaven I'm going to meet people who have come to Christ through my sharing, but I must reduce my support because my utility bills have gone up. Please pray for me that I will find a way to give my full support again."

When my wife, Gisela, showed me the letter, I was deeply touched. I called the woman and told her she need not feel guilty — she was doing all she could. I even advised her not to give if it became a greater hardship.

Two weeks later, another letter came. "Every day," she wrote, "I've been praying for a way to find some more money for my missionary. As I prayed, the Lord showed me a way — I've disconnected my phone."

I looked at the check. Tears came to my eyes as I thought how much this woman was sacrificing. She must be lonely, I thought. What would happen if she got sick? Without a phone, she would be cut off from the world. "Lord," I prayed, as I held the check in both hands, "help us to remain true to You and honor this great sacrifice." Another gift, this time from a thirteen-year-old boy named Tommy, shows the same spirit of sacrifice.

For over a year Tommy had been saving for a new bicycle for school. Then he read about the value of bicycles to native missionaries like Mohan Ram and his wife from Tamil Nadu State. Since 1977, Ram had been walking in the scorching sun between villages. He and his wife were engaged in church planting. With his family, he lived in one rented room and had to walk for miles or ride buses to do gospel work.

His outreach (Bible classes, open-air evangelism, tract distribution, children's classes and Bible translation) was directly dependent on his ability to travel. A bicycle would mean more to him than a car would mean to someone in suburban America.

But a new Indian-made bicycle, which would cost only ninety-two dollars, was totally out of reach of his family budget. What amazed me when I came to America is that bikes here are considered children's toys or a way to lose weight. For native missionaries they represent a way to expand the ministry greatly and reduce suffering.

When Tommy heard that native missionaries use their bikes to ride seventeen to twenty miles a day, he made a big decision. He decided to give to GFA the bike money he had saved.

"I can use my brother's old bike," he wrote. "My dad has given me permission to send you my new bike money for the native missionary."

Another teenager, seventeen-year-old Todd, sponsored five missionaries a month. To accomplish this task, he worked two part-time jobs and gave up ice cream and other treats. Not satisfied, he organized a walk-a-thon among friends and sent us twelve hundred dollars more.

A tireless volunteer, he actively distributed *SEND* in local churches and Christian organizations. Seeking to enlist others as sponsors, he wrote twenty-five letters by hand to friends. We received a check for six hundred dollars from such activity.

Seeing his zeal, we expected to meet an extreme extrovert. But instead, he was shy and quiet — someone who made an intelligent decision to set goals rather than accumulate wealth.

Several times we have received large gifts — as much as twenty thousand dollars and thirty thousand dollars at one time — with unusual explanations attached.

One couple wrote, "We have prayed, and we don't want to leave our money to the world. We want to give everything for eternity. The way we can do this is *not to leave it to our kids*. Here is what we had laid aside for them."

Another woman wrote a similar letter: "The Lord has for some time been speaking to me about money I've been saving up for a rainy day. I want to give it now while I can. Please use it for the native brethren."

Sometimes people find unusual ways to raise extra support. One factory worker goes through all the trash cans at his workplace collecting aluminum beverage cans. Each month we get a check from him — usually enough to sponsor two or more missionaries.

Many churches and pastors also have started to include native evangelists in their mission budgets.

One pastor, Skip Heitzig of the Calvary Chapel in Albuquerque, New Mexico, now supports several missionaries. Like other pastors, he has been sent overseas by his congregation to learn about the native work there. Through Skip's influence, a number of other pastors also have started to include GFA in their regular mission budgets.

In addition to his congregation's ever-increasing monthly support, he has had GFA staff make several presentations at the church. As a result, two dozen individual families in the church also have taken on a family sponsorship.

Churches in nearly every state of the United States now include GFA in their regular mission budgets. One church in Florida sends more than a thousand dollars a month. Another in Plano, Texas, gives 5 percent of the church's gross income to the native missionary movement. (That church, a non-denominational congregation, made their decision after telephone calls to several sources to check on the validity of our work. I had never met the pastor.)

When a congregation in Kelso, Tennessee, made a decision to disband and merge with another church, they sold their property and sent the total proceeds to GFA — one of the largest single donations we've ever received.

Missionaries and former missionaries are among some of our most ardent supporters.

Nina Drew, a retired missionary who spent thirty years in India as a medical volunteer, is so excited about the native missionary movement she says she never would go back to India as a missionary again.

"I believe in this work," she told me. "You are getting more results than we ever did in all our years. I wouldn't return on the same basis again.... Native missionaries are the only way. I think God raised us up as an interim thing only. What is happening now is the permanent reality."

Miss Drew, who came to work among Muslims in a difficult area of North India, was a nurse and certified midwife. In her thirty years of work in India, she saw only one family converted. And she says now they are not living openly for the Lord.

"Sometimes I wonder if it was worth it," she admits.

When Miss Drew came to India in 1945, the British empire already was disintegrating, and she was an eyewitness to the terror and bloodshed of partition — when India and Pakistan were separated from each other in bloody, religious warfare.

Now she works in her native New Zealand, raising money for the native missionary movement in India.

"I feel my ministry at home today is much more productive than most of the work I did while in India," she declared.

Miss Drew said the native missionary movement is the biggest change in modern India.

"This is tremendous!" she exclaimed. "God is raising up hundreds of native brethren in our places."

When asked what strategy she believes the Western church should follow to evangelize India, Miss Drew has only one message:

"Tell God's people in America to support the native workers. It is the only way...the only way."

Another young woman, whose missionary parents have served in India for thirty years, said, "I always wondered why my parents didn't see people coming to Jesus in their work. Now I'm glad I can sponsor a native missionary who is fruitful."

Another "missionary kid" wrote, "My parents were missionaries in Maharashtra for thirty-seven years. I had the opportunity of living the first sixteen of my life there.

"I know something of the difficulty of witnessing for Christ in that dark land. Having looked at your criteria for native missionaries and realizing the many advantages they have over Western missionaries — as well as the fact that the doors are still open to them — I am enclosing a check for the first year of support of a new missionary in India. This will, prayerfully, be a long-time commitment to the continued evangelization of that great land."

Some of the most interesting support for the work has come from other Christian organizations in the United States. Some have loaned us mailing lists or allowed us to participate in their programs and special events.

For example, we were invited to participate in the Keith Green Memorial Concert Tour as the official representative of Third World missions. Melody Green, the widow of recording artist Keith Green, has personally sponsored two native missionaries.

One of the dearest friends of the work has been David Mains of Chapel of the Air in Wheaton, Illinois. Through my guest visits on the Chapel broadcast, sponsors have joined our family from all over the United States. David and Karen have advised and helped us in a number of much-needed areas — including the publishing of this book.

While David and Karen never have said anything about sacrificial giving, I know they have helped us during periods when their own ministry was experiencing financial stress. But Scripture is true when it says, "Give, and it shall be given unto you" (Luke 6:38). One of the unchanging laws of the kingdom is that we must always be giving away from ourselves — both in good times and bad.

How many North American churches, Christian ministries and individuals are experiencing financial difficulties because they have disobeyed these clear commands of God to share?

I could list many others who have helped, but one more whom I must mention is Bob Walker, the long-time publisher and editor of *Christian Life* magazine. Sensitive to the Holy Spirit, Bob was willing to give us a chance to tell our story when many others took a wait-and-see attitude toward our new ministry.

Although we were completely unknown in the early days, Bob didn't turn me away as other publishers did. He prayed about us and said he felt led of God to run articles and reports on the work. Bob also shared his mailing list with us, endorsing our ministry and urging his readers to support the native missionary movement.

It is this kind of open-handed sharing that helped launch the work in the beginning and keeps us growing now. In our weekly nights of prayer and in regular prayer meetings, we constantly remember to thank God for these kinds of favors — and pray that more leaders will be touched with the need of sharing their resources with the Third World.

Perhaps the most exciting long-range development has been a slow but steady shift in the attitude of North American mission agencies and denominations toward native mission movements.

One after another, older missions and denominations have changed anti-native policies and are beginning to support native missionary movements as equal partners in the work of the gospel. The old racism and colonial mind-set are slowly but surely disappearing.

This, I believe, could have long-range impact. If North American denominations and older mission societies would use their massive networks of support to raise funding for native missions, it would be possible for us and similar native missionary ministries to support several hundred thousand more native missionaries in the Third World.

Asks John Haggai, "In a day when an estimated three-fourths of the Third World's people live in countries that either discourage or flatly prohibit foreign missionary efforts, what other way is there to obey Jesus Christ's directive to evangelize all the world?

"For many thoughtful Christians the answer is becoming more and more clear: In those closed countries, evangelization through trained national Christian leaders is the logical way.... Some observers have gone so far as to say it may be the only way."

Haggai's viewpoints are becoming more and more common, and a shifting of opinion and strategy is taking place that I believe will change the complexion of missions almost completely by the end of this decade.

The day of the native missionary movement has come. The seeds have been planted. Ahead of us lie much cultivation and nurture, but it can happen if we will share our resources as the apostle Paul outlined in 2 Corinthians 8 and 9.

There Paul urges the wealthy Christians to collect monies and send support to the poor churches in order that "equality may abound" in the whole body of Christ. Those who have are obligated to share with those who have not, he argues, because of Christ's example.

"For you know the grace of our Lord Jesus Christ, that though he was rich, yet for your sakes he became poor, so that you through his poverty might become rich" (2 Cor. 8:9).

This is the New Testament cry I'm repeating to the wealthy and affluent Christians of the West. Many are becoming more willing to follow the example of our Lord Jesus. He made Himself poor for the salvation of others.

How many are ready to live for eternity and follow His example into a more sacrificial life-style? How many will join in the spirit of suffering of the native brethren?

They are hungry, naked and homeless for the sake of Christ.

I'm not asking North Americans to join them — sleeping along roadsides and going to prison for their witness. But I am asking believers to share in the most practical ways possible — through financial sharing and intercessory prayer.

Here is the true story of a couple who has demonstrated real spiritual understanding. Recently they wrote, "While reading your *SEND* publication, the Lord began to speak to us about going to India. As we pondered this and asked the Lord about it, He spoke again and said, 'You're not going physically, but you're going spiritually and financially.'

"Well, praise the Lord — here is our 'first trip' to India. Please use this money where you see the greatest need. May God's richest blessing be upon you and your ministry."

Enclosed was a check for one thousand dollars. It was signed, "Fellow workers in Christ, Jim and Betty."

My prayer? For several hundred thousand more like Jim and Betty. This dedicated couple has what it takes: the spiritual sensitivity to hear what the Lord is really saying today to the North American church.

20

We Are Walking
in the Narrow Way

He smiled warmly at me from across his big polished desk. I was very impressed. This man led one of the greatest ministries in America. I had admired his ministry for years. He was a great preacher, author and leader. I knew he had a huge following, both among clergy and lay people. (To protect his identity in these pages, I'm going to change some details in the story and not give his name. This incident took place in the very early days of our ministry.)

I was flattered that he had sent me a plane ticket and had invited me to fly across the country to advise him on expanding his work in India. His interest in GFA and the native missionary movement pleased me much more than I was willing to let him believe. From the minute he had first called me, I sensed that here was a man who could be a valuable friend to us in many ways. Perhaps he would open the doors and help us provide sponsorships for some of the hundreds of native missionaries waiting for our support.

But I really wasn't ready for the generous offer he made — one which would turn out to be the first of many tests for me and our mission.

"Brother K.P.," he said slowly, "would you consider giving up what you're doing here in the United States and go back to India as our special representative? We believe that God is calling you to work with us — take the message of our church back to the people of India. We'll back you up 100 percent to do it.

"Whatever you need," he went on without pausing for breath. "We'll give you a printing press and vans and literature. We're prepared to provide you with all the funding, many times what you can raise yourself."

It was an exciting offer. He made it sound even sweeter while I listened. "You can give up all this traveling and raising money. You won't need an office and staff in the States. We'll do all that for you. You want to be in Asia, don't you? That's where the work is — so we'll free you to go back and run the work there."

Weakened by the thought of having so many of my prayers answered in one stroke, I let my mind play with the possibilities. This could be the biggest answer to prayer we've ever had, I thought. As we talked, my eyes unconsciously wandered across the desk to an album of his best-selling teaching tapes. They were well-done, a series on some controversial issues that were sweeping across the States at that time. However, it was irrelevant to our needs and problems in Asia.

But seeing what appeared to be my interest in the cassettes, he spoke with a sudden burst of self-assurance. "We'll start with these tapes," he said as he handed them to me. "I'll give you the support you need to produce them in India. We can even have them translated in all the major languages. We'll produce millions of copies and get this message into the hands of every Indian believer." I'd heard other men with the same wild idea. The tapes would be useless in India. Millions were going to hell in India. They didn't need this man's message at all. Although I thought his idea was insane, I tried to be polite.

"Well," I offered lamely, "there might be some material here that could be adapted for India and printed as a booklet."

Suddenly his face froze. I sensed that I had said something wrong. "Oh, no," he said with an air of stubborn finality, "I can't change a word. That's the message God gave me. It's part of what we're all about. If it's not a problem in India now, it soon will be. We need you to help us get the word out all over Asia."

In an instant this basically good man of God had shown his real colors. His heart wasn't really burning with a passion for the lost at all — or for the churches of Asia. This man had an axe to grind, and he thought he had the money to hire me to grind it for him overseas. It was the same old story — a case of religious neo-colonialism.

So here I was, face-to-face again with pride and flesh in all its ugliness. I admired and liked this man and his ministry, but he had only one problem. He believed, as many before him have, that if God was doing anything in the world, He would do it through him.

As soon as I could, I excused myself politely and never called him back. He was living in a world of the past, in the day of colonial missions when Western denominations could export and peddle their doctrines and programs to the emerging churches of Asia.

The body of Christ in Asia owes a great debt to the wonderful missionaries who came in the nineteenth and twentieth centuries. They brought the gospel to us and planted the church. But the church now needs to be released from Western domination.

My message to the West is simple: God is calling Christians everywhere to recognize that He is building His church in Asia. Your support is needed for the native missionaries whom God is raising up to extend His church — but not to impose your man-made controls and teachings on the Eastern churches.

And we've faced other tests. The biggest perhaps came from another group that also shall remain unidentified. This time it involved the biggest single gift ever offered us.

Our friendship and love for these men have developed over the last few years. We have seen God birth into their hearts a burden to see the gospel of the Lord Jesus preached in the demonstration of the power of God throughout the world. God has given them a desire to be involved in the equipping of these native pastors and evangelists, and they have helped GFA financially with projects over the last several years.

Once, by apparent chance, I accidentally ran into a delegation of four of their American brothers in India. After meeting some of our native missionaries, I could see that the visitors were significantly challenged by the lives of the Indian evangelists.

Privately, they exclaimed how deeply touched they were by the effectiveness of the native workers and with the work God was doing through them. When I returned home, letters of thanks were waiting for me, and a couple of the men offered to sponsor a native missionary. This gesture was amazing to me because these same men also were voting to give us financial grants for other projects. It convinced me they really believed in the work of the native brethren — enough to get personally involved beyond their official duties as trustees.

Imagine the way I shouted and danced around the office when I got another call from the chairman of this board two weeks later.

They had decided, he said, to give us a huge amount from their missionary budget! It was beyond my comprehension even to imagine a gift that size. When I hung up the phone, the staff in our office thought I'd gone crazy. How desperately we needed that money. In fact, in my mind I already had it spent. The first part would go, I thought, to start the intensive missionary training institute for new missionaries.

And that's why, perhaps, the next development was such a blow. As members of their board discussed the project among themselves, questions arose about accountability and control. They phoned me. The leaders expressed that probably the only way the board would agree to support the project would be for a representative of their organization to be on the board of the institute in India. After all, that large amount of money just could not be released with "no strings attached."

The request went through my heart like a knife. This was a real surprise. I couldn't do that. Through all the years, I always personally had refused to sit on any of the native mission boards we support in Asia. To suggest an outsider sit on the board of this new indigenous work would betray my brethren and take them back into bondage of men. We always have given our aid without demanding control of an indigenous ministry.

Taking a deep breath and asking the Lord for help, I tried to explain why we don't sit on native boards and why I couldn't accept a gift that required one of their directors to sit on the indigenous board.

"Our leaders overseas fast and pray about every decision," I said. "We don't have to sit on their boards to protect our monies. It's not our money, anyway; it belongs to God. He is greater than GFA or your organization. Let God protect His own interests. The native brethren don't need you or me to be their leader. Jesus is their Lord, and He will lead them in the right way to use the grant."

The silence on the other end of the line was long.

"I'm sorry, Brother K.P.," said the director finally. "I don't think I can sell this idea to our board of directors. They want accountability for the money. How can they have that without putting a man on the board? Be reasonable. You're making it very hard on us to help. This is standard policy for a gift this size."

My mind raced. A little voice said, "Go ahead. All they want is a worthless piece of paper. Don't make an issue of this. After all, this is the biggest grant you've ever received. Nobody gives big money away like this without some control. Stop being a fool."

But I knew I could not consent to that proposal. I couldn't face the Asian brethren and say that in order to get this money, they had to have an American fly halfway around the world to approve how they spent it. "No," I said, "we cannot accept your money if it means compromising the purity of our ministry. We have plenty of accountability through the trusted godly men who have been appointed to the native board. Later, you can see the building yourself when you go to Asia. I can't compromise the autonomy of the work by putting an American on the native board.

"What you are suggesting is that you want to 'steady the ark' as Uzzah did in the Old Testament.

God slew him because he presumed to control the working of God. When the Holy Spirit moves and does His work, we become restless because we want to control it. It is an inherent weakness of the flesh. The bottom line of your offer is to control the work in Asia with hidden strings attached to your gift. You have to learn to let your money go, because it is not your money but God's."

Then, with my heart in my mouth, I gave him one last argument, hoping it could save the gift — but willing to lose all if I was unable to convince them.

"Brother," I said quietly, "I sign checks for hundreds of thousands of dollars and send them to the field every month. Many times as I hold those big checks in my hand, I pray, 'Lord, this is Your money. I'm just a steward sending it where You said it should go. Help the leaders on the field use this money to win the lost millions and glorify the name of Jesus.'

"All we must be concerned about is doing our part. I obey the Holy Spirit in dispensing the Lord's money. Don't ask me to ask the native brethren to do something I won't do."

I paused. What more could I say?

"Well," the voice at the other end of the line repeated, "we really want to help. I will make the presentation, but you're making it very hard for me."

"I'm sure," I said with conviction, "there are other organizations that will meet your requirement. I just know we can't. Fellowship in the gospel is one thing — but outside control is unbiblical and in the end harms the work more than helping it."

I said it with conviction, but inside I was sure we had lost the grant. There was nothing more to say, so we both said good-bye. I waited for some word. Two weeks passed without a contact. Every day I prayed God would help the whole board of directors understand. Our inner circle — people who knew about the expected gift — kept asking me if I'd heard anything. Our whole office was praying.

"We're walking in the narrow way," I said bravely to the staff, "doing what God has told us." Inside I kept wishing God would let me bend the rules a little this time.

But our faithfulness paid off. One day the phone rang, and it was the director again. The board had met the night before, and he had presented my position to them.

"Brother K.P.," he said with a smile in his voice, "we have met and discussed the project quite extensively. I shared the importance of autonomy of the national brothers. They have voted unanimously to go ahead and support the project without controls."

There's no guarantee you'll always have that kind of happy ending when you stand up for what's right. But it doesn't matter. God has called us to be here in the West, challenging the affluent people of this world to share with those in the most desperate need of all.

God is calling Christians in the West to recognize He is building His church as a caring, sharing and saving outreach to dying souls. He is using many North Americans who care about the lost to share in this new movement by supporting the native missionary leaders He has called to direct it.

God is calling the body of Christ in the affluent West to give up its proud, arrogant attitude of "our way is the only way" and share with those who will die in sin unless help is sent now from the richer nations. The West must share with the East, knowing that Jesus said, "Whatever you did for one of the least of these brothers of mine, you did for me" (Matt. 25:40, NIV).

Have native missionaries made mistakes? Yes. And it would be unwise stewardship to give away our money freely without knowledge of the truthfulness and integrity of any ministry. But that doesn't mean we shouldn't help the native missionary movement.

North America is at the crossroads. We can harden our hearts to the needs of the Third World — continuing in arrogance, pride and selfishness — or we can repent and move with the Spirit of God. Whichever way we turn, the laws of God will continue in effect.

If we close our hearts to the lost of the world who are dying and going to hell, we invite the judgment of God and a more certain ruin of our affluence. But if we open our hearts and share, it will be the beginning of new blessing and renewal.

This is why I believe that the response of North American believers to the cry of my heart is more than a missions question that can be shrugged off like another appeal letter or banquet invitation. Response to the needs of the lost world is directly tied to the spiritual beliefs and well-being of every believer.

Meanwhile, the unknown brethren of Asia continue to lift hands to God in prayer, asking Him to meet their needs. They are men and women of the highest caliber. They cannot be bought. Many have developed a devotion to God that makes them hate the idea of becoming servants of men and religious establishments for profit.

It is the highest privilege of affluent Christians in the West to share in their ministries by sending financial aid.

Without visible support, they are the true brethren of Christ about which the Bible speaks. Today they are walking from village to village facing beatings and persecution to bring Christ to Animists, Buddhists, communists, Hindus, Muslims and many other people who have still not received the good news of His love.

Without fear of men they are willing, like their Lord, to live as He did — sleeping on roadsides, going hungry and even dying in order to share their faith.

These are the men who go even though they may be told the mission fund is used up. They are determined to preach even though they know it will mean suffering. Why? Because they love the lost souls who are dying daily without Christ.

They are too busy doing the will of God to get

involved in church politics, board meetings, fund-raising campaigns and public relations efforts.

If we do not care enough to sponsor them — if we do not obey the love of Christ and send them support — we are sharing in the responsibility for those who go to eternal flames without ever hearing about the love of God. If native evangelists cannot go because no one will send them, the shame belongs to the body of Christ here because it has the funds to help them.

If those funds are not given to the Lord, they soon will disappear. If the Western church will not be a light to the world, the Lord will take the candlestick away.

Pretending the poor and lost don't exist may be an alternative. But averting our eyes from the truth will not eliminate our guilt.

Gospel for Asia exists to remind the affluent Christian that there is a hungry, needy, lost world of people out there whom Jesus loves and for whom He died. Will you join us in ministering to them?

A Third World Response

Those most concerned about missions have grown up hearing the classic approach of "send Americans" and never have been asked to consider alternatives better suited to changed geo-political conditions. It is hard for some to hear me reinterpret the stories told by Western missionaries of hardship and fruitless ministry as indicators of outdated and inappropriate methods.

But the biggest hurdle for most North Americans is the idea that someone from somewhere else can do it better. Questions about our methods and safeguards for financial accountability, while often sincere and well-intentioned, sometimes emanate from a deep well of distrust and prejudice.

On one of my trips to the West Coast I was invited to meet with the mission committee of a church that supported over seventy-five American missionaries. After I shared our vision for supporting native missionaries, the committee chairman said, "We have been asked to support national missionaries before, but we haven't found a satisfactory way to hold these nationals accountable for either the money we send or the work they do." I sensed he spoke for the entire committee.

I could hardly wait to respond. This issue of accountability is the objection most often raised about supporting native missionaries to the Third World, and I can understand why. Indeed, I agree it is extremely important that there be adequate accountability in every area of ministry. Good stewardship demands it.

Then I detailed how we handle the subject.

"In order to make people accountable we need some norm by which to measure their performance," I said. "But what criteria should we use? Would the yearly independent audit our missionaries submit be adequate to see that they handled money wisely?"

In addition I raised other questions. "What about the churches they build or the projects they have undertaken? Should they be judged according to the patterns and goals some mission headquarters or denomination prescribed? What about the souls they've won and the disciples they've made? Would any denomination have criteria to evaluate those? How about criteria to evaluate their life-style on the field or the fruit they produce? Which of these categories should be used to make these native missionaries accountable?"

Those who had been leaning back in their chairs

now were leaning forward.

I had laid a foundation for a thought I was sure they hadn't considered before. I continued: "Do you require the American missionaries you send overseas to be accountable to you? What criteria have you used in the past to account for the hundreds of thousands of dollars you have invested through the missionaries you support now?"

I looked to the chairman for an answer. He stumbled through a few phrases before admitting they never had thought of requiring American missionaries to be accountable nor was this ever a concern to them.

"The problem," I explained, "is not a matter of accountability but one of prejudice, mistrust and feelings of superiority. These are the issues that hinder love and support for our brothers in the Third World who are working to win their own people to Christ." I followed with this illustration.

"Three months ago I traveled to Asia to visit some of the brothers we support. In one country I met an American missionary who had for fourteen years been developing some social programs for his denomination. He had come to this country hoping he could establish his mission center. In this regard he had been successful. As I walked into his mission compound I passed a man with a gun, sitting at the gate. The compound was bordered by a number of buildings with at least half a dozen imported cars. The staff members were wearing Western clothes, and a servant was caring for one of the missionary children. The scene reminded me of a king living in a palace with his court of serfs caring for his every need. I had, in eighteen years of travel, seen this scene repeated many times," I explained.

"From conversation with some of the native missionaries, I learned that this American and his colleagues did live like kings with their servants and cars," I said. "They had no contact with the poor in the surrounding villages. While God's money is invested on missionaries like this who enjoy a life-style they could not afford in the United States — a lifestyle of a rich man, separated by economy and distance from the native missionaries walking barefoot, poorly dressed even by their own standards and sometimes going for days without eating. These nationals, in my opinion, are the real soldiers of the cross. Each one of the brothers we support in that country has established a church in less than twelve months, and some have started more than twenty churches in three years."

I told of another incident from my own country of India. Although India is closed to new missionaries, there are some Western missionaries living there from past times. And, of course, some denominations get a few new professional people in such as doctors or teachers. I was visiting one of the mission hospitals in India where some of these missionary doctors and their colleagues worked. All lived in richly furnished mansions. One had twelve servants to care for him and his family. One looked after the garden, another cared for the car, another cared for the children, two cooked in his kitchen, one took care of his family's clothes, and so on. And in eight years this missionary had won no one to Jesus nor established one church.

"What criteria," I dared to ask, "has been used by the two evangelical denominations that have sent these men to hold them accountable? In another place," I continued, "there is a hospital costing millions to build and more millions to keep staffed with Europeans and Americans where, in seventy-five years, not one living, New Testament church has been established. Did anyone ever ask for an account of such fruitless labor?

"These illustrations are not isolated instances," I assured them. "During my eighteen years of travel throughout Asia I have seen Western missionaries consistently living at an economic level many times above the people they work with. And the nationals working with them are treated like servants and live in poverty while these missionaries enjoy the luxuries of life."

I contrasted these examples with what the nationals are doing.

"Remember the illustration of the multi-million dollar hospital and no church?" I asked. "Well, four years ago we started supporting a native missionary and thirty co-workers who have started a mission only a few miles from the hospital. His staff has grown to 349 co-workers, and hundreds of churches have been started. Another native missionary, one of his co-workers, has established over thirty churches in three years. Where do these brothers live? In little huts just like the people with whom they work. I could give you hundreds of stories that illustrate the fruit of such dedicated lives. It is like the book of Acts being written once again.

"You are seeking accountability from native missionaries, accountability that is required for you to give them support? Remember that Jesus said, 'For John came neither eating nor drinking, and they say, He hath a devil. The Son of man came eating and drinking, and they say, Behold a man gluttonous, and a winebibber, a friend of publicans and sinners. But wisdom is justified of her children' [Matt. 11:18-19]."

Fruit, I pointed out, is the real test. " 'By their fruits ye shall know them,' Jesus said [Matt. 7:20].

"Paul told Timothy to do two things regarding his life. And these two things, I believe, are the biblical criteria for accountability. He told Timothy to watch his own life and to care for the ministry that was committed to him. The life of the missionary is the medium of his message."

Three hours had passed, yet the room remained quiet. I sensed I had their permission to continue.

"You asked me to give you a method to hold our native missionaries accountable. Apart from the issues I have raised, Gospel for Asia does have definite procedures to insure that we are good stewards of the monies and opportunities the Lord commits to us. But our requirements and methods reflect a different perspective and way of doing missions.

"First, Gospel for Asia assumes that we who are called are called to serve and not to be served. We walk before the millions of poor and destitute in Asia with our lives as an open testimony and example. I breathe, sleep and eat conscious of the perishing millions the Lord commands me to love and rescue."

Then I explained how God is reaching the lost, not through programs but through individuals whose lives are so committed to Him that He uses them as vessels to anoint a lost world. So we give top priority to how the missionaries and their leaders live. When we started to support one brother, he lived in two small rooms with concrete floors. He, his wife and four children slept on a mat on the floor. That was four years ago. On a recent visit to India I saw him living in the same place, sleeping on the same mat even though his staff had grown from 30 to 349 workers. He handles hundreds of thousands of dollars to keep this enormous ministry going, yet his lifestyle has not changed. The brothers he has drawn into the ministry are willing to die for Christ's sake because they have seen their leader sell out to Christ just as the apostle Paul did.

"In the West, people look to men with power and riches. In Asia our people look for men like Gandhi who, to inspire a following, was willing to give up all to become like the least of the poor. Accountability begins with the life of the missionary."

The second criteria we consider, I explained, is the fruitfulness of that life. Our investment of money shows in the result of lives changed and churches established. What greater accountability can we require?

When Western missionaries go into Third World countries, they are able to find nationals to follow them. But these nationals too often get caught up in denominational distinctives. Like produces like. Missionary leaders from denominations who fly into these countries and live in five-star hotels will draw to themselves so-called national leaders who are like themselves. Then, unfortunately, it is the so-called national leaders who are accused of wasting or misusing great amounts of money, while they have often merely followed the example provided by their Western counterparts.

Again I addressed the chairman: "Have you studied the lives and ministries of the American missionaries you support? I believe you will find that very few of them are directly involved in preaching Christ but are doing some sort of social work. If you apply the biblical principles I have outlined, I doubt you would support more than a handful of them."

Then I turned and asked the committee members to assess themselves. "If your life is not totally committed to Christ, you are not qualified to be on this committee. That means you cannot use your time, your talents or your money the way you want to. If you do and still think you can help direct God's people to reach a lost world, you mock God Himself. You have to evaluate how you spend every dollar and everything else you do in the light of eternity. The way each one of you lives is where we begin our crusade to reach the lost of this world."

I was gratified to see that the Lord spoke to many of them. There were tears and a feeling of Christ's awareness among us. This had been a painful time for me. I was glad when it was over.

GET INVOLVED!

See coupons at the back of this book.

22

Answers to Your Questions

One of the most educational and pleasurable moments for me in our meetings is the question-and-answer period. From the beginning of our ministry, I have found that a two-way exchange is an effective method to communicate with my audience.

Many ask about current conditions and Asian lifestyle. Others pose some very provocative questions which show they have been thinking seriously about the implications of the message. Some questions seek details about our policies and practices. Others deal with church growth or the strategy of the native missionary movement.

Certain questions come up repeatedly, and the following are my responses.

Question: What are the qualifications of missionaries you support?

Answer: By turning to the books of 1 and 2 Timothy in the New Testament, you will find a complete overview of the qualifications for a missionary evangelist.

However, there are five areas which I feel are especially important in the life of one applying to be a missionary evangelist:

Calling. We are not looking for hirelings, but for men of faith who are certain they are called to be an evangelist. *It's not a job.* A hireling quits when the going gets tough. We are not looking for a man who wants to represent a denomination, Gospel for Asia or K.P. Yohannan. We look for people who know they are called to represent Christ — people who will not seek to please men but God, seeking only God's glory, and who cannot be bought with money or influence. We are looking for people dedicated to winning whole nations to Christ — who believe in the Great Commission.

Walk. We are interested only in people who have a mature walk with the Lord. When the world sees such workers, they see the beauty of Jesus — the compassion and purity of our Lord. The only ones who can win others to Christ are men and women who are so lost in Jesus that they are like Him. This kind of person will not be a gossip or critical and judgmental of others. He is a person who is a giver, one who makes generosity and sharing a normal way of life. Most of all, this person has a love for the lost.

Life-style. Only people who live by kingdom principles can be successful native evangelists. This kind of person will live a life of righteousness and separation from the world. Such a person must be free from addiction to alcohol or drugs, free from lust and free from the love of money.

Fatherhood. Successful missionary evangelists are men whose wives and children love and respect them. If a man is not having a fruitful ministry in his own family, he can never plant churches. Such men will be modeling Christ to their own sons, and their ambition will be to send them someday to the most dangerous and neglected regions of their lands. They must model Christ to their families and dedicate their children to Christian service, raising them to minister. We cannot support a man who is not leading his family in the right way. Such a person is not qualified to preach.

Leadership. A successful native missionary is a man who loves the brethren and proves it with a servant spirit. He loves peace, is quick to forgive and is quick to ask forgiveness. Such a person knows how to cooperate and work with others, prays for them, and is a blessing to the group. This doesn't mean he is a compromiser. He loves the Word of God and correct doctrine and obeys the Scripture in all matters without question. A shepherd always is concerned about holding the flock together and protecting them, and this is what makes a missionary evangelist a productive church planter.

Question: What screening process do you use to select new native missionaries?

Answer: After we receive a completed application, inquiries are made among pastors and older Christian leaders who know the applicant and are able to evaluate him or her. Then, if the candidate is not already involved in ministry, he will be assigned an internship to work under an older missionary evangelist and become a "Timothy." As the disciple gains more experience and is able, he will do more and more outreach. When 1) support is pledged by a sponsor in the West, and 2) the intern is qualified and accepted by the mission board where he will be working, then he will go to the pioneer area where God is leading him to go.

Question: How are native missionary evangelists trained?

Answer: While we have several formal training programs, which I will explain in a moment, let me say that our most productive workers have not been trained in Bible schools or seminaries.

We have found in Asia that the best training is to use the disciple method Jesus used in New Testament days. This method is indigenous to our culture. Our most successful native missionaries are the ones who were trained on the field by older men whose lifestyle can be followed. These teachers are "born to reproduce."

Disciples are made on the field, not in the classroom. It is dangerous to isolate the leadership and train them in sterile and artificial situations away from the masses of people in our villages. (This is why I especially oppose bringing most native missionaries to the West for training.)

Therefore, we have been funding and supporting missionary training programs which are short-term and involve internship with actual local churches. A missionary trainee will have the opportunity to attend classroom sessions as well as implement his studies in local evangelism. The mobile evangelistic team is still one of the best methods to combine training and outreach at the same time. Before a church planting assignment is given a missionary, I believe he needs to have some time doing intensive evangelism.

All this is supplemented by annual and regional conferences held throughout the area where native missionaries gather for prayer, Bible teaching and fellowship.

Question: To whom are native missionary evangelists accountable?

Answer: In almost all cases, they are being supervised by local indigenous mission boards or elders under whom they work. It is the quality of field leadership which is at the core of all accountability in Gospel for Asia.

On my frequent journeys to Asia, I spend much of my time meeting with the leaders of these indigenous missions in the various nations where we are working. Sometimes I will play a role in forming new boards — usually on a state or regional basis. But we want no operating control over the day-to-day affairs of these autonomous missions.

In searching for local mission boards on the field, my staff and I look for certain characteristics:

First, I look for boards that are made up of older, godly leaders who have successfully planted churches themselves and are proven evangelists.

Second, I look for men who are willing to meet regularly with the native missionaries for prayer, fellowship and sharing.

Third, I look for men who are not sectarian in outlook. We are not eager to spread any one particular denominational or doctrinal position.

Fourth, I look for men who live a life of simplicity, purity, holiness, love and faithfulness to the work.

Finally, I avoid boards that are controlled by men with a power-hungry attitude.

However, I do expect men on the board to be looking out for two things in the lives of the native evangelists we support: life-style and doctrine according to 2 Timothy 4:16. I believe that by simply reading 1 and 2 Timothy you get a pretty good idea of how a person is qualified to be a missionary evangelist.

In this sense, the local boards are responsible to see that native missionaries are qualified when they are first approved for support and remain so throughout their years of service.

Question: What about grand strategy? Who is

directing the efforts of the native missionaries?

Answer: Experienced elders help make these kinds of tactical decisions. But in the day-to-day affairs of the work we are trusting the Holy Spirit to guide us about where to go and when. The native missionaries must wait on God for personal direction. If they cannot do this, they are not ready to be released into the field.

Question: What are the methods used by native missionaries?

Answer: While films, radio, television and video are becoming more common in Asia, the most effective methods still sound more as if they came from the book of Acts!

The most effective evangelism is done face-to-face in the streets. Most native missionaries walk or ride bicycles between villages much as the Methodist circuit riders did in America's frontier days. A bicycle is one of the most important tools any native evangelist can own.

Street preaching and open-air evangelism, often using World War II style megaphones, is the most common way to proclaim the gospel. Sometimes evangelists arrange witnessing parades and/or tent campaigns and distribute simple gospel tracts during week-long village crusades.

Since the majority of the world's one billion illiterates live in Asia, the gospel often must be proclaimed to them without using literature. This is done with small hand-cranked card-talk phonographs, cassette tapes, flip charts and films.

Kowvali songfests, a folk tradition, are popular in the villages of North India. Lasting for hours, they attract large crowds. In a Kowvali, the leader tells a story in song while pumping the bellows of a harmonium. A chorus of friends, chanting humorous responses, plays drums and rattles. A number of gospel and Bible stories have been adapted to this medium, and it is a good example of effective evangelism coming out of northwest India.

Trucks, vans, primitive loud-speaker systems, bicycles, leaflets, pamphlets, books, banners and flags are the most important tools. Easy to use and train with, they now are being supplemented with radio broadcasting, cassette players, film projectors and television.

These types of communication tools are available in Asia at low cost, and the native evangelists are familiar with them. They don't shock the culture, and we can buy them locally without paying import duties.

Question: Are native missionaries prepared to carry on cross-cultural evangelism?

Answer: Yes, with great effectiveness. Most of the native missionaries we support, for example, are involved in cross-cultural evangelism. Often, GFA evangelists find they must learn a new language, plus adopt different dress and dietary customs. However, since the cultures are frequently neighbors or share a similar heritage, the transition is much easier than it would be for someone coming from the West.

Even though my homeland has sixteen major languages and 1,650 dialects — each representing a different culture — it is still relatively easy for an Indian to make a transition from one culture to the other. In fact, almost anyone in Pakistan, India, Bangladesh, Burma, Nepal, Bhutan, Thailand and Sri Lanka can rather quickly cross-minister into a neighboring culture.

Question: What kind of churches are native evangelists planting?

Answer: First of all, and most important, indigenous missionaries establish local congregations which are part of the life-style and needs of the country and community they serve. We're not using Western labels and building churches along denominational traditions. Why should we be concerned about denominational names when most of the people haven't yet heard the name of Jesus?

We believe that Christ came to change the hearts of our people, not our culture. So we are concentrating our energies on building congregations which spring out of our own way of life.

Most evangelists in the native missionary movement will call their new congregations after the name of the village or perhaps some place in the Bible.

The building may be of stone or mud, or it may be

just a roof of coconut or banana leaves. There are no benches or chairs. Straw mats are spread over the ground so the congregation may sit. The people usually are divided into three groups — the children sit in front, the men on one side and the women on the other.

As you approach a service in progress, the singing and handclapping can be heard from a distance. Usually it is accompanied by drums, tambourines, rattles and other local instruments.

The words of the songs, sung in native dialects, reflect a specific situation in the life of the believer — giving them immediate meaning to all who participate and hear.

Each believer has a part in the service, which usually begins with one or two hours of worship and singing. One after another, believers stand to testify about what the Lord has done for them during the past week. There is much joy in this kind of meeting, and it is likely to last three or four hours.

Frequently, there may be two sermons presented. The approach to the Scriptures is made in reverence. The goal is not to study them in order to isolate doctrines, but to learn how God would have the new believer walk.

This kind of native church service is very different from worship in the West, yet it serves the same purpose — to allow believers to worship God, to be a witness to the community, to live the Christian life better and to bring many souls to Christ. It is the liturgy of a growing church determined to reach out to the lost masses.

Question: In light of the fact that you will be needing at least 200,000 missionaries to reach Asia, are there enough missionaries available to do the work?

Answer: The answer is yes. Since the current movement began, we never have had a problem finding enough native missionary evangelists. Right now we know of ten thousand evangelists on the field who need support to improve their ministry — with bicycles, bull horns, Christian literature, and so on. By the time these ten thousand are sponsored, I believe we will have another ten thousand waiting.

An amazing phenomenon is taking place throughout what I call the real Asia. At the village level, where masses of people live and die in anonymous poverty, God is doing a supernatural work. Hundreds of thousands are coming to Christ. And as fast as they do, they are being formed into little worshipping cells of believers. There the native missionary evangelists are able to train new disciples to take their place so they can multiply the work in new villages. As we have the support, these new disciples can go into the harvest fields themselves as evangelists.

Many of these new converts are willing to give up their jobs in order to take the gospel to the unreached. Plainly, there is no shortage of people power in Asia. The need is for money to send these workers out properly trained and equipped.

Question: With your emphasis on the native missionary movement, don't you feel there is still a place for Western missionaries in Asia?

Answer: Yes, there still are places for Western missionaries. First, there are still countries with no existing church from which to draw native missionaries. Morocco, Afghanistan and the Maldives Islands come to mind. In these places, missionaries from outside — whether from the West, Africa or Asia — are the only possible way the gospel can be spread.

Second, Christians in the West have technical skills which may be needed by their brothers and sisters in Third World churches. The work of Wycliffe Bible Translators is a good example. Their help in translation efforts in the nearly forty-five hundred languages still without a Bible is invaluable. So when Third World churches invite Westerners to come and help them, and the Lord is in it, the Westerner obviously should respond.

Third, there are short-term discipleship experiences that I think are especially valuable. Organizations like Operation Mobilization and Youth With a Mission have had a catalytic impact on both Asian and Western churches. These are discipleship-building ministries that benefit the Western participants as well as Asia's unevangelized millions.

Also, it must be noted that OM, headed by George

Verwer, has recruited thousands of young people from India and other Asian nations for discipleship training with an emphasis on literature evangelism.

During the last twenty years, OM has done more to challenge the church in India (and other Asian nations) for pioneer evangelism among the most unreached than any other group I know. I personally was recruited by the brothers of OM in 1966 to go to North India.

Through cross-cultural and interracial contact, such ministries are especially helpful because they allow Westerners to get a better understanding of the situation in Asia. Alumni of these programs are helping others in the West understand the real needs of the Third World.

And, of course, there is the simple fact that the Holy Spirit does call individuals from one culture to witness in another. When He calls, we should respond.

Question: Why don't indigenous churches support their own missionaries in the Third World?

Answer: They do. In fact, I believe most Asian Christians give a far greater portion of their income to missions than do Americans. Scores of times, I have seen them give chicken eggs, rice, mangos and tapioca roots, since they frequently don't have cash. The fact of the matter is, growing churches of Asia are made up of people from the poor masses. Often they simply don't have money. These are people from among that one-fourth of the world's population who live on just a few dollars each week.

Many times we find that a successful missionary evangelist will be almost crippled by his own dynamic growth. When a great move of the Holy Spirit occurs in a village, the successful missionary may find he has trained several gifted co-workers as "Timothys" who are ready to establish sister congregations. However, the rapid growth almost always outstrips the original congregation's ability to support additional staff. This is where outside help is vitally needed.

As God's Spirit continues to move, many new mission boards are being formed. Some of the largest missionary societies in the world are now located in Asia. For example, at the time of the revision of this book in 1992, Gospel for Asia alone was helping to support seven thousand native missionary staff members — and this number is increasing at an astonishing rate. But in light of the need, we literally need hundreds of thousands of additional missionaries who will in turn require more outside support.

Regrettably, there are some indigenous churches which don't support native evangelists for the same reason some American congregations don't give — lack of vision and sin in the lives of the pastors and congregations. But this is no excuse for American Christians to sit back and lose the greatest opportunity they've ever had to help win a lost world to Jesus.

Question: Is there a danger that native missionary sponsorships will have a reverse effect by causing native evangelists to depend on the West for support rather than turning to the local churches?

Answer: The truth is, of course, that it is not outside money that weakens a growing church, but outside *control*. Money from the West actually liberates the evangelists right now and makes it possible for them to follow the call of God.

After generations of domination by Western colonialists, most Asians are acutely conscious of the potential problem of foreign control through outside money. It is frequently brought up in discussions by native missionary leaders, and most native missionary boards have developed policies and practices to provide for accountability without foreign control.

In Gospel for Asia, we have taken several steps to make sure money gets to the local missionary evangelist in a responsible way without destroying valuable local autonomy.

First, our selection and training process is designed to favor men and women who begin with a right attitude — missionaries who are dependent on God for their support rather than on men. In fact, many of the native missionaries we support have worked for long periods in near-starvation situations before any support has arrived.

Second, there is no direct or indirect supervision of the work by Western supporters. The donor gives the Lord's money to the missionary through Gospel for Asia, and we in turn send the money to his board. GFA does not usually send the money directly to a native missionary but to a group of leaders who oversee the financial affairs on each field. Therefore, the native evangelist is twice-removed from the source of funds. This procedure is being followed by several other organizations which are collecting funds in the West for native support, and it seems to work very well.

Finally, as soon as a new work is established, the native missionary should be moving on to begin in another area. The new congregation usually has enough financial responsibility to support the gospel worker he leaves behind, but they still are giving sacrificially to support evangelism. Eventually, I am sure the native churches will be able to support most pioneer evangelism, but the job is too big now without Western aid.

The quickest way to help Asian churches become self-supporting, I believe, is to support a growing native missionary movement. As new churches are planted, the blessings of the gospel will abound, and the new Asian believers will be able to support greater outreach. Sponsorship monies are like investment capital in the work of God. The best thing we can do to help make the Asian church independent now is to support as many native missionaries as possible.

Question: How can Gospel for Asia support a

native missionary evangelist for only $360 to $1,200 a year when my church says it takes $43,000 to support an American missionary on the same fields?

Answer: There is a vast difference between living at the same level as an Asian peasant — as native evangelists do — and living at even a modest Western standard. In most of the nations where we support local missionaries, they are able to survive on one to three dollars a day. This is approximately the same per capita income of the people to whom they are ministering in most cases.

A North American missionary, however, is faced with many additional costs. These include international air transportation, language schools, special English-language schools for children, and Western-style housing. Native missionaries, on the other hand, live in villages on the same level as others in the community whom they are seeking to reach for Christ.

The Western missionary also is faced with visa and other legal fees, costs of communication with donors, extra medical care, import duties, and requirements to pay Social Security and income taxes back in the States. The cost of food can be very high, especially if the missionary entertains other Westerners, employs servants to cook, and eats imported foods. Frequently, host governments require foreign missionaries to meet special tax or reporting requirements, usually with payments required.

Clothing, such as shoes and imported Western

garments, is costly. Many native missionaries choose to wear sandals and dress as the local people do.

For a Western missionary family with children, the pressure is intense to maintain a semblance of American-style living. Frequently this is increased by peer pressure at private schools where other students are the sons and daughters of international businessmen and diplomats.

Finally, vacations and in-country travel or tourism are not considered essential by native missionaries as they are by most Americans. The cost of imported English books, periodicals, records and tapes is also a big expense not part of a native missionary's lifestyle.

The result of all this is that American missionaries often need thirty to forty times more money for their support than does a native missionary.

Question: It seems as if I'm getting fund-raising appeals every day from good Christian organizations. How can I know who is genuine and really in the center of God's will?

Answer: Many Christians receive appeal letters each month from all kinds of religious organizations.

Obviously, you can't respond to all the appeals, so what criteria should you use to make your decision? Here are a few guidelines we have developed for missions giving which I believe will help:

• Do those asking for money believe in the fundamental truths of God's Word, or are they liberal theologically? Any mission that seeks to carry out God's work must be totally committed to His Word. Is the group asking for money affiliated with liberal organizations which deny the truth of the gospel, while keeping the name "Christian"? Do their members openly declare their beliefs? Too many today walk in a gray area, taking no stands, trying to offend as few as possible so they can get money from all, whether friends or enemies of the cross of Christ. The Word of God is being fulfilled in them: "...having a form of godliness, but denying the power thereof" (2 Tim. 3:5).

• Is the goal of their mission to win souls, or are they only social-gospel oriented? One of the biggest lies the devil uses to send people to hell is, How can we preach the gospel to a man with an empty stomach? Because of this lie, for a hundred years much of missions money has been invested in social work rather than in spreading the Word.

Ask before you give, Is this mission involved in preaching the gospel of Jesus Christ? The liberal believes man is basically good; therefore, all that is needed to solve his problems is to change his environment. The Bible says all — rich and poor — must repent and come to Christ or be lost. Which gospel is being preached by the mission group asking for your support? (I have explained this in greater detail elsewhere in this book.)

• Is the mission organization financially accountable? Do they use the money for the purpose for which it was given? At Gospel for Asia every penny given for support of a missionary is sent to the field for that purpose. Our home office is supported with funds given for that purpose. Are their finances audited by independent auditors according to accepted procedures? Will they send an audited financial statement to anyone requesting it? Gospel for Asia meets both standards.

• Do members of the mission group live by faith or by man's wisdom? God never changes His plan: "The just shall live by faith." When a mission continually sends out crisis appeals for its maintenance rather than for outreach, there is something wrong with it. They seem to say God made a commitment, but now He is in trouble, and we must help Him out of some tight spot. God makes no promises He cannot keep. If a mission group constantly begs and pleads for money, you need to ask if they are doing what God wants them to do. We believe we must wait upon God for His mind and do only what He leads us to do, instead of taking foolish steps of faith without His going before us. The end should never justify the means.

• Finally, a word of caution. Don't look for a reason for not giving to the work of God. Remember, we must give all we can, keeping only enough to meet our needs so the gospel can be preached "before the night comes and no man can work." The problem for most is not that we give too much, but that we give too little. We live selfishly and store up treasures on this earth which will be destroyed soon, while precious souls die and go to hell.

Question: How can I sponsor a native missionary evangelist?

Answer: There are several American-based organizations, including Gospel for Asia, that now are channeling support to the native missionary movement. It is not advisable to send money directly to the field, since agencies like ours have elaborate systems to evaluate, train and hold local missionaries accountable.

To sponsor a native missionary through Gospel for Asia, here's all you need do:

• Write Gospel for Asia using the tear-out coupon at the end of this book. Let us know you want to help sponsor a native missionary.

• Enclose your first pledge payment. Most of our friends sponsor missionaries for between $30 and $120 a month.

• As soon as you receive information about your missionary, pray for him and his family every day.

Question: Are financial records audited on the field?

Answer: Yes, we inspect financial records to ensure that funds are used according to the purpose intended. A detailed accounting in writing is required for projects such as village crusades, training conferences and special programs. Missionary support funds are signed for as received both by leaders and the missionaries involved, and these receipts are checked.

All financial records on the field are also audited annually by certified public accountants.

Epilogue

Even as our ministry has expanded and grown, my own life has not become easier. I am now traveling halfway around the world half a dozen times a year meeting with our leaders on the field. In addition, when I am in the United States, I am often on speaking tours of up to two weeks' duration. In fact, in one recent year I spoke in ninety cities across the country.

Without the spiritual support of my wife, Gisela, it would not be humanly possible for me to keep up the pace. But she encourages me so completely that I keep on going. In fact, there are times when I am so weary I feel I cannot face another trip, and I feel bad for leaving my family again. But Gisela urges me to go because it is what the Lord has called me to do, and she sustains me with her prayers.

Our life as a couple, and as a family, is consumed with one thought: to do everything we can to support the native missionaries as they seek to win the lost millions of Asia to Christ. Eternity is very real to us. We evaluate everything we do against the reality of the millions who will perish forever unless we reach them with the gospel.

So we have made a deliberate decision to suffer so the gospel can be furthered. This decision was not enjoined upon us — we make it daily with prayerful joy. We have continued to maintain a simple lifestyle. We have made a covenant not to save up riches or accumulate the things of this world for our children, but that everything we have should be continually spent to reach the lost souls who have never heard the name of Jesus.

And in this life we must go on, until we see the Lord face to face.

A while ago, as I put my children to bed, as usual each one took his or her turn to pray. But that night my son, Daniel, age nine, added a new sentence to his prayers: "...and, Jesus, please help me to be a missionary."

A few days later, Sarah, age six, also prayed the same prayer. From the day they were born we prayed that the Lord would save them and call them to be missionaries and follow in their parents' footsteps.

In everything we do in our family, we teach our children to ask: What will this do to help us further the gospel by helping our brothers on the field who are going through much suffering in their commitment to preach?

We acknowledge we are in a real spiritual war,

with millions of lives at stake to spend eternity without God.

Sometimes I think I am a madman, but then I know it is not madness as some may think — it is a total obedience to Christ and His call. I believe this is a normal life-style for anyone who seeks to follow Him, knowing that time will soon run out, and eternity is real.

A Prayer

Dear Lord, we acknowledge that our commitment to You is so shallow. We say we love You, but our actions betray us.

Open our eyes so that we see time and eternity as You see them. Forgive us for forgetting we are only strangers and pilgrims on this earth.

How foolish we are, O Lord, to store up treasures on this earth and fight to save our lives and preserve them, when You tell us we will lose our lives if we try to do that.

We ask You, dear Lord, to forgive us and help us to walk in Your footsteps — forsaking all, denying ourselves, carrying our crosses daily and loving You supremely so Your causes might be furthered in this dark and dying world.

In Jesus' name, Amen.

You Can Become a Sender!

Yes! I care about the lost and forgotten millions of Asia. I will help native missionaries reach their own people for Jesus. I understand that it takes $30 to $120 per month to support a native missionary fully, depending on his or her marital status, family size and location of service.

To begin sponsoring today call toll free:
1-800-WIN-ASIA
(1-800-946-2742)
(in the USA or Canada)

Or mail the coupon on the back of this page to:

Gospel for Asia
USA: 1932 Walnut Plaza, Carrollton, TX 75006
Canada: P.O. Box 4000, Waterdown, ONT L0R 2H0
Germany: Karsauer Str. 15A, D7888 Rheinfelden

*You will receive a photo and testimony of each
native missionary you help sponsor.*

**Gospel for Asia sends 100% of your
missionary support to the mission field.**
Nothing is taken out for administrative expenses.

All donations are tax-deductible.

S921-WCB1

H925-RB1S

You Can Become a Sender!

☐ Starting now I will prayerfully help sponsor:

    ☐ 1 missionary at:

        ☐ $120 monthly

        ☐ $90 monthly

        ☐ $60 monthly

        ☐ $30 monthly

        ☐ $_____ monthly

    ☐ _____ missionaries at $_____ each monthly

      (total $_____ monthly)

    Total enclosed $_____

☐ **Please send me more information** about how to help sponsor a native missionary, including a FREE one-year subscription to *SEND!* — the newspaper voice of native missions.

Name_____

Address_____

City_____

State/Province_____

ZIP/Postal Code_____

Telephone (_____)_____

S921-WCB1

H925-RB1S

IF YOUR HEART HAS BEEN TOUCHED

consider adding more materials by K. P. Yohannan to your library.

BOOKS ──────────────────────────────

The Road to Reality — For those who hunger for spiritual reality and long to live consistently with what they believe, this book provides a fresh perspective and practical solutions. 203 pgs. Pocket-size. Suggested donation: $2.

Why the World Waits — K. P. Yohannan asks some disturbing questions about the effectiveness of today's traditional missions. A compelling and convincing case for the native missionary movement. 244 pgs. Suggested donation: $6.

Living in the Light of Eternity — In the tradition of Christ's "hard sayings," K. P. Yohannan lovingly, yet candidly, reminds Christians of their chief work while here on earth: harvesting souls. A contrast between the stark realities of New Testament Christianity and the comfortable lifestyles of contemporary Christians. 262 pgs. Suggested donation: $6.

VIDEOS──────────────────────────────

Cry of the Unreached — A message preached by K. P. Yohannan at Charles Stanley's church in Atlanta, this video has touched the lives of thousands of Christians. This is a must-see! Suggested donation: $5.

Glad Sacrifice — A colorful, moving documentary about the work of Gospel for Asia. You'll see native missionaries taking the gospel to some of the most unreached people. You'll be encouraged to see what God is doing in the Third World. Suggested donation: $5.

See other side for order information

Order Form

Call toll-free **1-800-WIN-ASIA** (946-2742)
or complete the information below
and mail with payment to:

Gospel for Asia
1932 Walnut Plaza, Carrollton, TX 75006
Canada: P. O. Box 4000, Waterdown, ON L0R 2H0

☐ Please send the following materials:

	Item	Donation*	Qty.	Total
Books	Revolution in World Missions	$1		
	The Road to Reality	$2		
	Why the World Waits	$6		
	Living in the Light of Eternity	$6		
Videos	Cry of the Unreached	$5		
	Glad Sacrifice	$5		

*Please add 25% for Canadian funds.

Total enclosed $_____

Send order to:

Name_____

Address_____

City_____

State/Province_____

ZIP/Postal Code_____

Telephone (_____)_____

H942-POP1

HELP US INVOLVE OTHERS

Give your Christian friends and relatives a FREE subscription to *SEND!* — the voice of native missions. Help give them a missions vision! Just fill out their names and addresses below. Use additional sheets of paper if necessary. Please print clearly.

❖ ❖

Name_____

Address_____ Apt. #_____

City_____ State_____

ZIP Code_____ Telephone (_____)_____

❖ ❖

Name_____

Address_____ Apt. #_____

City_____ State_____

ZIP Code_____ Telephone (_____)_____

❖ ❖

❏ Please identify me as the gift subscription donor. My name is
_____

Please send your list of mission-minded friends to:
Gospel for Asia
USA: 1932 Walnut Plaza, Carrollton, TX 75006
Canada: P.O. Box 4000, Waterdown, ONT L0R 2H0

F925-PB10

S921-WCB1

Notes

Chapter 4

1. Robert L. Heilbroner, *The Great Ascent: The Struggle for Economic Development in Our Time* (New York: Harper & Row, 1963), pp. 33-36.

Chapter 5

1. Rochunga Pudaite, *My Billion Bible Dream* (Nashville: Thomas Nelson Publishers, 1982), p. 129.
2. Ref. (Pasadena: U.S. Center for World Mission).

Chapter 8

1. 1980 World Population Data Sheet, Population Reference Bureau, 1337 Connecticut Avenue, N.W., Washington, D.C.

Chapter 10

1. William McDonald, *True Discipleship* (Kansas City: Walterick Publishers, 1975), p. 31.

Chapter 11

1. C. Peter Wagner, *On the Crest of the Wave* (Ventura: Regal Books, 1983), p. 150.
2. Watchman Nee, *Love Not the World* (Fort Washington: Christian Literature Crusade, 1968), pp. 23, 24.

Chapter 12

1. A.W. Tozer, *Of God and Man* (Harrisburg: Christian Publications Inc., 1960), p. 35.

Chapter 14

1. *India Journal*, published by Bibles for India, 1984.
2. David B. Barrett, *World Christian Encyclopedia* (New York: Oxford University Press, 1982), pp. 133, 135.
3. *Ibid.*, pp. 165, 166.
4. *Ibid.*, pp. 179, 180.
5. *Ibid.*, pp. 202-204.
6. *Ibid.*, pp. 360-363.
7. *Ibid.*, pp. 381-388.
8. *Ibid.*, pp. 419-426.
9. *Ibid.*, pp. 440-445.
10. *Ibid.*, pp. 472-476.
11. *Ibid.*, pp. 476-477.
12. *Ibid.*, pp. 507-508.

13. *Ibid.*, pp. 542-545.
14. *Ibid.*, pp. 562-568.
15. *Ibid.*, pp. 613-616.
16. *Ibid.*, pp. 634-638.
17. *Ibid.*, pp. 235-238.
18. *Ibid.*, pp. 664-667.

Chapter 16

1. Allen Finley, Lorry Lutz, *Mission: A World-Family Affair* (San Jose: Christian National Press, 1981), pp. 38, 39.

Chapter 17

1. Dennis E. Clark, *The Third World and Mission* (Waco: Word Books, 1971), p. 70.
2. C. Peter Wagner, *On the Crest of the Wave* (Ventura: Regal Books, 1983), p. 93.
3. Roland Allen, *The Spontaneous Expansion of the Church* (Grand Rapids: William B. Eerdmans, 1962), p. 19.

Chapter 18

1. George Verwer, *No Turning Back* (Wheaton: Tyndale House Publishers, 1983), pp. 89, 90.